Where Two Worlds Met

Where Two Worlds Met

The Russian State and the Kalmyk Nomads, 1600–1771

MICHAEL KHODARKOVSKY

CORNELL UNIVERSITY PRESS

Ithaca and London

Publication of this book was made possible,
in part, by a grant from
Loyola University of Chicago.

First published 1992 by Cornell University Press.

International Standard Book Number 0-8014-2555-7
Library of Congress Catalog Card Number 92-5282
Printed in the United States of America
Librarians: Library of Congress cataloging information
appears on the last page of the book.

♾ The paper in this book meets the minimum requirements
of the American National Standard for Information Sciences—
Permanence of Paper for Printed Library Materials, ANSI Z39.48-1984.

To my parents

Бийин үнр биид медгддг уга.
(One does not know one's own smell)

A Kalmyk proverb

Не сошлись обычаем, не бывать дружбе.
(If customs are different, friendship is impossible)

A Russian proverb

Contents

Maps and Illustrations

Maps

Illustrations

Acknowledgments

I owe debts and thanks to many people who in different ways made this book possible. Some offered friendship and support, others engaged me intellectually. My foremost gratitude is to my teachers at the University of Chicago, Richard Hellie and Halil Inalcik. An Ottoman historian, Halil Inalcik introduced me to the world of Turkish culture and history, which opened new vistas of research. Richard Hellie was more than a teacher, always ready to extend his hand in support at the most critical moments. He was and remains an example of hard work, fairness, and uncompromisingly high standards. I am grateful to the late Alexandre Bennigsen, who encouraged my interest in Kalmyk and Turkish history. My special thanks are to Robert Dankoff, who taught me Turkish and much more.

I extend my thanks to many of my colleagues whose work and advice benefited me greatly, and particularly to those who took the time to read and comment on various parts of the manuscript: Thomas J. Barfield, Arash Bormanshinov, Bernard Cohen, Robert Dankoff, Chester Dunning, Valerie Kivelson, Beatrice Manz, Victor Ostapchuk, and Frank E. Sysyn. I am particularly grateful to John Masson Smith of the University of California at Berkeley. His comments were an example of truly constructive and helpful criticism. My thanks also to Stephen R. Meyer and my editor for Cornell University Press, Trudie Calvert, who painstakingly edited the manuscript.

I am grateful to the publishers who kindly permitted the use of materials from articles of mine that appeared in *Central Asian Survey* 7, no. 4 (1988), and *Russian History* 15, no. 2-4 (1988), and on which Chapters 3 and 5 are based.

This book would not see the light at this time without the generous support of several agencies and foundations. A Fulbright-Hays Fellowship from the U.S. Department of Education provided me with an opportunity to conduct research at the Ottoman archives in Istanbul, Turkey. Social Science Research Council Dissertation and Postdoctoral Fellowships supported me throughout the critical stages of the manuscript preparation. The Russian Research Center at Harvard University provided a congenial and comfortable environment, where the final revisions were made. Finally, Kalamazoo College and my former colleagues in the department supported me wholeheartedly in this endeavor, as has, more recently, Loyola University of Chicago.

MICHAEL KHODARKOVSKY

Chicago, Illinois

Abbreviations

AGS *Arkhiv gosudarstvennogo soveta.* 5 vols. St. Petersburg: Tip. II-go sobstv. Ego Imp. Vel. otdeleniia, 1869–1904.

AI *Akty istoricheskie, sobrannye i izdannye Arkheograficheskoi komissiei.* 5 vols. and index. St. Petersburg, 1841–43.

AIuB *Akty, otnosiashchiesia do iuridicheskogo byta drevnei Rossii, izd. Arkheograficheskoi komissiei.* 3 vols. and index. St. Petersburg, 1857–1901.

AIuZR *Akty, otnosiashchiesia k istorii Iuzhnoi i Zapadnoi Rossii.* 15 vols. St. Petersburg, 1861–92.

AKAK *Akty, sobrannye Kavkazskoiu arkheograficheskoiu komissiei.* Edited by Ad. Berzhe. 12 vols. Tiflis: Tip. Glavnogo upravleniia namestnika kavkazskogo, 1866–1904.

AKV *Arkhiv kniazia Vorontsova.* 40 vols. Moscow: Tip. A. I. Mamontova, 1870–95.

AMG *Akty Moskovskogo gosudarstva, izdannye Imp. Akademiei nauk.* Edited by D. Ia. Samokvasov. 3 vols. St. Petersburg: Tip. Imp. AN, 1890–1901.

AVD *Akty, otnosiashchiesia k istorii Voiska Donskogo.* 3 vols. Novocherkassk: Tip. A. A. Karaseva, 1891–94.

BA *Bashbakanlik Arshivi,* Istanbul, Turkey.

ChOIDR *Chteniia v imperatorskom obshchestve istorii i drevnostei rossiiskikh pri Moskovskom universitete. Sbornik.* Moscow, 1845–1918.

DAI *Dopolneniia k aktam istoricheskim, sobrannye i izdannye Arkheograficheskoi komissiei.* 12 vols. and index. St. Petersburg, 1846–75.

DRV *Drevniaia rossiiskaia vivliofika.* Compiled by Nikolai Novikov. 2d ed. 22 vols. Moscow: Tip. kompanii tipograficheskoi, 1788–91. Reprint. Slavic printings and reprintings, 250/1, ed. C. H. van Schooneveld. The Hague and Paris: Mouton, 1970.

HJAS *Harvard Journal of Asiatic Studies.*

KNIIaLI *Kalmytskii nauchno-issledovatel'skii institut iazyka, literatury i istorii.* Elista, 1960–.

ODAMM *Opisanie del Arkhiva morskogo ministerstva za vremia s poloviny 17 do nachala 19 stoletiia.* 9 vols. St. Petersburg: Tip. V. Dimakova, 1877–1906.

ODB   *Opisanie dokumentov i bumag, khraniashchikhsia v Moskovskom arkhive Ministerstva iustitsii.* 21 vols. Moscow: Sinodal'naia tip., 1869–1921.

ODD   *Opisanie dokumentov i del, khraniashchikhsia v Arkhive sviateishego pravitel'stvuiushchego sinoda.* St. Petersburg, 1868–1914.

PB   *Pis'ma i bumagi imperatora Petra Velikogo.* 12 vols. St. Petersburg and Moscow, 1887–1977.

PDRV   *Prodolzhenie drevnei rossiiskoi vivliofiki.* 11 vols. St. Petersburg: Imp. Akademiia nauk, 1786–1801. Reprint. Slavic printings and reprintings, 251, ed. C. H. van Schooneveld. The Hague and Paris: Mouton, 1970.

PDS   *Pamiatniki diplomaticheskikh snoshenii drevnei Rossii s derzhavami inostrannymi.* 10 vols. St. Petersburg, 1851–71.

PSPR   *Polnoe sobranie postanovlenii i rasporiazhenii po vedomstvu pravoslavnogo ispovedaniia Rossiisskoi imperii.* 19 vols. St. Petersburg, 1869–1915.

PSZ   *Polnoe sobranie zakonov Rossiiskoi imperii. Sobranie pervoe.* 45 vols. St. Petersburg, 1830.

RIB   *Russkaia istoricheskaia biblioteka.* 39 vols. St. Petersburg and Leningrad, 1872–1927.

SA   *Senatskii arkhiv.* 15 vols. St. Petersburg, 1888–1913.

SK   *Süleymaniye Kütüpkhanesi,* Istanbul, Turkey.

SRIO   *Sbornik Russkogo istoricheskogo obshchestva.* 148 vols. St. Petersburg, 1867–1916.

TOEM   *Tarikhi Osmani Enjümeni mejmuasi.* 8 vols. Istanbul: Devlet Matbaasi, 1910–31.

ZhMNP   *Zhurnal Ministerstva narodnogo prosveshcheniia.* St. Petersburg, 1834–1917.

ZIOOID   *Zapiski Imp. Odesskogo obshchestva istorii i drevnostei.* 33 vols. Odessa, 1844–1919.

ZIRGO   *Zapiski Imp. Russkogo geograficheskogo obshchestva.* 13 vols. St. Petersburg: Imp. Akademiia nauk, 1846–59.

ZIRGOOE   *Zapiski Imp. Russkogo geograficheskogo obshchestva po otdeleniiu etnografii.* 44 vols. St. Petersburg, 1867–1917.

ZIRGOOG   *Zapiski Imp. Russkogo geograficheskogo obshchestva po obshchei geografii.* 52 vols. St. Petersburg, 1867–1917.

ZVOIRAO   *Zapiski Vostochnogo otdeleniia Imp. Russkogo arkheologicheskogo obshchestva.* 25 vols. St. Petersburg, 1886–1921.

Note on Transliteration

Inevitably, difficulties arise if one attempts to use a unified transliteration system for the Russian, Turkish, Mongol, and Chinese languages. For the Russian terms I chose to use the Library of Congress system. For Turkic and Mongol words I used the Turkish language transliteration system found in the *Encyclopaedia of Islam*, new ed. (Leiden: E. J. Brill, 1960–), except that I have employed ch instead of ç and j instead of c. Finally, Chinese words are transcribed in the pinyin system.

Kalmyk and Oirat Rulers

Kalmyk/Torgut Rulers

Kho-Urlük (chief tayishi) (?–1644)
Daichin Khan (1647–61)
Puntsuk (chief tayishi) (1661–69)
Ayuki Khan (1669–1724)
Cheren-Donduk Khan (1724–35)
Donduk-Ombo Khan (1735–41)
Donduk-Dashi Khan (1741–61)
Ubashi (viceroy) (1761–71)

Oirat/Jungar Rulers

Kharakhula (chief tayishi) (?–1634)
Erdeni Batur khong tayiji (1634–53)
Senge Khan (1653–70)
Galdan Boshoktu Khan (1671–97)
Tsevang Rabtan Khan (1697–1727)
Galdan Tseren Khan (1727–45)
Aji Khan (1746–49)
Erdeni Lama Batur khong tayiji (1749–53)
Davachi Khan (1753–55)

Where Two Worlds Met

Introduction

Throughout the centuries the steppes of the North Caspian region, with their lush pastures, plentiful rivers, and mild climate, were a preferred habitat of numerous nomadic peoples. The "nomadic factor" was ever-present in the history of Russia from the days of Kievan Rus' to the late eighteenth century, when this western corner of the Inner Asian steppes became South Russia. The appearance of the Kalmyks near the Volga River in the early seventeenth century represented the last wave in the traditional pattern of migration of nomads from their homelands in Inner Asia to the Caspian steppes.

This book tells the history of the Kalmyk people, their relations with Russia, and the impact of this relationship on both societies in the seventeenth and eighteenth centuries. Because the Kalmyks' arrival at the Caspian steppes occurred in the seventeenth century, their relations with Russia were far better documented than Russia's contacts with other nomadic peoples had been in the past. We have, therefore, a rare opportunity to study a nomadic people from the moment of their arrival at Russia's southern frontier to their ultimate political and military demise. An examination of the Kalmyks throughout this period confirms previous anthropological findings in regard to other societies on several crucial issues. It clearly demonstrates that the increasing power of the Kalmyk khan and the centralization of authority in Kalmyk society were not indigenous phenomena but rather a function of the Kalmyks' relations with the Russian state. It also demonstrates that sedentarization among the Kalmyks came as a result of major social changes brought about by their contacts with Russia. Some members of the Kalmyk elite chose to seek power outside their own society and turned to the Russian government for patronage and favors, while the impoverished ordinary Kalmyks found means for survival in the Russian markets. Among the Kalmyks sedentarization was a process of downward mobility.

This book is also a study of the Russian government's policies in its southern borderlands. Although the government's goals of stabilizing the frontier and using the Kalmyk military against its adversaries remained the same throughout the period under examination, its policies toward the Kalmyks underwent substantial changes, evolving from mere containment to the ultimate goal of incorporating them into the Russian empire.

In the initial stages, Moscow, unable to exercise control over the Kalmyks, had to rely on a system of payments and rewards, but by the early eighteenth century the expanding frontier and modernized Russian military allowed the government to exert more direct military and economic pressure. The Kalmyks' increased dependence on Russian markets and military support caused the government to resort to a broad range of policy tools. These included the continuous co-optation of the Kalmyk elite, increasing benefits to those who converted to Orthodox Christianity, incentives to settle down and join the military payroll, the provision of employment for destitute Kalmyks, and the introduction of Russian laws and institutions. It may be argued that these policies were typical of Russia's relations with the nomadic peoples along its southern frontier throughout the centuries.

Yet there were differences as well, and even though the migration of the Kalmyks continued the pattern of nomadic movement from Inner Asia, their arrival did not have the same significance for Russia as had the previous migrations of nomadic Turkic and Mongol peoples. The military superiority of the nomadic archers of the past was ended by the firepower of musketry and cannons in the seventeenth century. When in the next century the Chinese military destroyed the Oirats—the last powerful nomadic confederation in Inner Asia—and the Russian settlers achieved the same purpose by compelling the Kalmyk nomads to flee in 1771, the era of the nomad effectively came to an end. The bow and arrow were no match for the cannon and the plow.

The study of nomadic-sedentary interaction traditionally has been the domain of anthropologists. A number of anthropological works have examined specific cases to determine the links between nomads and sedentary states, as well as to address the question of sedentarization.[1]

---

[1]Only a few important works are Fredrik Barth, *Nomads of South Persia: The Basseri Tribe of the Khamseh Confederacy* (Oslo: Universitetsforlaget, 1964); Jacob Black [Black-Michaud], "Tyranny as a Strategy for Survival in an 'Egalitarian Society': Luri Facts versus an Anthropological Mystique," *Man* 7 (1972): 614–34; William Irons, "Nomadism as a Political Adaptation: The Case of the Yomut Turkmen," *American Ethnologist* 1 (1974): 635–58.

Such studies usually approach the nomad-settler relationship at a particular time and do not attempt to examine its evolution over a longer period.[2]

Several attempts have been made to write the history of the Kalmyk people. N. N. Pal'mov, for example, wrote a monumental five-volume study in the 1920s, but his reliance on Russian archival sources alone, as he admits in his introduction, inevitably led him to a Russocentric view of Russo-Kalmyk relations. Soviet historiography followed this traditional approach. Two volumes of *Ocherki istorii Kalmytskoi ASSR*, published in the late 1960s, as well as numerous articles published by the Kalmyk Research Institute of Language, Literature, and History (KNIIaLI) in Elista, USSR, all portray the Kalmyks as the sometimes nefarious subjects of an always benevolent Russian suzerain. The only serious and systematic attempt to acquaint Western readers with Kalmyk history was undertaken by Charles Riess in his dissertation "The History of the Kalmyk Khanate to 1724," completed at Indiana University in 1983. Like many before him, however, he shied away from exceeding the cultural boundaries of a Russocentric approach and chose to follow Pal'mov and his interpretation.

The focal point of this book is the history of the Kalmyk people and their relations with Russia, not only from the Russian viewpoint but from the Kalmyk as well. By giving validity to the point of view of the nomads and by showing how Kalmyk society functioned and perceived itself and its neighbors, I intend to demonstrate why the notions and values of a sedentary, state-organized society such as that of Russia could not automatically be applied to the nomadic, tribal society of the Kalmyks. Each society saw in the other a reflection of its own political system with its intrinsic values. This projection of cultural values and political notions led to fundamental misunderstandings and unrealistic expectations on both sides.

My methodology rests on the fundamental thesis that Kalmyk society must be approached and understood on its own terms, that is, from within the conceptual bounds of a traditional Kalmyk-Mongol view. The major obstacle to developing such an approach is that one has to rely predominantly on sources compiled in the sedentary societies, which are necessarily biased. To rectify the situation, I attempted to discern from a variety of sources a broad range of sociopolitical and economic categories that existed in Kalmyk-Mongol nomadic society. I then constructed a frame of reference through which to view Kalmyk society.

---

[2]The most notable exception is the recent study by Thomas J. Barfield, *The Perilous Frontier: Nomadic Empires and China* (Cambridge, Mass.: Basil Blackwell, 1989). This is the most comprehensive and sophisticated examination of the history of interaction between Inner Asian nomads and China.

Applying such a framework to Russian sources shows that Russian documents are often misleading and must be approached critically. Further to reduce the bias of the sources, I compared, whenever possible, Russian documents with Ottoman-Crimean ones. Ottoman sources often interpret the same event differently and thus provide a valuable corrective to the Russian materials.

Chapter 1 offers a historico-anthropological reconstruction of Kalmyk nomadic society. It aims to lay the theoretical ground for an understanding of Kalmyk society and to give the reader an idea of its organization and functions. The chapter deals with such aspects of Kalmyk society as its socioeconomic and military organization, law, and religious beliefs. Chapter 2 addresses the issues of diplomacy and political ideology in both Kalmyk and Russian societies and reveals that each had fundamentally different goals for, and expectations of, their relationship. Chapters 3–7 deal with two centuries of Kalmyk history, focusing in particular on relations with Russia. The account begins with the arrival of the Kalmyks in the Caspian steppes in the 1630s—a landmark in the history of both the Kalmyks and Russia—and ends in 1771, the year of the Kalmyks' departure for their traditional homeland in Jungaria.

The history of the Kalmyk people and their relations with the Russian state reveals numerous parallels with the history of other nomadic peoples. The dynamics of Russo-Kalmyk relations thus point to a pattern in the relationship between nomads and the sedentary state, suggesting that it was the Kalmyks' growing dependence on Russia that caused profound changes in Kalmyk society and ultimately resulted in its sedentarization.

Moreover, this book raises the issue of the role of the southern frontier in Russian history. I suggest that the Kalmyks, along with other nomadic peoples who preceded them, made a substantial impression on Russian society. The Russian state was forced to adapt to meet the challenges posed by the southern frontier, with its open steppes and constant exposure to the threat of raids by the highly mobile nomads. The losses sustained as a result of numerous nomadic incursions and the efforts to stabilize this frontier by both constructing a chain of defense lines and paying off the nomad elites took an enormous human and material toll on Russian society. The identity of the Russian state and its political ideology were also crystallized in the course of the constant struggle with the "infidel" nomadic peoples, which ended only with their incorporation into a multiethnic Russian empire.

1

Kalmyk Nomadic Society

The People and Their Name

During the seventeenth and eighteenth centuries, the Mongol people were scattered across a large region of modern Outer Mongolia, Inner Mongolia, the northwestern provinces of China, and some adjacent areas of the former Soviet Union. Eastern Mongols were known as Khalkha-Mongols, while Western Mongols were called Oirats and were concentrated in Jungaria (now Xinjiang province in China) (see Map 1).[1]

The Kalmyks were Western Mongols, or Oirats. The name *Kalmyk* in reference to the Oirats was first used by their Turkic neighbors and can be traced back to the mid-fourteenth-century work of the Arab geographer Ibn al-Wardi.[2] Traditional etymology derives the name from the Turkish verb *kalmak*—to stay, to remain. No one, however, has succeeded in attaching a relevant historical meaning to this etymology. Other scholars have attempted to trace the meaning of the name back to various Mongol roots.[3] It is reasonable to assume, however, that the

[1] A competent discussion of the Chinese sources concerned with the ethnic composition of the Oirats and the origins of the name is offered by Ch'i Yü Wu, "Who Were the Oirats?" *Yenching Journal of Social Studies* 3, no. 2 (1941): 174–219. The same issues have been thoroughly discussed by Hidehiro Okada, "Origins of the Dörben Oyirad," *Ural-Altaische Jahrbücher* 7 (1987): 181–211.

[2] E. V. Bretschneider, *Medieval Researches from Eastern Asiatic Sources*, 2 vols. (London: Kegan Paul, Trench, Trübner, 1910), 2:167.

[3] N. N. Poppe cited Gegen Dilova-Khutukhtu, who suggested that *Kalmyk* came from the Mongol *khal'kh*, meaning overflow, spill over (Poppe, "Rol' Zaya-pandity v kul'turnoi istorii mongol'skikh narodov," in Kalmyk Monograph Series, no. 2, *Kalmyk-Oirat Symposium* (Philadelphia: Society for Promotion of Kalmyk Culture, 1966), 60. A. Sh. Kichikov suggested

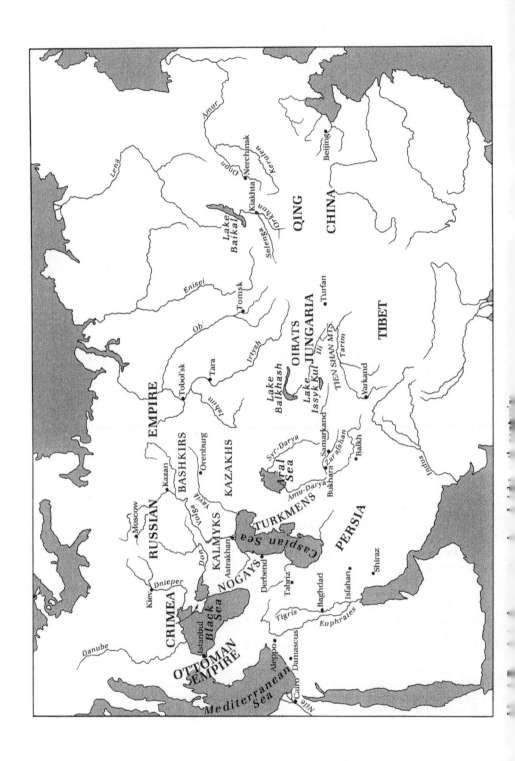

name indeed came from the Turkish *kalmak*. The most important distinction between the various Mongol tribes was between those who traced their lineage in the male line to Chinggis Khan and others outside this lineage. Until the seventeenth century only direct descendants of Chinggis could bear the title of khan. This unwritten law was so inviolable that even the all-powerful Tamerlane did not dare to appropriate the title for himself.

The Oirats, unlike other Mongols, were not descendants of Chinggis Khan, which prevented them from making any legitimate claims to supremacy.[4] That is why the Mongols proper referred to the Oirats as "aliens."[5] In addition, the expression *Döchin Dörben khoyar*, that is, forty and four,[6] meant forty *tümen* of the Mongols and four of the Oirats and thus clearly drew the line between the two. Some structural differences also remained, as the Oirats were least affected by Chinggis Khan's newly introduced military division into "thousands," which dealt a severe blow to the traditional kinship organization of the Mongol tribes.[7] These points suggest that the word *kalmyk* is likely to be a calque or a corruption of some Mongol or Chinese word used to refer to the Oirats since the time of Chinggis Khan. In this context the meaning of the term *kalmyk* as to stay, to remain behind acquires some historical validity. Whether it was the actual case, however, still remains to be shown.

To avoid confusion, I will follow W. L. Kotwicz and reserve the name *Kalmyk* only for the group of Oirats who came from Jungaria to roam the Caspian steppes in the early seventeenth century.[8] In the period under discussion, the Kalmyks consisted of four main tribes: the Torgut, Derbet, Khoshut, and Jungar.[9] The majority of the Kalmyks who left Jungaria belonged to the Torgut and Derbet tribes. By the 1630s to 1640s they had

an etymology from the Mongol word *khal'mag* meaning swift, headlong, flying (Kichikov, "K voprosu o proiskhozhdenii slova 'kalmyk,' " *Uchenye zapiski KNIIaLI* 5 [1968]: 133–34).

[4]Bretschneider, *Medieval Researches*, 2:171.

[5]Junko Miyawaki, "On the Oyirad Khanship," in *Aspects of Altaic Civilization*, vol. 3, ed. Denis Sinor (Bloomington: Indiana University Press, 1990), 143.

[6]Batur-Ubashi Tümen, "Skazanie o derben-oiratakh," trans. Iu. S. Lytkin, in *Kalmytskie istoriko-literaturnye pamiatniki v russkom perevode* (Elista: N.p., 1969), 19; B. Ia. Vladimirtsov, *Obshchestvennyi stroi mongolov. Mongol'skii kochevoi feodalism* (Leningrad: AN SSSR, 1934), 135. This expression was still remembered by the Oirats and Mongols in the middle of the seventeenth century (*Ikh Tsaaz* ["Velikoe ulozhenie"]. *Pamiatnik mongol'skogo feodal'nogo prava 17 v.*, trans. S. D. Dalykov [Moscow: Nauka, 1981], 13).

[7]Vladimirtsov, *Obshchestvennyi*, 109–10.

[8]W. L. Kotwicz, "Russkie arkhivnye dokumenty po snosheniiam s oiratami v 17–18 vekakh," *Izvestiia Rossiiskoi akademii nauk*, nos. 12–15 (1919): 791.

[9]V. P. Sanchirov, "Etnicheskii sostav oiratov 15–18 vv. po dannym 'Iletkhel shastir'," in *Iz istorii kapitalisticheskikh otnoshenii v Kalmykii* (Elista: N.p., 1977), 3–33; Paul Pelliot, *Notes critiques d'histoire kalmouke* (Paris: Librairie d'Amerique et d'Orient, 1960).

succeeded in driving out the Nogay people of the Caspian steppes[10] and took over their pastures along the Emba, the Yayik, and the Volga rivers. By the end of the century the Torguts and the Derbets were joined by two other tribes.

Contemporary Russian sources often failed to differentiate between the Kalmyks of the Caspian steppes and those of Jungaria. An apparent lack of consensus among the different Kalmyk tribes only added to this confusion. As late as 1761 the Khoshut and Jungar referred to themselves and the Torgut tribe as Oirats, not Kalmyks. The Torguts used the name Kalmyks for themselves, as well as for the Khoshuts and the Jungars, but believed that this name had been given to them by the Russians.[11] Ninety years later, the Khoshuts still referred to themselves as Oirats, as the nineteenth-century Russian ethnographer Pavel Nebol'sin observed.[12]

It was only in the course of the nineteenth century that the Kalmyks adopted the name *Kalmyk* to identify themselves. Even then it was predominantly used in relations with outsiders and with neighboring states. The most important criteria for differentiating among themselves remained tribal and clan affiliation and location of pastures.[13]

In summary, the name *Kalmyk* was used by the Kalmyks' neighbors as a generic term to include several tribes. The name was imposed from the outside and in time included not only the Kalmyks proper but also the Mangyshlak Turkmen and various Nogay tribes, which at various times joined them. As it was used by the Kalmyks' sedentary neighbors in the

[10]The area was known to various Turkic peoples under its Persian name, Desht-i Kipchak, i.e., the steppes of the Kipchak people. Others called it the Sarmatian, Nogay, or Kalmyk steppes after the names of the peoples who inhabited the area at the time. I chose to call these steppes Caspian to give the name a more permanent sense.

[11]This observation was made by Vasilii Bakunin, a Russian official who dealt with the Kalmyks at length and knew them well (Bakunin, "Opisanie istorii kalmytskogo naroda," *Krasnyi arkhiv. Istoricheskii zhurnal* 3 [1939]: 194).

[12]Pavel Nebol'sin, *Ocherki byta kalmykov khoshoutovskogo ulusa* (St. Petersburg: Tip. Karla Kraia, 1852), 10. This makes sense because the Khoshuts, unlike three other Kalmyk tribes, were originally a Mongol tribe that joined the Oirat confederation in Jungaria relatively late, in the mid-fifteenth century (Okada, "Origins," 203–7). It is also remarkable that the Kalmyk historical accounts of Gabang Sharab and Batur-Ubashi Tümen, written in 1737 and 1819, respectively, are entitled "A Tale of the Oirats," and refer to well-known *noyons* and khans of the Caspian steppes as Oirats. Only the anonymous chronicle written in the 1840s uses the name *Kalmyk* in reference to these *noyons* and khans. Yet this chronicle too was originally written in the Oirat language and only later translated into Kalmyk (Iu. S. Lytkin's introduction to "Istoriia kalmytskikh khanov," trans. Iu. S. Lytkin, in *Kalmytskie istoriko-literaturnye*, 50).

[13]When a Kalmyk or Mongol nomad met another, the first questions were: "What clan and tribe do you belong to? Where are your pastures? What are your father's and mother's names? What is your name?" (Shara-Bodon, in *Mongolo-oiratskii geroicheskii epos*, trans. B. Ia. Vladimirtsov [Petersburg and Moscow: Gos. izd-vo, 1923], 237, 243; also David F. Aberle, *The Kinship System of the Kalmuk Mongols* [Albuquerque: University of New Mexico Press, 1953], 40).

seventeenth and eighteenth centuries, the name implied the existence of a consolidated ethnic group, the Kalmyk nation. Such a concept was as yet alien to the Kalmyk people and in reality stood for a confederation of different Oirat and some Turkic tribes with different degrees of consolidation at different times.

Socioadministrative System

Historical sources of the seventeenth and eighteenth centuries contain little information concerning the social structure of Kalmyk society. Yet some principal social categories can be discerned, and I briefly outline them here, proceeding from compound to elementary units.

In classical Mongol times a tribe was equated with the category of *ulus*—the largest organizational entity composed of a variety of kin groups and united by their political allegiance to the chief, who bore the Chinese title of *tayishi*.[14] Territory occupied by such a tribe-ulus was called *nutug* (*yurt*), and its pastures were in common tribal possession.[15] In the middle of the seventeenth century, perhaps under pressure from the growing numbers of people and herds, it became common practice for a Kalmyk tayishi to divide the tribe-ulus equally among his sons, without regard to seniority.[16] The name *ulus*, then, began to mean a social and administrative unit. It became the property of a certain tayishi, his appanage. It is in this sense of an appanage organized on social and political principles that the word *ulus* was used in seventeenth- and eighteenth-century sources.

The ulus consisted of a number of *ayimag*—a group united by a patrilineal descent and sharing a common pasture ground.[17] At the head of the ayimag was the *zayisang*.[18] Some claimed that the ayimag was

---

[14]In Russian documents and in most of the critical literature of the Russian and Soviet periods, the word *taisha* is incorrectly used as a singular noun, perhaps because of the association of the ending "-i" with the Russian plural. The correct rendering for the singular is *tayishi*, from the Chinese *tay-ishi*—literally grand preceptor (Vladimirtsov, *Obshchestvennyi*, 138; Charles O. Hucker, *A Dictionary of Official Titles in Imperial China* [Stanford, Calif.: Stanford University Press, 1985], 481, no. 6213). For the history of this term see Henry Serruys, "The Office of Tayishi in Mongolia in the Fifteenth Century," *HJAS* 37, no. 2 (1977): 353–81.

[15]Vladimirtsov, *Obshchestvennyi*, 111.

[16]The Torgut tayishi Daichin seems to be the first to have divided his ulus equally among his three sons, although he left a larger part for himself (Gabang Sharab, "Skazanie ob oiratakh," trans. Iu. Lytkin, in *Kalmytskie istoriko-literaturnye*, 151).

[17]Vladimirtsov, *Obshchestvennyi*, 136–37.

[18]Like the tayishi, this term is also of Chinese origin (Vladimirtsov, *Obshchestvennyi*, 138); David Aberle stated that according to his informants, the ayimag was made up of people sharing the same grazing area and not based on kinship (Aberle, *Kinship System*, 8).

divided into *änge*—clans—which had disappeared by the nineteenth century.[19] Other observers thought that the *änge* was a larger unit comprising several ayimags.[20] The number of households or tents per ayimag varied. In the middle of the eighteenth century, an ayimag could include anywhere from one hundred to one thousand tents.[21] As the number of people and herds dramatically diminished at the end of the eighteenth century, one ayimag was reported to have two hundred to three hundred tents.[22]

One step down in this administrative hierarchy was the division into *khoton* headed by an elder or headman called *akha.* In terms of kinship the khoton was a compound and not a clearly delimited group, politically structured around the headman.[23] The khoton consisted of several *ger*—tents situated around the central tent of the akha.[24] In the late eighteenth and early nineteenth centuries a khoton consisted of ten to twelve tents.[25] The khoton was the basic economic and social group of Kalmyk society.

As well as the classification into ulus-ayimag-khoton, the Kalmyks had other ways of distinguishing among themselves. For instance, the Kalmyks were divided by *yasun*—"bone"—a notion with different meanings at different times. By the seventeenth century, it had become primarily a social category, classifying the Kalmyks into *tsakhan yasun* ("white bone") and *khara yasun* ("black bone"), that is, nobility and commoners.[26]

Another traditional system of organization in Mongol society was the

[19]G. Bembeev, "O rodo-plemennykh izmeneniiakh u kalmykov," in *Problemy etnogeneza kalmykov* (Elista: N.p., 1984), 69.

[20]Nebol'sin, *Ocherki byta kalmykov,* 8.

[21]Bakunin also mentioned some ayimags that included five or ten tents. He probably confused it with *khoton,* for it is unlikely that an ayimag could be that small (Bakunin, "Opisanie," *Krasnyi arkhiv* 3 [1939]: 241).

[22]Benjamin Bergmann, *Nomadische Streifereien unter den Kalmüken in den Jahren 1802 und 1803,* 4 vols. (Riga: Hartmann, 1804–5), 2:35.

[23]Vladimirtsov, *Obshchestvennyi,* 170. Barth, *Nomads of South Persia* 61.

[24]On various forms of the ger and its evolution see D. Maidar and D. Piurveev, *Ot kochevoi do mobil'noi arkhitektury* (Moscow: Stroiizdat, 1980), 12–36; also I. A. Zhitetskii, *Ocherki byta astrakhanskikh kalmykov: Etnograficheskie nabliudeniia 1884–1886 gg.* (Moscow: Tip. M. G. Volchaninova, 1893), 1–17; Peter Simon Pallas, *Reise durch verschiedene Provinzen des Russischen Reichs,* 3 vols. (St. Petersburg: Kaiserl. Akademie der Wissenschaften, 1771–76; rpt. Gratz-Austria: Akademische Druck-und Verlagsanstalt, 1967), 1:312–14. For more about the khoton and the arrangement of the tents in it, see Zhitetskii, *Ocherki byta,* 33–35; F. I. Leontovich, *K istorii prava russkikh inorodtsev: Drevnii mongolo-kalmytskii ili oiratskii ustav vzyskanii (Tsaadzhin-Bichig)* (Odessa: N.p., 1879), 159.

[25]Pallas, *Reise,* 1:328; Bergmann, *Nomadische,* 2:36.

[26]Bembeev, "O rodo-plemennykh," 63; Vladimirtsov, *Obshchestvennyi,* 153.

1. A Kalmyk encampment in the nineteenth century (from *Kalmytskaia step'* *Astrakhanskoi gubernii po issledovaniiam Kumo-Manychskoi ekspeditsii.* St. Petersburg: Tip. V. Bezobrazova, 1868).

division into thousands, a military system used in times of warfare or large-scale migrations. Each ulus corresponded to tümen and was supposed to provide ten thousand warriors. *Otog* is described sometimes as a military division, a banner,[27] and sometimes as a social and administrative unit corresponding to the military corps.[28] Ayimag was equated with the military unit *khoshun*—a regiment with a varying number of horsemen depending on the size of the ayimag.[29]

The division into thousands and hundreds with their strict correspon-

[27]Peter Simon Pallas, *Sammlungen Historischer Nachrichten über die Mongolischen Volkerschaften* (St. Petersburg: Akademie der Wissenschaften, 1776), 1:221–22, as cited in Paula G. Rubel, *The Kalmyk Mongols: A Study in Continuity and Change,* Uralo-Altaic Series, vol. 64 (Bloomington: Indiana University Press, 1967), 60–61; Leontovich, *K istorii prava,* 165.

[28]Vladimirtsov, *Obshchestvennyi,* 132.

[29]Ibid., 133; Bembeev, "O rodo-plemennykh," 67.

dence to certain socioadministrative units was not used by the Kalmyks in the seventeenth and eighteenth centuries. Presumably, even if such a system had existed among them earlier, it could no longer have been possible once the uluses were increasingly subdivided among various tayishis. The military organization of the Kalmyks is discussed in greater depth later in this chapter.

The socioadministrative organization of Kalmyk society is not clear, in part because of the extreme vagueness of contemporary sources on these issues but also because the classifications described were closely interwoven and the Kalmyks frequently used them interchangeably. The blending of terms and the contradictory evidence eloquently reflect the decentralized and fragmentary character of the Kalmyk pastoral nomadic society of the seventeenth and eighteenth centuries, which had a complex, multifunctional social organization with the often undifferentiated and intermittent institutions typical of tribal society.

The Social Ladder

Russian historical records of the seventeenth and eighteenth centuries dealt only with such social groups as tayishis, zayisangs, and commoners. The Mongol-Oirat law code of 1640 and the laws compiled by the Kalmyk khan Donduk-Dashi in the 1740s present a more complex picture of a stratified nomadic society. The laws clearly distinguished between the various social strata, and as in many premodern societies, social status carried moral assumptions so that the law referred to people of high status as "noble" or "good" and to those of inferior status as "low" or "bad."

The Donduk-Dashi code reveals a Kalmyk society divided into four different groups (clergy are considered separately below): (1) ruling aristocracy—tayishis; (2) "noblemen"—zayisangs; (3) "people who are well-known to many"—presumably akhas; and (4) commoners—*albatu*.[30] The tayishi, as a leader of the ulus, has been mentioned. With the division of the ulus among the tayishi's sons, the number of tayishi grew, as did the number of uluses. The law code of 1640 distinguished three different types of tayishi according to their wealth and power: (1) chief tayishi; (2) "tayishis similar to Mergen-Daichin and Chouker" (perhaps

---

[30]These groups were distinguished by the different penalties they had to pay if they failed to appear on time for a military campaign (Donduk-Dashi's laws in K. F. Golstunskii, *Mongolo-oiratskie zakony 1640 goda, dopolnitel'nye ukazy Galdan Khun-Taidzhiia i zakony, sostavlennye dlia volzhskikh kalmykov pri kalmytskom khane Donduk-Dashi* [St. Petersburg: Tip. Imp. Akademii nauk, 1880], 62).

meaning wealthy and important tayishis); and (3) minor tayishi.[31] The title of chief tayishi, and later that of khan, implied possession of the largest ulus and the position of political leader of the tribal confederation.

The zayisangs constituted a group of lesser Kalmyk nobility. An eighteenth-century Russian official and translator from Kalmyk, Vasilii Bakunin, mentioned that each *noyon* (that is, chief or minor tayishi) had a few zayisangs, and each zayisang had in his possession an ayimag, just as a Russian noble had a village.[32] Little is known about the akha—an elder or a headman—except that in the court procedures he was responsible for his khoton. If a theft was committed by a person from his khoton, the akha had to pay a penalty—one four-year-old camel.[33]

According to an early nineteenth-century observer, commoners, or albatu,[34] were so disdained by higher-class Kalmyks that no respected Kalmyk would drink from the same bowl as such a person.[35] The ruling elite—the noyons—were responsible for their albatu, who were bound to their respective khotons and ayimags and had to be returned if they fled.[36] The albatu was also personally bound to the noyon, who had complete rights over him, except for the right to kill him in public.[37] The albatu had to pay the noyon an annual tithe in livestock and provide various services, such as supplying horses, wagons, and food for passing court officials and envoys; collecting dry manure for heating; and participating in the noyon's militia.[38] In rare cases—for example, if he saved the noyon's life in battle—an albatu could be relieved from his obligations to the noyon and thus assume the title of *darkhan/tarkhan*.[39]

Below the albatu was another social group, the *bogol*, whose position B. I. Vladimirtsov characterized as part slave and part servant.[40] The 1640 law code considers the bogol equivalent to a classical slave. In one case, a slave woman was not considered a viable witness in a burglary case. In another, a slaveowner was allowed to exercise unlimited rights over the

---

[31]*Ikh Tsaaz*, 14, no. 13.

[32]Bakunin, "Opisanie," *Krasnyi arkhiv* 3 (1939): 241.

[33]Donduk-Dashi's laws, in Golstunskii, *Mongolo-oiratskie*, 64.

[34]*Albatu* is derived from the Mongol alba(n)—homage, service (Vladimirtsov, *Obshchestvennyi*, 159).

[35]Bergmann, *Nomadische*, 2:36–37.

[36]*Ikh Tsaaz*, 14, nos. 10–12. Donduk-Dashi's laws, in Golstunskii, *Mongolo-oiratskie*, 70.

[37]*Ikh Tsaaz*, 20, no. 69; Pallas, *Reise*, 1:328; Vladimirtsov, *Obshchestvennyi*, 163.

[38]Pallas, *Reise*, 1:328; *Ikh Tsaaz*, 17, no. 35; Donduk-Dashi's laws, in Golstunskii, *Mongolo-oiratskie*, 70; Vladimirtsov, *Obshchestvennyi*, 164. A thorough discussion of the alba(n) in comparison with other taxes is found in John Masson Smith, Jr., "Mongol and Nomadic Taxation," *HJAS* 30 (1970): 78–81.

[39]*Ikh Tsaaz*, 15, no. 15; Vladimirtsov, *Obshchestvennyi*, 164.

[40]Vladimirtsov, *Obshchestvennyi*, 165–66.

slave and had to pay a hefty penalty only if charged with the slave's murder.[41]

Numerous officials existed to perform various functions in Kalmyk society. For instance, there was the *daruga*, who, in one account, is described as an envoy from one ulus to another, and, in another account, as a governor or steward appointed by the noyon to supervise various work and collect taxes.[42] The *demchi*, an assistant to the daruga, was in charge of collecting taxes from forty tents.[43] A headman in charge of twenty tents was called *shülenge*.[44]

Two other important positions close to the noyon were the *elchi*, envoy, and the *köteji*, an equerry, both personal servants of the noyon.[45] A special position was occupied by the *nökör*—a close associate of the noyon, a trusted follower who pledged to serve him but was free to leave him.

I observed earlier that the socioadministrative system of Kalmyk society consisted largely of typical tribal institutions. What emerges here, however, is a stratified society with a close resemblance to a premodern social hierarchy. This amalgam of tribal institutions permeated by the elements of more complex social hierarchies characterized Kalmyk nomadic society in the seventeenth and eighteenth centuries.

Political Organization: Khanate, Chiefdom, or Tribal Confederation?

In the literature on the Kalmyks or Oirats, the word *khanate* is customarily used to denote the Kalmyk or Oirat political entity.[46] It was used in such a context either because of a traditional association or a stubborn ideological bias. I will show that the word *khanate* needs to be carefully qualified and can be misleading when applied to Kalmyk society.

The term *khanate*, as it was used in the contemporary sources as well as by scholars more recently, implies the notion of statehood. It suggests

---

[41]The penalty for killing a female slave was less than that for a male slave (*Ikh Tsaaz*, 18, no. 46; 27, no. 169).

[42]The first definition belongs to the late eighteenth-century German traveler and scientist Peter Pallas, *Reise*, 1:329. The latter one is found in Vladimirtsov, *Obshchestvennyi*, 140.

[43]*Ikh Tsaaz*, 18, no. 52.

[44]Vladimirtsov, *Obshchestvennyi*, 140, 162.

[45]Ibid., 162–63.

[46]*Ocherki istorii Kalmytskoi ASSR*, vol. 1: *Dooktiabr'skii period* (Moscow: Nauka, 1967); Charles A. Riess, "The History of the Kalmyk Khanate to 1724" (Ph.D. diss., Indiana University, 1983); I. Ia. Zlatkin, *Istoriia Dzhungarskogo khanstva, 1635–1758*, 2d ed. (Moscow: Nauka, 1983).

the existence of at least rudimentary state structure, with some urban centers, defined territory, sovereign jurisdiction, and effective legal authority, which allows the khan to use a coercive power superior to that possessed by any individuals or groups within the state. Previous classic examples of such khanates were the Khazar khanate in the eighth through tenth centuries and the Golden Horde in the thirteenth through fifteenth centuries.

The Kalmyks were organized into a loose confederation of tribes with no urban centers or even winter headquarters where hay could be stored. Instead, they followed seasonal migration routes throughout the entire year. Kalmyk society of the seventeenth and eighteenth centuries was totally nomadic society. The power of the Kalmyk chief tayishi, or later khan, rested largely on the support of other Kalmyk tayishis, who were economically and politically independent of the khan. The khan's limited power was most eloquently defined by the zayisang Yaman in 1722. Upon Ayuki Khan's death, the Astrakhan governor Artemii Volynskii asked the zayisang who, in his view, would be an appropriate candidate to become khan. Yaman replied that the Kalmyks could not agree on this: "Who becomes khan does not matter. All he gains is a title and prominence; his income comes only from his own ulus. Other tayishis have their own uluses and they govern them themselves. The khan is not supposed to interfere, and if he does, no one will obey."[47]

The title of khan at this time carried mostly political prestige, which did not always translate into increased power. Since the middle of the seventeenth century the title of khan had been largely devalued and often liberally granted by the new rulers in Tibet. Contrary to established practice, one was no longer required to be a descendant of Chinggis Khan to become a khan. In the early 1650s the chief tayishi Daichin received a diploma confirming the title and the khan's seal from Tibet. Yet he chose to return the seal and diploma to the Dalai Lama, saying that there were many tayishis like him, and he, therefore, could not accept the title.[48] Forty years later, Daichin's grandson Ayuki requested and received the title of khan from the Dalai Lama, thus becoming the first Kalmyk khan.[49] The title was given in a postfactum recognition of

[47]N. N. Pal'mov, *Etiudy po istorii privolzhskikh kalmykov 17 i 18 veka,* 5 vols. (Astrakhan': Tip. Kalmoblitizdata, 1926–32), 3–4:289–90.

[48]Gabang Sharab, "Skazanie ob oiratakh," 147.

[49]"Istoriia kalmytskikh khanov," trans. Iu. Lytkin, in *Kalmytskie istoriko-literaturnye,* 70. As careful an observer as Vasilii Bakunin noted that after Ayuki's military victories over the Kazakhs and the Turkmens, his authority over the Kalmyks and their subjects the Nogays grew to such an extent that he requested the title of khan from the Dalai Lama (Bakunin, "Opisanie," *Krasnyi arkhiv* 3 [1939]: 198).

Ayuki's accumulation of wealth and prestige, unequaled by any other tayishi. His increased stature was a function of his relationship with Russia, in which he became the main "redistribution center" of Russian goods and military power. Now he was able to send more generous gifts to the Dalai Lama of Tibet and to donate more albatu to the Kalmyk monasteries and lamas, who had advised the Dalai Lama of the political expediency of bestowing upon Ayuki the title of utmost honor.

The Russian government, however, considered Ayuki its subject and was not willing to recognize his new status. Only the growing need for his military assistance forced the authorities finally to address Ayuki as khan in 1708.[50] By association the khan was supposed to be the ruler of a khanate; thus the word *khanate* came into use in reference to the Kalmyks. At the time, Russian officials were hardly able to comprehend that to refer to the Kalmyks as "a khanate" was in fact to superimpose the notion of a centralized and bureaucratic political system of Russia onto Kalmyk society. The Russian government did not realize that although the role of the khan had grown substantially, his real power was still limited; Kalmyk society remained a decentralized confederation of several tribes.

Placing Kalmyk society in the evolutionary scheme offered by Elman Service and Marshall Sahlins, that of "band—tribe—chiefdom," it becomes obvious that Kalmyk society does not precisely fit any single category, but rather combines features of the last two. According to Service, "A tribe is a loosely integrated and more variably constituted entity than a chiefdom. A chiefdom has centralized authority and a ramification of the subsidiary, connected authority that extends toward the boundary of the society."[51] He then observes: "Chiefdoms seem to have boundaries or borders. Territoriality or at least some criteria of membership in the society which are not based merely on sentiments of kinship and voluntary association seem to be emerging at the chiefdom level."[52] The nomadic society of the Kalmyks lacked any of the important criteria necessary to acquire the full features of chiefdom.

Marshall Sahlins, observing the chiefdoms formed by the pastoral nomads in contention with agrarian centers in southwest Asia, noticed that such chiefdoms were "not entirely *sui generis* but crystallized by external pressure. The body politic may then retain features of a primitive organism, covered by a protective exoskeleton of chiefly authority

---

[50]*Materialy po istorii Bashkirskoi ASSR*, vol. 1: *Bashkirskie vosstaniia v 17 i pervoi polovine 18 vekov* (Moscow and Leningrad: Izd-vo AN SSSR, 1936), 238, no. 104.

[51]Elman R. Service, *Primitive Social Organization: An Evolutionary Perspective* (New York: Random House, 1966), 167.

[52]Ibid., 168.

but fundamentally uncomplicated and segmented underneath. That is to say, a structural gap appears between the central chieftainship and underlying local groups."[53] Such a "structural gap" was indeed inherent in Kalmyk nomadic society. The nature of nomadism, with its centrifugal forces, prevented the establishment of a tightly controlled, centralized authority able to reach the periphery of the society. Such a structure became possible only when a certain degree of sedentarization had occurred, the establishing of territoriality, or some criteria of common membership other than kinship and voluntary association. This structural gap was not closed in Kalmyk society until the late nineteenth century. At this time, with the growing process of sedentarization, the increasing role of the central authority, and a rising sense of corporate identity, Kalmyk society obtained the full features of the chiefdom—the khanate. Since this book is concerned with the seventeenth and eighteenth centuries, the term *Kalmyk society* appears to be much more precise than *Kalmyk khanate*.

Environment and the Way of Nomadism

The size of the Kalmyk pastures in the Caspian steppes varied greatly depending on both the climatic conditions and the political situation. In the chapters to follow I will discuss how the size and the location of Kalmyk pastures changed as political circumstances changed. Here, I will simply show the relevance of climatic and geographic conditions of the area in defining the general pattern of the nomadic movement of the Kalmyks.

The North Caspian steppes are formed by five main rivers which empty into the Caspian Sea. The easternmost river is the Emba, followed by the Yayik (today called the Ural), the Volga (by far the largest river in the area), and then the Kuma and Terek. The northwestern corner of these vast plains is bounded by the rivers Don and Manych. The northern boundary of the steppes is the Samara River, a tributary of the Volga. In the south the steppes are confined by the shores of the Caspian Sea. The steppes' main divide is the Volga River. Russian sources called land east of the Volga "the Nogay side" or "the lowland" (*lugovaia*) side; land west of the river was "the Crimean side" or "the upland" (*nagornaia*) side. Despite some desert areas, the Caspian steppes have extremely rich,

---

[53]Marshall D. Sahlins, *Tribesmen* (Englewood Cliffs, N.J.: Prentice-Hall, 1968), 45–46. Also see Sahlins, "The Segmentary Lineage: An Organization of Predatory Expansion," *American Anthropologist* 63, no. 2 (1961): 322–45.

lush grass which is ideal for grazing herds. These steppes were a sort of pastoral El Dorado, glorified in the songs and epics of many nomadic peoples. From time immemorial the nomads came here to roam and to herd. The Sarmatians and the Cumans, the Khazar khanate and the Golden Horde all were attracted to this rich grassland. Now it was the Kalmyks' turn.

The Kalmyks first arrived in this area in the 1630s, and twenty years later they were in firm possession of the pastures along the Emba, the Yayik, and the Volga (see Map 2). By the end of the century Kalmyk uluses were roaming in the steppes as far west as the Don and Medveditsa rivers and advancing further south toward the Kuma river. In the eighteenth century, under growing pressure from the Kazakhs in the east and Russian colonists in the north, the Kalmyks found themselves more and more confined to the southwestern part of the steppes—the Volga-Kuma area (see Map 3). They were true nomads with no sedentary centers, no agricultural basis, and no winter headquarters. Consequently, they depended on large grazing areas and practiced an extensive nomadism.

Unless disrupted by political turmoil, the Kalmyks' annual migration cycle was meridional, that is, along the north-south axis. They usually spent autumn and winter in the southern parts of the steppes. During the seventeenth century they would be found in the basins of the Yayik and the Volga and by the eighteenth century along the Caspian shores from the Volga to the Kuma. Since there was less snow in these regions, it was easier for the animals to find food. Reeds provided warm shelter for the herds and abundant fuel for people. When spring came the Kalmyks moved north and waited until the Volga returned to its former level and the land offered rich fodder.[54] The Kalmyk uluses spent the summers with their herds farther north, roaming along the Volga and the Akhtuba or in the nearby steppes. Finally, at the end of summer and early autumn, the Kalmyks would move back to their winter pastures, thus completing an annual cycle.

Living in accordance with a full ecological cycle, the Kalmyks and their herds were at the mercy of nature. The richness of pastures depended on weather conditions, herds depended on pastures, and people depended on herds. Needless to say, any natural calamity could spell disaster for such a fragile economy. The most devastating phenomenon

---

[54]According to Pallas, the Kalmyks called this marshy area of reeds and rushes *matsak*, from which originated the corrupted Russian *mochag* (Peter Simon Pallas, *Travels through the Southern Provinces of the Russian Empire in the Years 1793 and 1794*, 2d ed., 2 vols. [London: Printed for John Stockdale, 1812], 1:289, 326).

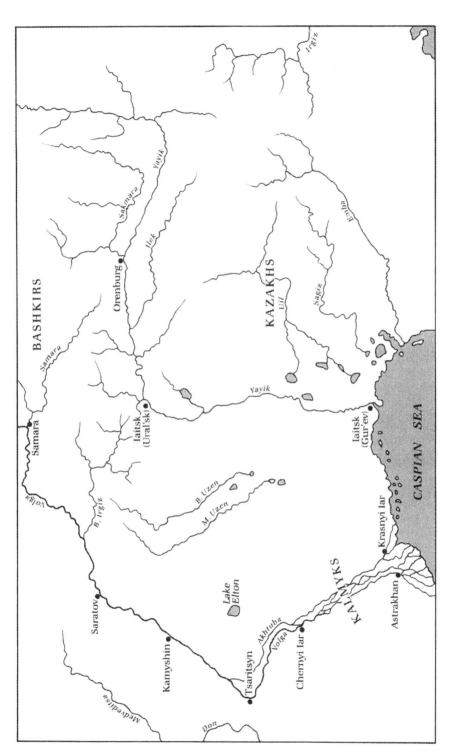

Map 2. Volga-Yayik-Emba region.

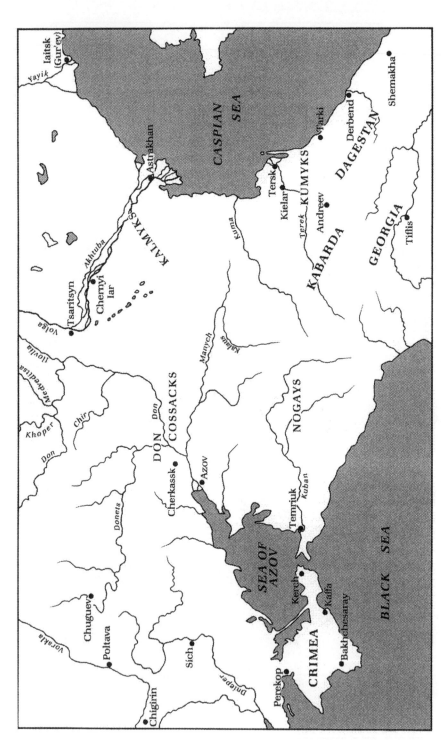

Map 3. Black Sea–Caucasus–Caspian Sea region.

was known as *zud* (*jud*)—a lack of fodder in winter resulting in the depletion of the herds.[55]

Besides pastures, water was another element vital to the nomadic way of life. Most of the nomadic routes lay along the available supplies of water—rivers, brooks, and lakes. To cross a river, the Kalmyks would make bridges out of reeds, which they bound into big bundles resembling barrels. These bundles were then tied firmly together and placed across the river to transport herds and people.[56] Another way of crossing a river was to make rafts out of bundles of reeds, to which air-filled sheepskins were attached.[57] The Kalmyks preferred, however, to cross rivers in winter on the ice.

In the search for fodder, the nomads often had to go deep into the steppes where there was no visible water supply. One such area was a large stretch of sand dunes called Rin-"sands" between the lower Volga and the lower Yayik. Water was available only from wells—*khuduk*—and could be found a foot below surface. The Kalmyks usually chose as a campsite marshes with small reeds in an area in which wells had been dug in earlier years so they needed only to clear the wells and dig a little deeper for water. One of these campsites was described as having had more than a hundred such wells, each one from twenty to fifty paces in diameter and about four fathoms deep.[58]

Another indispensable ingredient in the diet of both men and animals was salt, which the people usually obtained from the numerous salt lakes near Astrakhan, and later, in the eighteenth century, mostly from Lake Elton about sixty-five miles east of Tsaritsyn. The herds supplemented their diet with numerous salty plants growing abundantly in these steppes.

The constant search for new pastures required frequent moving. When the pastures were sufficiently depleted, the Kalmyks took down their tents, loaded them on camels or ox-drawn wagons, and moved on

[55]The Kalmyks distinguished at least three different types of *zud*. The phenomenon of herds' perishing from lack of snow in the waterless region was called *khar* ("black") *zud*. During *tsahan* ("white") *zud* the herds were decimated when the ground was covered with too much snow and animals could not find sufficient fodder. An event in which a pasture was damaged by excessive grazing was known as a *turun* ("hoof") *zud* (*Kalmytsko-russkii slovar'*, ed. B. D. Muniev [Moscow: Izd-vo "Russkii iazyk," 1977], 255).

[56]*Dnevnye zapiski puteshestviia kapitana Nikolaia Rychkova v kirgis-kaisatskoi stepi, 1771 godu* (St. Petersburg: Imp. Akademiia nauk, 1772), 52.

[57]U. E. Erdniev, *Kalmyki (konets 19-nachalo 20 vv.). Istoriko-etnograficheskie ocherki* (Elista: Kalm. knizhnoe izd-vo, 1970), 52.

[58]Pallas, *Reise*, 1:320; H. A. Zwick and J. G. Schill, *Reise von Sarepta in verschiedene Kalmücken-Horden des Astrachanischen Gouvernements im Jahr 1823 von 26ten Mai bis 21ten August Stils in Angelegenheiten der Russischen Bibel-Gesellschaft unternommen* (Leipzig: Paul Gottheif Rummer, 1827), 30.

to a new site. The process of breaking camp took about two hours. While women and children were driving the herds and singing gay songs, men were occupied with hunting and scouting the area. Changing pastures was one of the few highlights of the otherwise monotonous life of a nomad. In one day the Kalmyks could cover from fifteen to twenty five *verst* (ten to seventeen miles), but rarely more than that.[59]

There were traditionally two different types of nomadism known as the *küriyen* (from which the cossack *kuren* originated) and the *ayil*. The *küriyen* consisted of a large group of *gers*—tents. When such a group arrived at a new site, they would form a circle with their wagons. The tents were pitched inside, with the tent of the leader in the center. Thus the people and the herds were protected against enemy raids. *Ayil* consisted of a small number of tents, whose inhabitants roamed together.[60]

Available circumstantial evidence indicates that in the seventeenth and eighteenth centuries, the Kalmyks practiced the *ayil* type of nomadism. Usually different uluses were reported to roam at different locations. Each ulus had its own *nutug*—pasture. A tayishi then divided a pasture among each of his zayisangs with their respective ayimags, who in turn divided it among khotons. Later, in the 1760s, the *zargo* (a council and legislative body at the khan's headquarters) allotted winter and summer pastures to each tayishi and his ulus. The decision was confirmed by the khan and was not disputed by the tayishis.[61] The Russian sources frequently mention that the tayishi "was gathering his ulus" at a time of military threat—perhaps another indication that the ulus was using an *ayil* type of nomadism. The *küriyen* type, as in the old days, was used mainly in times of immediate military danger.

The migration routes of the Kalmyks, their favorite pastures, and their life-style all reveal the similarities between the Kalmyks and their various nomadic predecessors in these steppes—the Sarmatians, the Cumans, the Mongols, and the Nogays. From the earliest times, these children of the steppe seemed to have found the most efficient ways of using the scarce gifts of nature. Their adaptations vividly demonstrate the impact that the geographic and climatic conditions of the region had on the life of the people, who became an intrinsic part of its ecological system.

---

[59]Pallas, *Reise*, 1:327; Zhitetskii, *Ocherki byta astrakhanskikh*, 37. During their migrations nomadic Kirgiz covered the same distance (Ch. Ch. Valikhanov, "Zapiski o kirgizakh," in *Sobranie sochinenii v piati tomakh* [Alma-Ata: GRKSE, 1985], 2:36).

[60]Vladimirtsov, *Obshchestvennyi*, 37; G. E. Markov, *Kochevniki Azii* (Moscow: Izd. Mosk. Univ., 1976), 56–58.

[61]Zlatkin, *Istoriia Dzhungarskogo*, 259–60.

Economy and Trade

Throughout the seventeenth and eighteenth centuries, herds remained the sole, fundamental base of the Kalmyk economy. For the Kalmyk nomad, the herd provided food, clothing, transportation, and the principal source of wealth and prestige. The herd consisted mainly of horses, sheep, cattle, and camels. Horses and sheep were by far the most numerous. Cows supplied meat, milk, and hides, and oxen were primarily used for transportation. A few goats were always mixed in with the sheep herd.[62] The number of camels had drastically diminished by the mid-eighteenth century as part of the general reduction of the Kalmyk herds caused by the social upheavals that shook Kalmyk society in the 1720s and 1730s. The law code of 1640 does not place any special value on camels, whereas in the laws of Donduk-Dashi of the 1740s a four-year-old camel seemed to be the single most valued animal. Despite the small number of camels, the Kalmyks occasionally brought them for exchange in the cities of Orenburg and Bukhara.[63]

The Kalmyk nomads depended most of all on horses. The great value the Kalmyk placed on his horse compared to his wife is clear from a Kalmyk proverb: "The idiot praises his wife, the fool praises himself, the wise man praises his horse."[64] A horse was a Kalmyk's vehicle and his food, his friend and his pride. Whether a peaceful shepherd or an imposing warrior, the Kalmyk had always to rely on his horse, on which his life often depended in battle. The importance attached to the horse was so great that on occasion a military victory was credited to stealing or taking by force the enemy's herds of horses.[65]

Horses were herded in groups called *tabun* (*adun* in Kalmyk). The tabun consisted of several smaller groups, each containing from twelve to fifteen mares, one stallion, and several foals—altogether around thirty to fifty horses. The complete tabun could contain one hundred to two hundred horses. To distinguish one tabun from another, the owner branded his horses on the thigh or sometimes on the neck.[66]

---

[62]*Dzhangar. Kalmytskii geroicheskii epos*, trans. Semen Lipkin (Elista: Kalmytskoe knizhnoe izd-vo, 1978), 76; Bergmann, *Nomadische*, 2:63; Zwick, *Reise von Sarepta*, 24; Pallas, *Reise*, 1:325.

[63]A fine amounting to a four-year-old camel was one of the heaviest penalties that could be imposed (Donduk-Dashi's laws, in Golstunskii, *Mongolo-oiratskie*, 62). In 1803 the Kalmyks were reported to have only two-humped camels (Bergmann, *Nomadische*, 2:66); Pallas, *Reise*, 1:326.

[64]W. L. Kotwicz, *Kalmytskie zagadki i poslovitsy* (St. Petersburg: Tip. Imp. Akademii nauk, 1905), 71, no. 29.

[65]*Dzhangar*, 39, 99.

[66]Nebol'sin, *Ocherki byta kalmykov*, 160, 164.

The Kalmyks' horses were small because they were maintained entirely by grazing. Too wild and not powerful enough to be used as draft animals, they were mostly known for their great speed and endurance.[67] These horses enabled the Kalmyk nomad to move and maneuver swiftly and thus gave him a tremendous advantage in warfare.

Horses also provided food for the Kalmyks' diet. The meat of foals was tender and delicious. Horse meat was also often eaten, particularly during raids, when there was no other readily available food. Mares supplied the Kalmyks with rich and refreshing milk. Fermented mare's milk was known under its Turkic name, *kumis* (*kimiz*). For a feast, the milk could be turned into *arza* or *khurza*—alcoholic beverages differing in strength depending upon how many times they were distilled.[68]

Sheep were also an intrinsic part of the Kalmyk nomadic economy. Peter S. Pallas observed that the Kalmyk sheep was a "fat rump" (*kurdiuk*) type of sheep similar to the Kirgiz but a little smaller. Sheep provided wool for clothing and felt. Pelts could be used in manufacturing clothing, shoes, containers for liquids, quivers, and numerous other items. Sheep also provided fat and milk, and mutton was a staple in the Kalmyk diet.

Although herds provided most of the Kalmyks' needs, hunting served as a means to supplement the diet and was a favorite pastime. Even more important, hunting was a school of military training through which horsemen sharpened their skills for use in battle. A mid-nineteenth-century description of hunting the *saigak*—a large, horned antelope—is remarkably similar to some of the military tactics used by the Kalmyks. A group of four to eight Kalmyks in two lines approached the *saigak* herd from upwind. When they got within a few hundred meters, the group in the second line jumped off their mounts, while the remainder took their horses and continued the pursuit. After a short time they stopped the chase, split by making two semicircles, turned left and right, and returned by the same road. Curious *saigaks*, intrigued by the spectacle of the fleeing hunters, would turn around and follow the hunters as they disappeared from view. Soon they ran into an ambush where the first group of Kalmyks was hiding.[69]

The Caspian steppes were not known to support a greatly varied animal population. Among other game were the wild boars that were often hunted along the Caspian shores, and foxes and beavers were caught in snares and traps. Bird hunting with falcons and hawks was

[67]Pallas, *Reise*, 1:325.

[68]For the process of manufacturing the three alcoholic beverages (*arak, arza,* and *khurza*) see E. I. Kychanov, *Povestvovanie ob oiratskom Galdane Boshoktu-Khane* (Novosibirsk: Nauka, 1980), 51.

[69]Nebol'sin, *Ocherki byta kalmykov*, 154–55.

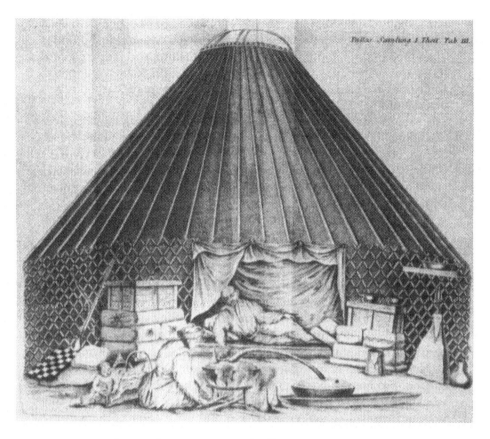

2. An interior of a tent, showing a woman distilling *arza* (from Peter Simon Pallas, *Sammlungen Historischer Nachrichten über die Mongolischen Volkerschaften*. St. Petersburg: Akadamie der Wissenschaften, 1776, Plate III).

another favorite pastime. In the late seventeenth century fishing began to play a greater role in Kalmyk economy. It became even more important in the eighteenth century, when disputes over fishing rights between the Kalmyks and the Russian authorities often emerged as a thorny issue. To be sure, no Kalmyk nomad voluntarily took up fishing over herding or even combined the activities. Fishing was a last resort for the impoverished Kalmyks. The significantly increased number of Kalmyks involved in fishing in the eighteenth century reflected such impoverishment.

Animal husbandry was a fundamental economic underpinning of Kalmyk society. Most of the available labor force was consumed by extensive nomadism, with no labor specialization other than cattle breeding. Production was a domestic function; each household or, perhaps, khoton cared for its own needs. Men were free to engage in military affairs because most of the labor was performed by women and children. They prepared the food, made clothing and shoes, and tanned animal hides and pelts. There were few artisans among the Kalmyks, although some evidence suggests that they knew the rudiments of carpentry and blacksmithing.[70]

No significant exchange of goods took place within Kalmyk society. Traditional economy allowed only for ritual exchange, such as the exchange of gifts and dowries, and bestowal of rewards. Animals were the principal exchange unit. In the seventeenth century the unit was called a "nine." Each nine usually included four head of cattle and five sheep, with possible variations.[71]

By the late seventeenth century, Russian money began to play a prominent role in the Kalmyk economy but was mostly concentrated in the hands of the noyons. By the 1730s and 1740s money appeared to have filtered down to all levels of Kalmyk society, although it still was clearly secondary in importance to the herds. In Donduk-Dashi's laws the heaviest penalty for the "rich and famous" was to pay with a number of animals, while the rest could pay cash.[72]

The vulnerability of the Kalmyk economy in the face of potential natural calamities and a system of domestic production that prevented any significant economic differentiation and provided little incentive for surplus production were among the reasons for the Kalmyks' overwhelming dependence on external markets. To obtain agricultural products, numerous items of everyday life, and luxury goods, the Kalmyks relied on trade with their sedentary neighbors, among which Russia emerged as the most important partner.

From the beginning of Russo-Kalmyk relations in the early seventeenth century, the Kalmyks insisted on access to Russian markets to barter their livestock. The Kalmyks offered a great variety of products of the cattle-breeding economy. They brought to the market sheep, horses, cattle, wool, and different types of hides and pelts, as well as the furs of the animals they hunted—foxes and beavers. They also brought items obtained from different parts of the world such as Chinese tea, paper, and musks or expensive Persian cloth and silks.

---

[70]Pallas, *Reise*, 1:314, 324; *Ikh Tsaaz*, 25, no. 137.

[71]*Ikh Tsaaz*, 37. A nine was a common exchange unit in other nomadic societies as well, although its composition could vary. For example, a nine for the nomadic people of eastern Tibet (Dza-chiu-kava) consisted of a horse, a gun, skins of leopard, lynx, wolf, fox, Kirgiz fox (*korsak*), fifteen meters of Chinese cloth, and a silk kerchief or scarf (P. K. Kozlov, *Mongoliia i Kam. Trekhletnee puteshestvie po Mongolii i Tibetu [1899–1901]*, 2d ed. [Moscow: OGIZ, 1947], 344).

[72]Donduk-Dashi's laws, in Golstunskii, *Mongolo-oiratskie*, 61, 62.

In exchange the Kalmyks sought a variety of items, including metal products—pots, tin boxes, buckets, plates, cups; petty merchandise—combs, needles, mirrors, and buttons; linen, wool, and felt; ready-made clothes such as pants, tunics (*kaftan*), girdles, boots, and other leather items. The Kalmyks could produce many of these products, such as wool, felt, and boots, by themselves, but they preferred Russian-made products for the Russians used improved manufacturing processes and different dyes, producing fine-quality, brightly colored merchandise. Russian vodka and tobacco also came into great demand among the Kalmyks.

With the growing realization of the power of firearms, the Kalmyks showed increasing interest in obtaining these weapons. Throughout the seventeenth century, however, the Russian government had a strict policy of not allowing any arms, particularly firearms, to end up in the hands of their unruly neighbors, be they Kalmyks, Bashkirs, or Kazakhs. This banned merchandise (*zapovednye tovary*) was not limited to gunpowder, bullets, guns, and armor but also included iron, money, gold and silver, slaves, and hunting birds.[73]

In the 1670s Astrakhan was the main trading center for the Kalmyks. The importance of Kalmyk trade for Astrakhan was reflected in the name of the place known until recently as Kalmytskii bazar, located a few miles north of Astrakhan, on the Volga's west bank.[74] A few other sites near major Volga towns had the same name. Indeed, at the end of the seventeenth century the Kalmyks were widely trading their products not only in Astrakhan but also in the towns of Saratov, Tsaritsyn, Chernyi Iar, and Krasnyi Iar on the Volga and the Iaitsk town (*gorodok*) on the Yayik. In the 1720s Makar'ev Fair near Saratov became an annual event, where a large volume of Kalmyk and Russian goods were sold and bartered. At times, to stimulate trade and especially to win political favors from the Kalmyks, the Russian government ordered that customs duties not be collected from the herds brought by the Kalmyks or the Tatars, as was the case in 1691 in the town of Iaitsk (Gur'ev).[75] A senate decree of February 26, 1719, declared that the envoys of Ayuki Khan who traveled with the knowledge of the Chancellery of Foreign Affairs could sell goods worth up to three thousand rubles duty free.[76]

Most of the Kalmyk trade with Russia and other neighbors in the area was handled by intermediaries, predominantly Tatars. Later, in the eigh-

---

[73]*PSZ* 3:313, no. 1585.

[74]*Kaspiiskaia ekspeditsiia K. M. Bera 1853–1857* gg., comp. T. A. Lukina, Nauchnoe nasledstvo, vol. 9 (Leningrad: Nauka, 1984), 195.

[75]*AI* 5:361–62, no. 210.

[76]*PSZ* 5:no. 3314.

teenth century, Armenian and Russian merchants appear to have occupied a prominent role in the Kalmyk trade. Faithful to the traditions of true nomads, the Kalmyks despised trading, and it is not until the early nineteenth century that the names of a few Kalmyk merchants appear in the records.

If the horse was the most valued animal for the Kalmyks, in the seventeenth and eighteenth centuries it was of significant economic and military value to the Russians as well. For many centuries Moscow was a traditional horse market. A Russian official of the 1660s, Grigorii Kotoshikhin, recalled that the Nogays and the Tatars annually drove herds estimated at between thirty thousand and fifty thousand horses to Moscow, where they were sold at a price of five, seven, ten, or fifteen rubles per horse.[77] In the second half of the seventeenth century, the Kalmyks took over the role of the Nogays as the major suppliers of horses to Russia. They used the same old route via the Russian towns of Tambov, Kasimov, and Vladimir. In August 1688, for instance, 6,400 Kalmyk horses were driven to Moscow for sale.[78] In the beginning of the eighteenth century the Russian government decided that it would be more expedient for the Kalmyks to sell their horses in the traditional markets in the Volga towns. Sometimes, a Russian officer, instructed to purchase a certain number of horses at a price ranging from five to ten rubles, was dispatched directly to the Kalmyk ulus. Throughout the 1730s in Saratov alone the Russian merchants spent around seven thousand rubles annually to purchase Kalmyk horses for the dragoon regiments.[79]

The Kalmyks remained the principal suppliers of horses for the Russian cavalry until the 1740s. Then the situation changed, as the Kalmyk herds diminished substantially because of the unfavorable weather conditions, internal wars, and Russia's ceaseless demands for large-scale Kalmyk participation in military campaigns. The Kalmyks never fully recovered from the severe crisis of the 1720s–1730s. Henceforth their economic significance diminished by comparison with their more numerous and powerful nomadic neighbors in the east, the Kazakhs. By the 1740s the Volga markets through which various animal products entered Russia were secondary in importance to the newly built fortress of Orenburg, where the buoyant trade between the Russians and the Kazakhs continued to grow.

Payments and rewards for participation in Russian military cam-

[77]Grigorii Kotoshikhin, *O Rossii v tsarstvovanie Alekseia Mikhailovicha,* 4th ed. (St. Petersburg: Tip. glavnogo upravleniia udelov, 1906), 92.

[78]*PSZ* 1:927, no. 540; *DAI* 12:222, no. 33.

[79]*Ocherki istorii Kalmytskoi,* 1:168–69.

paigns constituted an important part of the Kalmyk economy. Annual payments at first consisted partially of cash and partially of expensive cloth, fur hats, and coats. By the late seventeenth century, payments were mostly made in cash. According to a 1677 agreement, Ayuki and other tayishis were promised an annuity of 590 rubles in cash. In reality, such payments were made only occasionally, not annually as promised. In time the payments increased, and by 1737 the Kalmyk tayishis were allocated 7,400 rubles.[80]

Substantial sums of money and expensive items were sent only to tayishis. Ordinary Kalmyk horsemen participating in campaigns were rewarded with vodka and tobacco and occasionally with cloth and some cash. Tayishis, though, had other ways of increasing their income. At various times they were paid a monetary compensation for those Kalmyks who, after fleeing their ulus, were forcibly baptized. Such compensations could amount to as much as thirty rubles per person.[81] Tayishis were also pleased if they could send numerous embassies to the local governors of Astrakhan, Tsaritsyn, and Saratov or to Moscow. Such embassies generally brought gifts that had to be reciprocated. This also provided an alternative trading relationship, although in a different form and on a smaller scale. Members of these embassies were given personal gifts and cash, particularly in Moscow.[82]

Typically, slave trading represented an important source of income in many nomadic societies. The special tax in Russia throughout the sixteenth and seventeenth centuries to ransom Russian slaves vividly illustrates the extent of this problem for the Russian state. Yet the Kalmyks' involvement in the slave trade seems to have been relatively insignificant. For instance, out of seventy-seven Russian slaves ransomed from Bukhara, Khiva, and Balkh in 1678, only six had been captured and sold by the Kalmyks. Usually, Russian captives were held in the Kalmyk ulus until merchants returning home from Bukhara and Khiva stopped and bought them.[83] In the middle of the eighteenth century the situation was reversed when many impoverished Kalmyks had to sell their children into slavery.

Raids and control of the trade routes generated significant income for the Kalmyk economy. The actions of the Kalmyks along the trade routes connecting Astrakhan with Khiva or Tersk were crucial for Russia's trade

---

[80]*PSZ* 2:no. 672; *SRIO* 28:96.

[81]*PSZ* 3:no. 1591.

[82]*PSZ* 5:no. 3046.

[83]*Materialy po istorii Uzbekskoi, Tadzhikskoi i Turkmenskoi SSR*, vol. 1: *Torgovlia s Moskovskim gosudarstvom i mezhdunarodnoe polozhenie Srednei Azii v 16–17 vv.* (Leningrad: AN SSSR, 1932), 386–97, table 7.

with Central Asian khanates, India, and Persia. At times of increased Kalmyk raids along the routes, trade was heavily disrupted.[84] Conversely, the Kalmyks' protection was essential to the safety of the merchant caravans and embassies passing through the area.[85] Merchants often had to pay exorbitant sums to secure safe passage for their caravans. Thus, according to the senate's 1726 report, the Kalmyk Dorji-Nazar and Lubji tayishis in the period from 1717 to 1726 received goods worth six hundred thousand rubles for protecting small caravans.[86] Such large incomes were rarely sustained and in this rather exceptional case resulted from Russia's ban on trade with Bukhara after the massacre of Prince Alexander Bekovich-Cherkasskii's expedition in 1717. Already in 1726 the Russian government realized that the losses it suffered from its prohibitive policies were too great and ordered that the caravans be protected by the troops from the Astrakhan regiment.[87] Nonetheless, at various times the Kalmyks continued to collect ransom from the passing traffic.

Military and political aspects of the raiding activity will be discussed later. Here, let us consider only its economic implications. Historical records of the seventeenth and eighteenth centuries registered an almost infinite number of raids by small bands of Kalmyks, both on their sedentary neighbors such as Russian peasants, the Bashkirs, and the Don cossacks and on their nomadic neighbors such as the Kuban Nogays, the Crimean Tatars, and the Kazakhs. Traditionally, such frontier raids have not been accorded much historical importance. Historians of sedentary societies, whose value lies in land, money, and population centers, are usually concerned with major battles and the conquest of cities and territories. For nomadic societies, however, which have no cities to conquer and no land to capture and the real value lies in herds, these "minor" raids take on considerable importance.

A specific case will illustrate this point. In October 1721, in a raid on a small cossack settlement on the Don, twenty-six Kalmyks captured thirty horses. While crossing the Volga, they met ten other Kalmyks who were driving home a tabun stolen from the Don cossacks.[88] In the middle of the seventeenth century the price of horses ranged from 5 to 15 rubles

[84]Ibid., 142, no. 33; 256–57, no. 128; B. G. Kurts, "Sostoianie Rossii v 1650–55 gg. po doneseniiam Rodesa," *ChOIDR* 253, bk. 2 (1915): 136–37.

[85]*Materialy po istorii Uzbekskoi*, 227, no. 89; *RIB* 15:21, pt. 6; *Russko-indiiskie otnosheniia v 17 v. Sbornik dokumentov* (Moscow: Izd-vo vostochnoi literatury, 1958), no. 126; *Materialy po istorii russko-gruzinskikh otnoshenii: (80-90-e gody 17 veka)*, comp. C. G. Paichadze, vol. 3 (Tbilisi: Metsniereba, 1974), p. 98, no. 1; *AI* 5:no. 227.

[86]*SRIO* 63:366, no. 143.

[87]*PSZ* 7:no. 5045.

[88]*AVD* 1:290, no. 186.

per horse, from 3 to 10 rubles by the end of the century, and from 5 to 11 rubles in the first quarter of the eighteenth century.[89] Sometimes a sudden massive supply of horses would depress prices to very low levels.[90] Prices also differed depending on the age and type of the horse. Apparently, prices were lower for "hot items," that is, stolen horses, ranging from 4 to 6 rubles per horse.[91] If the stolen cossack horses were sold at an average price of 5 rubles per horse, the profit of such a raid would amount to 150 rubles in total, or almost 6 rubles per person. The result of such a small-scale single raid was twice as much as the Russian government was able to offer each Kalmyk horseman for the entire season of military campaigns.[92]

Larger raids involved from one hundred to three hundred horsemen. Such a band of Kalmyks, in a typical raid on the Crimea, the Kazakhs, the Bashkirs, or the Nogays, would usually drive home at least several hundred horses and one or two dozen captives. The price of the captives in the slave market in Khiva at the end of the seventeenth century was from 40 to 50 rubles per person.[93] To redeem the Russian slaves from captivity, the Russian government would pay from 15 to 50 rubles, depending on the person's status.[94] The monetary value of even a single such raid was at least twice as much as the 590 rubles negotiated in 1677 as the tayishis' annuity. The incentives to disregard the wishes of the Russian government were too strong for the Kalmyk tayishis to resist.

Growing dependence on Russia brought about dramatic economic, political, and social changes in Kalmyk society. Specifically, trade with Russia provided new incentives to produce a surplus of herds, which then could be sold or bartered for necessities or luxury goods. Such a surplus was often achieved by taking over the herds of others, either by waging internal wars, as happened throughout the 1720s and 1730s, or by increasing raiding warfare against other nomadic peoples such as the Crimean Tatars, Kuban Nogays, Kazakhs, and Karakalpaks. Such raids, indeed, took place constantly throughout the period. The growing im-

[89]Kotoshikhin, *O Rossii v tsarstvovanie*, 92; *PSZ* 1:156–57; *AIuB* 2:17; *Ocherki istorii Kalmytskoi*, 1:168.

[90]The inhabitants of Astrakhan witnessed such a situation in 1698. As a result of the Kalmyks' campaign against the Kuban Nogays, in which many Nogays were butchered and a great number of their horses captured, the price of horses in Astrakhan fell to fifteen kopecks per horse (*PB* 1:698, note to no. 228).

[91]*AIuB* 3:278, no. 332.

[92]At the time, cash rewards to the Kalmyks were rarely more than three rubles (*AVD* 1:317, no. 210).

[93]N. Tsarykov, "Un Voyage dans l'Ouzbekistan en 1671," *Sbornik Moskovskogo glavnogo arkhiva Ministerstva Inostrannykh Del* 5 (1893): 59.

[94]Kotoshikhin, *O Rossii v tsarstvovanie*, 59.

portance of relations with Russia also heightened the struggle for the political office of khan, which had access to Russian luxury goods and political and military advantages.

The effects of trade, together with various payments, rewards, and gifts, introduced Russian money into the Kalmyk economy. In time, growing dependence on the Russian market and the continual shrinkage of Kalmyk pastures substantially undermined the extensive nomadic Kalmyk economy, which was incapable of coping with the new phenomena. Increasing impoverishment among the Kalmyks in the middle of the eighteenth century forced many of them to abandon their traditional economy and to seek employment at the fisheries, salt mines, and later, in the nineteenth century, in agriculture.

Human and Animal Population

The Kalmyks' pastoral economy clearly was conditioned by a precarious balance between pastures, herds, and households. Any significant shift in either of these variables—shrinkage of pastures, reduction of animal herds, or diminished population—could threaten the very existence of Kalmyk nomadic society.

No precise figures for the Kalmyk population are available until the second half of the eighteenth century, and only approximate estimates are possible. At the height of Kalmyk power at the end of the seventeenth century, the total number of Kalmyk tents (each housing four to five people[95]) together with Ayuki Khan's Nogay subjects appears to have been as large as 70,000.[96] In the late 1720s, in the middle of the Kalmyk civil war, Russian officials estimated that the Kalmyks numbered from 30,000 to 34,000 tents.[97] By the early 1740s the number diminished even further and is reported to have been between 20,000 and 30,000.[98] In 1767 the Kalmyks' own count placed the number of Kalmyk tents at 41,523.[99]

There is no statistical evidence as to how much livestock an average

[95]I calculated this average number using data from the following sources: *SA* 10:188; Pal'mov, *Etiudy*, 3–4:103; *Ocherki istorii Kalmytskoi*, 209; A. M. Pozdneev, "Astrakhanskie kalmyki i ikh otnosheniia k Rossii do nachala nyneshnego stoletiia," *ZhMNP* 244 (March 1886): 162.

[96]M. M. Batmaev, "Novye khoziaistvennye iavleniia v Kalmytskom khanstve v 40-60-godakh 18 veka," in *Obshchestvennyi stroi i sotsial'no-politicheskoe razvitie dorevoliutsionnoi Kalmykii* (Elista: N.p., 1983), 26; T. I. Belikov, *Kalmyki v bor'be za nezavisimost' nashei rodiny (17-nachalo 19 vv.)* (Elista: Kalmgosizdat, 1965), 103.

[97]*SRIO* 56:182, 196; Bakunin, "Opisanie," *Krasnyi arkhiv* 3 (1939): 223.

[98]Batmaev, "Novye khoziaistvennye," 26.

[99]*SRIO* 87:274–75.

Kalmyk family owned in the seventeenth and eighteenth centuries. Nevertheless, even a cursory look at the 1640 law code and Donduk-Dashi's laws reveals that the Kalmyk herds in the 1740s were far smaller than a hundred years before. According to the 1640 law code, a noyon could be fined as much as ten camels and one hundred horses, whereas in Donduk-Dashi's laws the heaviest penalty was one "nine."[100] In the 1830s an average Kalmyk household was reported to have from 60 to 150 sheep, 10 to 50 horses, 10 to 30 head of cattle, and 5 to 15 camels. A poor family had 2 to 3 horses, 5 head of cattle, and 20 sheep.[101] The last numbers represented a minimally adequate standard of a nomadic household's capitalization in animals. Falling below this standard meant that such a household had to seek other sources of income—a process that led to its eventual sedentarization.

Religion

"We bow in front of the Lamas and precious Buddhas, who are our guides, in front of the precious teachings, which give us means for achieving Nirvana."[102] Since the end of the sixteenth century, when the Mongols chose to bow down in front of the images of the Buddhas made in Tibet, Tibetan Buddhism was their religion. Shortly thereafter the Oirats, too, accepted the teachings of the Buddha.

Before the new religion could take root, the Kalmyks left Jungaria for the Caspian steppes. Throughout the seventeenth and early eighteenth centuries the Kalmyks kept up vital ties with Tibet. Kalmyk embassies brought sumptuous gifts to the Dalai Lama, and the Kalmyk noyons frequented Tibet both for short pilgrimages and for longer stays to partake of sacred knowledge. In return, the Dalai Lama dispatched his appointee to be chief lama of the Kalmyks and sent symbols of political power to the Kalmyk khans, together with divine books and various

[100]*Ikh Tsaaz,* 14, no. 13; Donduk-Dashi's laws, in Golstunskii, *Mongolo-oiratskie,* 62.

[101]*Ocherki istorii Kalmytskoi,* 1:164. The subsistence level appears to vary in different nomadic societies. In the 1920s the Mongols regarded 20 sheep or their equivalent (20 sheep=2 camels=4 horses=5 cattle=30 goats) as a threshold beyond which the household would be exempt from taxation (H. H. Vreeland, *Mongol Community and Kinship Structure* [New Haven: Human Relations Area File, 1954], 24), while at the same time the Basseris of South Persia found it impossible for a household to subsist with fewer than 60 sheep (Barth, *Nomads of South Persia,* 16). For the size of the herds in different nomadic societies also see A. M. Khazanov, *Nomads and the Outside World,* trans. Julia Crookenden (Cambridge: Cambridge University Press, 1984), 30.

[102]"Biografiia Zaya-Pandity," in *Kalmytskie istoriko-literaturnye pamiatniki v russkom perevode* (Elista: N.p., 1969), 159.

Buddhist artifacts. Such journeys from the Volga to Tibet usually took several years and were very costly. By the mid-eighteenth century, Kalmyk ties to Tibet and the Dalai Lama weakened as the threat of Kazakh raids rendered the route to Tibet unsafe and the Russian government, which saw the Kalmyks' relations with Tibet as a challenge to its supremacy, increased its political control.

Tibetan Buddhism—also known as Lamaism—places special emphasis on the role of the lama, a monk-preceptor.[103] A lama is a spiritual leader who knows all there is to know. He alone knows how man can save himself from suffering, and only he can bring Buddha's teaching to the hearts and minds of the initiated. Although all Tibetan sects emphasized the importance of the lama, one sect more than any other stressed the role of the clergy. This sect was called Ge-lug-pa—the virtuous way. It emphasized rituals and symbols, strict monastic discipline, pure morality, and aggressive propagation of the sacred teachings. The Mongols and the Oirats accepted the tenets of Tibetan Buddhism as taught by the Ge-lug-pa sect, which became the dominant sect in Tibet after 1640.

As a result of the growing isolation from Tibet, the Kalmyk Lamaist hierarchy developed somewhat differently from that of the Mongols and the Oirats. Among the peculiarities of the Kalmyk Lamaism were a lack of strong centralization, a less developed clerical hierarchy, and smaller numbers of monks and monasteries.

The Kalmyk nomadic monastery (khurul) consisted of three types of tents: temple-tents, tents for the clergy, and the tents of khurul laborers. Temple-tents were distinguished by their large size, central location, and white color.[104] To become members of the clergy, male children were dedicated to the khurul, sometimes at birth. To do so was considered a pious deed so that each family that could afford to dedicated at least one son, usually the youngest, to the clergy.

There were four basic priestly ranks: surgalin-kebün—a preparatory level for students from ten to twelve years of age; manji—a clerical apprentice, who kept the ten precepts; getsul—the novitiate monk, who kept the thirty-six rules; and, finally, gelüng—"virtuous beggar," or the fully ordained monk over twenty years of age, who kept the 253 rules.[105] According to Pallas, at the end of the eighteenth century there was one gelüng for every 150 to 200 tents. The head of the Kalmyk clergy was the

---

[103]Generally, the term lama is used to denote an ordained priest or monk. The Kalmyks reserved this term mostly for the leader of the Kalmyk Lamaist church.

[104]Zhitetskii, Ocherki byta astrakhanskikh, 43.

[105]Austin L. Waddel, Tibetan Buddhism: With Its Mystic Cults and Mythology, and in Its Relation to Indian Buddhism, 3d ed. (New York: Dover, 1972), 171; Zhitetskii, Ocherki byta astrakhanskikh, 50; Bergmann, Nomadische, 1:69.

3. A Kalmyk monastery (*khurul*) of the Khoshut ulus in the nineteenth century (from *Kalmytskaia step' Astrakhanskoi gubernii po issledovaniiam Kumo-Many-chskoi ekspeditsii*. St. Petersburg: Tip. V. Bezobrazova, 1868).

lama, who was a regent of the Dalai Lama. Next in rank to the lama was the *tsorji*, whom Pallas equated with a bishop.[106]

The tribal nature of Kalmyk society, with its lack of firm central authority, was clearly reflected in its clerical organization. The Kalmyk khurul, for instance, belonged to the tribe, and no person from any other tribe could be admitted to it. Sometimes different tribes used different terminology. Thus the *bagshi* for the Torguts was the head of the large khurul, while the Derbets used the word in its original meaning, teacher.[107] Perhaps it is not accidental that such deviations from the original meaning are mostly known among the Torguts, who were the first to leave Jungaria and thus diluted the ideas of the Lamaist precepts.

In the seventeenth and eighteenth centuries, khuruls developed into

[106]Pallas, *Reise*, 1:350–51.
[107]Zhitetskii, *Ocherki byta astrakhanskikh*, 50.

4. Kalmyk clergy in the mid-nineteenth century (from *Kalmytskaia step' Astrakhanskoi gubernii po issledovaniiam Kumo-Manychskoi ekspeditsii.* St. Petersburg: Tip. V. Bezobrazova, 1868).

important centers of economic activity. For pious purposes as well as for political reasons, noyons presented the khuruls and lamas with large donations of people and herds. Albatu—subjects of a noyon—who were given to the monastery became known as *shabinars* and were supposed to become students of Lamaism or servants. In reality, however, most of them were made the serfs of the khurul and its clergy. Once these people had been donated to the monastery, a khan or tayishi could under no circumstances resume authority over them.[108]

[108]*The World of Buddhism: Buddhist Monks in Society and Culture* (New York: Facts on File, 1984), 257. A Russian Mongolist of the late nineteenth century, A. Pozdneev, describes another curious way of becoming a *shabinar:* when a noyon was ill, he would choose a person to whom subsequently the lama would symbolically transfer this illness. This person, in turn, was expelled from the ulus to become a *shabinar* at the khurul that had sent the lama. Such exiles were united in small groups and had their own herds (Pozdneev,

Herds were donated to the khurul and clergy on a regular basis, but on occasion wealthy noyons made extraordinary donations numbering thousands of horses and hundreds of sheep and camels. This was not very different from an earlier tradition, when, upon the death of a well-to-do nomad, depending on his status, a number of horses and camels were sacrificed and buried with him. After the Kalmyks converted to Buddhism, these gifts had to be donated to the monastery.[109] Thus the khurul and its clergy constituted a large, independent economy and retained a position of significant political influence.

In time, some inherent contradictions in the Ge-lug-pa sect began to surface. Strict ascetic principles of celibacy and abstinence, coupled with the right to own private property, to have a personal income, and to be involved in trade, led to abuses. These abuses figured prominently in Donduk-Dashi's laws of the 1740s, in which several clauses were concerned with drinking problems and marriages among the clergy.[110]

The inclusion of laws concerning the clergy in civil legislation indicates a close relationship between clerical and secular authorities. Indeed, such laws could not have been compiled without the participation of Kalmyk clergy. They were the most learned men, and their khuruls were the centers of knowledge. The khurul was the only place where one could learn to read and write in the Oirat alphabet, invented by Zaya-Pandita in 1648.[111] If a pupil proved to be apt in learning, he could become a member of the clergy specializing in one of the four fields of knowledge. He could eventually become a *bagshi*—a teacher of divine knowledge—or *zurhachi*—an astrologer. He could also become an *emchi*—a medicine man—or a *zurachi*—an artist.[112]

Even though Buddhist teachings apparently spread among the Kalmyks throughout the seventeenth and eighteenth centuries, the character of Tibetan Buddhism, as it was practiced by the Kalmyks, remained largely superficial. Vladimirtsov called it "a popular Buddhism."[113] In-

---

Ocherki byta buddiiskikh monastyrei i buddiiskogo dukhovenstva v Mongolii v sviazi s otnosheniiami sego poslednego k narodu, ZIRGOOE vol. 16 [St. Petersburg: Tip. V. F. Kirshbauma, 1887], 456).

[109]See gifts offered to Zaya-Pandita in "Biografiia Zaia-Pandity," in *Kalmytskie istoriko-literaturnye*, 164, 167; "Vvedenie buddiiskogo ucheniia sekty zheltoshapochnikov mezhdu mongolami i oiratami," ibid., 127.

[110]Donduk-Dashi's laws, in Golstunskii, *Mongolo-oiratskie*, 62.

[111]The Oirat script remained in use until the 1920s. The kernel of the Kalmyk language was a Torgut dialect, which in time grew more distinct from the Oirat language based on a Jungar dialect (N. N. Ubushaev, "Torgutskii dialekt i ego otnoshenie k kalmytskomu literaturnomu iazyku," *Uchenye zapiski KNIIaLI, seriia filologicheskaia* 7 [1969]: 186–98).

[112]Zhitetskii, *Ocherki byta astrakhanskikh*, 51.

[113]B. Ia. Vladimirtsov, "Mongol'skaia literatura," in vol. 2, "Literatura Vostoka," *Vsemirnaia literatura* (Petersburg: N.p., 1920), 103.

deed, only a small number of the Tibetan philosophical and theological works were translated into the Oirat language, which acquired written form only in the middle of the seventeenth century and was known to a privileged few among a predominantly illiterate majority. Moreover, early separation of the Kalmyks from the mass of the recently converted Oirats, along with the costly, long, and dangerous journeys they had to undertake to maintain their ties with Tibet, resulted in their further isolation and growing autonomy. Deep and rapid dissemination of the Buddhist teachings could not be sufficiently enforced because of the decentralized character of tribal Kalmyk society. In the 1740s the laws of Donduk-Dashi attempted to induce the people to observe the religious rules more rigorously.[114]

As was the case with other world religions, the adoption of Tibetan Buddhism by the Oirats in the late sixteenth century was, most of all, a political act of the Oirat aristocracy and had little effect on the masses of common nomads, who continued to practice shamanism. Four articles of the 1640 law code imposed penalties on those who invoked the aid of a shaman-man or shaman-woman or in any way practiced shamanism.[115] In the late eighteenth and early nineteenth centuries travelers observed the persistence of shamanistic traditions, noting a number of primitive temples, *obo*, along the Kalmyk nomadic routes or near mountain passes.[116]

Most Kalmyks remained Tibetan Buddhists, but some chose to become Russian Orthodox. In the seventeenth century the issue of religious affiliation ignited occasional hostilities between the Russian authorities and the Kalmyk tayishis. By the eighteenth century it was one of the central issues in Russo-Kalmyk relations. Persistent attempts to

[114]Donduk-Dashi's laws, in Golstunskii, *Mongolo-oiratskie*, 62.

[115]*Ikh Tsaaz*, 28–29, nos. 182–85.

[116]The *obo* was a shamanistic temple consisting of a heap of stones honoring the local spirits, later incorporated into Buddhism. On top of it was placed an image of the pan-Mongol deity Tsakhan-Avga (the white elder). Such temples served as sites for various rituals, which usually ended in traditional contests of horse racing, wrestling, and arrow shooting (N. L. Zhukovskaia, *Lamaism i rannie formy religii* [Moscow: Nauka, 1977], 32, 43; Pallas, *Reise*, 1:326; Dorzhi Banzarov, "Chernaia vera ili shamanstvo u mongolov," in *Sobranie sochinenii* [Moscow: Izd-vo vostochnoi literatury, 1955], 67–69; G. N. Potanin, *Puteshestviia po Mongolii* [Moscow: Gos. izd-vo geogr. literatury, 1948], 140. A description of a slightly different type of *obo* is in G. Ts. Tsybikov, "Buddist-palomnik u sviatyn' Tibeta," in *Izbrannye trudy v dvukh tomakh* [Novosibirsk: Nauka, 1981], 1:40. Today, in some places, the sites of former *obo* have become the locales of annual fairs. For instance, the Nadam Fair in Inner Mongolia is held at such locations between mid-July and early August (Alan Samagalski and Michael Buckley, *China: A Travel Survival Kit* [Victoria, Australia: Lonely Planet Publications, 1984], 754).

convert the Kalmyks in the eighteenth century were largely unsuccessful, and only small numbers chose to convert. Poor Kalmyks did so in hope of gaining economic benefits. Bereft of their herds or unbearably oppressed by their own tayishis, a number of khotons and sometimes whole ayimags fled to embrace Christianity.[117]

The Kalmyk nobles, by contrast, sought in conversion support for their political ambitions. Thus Ayuki Khan's grandson Baksaday-Dorji for a long time cherished the idea of inheriting his grandfather's title and decided to achieve his goal by becoming a Russian Orthodox. In the spring of 1724, shortly after Ayuki's death, he was baptized in St. Petersburg and assumed a Christian name, Petr Taishin. After the ceremony he requested that his godfather Peter I make him a Kalmyk khan. The emperor promised to do his best.[118]

The Russian government encouraged conversion by all feasible means. Those Kalmyks who chose to convert and to settle down with the Don cossacks were put on the military payroll and for the next few years were paid a higher salary than the cossacks. On other occasions, the Kalmyks were granted tax exemptions for three to five years. The Kalmyk tayishis who chose to convert were rewarded with handsome salaries and could live in towns or settlements built especially for them. Yet Christianity among the converts remained largely superficial. The baptized Kalmyks continued to live by Buddhist, not Christian, laws and, frequently, a few years after conversion they chose to abandon their settlements and return to their former ulus.

Loss of people as a result of the government's conversion policies could not but provoke a furious reaction on the part of the Buddhist Kalmyk nobles. They raided the settlements of the converts, often razed

---

[117]*DAI* 12:276, no. 17 (XX). Some Kalmyks became Roman Catholics, but their numbers were insignificant. Converts to Islam, however, were more numerous. We are told of a group of Kalmyks called Tomuts, who were the offspring of mixed marriages between Kalmyk women and those Kazakhs and Bashkirs who resided among the Kalmyks. At the end of the 1730s the Tomuts numbered 600 tents. They practiced Islam and were employed by Donduk-Ombo Khan as his bodyguards. Another group of Muslim Kalmyks was called Sherets (from Shari'at?). This group consisted of 120 tents; in 1733 they fled from the Derbet tayishi Cheter and found refuge near Azov. Later they were transferred to the Crimea, where they converted to Islam (Bakunin, "Opisanie," *Krasnyi arkhiv* 5 [1939]: 201; I. V. Borisenko, "O rasselenii sheretov, tomutov, chuguevskikh i beliaevskikh kalmykov," in *Obshchestvennyi stroi i sotsial'no-politicheskoe razvitie dorevoliutsionnoi Kalmykii* [Elista: N.p., 1983], 50–53). In 1744, 233 men and 413 women were converted to Islam by the Astrakhan Tatars. Contrary to the request of the Kalmyk Donduk-Dashi Khan to return to him these Muslim Kalmyks, the senate decreed that they be sent to the Stavropol settlement near Saratov, to the bosom of the Russian Orthodox church (*PSZ* 13:no. 9722).

[118]Pal'mov, *Etiudy*, 3–4:139.

their buildings to the ground, and forcibly brought back the baptized
Kalmyks. The Russian government responded by resettling the baptized
Kalmyks further inside Russian territory. It is hardly surprising that the
issue of baptized Kalmyks was a thorny one in Russo-Kalmyk relations.

Women and Marriage

As in any patriarchal society, Kalmyk women were considered the property of men. They had few rights but many duties, performing the domestic labor and being responsible for care of the household and children. To enter into marriage, a Kalmyk woman had to be fourteen years
of age or older and usually had her parents' consent. Upon her marriage,
a bride would untie her braid and do her hair in two braids—a sign that
she was married. The groom's parents had to pay a bride-price, and the
bride's parents provided a dowry. The size of the bride-price and dowry
varied according to the social status of the married couple's parents.
Generally, it consisted of herds, household necessities, valuable goods,
clothing, and, later on, cash. After the wedding, the bride, with her
dowry, joined the khoton of her husband. It often happened that her
new father-in-law would physically abuse her, for which he would have
to pay a penalty. But her mother-in-law was permitted to inflict corporal
punishment for the purpose of moral admonition.[119]

Those who had insufficient means to marry off their sons or daughters
depended on the goodwill of their relatives and the law, which stipulated that every year four out of forty tents had to marry their available
bachelors and every ten tents had to assist in the marriage of one of
them.[120] A married couple could be divorced at the request of both
parties, but a woman's request for divorce had to be considered by the
relatives and was more difficult to achieve. The most common reason for
divorce was the wife's barrenness. After the divorce, the woman and her
dowry were returned to her family, and the marriage contract was
terminated.[121]

The 1640 law code contains clauses imposing fines for sexual assaults,
harassment, adultery, and the abduction of women—an indication of
the less-than-puritan morals of Kalmyk society. One such clause prescribes an unusual penalty for sexual harassment—a person who grabs

[119]*Ikh Tsaaz,* 18–19, nos. 42, 43, 50–57; Nebol'sin, *Ocherki byta kalmykov,* 77; Donduk-
Dashi's laws, in Golstunskii, *Mongolo-oiratskie,* 63.
[120]*Ikh Tsaaz,* 19, nos. 59, 59[1].
[121]Nebol'sin, *Ocherki byta kalmykov,* 82.

a girl over ten years of age by the breasts or kisses her is punished by one flick on the "secret spot."[122]

The anthropologist David Aberle was slightly puzzled by the finding that the Kalmyks' kinship system indicated the presence of nonsororal polygamy, and yet the Kalmyks were not polygamous. Although he could not determine how prevalent polygamy was, he nevertheless suggested correctly that the Kalmyks must have been polygamous in the past.[123] Actually, Kalmyk society in the seventeenth and eighteenth centuries knew both polygamy and monogamy. Monogamy was the lot of the poor, whereas polygamous marriage prevailed among the nobility. Only the noble and the affluent could afford to have more than one wife. The 1640 law code provided for the punishment of a wife who killed another wife in the case of a polygamous marriage.[124] Most of the Kalmyk khans and tayishis had several wives. Ayuki Khan, for instance, had four wives, and his son Chakdorjab, nine.[125] Wives were taken not only from different Kalmyk or Oirat tribes, but often from other peoples. Such marriages were supposed to create political and military alliances.

The Kalmyks were also allowed to have concubines captured on the battlefield. In the seventeenth century, the concubine's status was equal to that of a slave woman with no rights. By the nineteenth century, Nebol'sin observed that concubines enjoyed all the rights of legal wives.[126] One fundamental difference remained, however. A concubine was considered the personal property of her master-husband, whereas a wife was also the property of the whole family. On the death of the elder brother, the younger brother married the widow, but if the widow was childless, she was returned to her family. Under certain circumstances the injured party in a lawsuit could be awarded the offender's wife.[127]

Not every woman's fate was so bleak. The wives and widows of the Kalmyk khans and tayishis could become influential through political intrigues. On occasion, the widow of a noyon could assume power and become the leader of the ulus, but only temporarily, until the heir came of age.[128] Darma Bala, the widow of Ayuki Khan, and Jan, the widow of Donduk-Ombo Khan, played important roles in the struggle for political power.

[122]*Ikh Tsaaz*, nos. 106–9, 120, 189–91; 24, no. 122.

[123]Aberle, *Kinship System*, 44–45.

[124]*Ikh Tsaaz*, 18, no. 48.

[125]Bakunin, "Opisanie," *Krasnyi arkhiv* 3 (1939): 204.

[126]*Ikh Tsaaz*, 21, nos. 80, 82; 27, no. 169; Nebol'sin, *Ocherki byta kalmykov*, 80.

[127]Kotwicz, *Kalmytskie zagadki i poslovitsy*, 80, no. 92; *SRIO* 57:486; *Ikh Tsaaz*, 29, no. 191.

[128]In the 1670s, Dorji-Rabtan, a widow of Ochirtu-Tsetsen Khan, arrived from Jungaria at the head of one thousand tents of the Khoshuts. A childlesss widow could become chief of the ulus (Bakunin, "Opisanie," *Krasnyi arkhiv* 3 [1939]: 195, 204).

Law

In 1640 the *khurultay*—the assembly of the Oirat and Mongol nobles—convened near the Tarbagatay mountains in Jungaria to discuss the political situation and codify a set of laws for both the Mongols and the Oirats. The Torgut Kho-Urlük tayishi also attended the assembly with his sons and a grandson. Originally written in Mongol, the law code survived only in its Oirat version and appears to be the first written law of the Oirats and the Kalmyks.[129]

The code clearly reflected new political developments in Inner Asia in the 1630–1640s. Some provisions sought to reconcile former foes, the Oirats and the Mongols, but on the Oirats' terms—a clear sign of the growing political power of the Oirats of Jungaria.[130] This reconciliation could hardly have been achieved without the meticulous labor of the lamas of the Ge-lug-pa sect, who sought to consolidate their influence among the Oirats and the Mongols so as to make a strong bid for power in Tibet. Shortly after the *khurultay* took place, Tibet was conquered by the Oirat and Mongol armies, the fifth Dalai Lama was put on the throne, and the Ge-lug-pa became the dominant sect in Tibet.

Despite the role of the Ge-lug-pa sect in convening the representative assembly of the Mongol and Oirat noyons, neither Buddhist canonical law nor Buddhist teachings appear to have had a major effect on the code. The only sign of a Buddhist presence in the code was clauses concerning penalties imposed for offenses against the clergy.[131]

The recent discovery by a Mongolian scholar of Mongol legal monuments written on birchbark in the late sixteenth and early seventeenth centuries suggests that some previously unknown Mongol sources were used in the compilation of the 1640 law code.[132] Nevertheless, Mongol-Oirat customary law was its principal source. The code dealt with a wide range of subjects, codifying behavior on the battlefield and during the hunt, as well as setting marriage practices and court procedures. It imposed penalties for violations of these and other provisions and for sundry offenses, insults, and thefts. With few exceptions, offenses were punished by a single penalty—a fine paid in herds or sometimes in valuable goods. The number and type of herds depended on the gravity of the offense.

---

[129]For a bibliographical survey of the code's recensions and translations see M. I. Gol'man, "Russkie perevody i spiski mongolo-oiratskikh zakonov 1640 goda," in *Mongol'skii sbornik. Ekonomika, istoriia, arkheologiia* (Moscow: Izd-vo vostochnoi literatury, 1959), 139–62.

[130]*Ikh Tsaaz,* 14, nos. 2–5.

[131]Ibid., nos. 6, 24–26.

[132]Ibid., 8, 11.

An oath—in Mongol *shikhaga* (cf. Kalmyk *shükh*[133])—was used by the Kalmyks as a mean of mediation. The 1640 law code prescribes the oath as a last resort, mainly in cases when the defendant's guilt was not clearly established. The oath had to be administered by a person whose status in the social hiararchy was higher than that of the person who took the oath.[134] As was true of other peoples, the Kalmyks did not take the oath lightly. It was used infrequently and was seen as an extremely serious trial.[135] The prominence of the oath in Donduk-Dashi's laws must have been a result of the growing influence of the Russian judicial system.[136]

It is not known how many copies of the 1640 law code Kho-Urlük and his sons brought with them from Jungaria. Nor is it clear how widespread the application of this code was among the Kalmyks. The available evidence suggests that there were only a few copies, and a hundred years later Donduk-Dashi Khan could not locate a single one.[137] Unwritten customary law apparently carried more weight in guiding the Kalmyks throughout the seventeenth and early eighteenth centuries.

In the 1740s, a century after the compilation of the 1640 law code, the Kalmyk khan Donduk-Dashi thought it necessary to introduce new laws. These new statutes highlighted the impact of Kalmyk isolation from the main bulk of the Oirats, as well as Russia's increased influence. Compared with the 1640 code, the new laws sought to strengthen the role of Lamaism and the clergy. In addition to traditional fines paid in cattle, some fines now had to be paid in Russian money. Russia's economic inroads into the Kalmyk economy were also accompanied by tighter administrative control over the Kalmyks. Some Kalmyk-Russian disputes were to be investigated solely by the Russian authorities.[138] This often caused delays and injustices and incurred numerous Kalmyk complaints.

The 1740s laws also reflected the state of the Kalmyks' relations with

---

[133]Perhaps related to the oath, it means to investigate, to examine, to purify, to win (B. Kh. Todaeva, *Opyt lingvisticheskogo issledovaniia eposa "Dzhangar"* [Elista: Kalmytskoe knizhnoe izd-vo, 1976], 498; G. J. Ramstedt, *Kalmückisches Wörterbuch* [Helsinki: Suomalais-Ugrilainen Seura, 1935], 372; *Kalmytsko-russkii slovar'*, 688).

[134]*Ikh Tsaaz*, 16, no. 27³; 17, no. 37¹; 23, no. 101; 23, no. 101¹.

[135]N. N. Iomudskii, "Prisiaga u zakaspiiskikh turkmen," in "Sbornik v chest' semidesiatiletiia G. N. Potanina," *ZIRGOOE* 34 (1909): 219–36.

[136]Donduk-Dashi's laws, in Golstunskii, *Mongolo-oiratskie*, 64–68.

[137]The Kalmyk khan Donduk-Ombo wrote in his letter to the Astrakhan governor Tatishchev that the law code was lost during the Kalmyk internal wars and only half of the code could be found in the possession of the Russian official Bakunin (Nil Popov, Review of the book by F. I. Leontovich, *K istorii prava russkikh inorodtsev: Drevnii mongolo-kalmytskii ili oiratskii ustav vzyskanii [Tsaadzhin-bichig]* Odessa: N.p., 1879, in *ZhMNP* 205 [October 1879]: 307).

[138]Donduk-Dashi's laws, in Gostunskii, *Mongolo-oiratskie*, 61–62, 70.

Russia and other neighbors. The Kalmyks were penalized for raiding or stealing from the Russians, the Kazakhs, the Circassians, and the Crimean and Kuban Tatars. For the first time corporal punishment was introduced for certain thefts. A thief sentenced three times could be sold into slavery to the Crimea and the Kuban.[139]

Donduk-Dashi's laws contained numerous clauses concerning the zargo—an institution which in the eighteenth century began to play a more prominent role in Kalmyk society. The zargo was simultaneously a multifunctional council, an advisory body to the khan, and a court of law. It is not clear when the zargo came into being. Although it is not mentioned in the 1640 law code, this old Turko-Mongol institution must have been known to the Kalmyks.[140] In one of his well-known exhortations, probably based on his own experience, Daichin tayishi said to his grandson Ayuki: "It is hard for one person to have a knowledge of nine different subjects, for life is short. But if you have by yourself nine men, and each of them learned one of these subjects, you will be equal to a man who learned nine subjects."[141] Whether the zargo was already institutionalized is not clear. It is likely that at the time it existed as an unofficial advisory council to the chief tayishi or khan and had limited functions. Only later, when Kalmyk society became more stratified, did it become a multifunctional body with primary judicial and legislative power.

The omnipresent Bakunin described the zargo in the middle of the eighteenth century as a court or council situated in a special tent at the khan's headquarters. This council consisted of the eight most trustworthy zayisangs of the khan, among which one or two were from the clergy. Members of this council were called zargachi—counselor, judge. The zargo governed the Kalmyk people. The zargachis drafted edicts to the Kalmyk noyons on public affairs which, if approved by the khan, were rewritten and the khan's seal was stamped on them.[142] A zargachi was expected to dispense justice fairly. If a zargachi was found to favor someone three times, he was expelled from the zargo.[143] It is noteworthy that the zargo consisted of zayisangs solely from the khan's ulus. In 1762, in an attempt to undermine the authority of the khan and increase its own influence, the Russian government decided to reshape the traditional zargo by introducing the zayisangs from other Kalmyk uluses as

---

[139]Ibid., 63, 64, 71.

[140]In old Turkish it was called *yargu* and meant a legal tribunal, a lawsuit (Sir Gerard Clauson, *An Etymological Dictionary of Pre-Thirteenth Century Turkish* [Oxford: Clarendon Press, 1972], 963).

[141]Batur-Ubashi Tümen, "Skazanie," 31; Gabang Sharab, "Skazanie ob oiratakh," 147.

[142]Zlatkin, *Istoriia Dzhungarskogo*, 275–76; also *RIB* 51:540.

[143]Donduk-Dashi's laws, in Golstunskii, *Mongolo-oiratskie*, 66, 63.

well. This action had far-reaching consequences for Kalmyk society. The laws of Donduk-Dashi Khan remained in place until 1771, when, following the exodus of the majority of the Kalmyks to Jungaria, the Russian government abolished the zargo among the remaining Kalmyks.

One other traditional institution common to many nomadic peoples deserves mention. It was best known among the Kazakhs, who called it *barimta* (also known as *baranta;* Kalmyk—*bärmt*).[144] The barimta was a forceful seizure by an offended party of herds or goods to recover an unpaid debt or to avenge an insult. Barimta was sanctioned by customary law and was different from other raids or thefts, which were punished by *ayip*—a fine. It often happened that a rich and powerful individual refused to pay a fine for an offense that might range from insult to murder. The family of the offended party then would choose to undertake a barimta. It could be carried out overtly in the daytime or secretly at night. After a successful barimta, a settlement was usually reached and the captured herds or goods were returned. The barimta was a traditional means of self-administered justice when all other means failed.[145]

Similar institutions also existed among both the Mongols and the Oirats. One of the articles in the 1640 law code stipulated that disputes over debts should be mediated by an official. If a barimta was carried out, however, the debt was considered null and void. In addition, if such a barimta took place under the cover of dusk, those who undertook it were to be punished by a fine.[146] If the 1640 law code intended to eradicate barimta, it did not succeed in doing so. A hundred years later Donduk-Dashi's laws made another futile attempt to ban the barimta.[147] The ancient tradition continued to survive.

Succession

Throughout the seventeenth and eighteenth centuries Kalmyk society lacked a single strict law of political succession. Potentially any member of the ruling house could become a khan. As a general rule, the seat of a chief tayishi or a khan was reserved for the eldest son of the ruler. Because the Kalmyk tayishis had several wives, the eldest son of the first wife would be an heir apparent. Not infrequently, however, a khan

[144]According to Ramstedt, *bärmt* in the Oirat language meant a raid aimed at securing a pledge for future agreement from the raided party (Ramstedt, *Kalmückisches,* 39).

[145]A vivid description of barimta apppears in Ch. Ch. Valikhanov, "Zapiski o sudebnoi reforme," in *Sobranie sochinenii v piati tomakh* (Alma-Ata: GRKSE, 1985), 4:96–97.

[146]*Ikh Tsaaz,* 23, no. 102.

[147]Donduk-Dashi's laws, in Golstunskii, *Mongolo-oiratskie,* 68.

attempted to designate his favorite son as his heir. The khan's choice was not final, and more often than not, upon the khan's death, other pretenders laid claim to the khanship.

The struggle between the pretenders was usually a contest between uncles and nephews or between brothers. In 1661–62, after having become the chief tayishi, Puntsuk (Monchak) turned against his nephew Jalba (Yalba) in an effort to annihilate the rival. A decade later Ayuki tayishi did the same to his uncle Dugar. The incessant civil strife that plagued Kalmyk society throughout the eighteenth century was caused by feuds among the contending members of the ruling house. In the first half of the eighteenth century, Kalmyk emchi Gabang Sharab bitterly complained of the destructive internal conflicts, unambiguously attributing them to the unreliability of primogeniture among the Kalmyks and the resultant equal partition of property between the ruler's progeny.[148]

Eventually, it was not the law but the power and prestige of a candidate that were instrumental in securing the desired position. In this sense, war and the use of force were legitimate parts of the political system that determined the succession. But in Kalmyk nomadic society no single candidate was powerful enough to enforce his will on the rest of the people, and in the end an alliance of the tayishis would bring its candidate to power and retain him in his seat.

It thus appears that, like other pastoral nomadic societies, the Kalmyks' succession system was based on two mutually contradictory principles. Vertical succession from father to son was supposed to be the foremost model for the transfer of power. One advantage of this "prince-of-Wales" system was a clear designation of the successor. Such a system emphasized appointive succession and implied the centralization of the ruler's office. But the cost of such a determinate mode of succession was a hardening of the incumbent-successor tensions.[149] Lateral succession, in which the senior male of the ruling house inherited power, was no less legitimate and retained the strong corporate character of the ruling dynasty. A situation in which both vertical and lateral systems were regarded as legitimate put more emphasis on elective succession and implied the relative weakness of the ruling office and the stronger power of the tribal aristocracy. Such indeterminacy of succession provided an important legitimate check in Kalmyk society and allowed it to select

[148]Gabang Sharab, "Skazanie ob oiratakh," 155. For a more specific discussion of the issue see the section "The Struggle for Succession" in Chapter 6.

[149]Jack Goody offers a superb discussion of this subject in his introduction to *Succession to High Office*, ed. Goody (Cambridge: Cambridge University Press, 1966), 1–56. I am indebted to Thomas Barfield for calling some of these issues to my attention.

"the best man for the job."[150] Although the occupant of the office of the chief tayishi or khan as well as the Kalmyk clergy favored vertical succession, the tribal aristocracy preferred a more traditional lateral succession, thus creating a situation of uncertainty that allowed tribal leaders to curb the power of a khan and secure for themselves the right of selecting a candidate who would better represent their interests.[151]

The system of succession among the Kalmyks closely mirrored the structural organization of their society. The tribal leaders were best served by a lateral system or indeterminacy of succession, which allowed them to retain an elective power and exhibited a strong separatist tendency, whereas the ruling lineage, supported by the clergy, was more interested in making the dynasty hereditary. The ruler was best served by exercising his appointive authority and therefore gravitated toward centralization of the society. In the eighteenth century external powers, such as Russia, tended to lend their support to the khan's office, thus further promoting a tendency toward centralization. Vertical succession was a function of the growing hierarchical, centralized state structure in Kalmyk society, while the continued presence of the more ancient lateral succession suggested the presence of traditional society organized in a loose confederation.

The existence of the two structurally antagonistic tendencies, one propelling the top of the society toward increasing centralization, the other consolidating a separatist tendency, may explain the endless cycles of civil wars so often associated with nomadic society. It may also explain the meteoric rise and subsequent rapid demise of the nomadic empires throughout time. For it is only in sedentary societies that centralizing tendencies finally prevail.

Warfare and the Kalmyk Military

In the Kalmyk epic "Janggar," each song begins with the theme of Kalmyk heroes at an enormous feast. After having consumed much food and drink, they begin to boast of their strength, asking, "Can it really be

[150]Goody suggests five different elements accounting for uncertainty of succession (ibid., 27–28).

[151]For a more detailed discussion see Chapter 4 below. For a discussion of the succession in other Turco-Mongol societies see Joseph Fletcher, "Turco-Mongol Monarchic Tradition in the Ottoman Empire," *Harvard Ukrainian Studies* 3–4 (1979–80): 236–51; Halil Inalcik, "The Khan and the Tribal Aristocracy: The Crimean Khanate under Sahib Giray I," *Harvard Ukrainian Studies* 3–4 (1979–80): 445–66.; also his "Giray" in *Islam Ansiklopedisi*, vol. 4 (Istanbul: Milli Egitim Basimevi, 1945), 783–89.

true that there are no more battles in which to achieve renown and no *saigaks* to hunt, no country to fight, and no foe to defeat?"[152] This urge for combat was one of the main characteristics of the Kalmyks.

Erich Fromm explains the character of a warrior from a psychosocial point of view:

> The social character is that particular structure of psychic energy which is molded by any given society so as to be useful for the functioning of that particular society. The average person must want to do what he has to do in order to function in a way that permits society to use his energies for its purposes. . . . A member of a primitive people, living from assaulting and robbing other tribes, must have the character of a warrior, with a passion for war, killing, and robbing.[153]

An anthropological explanation suggests that "a segmentary lineage system consistently channels expansion outward, releasing internal pressure in an explosive blast against other peoples."[154]

Throughout the centuries the power of the Kalmyk military rested on its fast, daring cavalry. Horsemen were traditionally equipped with bows, sabers, and spears. The spread of firearms, however, inevitably affected on the Kalmyk military. The Oirats of Jungaria are reported to have used muskets in the early seventeenth century. Gunpowder was in short supply and was usually procured by forceful seizure from the Bukharians.[155] Nevertheless, the use of muskets was still insignificant, and traditional weapons were certainly preferred. In the 1640 law code the value of a musket was equated with that of a helmet or a good saber, while various types of armor or a good bow with ten arrows was valued from three to nine times higher.[156]

With the growing sophistication of firearms, and cannons in particular, the Kalmyks came to realize the advantages of gunfire. Time and again the Kalmyks attempted to procure guns, cannons, and gunpowder from Russia, but the government remained steadfast in its strict policy of banning the spread of firearms to its "tumultuous neighbors." It was not until the agreement of 1697 that Ayuki Khan was promised two light cannons and three mortars, together with gunners and an annual sup-

---

[152]*Dzhangar*, 39.

[153]Erich Fromm, *On Disobedience* (New York: Seabury Press, 1981), 27–28.

[154]Sahlins, "Segmentary Lineage," 340.

[155]*Russko-mongol'skie otnosheniia, 1607–1636. Sbornik dokumentov* (Moscow: Izd-vo vostochnoi literatury, 1959), 54, no. 18.

[156]*Ikh Tsaaz*, 19–20, nos. 62[1], 63.

ply of gunpowder and bullets.[157] Throughout the eighteenth century the Kalmyks occasionally received firearms, but the Russian authorities always remained cautious. They preferred having a unit of Russian musketeers or dragoons among the Kalmyks to supplying the Kalmyks with firearms.

The Kalmyk tayishis learned to appreciate the advantages of firearms, but their use and adoption presented genuine problems for the Kalmyk cavalry, and dissemination of firearms among the Kalmyks proceeded slowly. The musket was difficult to use and could shoot neither far nor accurately. It demanded new military tactics and required a horseman to dismount in order to shoot. Even then, in the middle of the seventeenth century, a musket could fire at most twelve rounds in a battle.[158] In comparison, a Kalmyk horseman could release an arrow with fair precision every few seconds, while rapidly closing in on the target. After all, he had practiced archery since early childhood—in contests, in hunting, and on the battlefield. Guns and muskets, even if useful tools, were still unfamiliar, alien, and not suitable to a true warrior by Kalmyk standards. Bows, sabers and spears remained the principal weapons of the Kalmyks throughout the seventeenth and eighteenth centuries.

Pallas has left a vivid description of Kalmyk weapons. The best and most expensive bows were made out of maple wood or horn. Different types of arrows served different purposes: short arrows with clublike heads for shooting small animals and birds; light arrows with narrow iron chisellike heads; large war arrows with heavy, broad-pointed arrowheads. The end of each arrow was fitted with three or four eagle tail feathers because straight flight was not possible with wing feathers. Different types of arrows were placed in different compartments of a quiver hanging on the right side of the saddle, while the bow was attached to the left side. The spear was used infrequently and was not of great value. A whip, however, was as powerful a weapon in Kalmyk hands as any other. Often witnesses were astonished by the Kalmyks' skillful use of the whip. There were several different strike techniques, and with one blow of a whip a Kalmyk could kill a wolf or dismount and mortally wound a horseman.[159]

The bow and arrow was the most typical weapon of both the commoner and the noble. The noble was best distinguished from the commoner by his armor. The Kalmyks had several kinds of armor—*khuyag*

---

[157]*PSZ* 3:no. 1591.

[158]S. K. Bogoiavlenskii, "Vooruzhenie russkikh voisk v 16–17 vekakh," *Istoricheskie zapiski* 4 (1938): 272.

[159]Pallas, *Reise*, 1:323–24; *Ikh Tsaaz*, 20, no. 63; Nebol'sin, *Ocherki byta kalmykov*, 156.

(in Kirgiz and Russian *kuyak*);[160] the most expensive was called *lübchi khuyag*[161] and consisted of a thick wool caftan with heavy metal plates sewn on top of it. A less expensive armor with short sleeves was *degeley khuyag*.[162] A suit of armor was always one of the most valued items among the Kalmyks, and a fine paid in armor was one of the heaviest penalties imposed by the 1640 law code. The same code prescribed that each forty tents had to produce two suits of armor annually.[163] Even though its practical use was declining, armor remained an important status symbol. At the end of the eighteenth century a suit of armor of poor quality could be exchanged for six or eight horses; Pallas once saw a suit of armor of Persian workmanship appraised at more than fifty horses.[164]

The use of cavalry armed with bows, sabers, and spears demanded specific tactics. Witnesses described a Kalmyk offensive in the early seventeenth century, mounted in three stages. First, the Kalmyks launched arrows at the enemy; then they charged with spears; finally, they used sabers in hand-to-hand combat. If the enemy was not bested by these attacks, the Kalmyks would retreat, though often retreat was staged to entrap the enemy.[165]

Although Russian observers have left only the above-mentioned brief account of Kalmyk military tactics, there are indications that they were far more sophisticated than they appeared to outsiders. One military formation was bow-shaped and called the bow-clasp. Its purpose was to encircle the adversary. Another formation called the ox horn was best used for attacking the enemy's flanks in short, powerful strikes.[166] Unfortunately, no detailed information is available on these or other formations.

As the Russian army increasingly used firearms, and particularly cannons, by the end of the seventeenth century, the Kalmyk offensives against Russian towns and forts proved ineffective. The Kalmyks were most successful against their seminomadic (the Crimean and Kuban Tatars and the Bashkirs) and nomadic (the Turkmen and Kazakhs)

---

[160]Ramstedt, *Kalmückisches*, 195; B. Kh. Todaeva, *Iazyk mongolov vnutrennei Mongolii. Materialy i slovar'* (Moscow: Nauka, 1981), 247.

[161]*Lübchi* (in Kalmyk *luvch*) meant a full armor (Todaeva, *Opyt lingvisticheskogo*, 327; *Kalmytsko-russkii slovar'*, 336).

[162]*Ikh Tsaaz*, 19–20, no. 63; Ramstedt, *Kalmückisches*, 85; Vladimirtsov, *Obshchestvennyi*, 167.

[163]*Ikh Tsaaz*, nos. 2, 6, 10, 59, 63.

[164]Pallas, *Reise*, 1:323.

[165]*Russko-mongol'skie otnosheniia, 1607–1636*, 54, no. 18.

[166]Kychanov, *Povestvovanie ob oiratskom*, 56.

neighbors. Steppe warfare favored raids on other people's ulus rather than pitched battles. The goal of a small raid conducted by a few hundred people was to prey on animal herds and, occasionally, on people. Such raids were the most common form of warfare among the nomadic peoples.

Several preconditions instigated launching a raid. If the precise location of the ulus to be preyed upon was identified and it was reasonable to expect that the ulus would remain at the present site for some time, a raid would be attempted. Speed and surprise were the crucial elements in the success of such a raid. Often larger raids were launched when it became known that the men of a targeted ulus had left on a military campaign and the ulus was insufficiently protected. Finally, a full-scale military campaign might be undertaken when it was learned that a certain ulus had become substantially weakened either by the constant incursions of outsiders or by internal bickering and therefore could be easy prey.

Larger-scale warfare was undertaken less frequently. The size and goals of such campaigns were fundamentally different from those of a raid. All-out war might include an army of several thousand and aim to seize the entire ulus of the victim, with all its herds and people. This ulus would then be driven away and forced to roam with the Kalmyks. As a rule, it was allowed to retain its administrative and political independence, but it had to pay taxes to the victors and provide men for the military campaigns. Having remained an independent entity, such an ulus would in time merge with the conquering tribe and assume its name. Occasionally the conquered people, if discontented, would succeed in breaking away from their captors, as the numerous Nogay tribes did in their 1696 flight from the Kalmyks to the Kuban.[167]

Warfare, like everything else in Kalmyk society, was seasonal. Raids or larger military campaigns were mostly undertaken in spring and summer. The Kalmyk horsemen could not set out for any significant raid before the month of April, when the new spring grass became sufficient to provide forage for horses. Winter raids were rare but not unprecedented. Although in winter the rivers could be conveniently crossed on the ice, scarcity of forage was a great handicap to any prolonged raid.[168]

Steppe warfare of the nomadic peoples was dramatically different from the conventional warfare of the sedentary states. Contemporary observers provided several insights into the tactics and organization of

---

[167]Silahdar Mehmed Aga Findiklili, *Nusretnâme*, comp. Ismet Parmaksizoglu, 2 vols. (Istanbul: Milli Egitim Basimevi, 1962–66), 1:251–53.
[168]*SRIO* 136:560.

such warfare. Bakunin described the defensive tactics of the Kalmyks which he witnessed at the time of a Kazakh raid:

> Since there is a constant danger from the Kalmyks' nomadic neighbors such as the Kuban Tatars and the Kazakhs, the Kalmyks always keep the scout parties at the edge of their uluses. Upon receiving the news that the enemy is approaching, the Kalmyks never set out to encounter the assailant. Instead each ulus runs away. While women and children drive horses, animal herds, and camels loaded with their belongings, the men, armed and on better horses, follow in the rear of the ulus to repel the enemy. The Kalmyks do not set out to encounter the approaching enemy. If they did so, they could miss the enemy, since there is wide-open steppe in all directions. The enemy meanwhile could raid the Kalmyk uluses, cause substantial damage, and then leave for home with captured booty. This is why, when the enemy returns home with or without booty, the Kalmyks gather their horsemen to pursue the raiders. Since the assailants and their horses are tired after the raid, the Kalmyks, having caught up with an enemy, have the advantage over them. Meanwhile, the Kalmyk reinforcements continue to arrive from other uluses.[169]

Different tactics were used during a move to new pastures or any large migration. In this case the Kalmyk horsemen took positions along the flanks of the ulus, thus forming a square with herds, belongings, women, and children in the middle.[170] Still other tactics were used by the Kalmyks while raiding. According to the Kalmyk tayishi Daichin, when the Kalmyks raided the Crimea they approached a target in separate groups from different directions and then gathered together in one place shortly before launching a raid.[171]

In the middle of the eighteenth century the Orenburg governor Ivan Nepliuev made another interesting observation on nomadic warfare. The attentive governor cautioned his superiors against driving the Kazakhs away from their pastures along the Yayik River: "For when they [Kazakhs] consider any ill-doing, then all their uluses usually move away to a secure distance, as indeed happened during their present raid on the Kalmyks—Abul Khayir [Khan] with the Lesser Horde roamed near the Emba River. . . . When they plan no mischief, their uluses roam close to the border, and there is no harm from them except for smaller raids."[172]

Neither a small raid nor a large military campaign could be under-

[169]Bakunin, "Opisanie," *Krasnyi arkhiv* 3 (1939): 226.

[170]*SRIO* 55:232.

[171]*Ocherki istorii Kalmytskoi*, 1:125.

[172]*Kazakhsko-russkie otnosheniia v 16–18 vv. Sbornik materialov i dokumentov* (Alma-Ata: AN Kazakhskoi SSR, 1961), 345, no. 135.

taken without a careful assessment of the enemy's military capability. Intelligence gathering in such warfare played a central role. Though knowledge of a potential target could be obtained in many ways, it was usually provided by informants among the targeted people or those captured by scouting parties. The latter were sent in all directions to collect information on both the possible targets and the approaching raiders. The sizes of such parties varied. At times of particular unrest they could be quite large, each group numbering as many as five hundred horsemen.[173] Most often, intelligence was obtained via the exchange of embassies and envoys or solicited from traveling merchants, who for a price would brief an interested party.

Not only warfare and raiding required careful intelligence assessment. Any movement of the ulus and, particularly, any significant migration could not be undertaken without knowledge of the geographical, political, and military situation at the new location. The early versions of the Kalmyk epic "Janggar" tell about Kho-Urlük tayishi sending scouts to the Emba, the Yayik, and the Volga rivers before the migration from Jungaria.[174] Historical records relate that just before Kho Urlük began his thrust toward the Volga, he was visited by an envoy from the Tatar Kanabey *mirza,* who informed him that the mirza would assist him in attacking Astrakhan.[175]

Raiding was a principal military activity of the Kalmyks, and a key element of the raid was swiftness, not only because a targeted ulus had to be taken by surprise but also because of concern for the safety of the raiders' own ulus. For these and other reasons the raiding parties tended to be relatively small, numbering from a few dozen to a few hundred horsemen. The best horses were chosen for the raid, and each horseman took with him as many as four or five horses.[176] The raiding party was sometimes led by a tayishi but more often by a zayisang. Other participants were the *nökörs*—a cohort of close associates, or bodyguards. For a specific raid such a group could be joined by some volunteers as well.

Raids undertaken by a small group of warriors played an important economic and social role in Kalmyk society. They provided spoils for the participants and presented an opportunity for a tayishi to demonstrate his valor. For a tayishi, peace was synonymous with idleness, whereas by accomplishing a successful raid, a tayishi could exhibit his knowledge of military craft, earn renown, strengthen his authority among his fol-

---

[173]*DAI* 12:250, no. 17.
[174]Nebol'sin, *Ocherki byta kalmykov,* 132.
[175]*Russko-mongol'skie otnosheniia, 1607–1632,* 189, no. 94.
[176]Pal'mov, *Etiudy,* 3–4:374.

lowers, and consequently attract more people to his side. These groups of tayishis and their retinues were the only standing military units in Kalmyk society. Such groups could be held together only by means of constant warfare.[177]

The Kalmyk army was essentially a self-equipped militia. In earlier times such a militia apparently consisted of volunteers, although there was no shortage of fighters attracted by the possibility of booty and the thrill of military adventure. In the middle of the eighteenth century, however, it was mandatory for the Kalmyk horsemen to participate in military campaigns. At the time of a large military campaign, a call was issued, and the Kalmyk horsemen had to gather immediately. Those who did not arrive on time had to pay fines in animal herds according to their social status.[178]

Such an irregular army driven by two major forces—the desire to seize booty and to demonstrate personal prowess—could not pride itself on strict discipline and organization. The laws of both the seventeenth and the eighteenth centuries contained many clauses aimed at strengthening discipline on the battlefield. These statutes penalized those who assailed the enemy prematurely or were too eager to go after booty, and more severe punishment awaited those who fled the battlefield. Most of the disciplinary penalties consisted of fines, but a warrior who fled the battlefield was castigated by the ultimate disgrace: he had to put on a woman's sleeveless blouse.[179]

Not much is known about the military organization of the Kalmyk army. There is no evidence to suggest that it was organized in hundreds and thousands according to the Mongol tradition, which dated back to the time of Chinggis Khan. Most likely it was organized on principles that mirrored the larger social patterns of Kalmyk society. Presumably, each tent had to provide one fully equipped horseman. The social unit of the ayimag equaled the military unit of the khoshun. As the size of the ayimag varied, so did the size of the khoshun. Thus one khoshun could number from a few hundred to a thousand fighters.

The size of the Kalmyk armies varied greatly. In discussing the Kalmyks' large military campaigns against their neighbors, Russian sources sometimes mentioned a Kalmyk army of forty thousand warriors.[180] Most likely, this figure had little to do with reality. The numbers four, forty, and forty thousand have a symbolic significance and are frequently

[177]See Owen Lattimore, *Inner Asian Frontiers of China* (New York: Capitol Publishing Co., 1951), 516–17.

[178]Donduk-Dashi's laws, in Golstunskii, *Mongolo-oiratskie*, 62.

[179]Ibid., 62; *Ikh Tsaaz*, 14–15, nos. 14–14[12].

[180]*AI* 5:138, no. 87 (V); *DAI* 10:69, no. 25 (I).

used in Turkic and Mongol epics. Forty thousand usually indicated any large number.[181] The Russians relied on their Tatar and cossack informants and had no way of verifying the information. It appears that at no time during the period could the Kalmyks muster an army more than twenty thousand strong.

In following chapters we will see that the Russian government often attempted to enlist the Kalmyk cavalry in Russian military campaigns, sometimes successfully but not to its complete satisfaction. Russian commanders complained that the Kalmyks often fled the battlefield during serious engagement, that the Kalmyk cavalry did not arrive on time, or that instead of fighting the enemy the Kalmyks looted nearby settlements.

Such acts did not necessarily represent deliberate sabotage against Russia, but rather reflected the Kalmyk style of warfare. The irregular Kalmyk military was not renowned for its discipline, and numerous clauses in Kalmyk law attempted to remedy the situation. Because the Kalmyks could operate only in wide open spaces and were very vulnerable to musket and artillery fire, they naturally tried to avoid pitched battles. In warfare against sedentary powers, the Kalmyks were most effective in swift surprise raids on the enemy's rear or under the cover of night, but even in this limited capacity they could not survive the rigors of a long campaign. After a few successful raids they set out for home overburdened with booty. Likewise, their looting of the villages was not prompted by the mere desire for spoils. The Kalmyk army was a light cavalry unit with no supply train and had to live off the land during its march. The Russian authorities did not always take sufficient care to provision the Kalmyks.[182]

As the Russian government came to realize, the Kalmyks were most successful against their steppe neighbors. Speed, endurance, and surprise were the noteworthy qualities of the Kalmyk horsemen—qualities the regular Russian army did not possess. These characteristics, eminently suitable to the harsh conditions of the steppes, made the Kalmyks an indispensable military force in campaigns against the Crimean and Kuban Tatars.

Kalmyk horsemen were known, above all, as wanton and ferocious

---

[181]Dzhangar, 30; Koblandy-batyr. Kazakhskii geroicheskii epos, trans. N. B. Kidaish-Pokrovskaia and O. A. Nurmagambetova (Moscow: Nauka, 1985), 238. On symbolic meaning of the number four, see Zeki Velidi Togan, Umumî Türk Tarikhi'ne Girish, vol. 1: En Eski Devirlerden 16. Asra kadar, 3d ed. (Istanbul: Aksiseda Matbaasi, 1981), 114.

[182]After an unfortunate experience, the Ukrainian hetman Samoilovich realized this and suggested that in the future guides should be provided for the Kalmyks and food and drink supplied by the local inhabitants (AIuZR 13:403, no. 93).

warriors. Their warrior mentality and notorious fierceness had specific economic and social roots. For Kalmyk nomads with no tradition of agriculture, artisanship, or trade, with cattle breeding as their only source of income, dependence on booty was far greater than among semisedentary steppe peoples. Thus the 1640 law code, in an attempt to prevent arguments over the spoils, furnished specific regulations on this account. Upon killing a combatant, the victor was allowed to take his wife or weapons. One such article stated: "If one kills a man in cuirass he should take his cuirass, and the one who arrives after him should choose one of the two—coat of mail or helmet. Those who arrive later should take whatever is left upon their arrival."[183] The laws provided the Kalmyks with strong incentives to manifest their zeal in battle.

Ordinarily, booty captured in a raid or a battle was shared among the participants, with military leaders receiving a larger share and those who showed exceptional valor receiving special rewards. The booty had to be distributed within three days. Those who stole a part of the booty during this period were punished by a relatively small fine. If a theft was committed after the three-day period, that is, after the distribution of booty had been completed, it was punishable according to the provisions concerning the theft of property.[184]

For an ambitious and skillful warrior or a young Kalmyk noble, peace meant stagnation. Only in times of war could they achieve renown by exhibiting their martial and organizational skills—the most cherished qualities in Kalmyk society. Only in combat could they hope to resemble the heroes glorified in the songs they had heard since childhood. War alone could strengthen and forge ties with their *nökörs*—a close circle of trusted men. Successful war brought abundant booty, which, when given away as generous gifts, helped to create a wide circle of devoted followers; generosity was the paramount quality of the leader. Only war could bring the popularity and support that were crucial in a bid for political power.

Warfare and raiding were, then, chronic phenomena of Kalmyk nomadic society. In bad times, when the herds were depleted by unfavorable weather, disease, or enemy forays, ever-larger segments of the population became dependent on booty and raids occurred more frequently. Even in times of relative economic prosperity, there were those who preferred raiding to peace and were ready to lead a raid to please their followers and gain personal fame. In either case, with no strong centralized authority in the society, these raids could not be stopped.

---

[183]*Ikh Tsaaz*, 21, no. 81.
[184]Donduk-Dashi's laws, in Golstunskii, *Mongolo-oiratskie*, 63; *Ikh Tsaaz*, 21, no. 86.

The Russian government repeatedly initiated efforts to find a means to check Kalmyk raids against the Russian towns and settlements. When the government chose to resolve the issues of pastures, trade, and payments in the Kalmyks' favor, it prevented large military campaigns along the Russian frontier. Small-scale raiding activity, though, could not be averted. In the seventeenth and early eighteenth centuries, Russia, for reasons of its own, could not fulfill its obligations as a suzerain toward the Kalmyks, and both large campaigns and small raids took place in abundance.

2

Mutual Perceptions

Diplomacy and Symbolism

"Every society," as Jacques Le Goff has remarked, "is symbolic to the extent that it employs symbols in its practices and that it may be studied with the aid of a symbolic type of interpretation."[1] Both Russian and Kalmyk societies were imbued with symbolism and rituals to which they attached an important political meaning. Compliance with required rituals and customs was always a sensitive issue. The semantics of political notions expressed through cultural symbolism was different in each society and was often misread and misinterpreted by both sides.

Exchange of envoys played an important role in relations between the two political entities. For Russia, sending an embassy was a political and diplomatic act. Such embassies from Moscow to the Kalmyks were dispatched infrequently. They usually arrived in early spring with one primary goal—to ensure the Kalmyks' participation in the summer military campaigns. Since material rewards possessed more persuasive power than mere promises, such embassies usually brought cash and gifts for the tayishis, as well as tobacco and wine.[2]

[1]Jacques Le Goff, *Time, Work, and Culture in the Middle Ages* (Chicago: University of Chicago Press, 1980), 237.

[2]In the seventeenth century diplomatic relations with the Kalmyks were under the auspices of the Chancellery of Foreign Affairs, while trade and annual payments were handled by the Kazan Chancellery. In 1661 the government created the Chancellery of Kalmyk Affairs, headed by the *d'iak* I. S. Gorokhov. This chancellery appears to have lasted for less than a year (Kotoshikhin, *O Rossii,* 87, 92; S. B. Veselovskii, *D'iaki i pod'iachie 15–17 vv.* [Moscow: Nauka, 1975], 127; M. Kichikov [Ochirov], "K voprosu obrazovaniia Kalmytskogo khanstva v sostave Rossii," *KNIIaLI, Vestnik instituta, istoriko-filologicheskaia seriia* 1 [1963]: 27).

In Kalmyk society, in addition to communicating a political message, the embassy had other important functions, one of which was to gather information. This is not to say that the Russian embassies had no such purpose. Russian envoys often used gifts and promises to solicit information from informants, or "well-wishers," as the Russians called them. The Kalmyks' reliance on such intelligence was far greater. If an embassy was sent to their allies, it was done with the expectation that the other party would share the latest political and military news.[3] A courtesy embassy to neighboring peoples served the same purpose but had to rely more on hearsay and informants.

Throughout the period, the Russian government, seeking to secure the Kalmyks' political loyalty, often demanded that the Kalmyks sever their relations with the Ottoman empire, the Crimea, and others among Russia's enemies. But the Kalmyks continued sending embassies to these and other powers in the area. The Russian authorities considered this to be an act of treachery and defiance. For the Kalmyks, however, compliance with Russian demands meant severing vital channels of communication and information, without which the relative safety of the Kalmyk uluses could not be secured.

Multipurpose Kalmyk embassies also played an important commercial role. To a certain extent, they functioned as traveling merchant companies. Ordinarily the members of the Kalmyk embassy brought horses, various products of the nomadic economy, and, on occasion, Chinese goods, including tea and tobacco, to sell.[4] Participation in such an embassy promised numerous economic benefits. Valuable gifts such as fur hats, coats, boots, and other garments were bestowed upon the envoys by the Russian officials.[5] In addition, the envoys were given cash allowances and permitted to sell their merchandise tax-free. With this money, embassy members could shop for prized Russian goods. Bringing home a piece of cloth or wool, a pair of brightly colored leather boots, or a fine knife (and perhaps some vodka) could not fail to impress their relatives and friends. Sending an embassy to Moscow not only meant direct communication with high officials, thus avoiding harassment from the local governors, but also promised better gifts and more money. It is understandable, therefore, that the Kalmyks' requests to send frequent and sizable embassies—often directly to Moscow—figured prominently in Kalmyk-Russian correspondence.

[3]In his letters of 1714 to the Astrakhan governor Chirikov, Ayuki consistently asked about the latest news from "the four sides" (Russko-kitaiskie otnosheniia v 18 veke. Materialy i dokumenty, vol. 1: 1700–1725 [Moscow: Nauka, 1978], 151–52, nos. 101–3).

[4]Johann George Korb, Dnevnik puteshestviia v Moskoviiu, 1698–1699 gg., trans. A. I. Malein (St. Petersburg: Tip. A. S. Suvorina, 1906), 139.

[5]Kotoshikhin, O Rossii, 69, 70, 74.

All major Kalmyk tayishis wished to send their own embassies, if not to Moscow, then at least to the governors of nearby towns. By appointing their favorite zayisangs to the embassy, the tayishis created a circle of political loyalty around themselves. The tayishis were interested in appointing as many people as possible to the embassy, which on occasion consisted of no fewer than two hundred people. The Russian authorities continuously attempted to regulate the number of Kalmyk embassies, as well as their size and destination.[6] Throughout the period such embassies were a recurring issue of contention between the Russian authorities and the Kalmyks.

Upon the arrival of an embassy, both the Russians and the Kalmyks paid great attention to the manner in which it was received. The ceremony, the gifts, the duration of the stay—everything was considered on a scale of honor and respect and interpreted in political terms. These interpretations, however, did not always coincide because Russian and Kalmyk diplomatic etiquette differed substantially.

After the embassy had arrived, it was assigned a place of residence, a food and drink allowance, and some cash. The Kalmyks, following Turko-Mongol tradition, regarded the reception of an embassy, the type and amount of its allowances, and its place of residence as particularly important symbols of respect. Yet the Russian authorities adopted a condescending attitude toward their nomadic neighbors. They commonly referred to them as "lightminded people" or "unwise, silly children" and tried to offer as little as possible to the Kalmyk embassy.[7]

Abuses on the part of Russian officials were common and were not limited to the local governors. Johann Korb, a secretary in the embassy of the Holy Roman Emperor, recalled in his diary that in 1698 a Kalmyk envoy with six other people arrived in Moscow. The envoy was put up in small rooms above the stables of the Chancellery of Foreign Affairs, given an allowance of thirty kopecks a day, and assured that all other envoys lived in the same fashion.[8]

In accordance with the common practice of decentralized Kalmyk society, a foreign embassy was free to move around the ulus and contact different people. Russian envoys always used the occasion to establish contacts with Kalmyk informants or "well-wishers." Conversely, the Rus-

---

[6]In February 1703 Peter I ordered that embassies of tayishi Munko-Temir should be limited to one a year and their size to five people (AVD 1:194–95, no. 128).

[7]In one instance, in 1691–92, Governor S. I. Saltykov of the Siberian town of Tobol'sk detained an embassy from the Oirat Galdan Boshoktu Khan for more than half a year. Instead of housing the envoys at the special ambassadorial quarters, he put them up in a Tatar village and gave them an allowance for four individuals, although the embassy consisted of ten persons (N. P. Shastina, Russko-mongol'skie posol'skie otnosheniia v 17 veke [Moscow: Izd-vo vostochnoi literatury, 1958], 171).

[8]Korb, Dnevnik puteshestviia, 139.

sian government, concerned with security and the possibility of a plot, did its best to prevent the Kalmyks from having contact with others, particularly the local Tatars residing in the Volga towns. The Kalmyks were confined to their quarters and guards were appointed to enforce the rule.[9]

Within several days of an embassy's arrival, it was given an audience. In Moscow, the embassy was usually received by a high official of the Chancellery of Foreign Affairs but rarely by the tsar himself. If the embassy had been sent to a local town, it was received by the governor. After speaking, the envoy presented a letter and offered gifts. The letter was addressed to the tsar without mentioning his full titles. The letters were usually brief because the main message was delivered orally by an envoy.[10]

The presentation of gifts was an important part of the diplomatic ritual. For the Kalmyks each gift had a symbolic significance. The most common Kalmyk gifts were horses, sabers, bows and arrows, and saddles. Offerings of Chinese or Bukharan handicrafts, expensive brocades, silk, or musk were rarer. Among the gifts carrying a strong symbolic meaning was a bay saddle horse of fine Oriental breed (argamak). This most valuable gift of the Kalmyk nomad was a sign of great honor and respect. Important meaning was attached to the number nine, which was considered sacred. The presentation of nine gifts meant particularly friendly intentions.[11] For example, among the gifts delivered from Ayuki Khan to the Ottoman Porte in 1710 were nine bottles of musk, nine Russian leather hides, one gray stallion, one gray horse, and one bay pack horse.[12] Sending an arrow meant an invitation to join a military campaign, while presenting a sword or bow and arrows served to underscore commitment to a military alliance between the two parties.[13] The subtle language of Kalmyk diplomatic etiquette was often misunderstood in seventeenth-century Muscovy.

Among the most precious presents brought by the Russian embassies and presented to the Kalmyk tayishis were fine Russian hides, wools, brocades, fabrics, and hunting birds. Furs and fur coats were presented less frequently. The Russian embassy had to learn painfully (often in the literal sense of the word) that it was not enough to bring presents only to a chief tayishi or khan. Each Kalmyk tayishi, being independent from the khan, expected to receive presents as well. A tayishi was offended if he

---

[9]Shastina, *Russko-mongol'skie posol'skie*, 134. Such treatment was not limited to Kalmyk embassies.

[10]Kotoshikhin, *O Rossii*, 38.

[11]Shastina, *Russko-mongol'skie posol'skie*, 92, 95.

[12]BA *Nâme-i Hümayun*, no. 6, p. 520.

[13]Shastina, *Russko-mongol'skie posol'skie*, 117.

did not receive gifts, or if he thought that the gifts were not appropriate to his status. This treatment often resulted in raids on Russian settlements, organized in revenge by the offended tayishi. To show his immediate displeasure, such a tayishi felt justified in beating the envoy or humiliating him in a variety of ways. The most effective Russian officials were those who realized the importance of the gifts when dealing with the Kalmyks, and they constantly insisted that the Russian government should allocate more money for gifts to the Kalmyks.

The exchange of gifts was an important symbol of political status. To reciprocate with equally valuable gifts was to emphasize parity between the parties involved. Refusal to accept gifts was construed as an act of blatant hostility or an opportunity to show dismay or anger. It could also be an assertion of victory. Acceptance of gifts without adequate reciprocation was an admission of subordinate status. Accepting gifts from a chief or a suzerain was a guarantee of future loyalty.[14]

The exchange of gifts also had a commercial aspect. Marcel Mauss defined gift exchange as "an aristocratic type of commerce characterized by etiquette and generosity; moreover when it is carried in a different spirit, for immediate gains, it is viewed with disdain."[15] During the initial stage of Kalmyk-Russian relations, before substantial trade took place, such a "gift economy" was particularly important for the Kalmyk tayishis.

Thus the exchange of embassies was an important part of Kalmyk-Russian relations. Each side, however, viewed the role of the embassy from a different perspective. The Russian view, based on the principles of Byzantine diplomacy, held that the embassy and the envoys were a respected and inviolate body fully representing its monarch. The Kalmyk view was similar to the principles of Manchu diplomacy, whereby "the ambassador was fundamentally only a messenger conveying his master's letters. His own person was not inviolate and he might, in fact, be harshly treated."[16] In many cases the tayishis' anger against the envoys was not unjustified. Russian envoys were notorious for embezzling the money and gifts they were supposed to deliver, and their complaints of beatings and abuse were sometimes fabricated to conceal their own misdeeds.[17]

---

[14]A. Ia. Gurevich, *Kategorii srednevekovoi kul'tury* (Moscow: Iskusstvo, 1972), 201.

[15]Marcel Mauss, *The Gift: Forms and Functions of Exchange in Archaic Societies,* trans. Ian Cunnison (Glencoe, Ill.: Free Press, 1954), 36.

[16]Mark Mancall, "The Ch'ing Tribute System: An Interpretive Essay," in *The Chinese World Order: Traditional China's Foreign Relations,* ed. John Fairbank (Cambridge, Mass.: Harvard University Press, 1968), 65.

[17]For example, a Russian envoy to the Crimea, Tarakanov, in 1682 complained that he had been beaten up by the Crimean *nureddin,* who demanded presents. The story was

Upon completing its mission, a Kalmyk embassy was expected to return promptly. Letters from the Kalmyk tayishis often contained a firm request not to delay the return of the embassy. In the language of Kalmyk diplomacy, the expeditious return of the embassy was a sign of friendship and good intentions.[18] Delaying the embassy was interpreted as an act of disrespect or outright hostility.[19] It meant that the envoys were suspected of being spies, or that one side was trying to prevent the other from receiving important news expeditiously.[20] Detaining the envoys could also mean that one side had unsettled claims against the other and had decided to keep the envoys until the dispute was settled according to the common laws of barimta.[21]

Not only ambassadorial exchanges but all aspects of communication between Russia and the Kalmyks were permeated with symbolism. In time, Moscow's failure to understand this semiotic language led to false presumptions and expectations.

Translating and Interpreting

Most of the Kalmyk correspondence addressed to Russian officials and the tsar has survived in Russian translation. Throughout the seventeenth and early eighteenth centuries translations from Kalmyk into Russian and vice versa were made in two steps. First, the documents were

---

most likely not true, as Tarakanov had been known to lie in the past. The Crimean documents contain numerous complaints about Tarakanov's lying and cheating (V. D. Smirnov, *Krymskoe khanstvo pod verkhovenstvom Otomanskoi Porty do nachala 18 veka* [St. Petersburg: Tip. A. S. Suvorina, 1887], 600–601). In another case, in February 1654, when the interpreter Afanasii Borisov arrived at the Kalmyk uluses from Astrakhan, he was tied up and beaten. The Kalmyks broke his right hand and told him that "he was sent to lie and to cheat, and not to tell the truth" (P. S. Preobrazhenskaia, "Iz istorii russko-kalmytskikh otnoshenii v 50-60-kh godakh 17 veka." *Zapiski KNIIaLI* 1 (1960): 62). When in 1747 the Kazakh Abul Khayir Khan was angry with the Orenburg governor Ivan Nepliuev, he ordered the Russian embassy detained and the interpreter lashed (I. I. Kraft, *Turgaiskii oblastnoi arkhiv. Opisanie arkhivnych dokumentov s 1731 po 1782 g. otnosiashchikhsia k upravleniu kirgizami* (St. Petersburg: Tip. A. P. Lopukhina, 1901), 19, no. 76.

[18]Silahdar Mehmed Aga Findiklili, *Silahdar Tarikhi*, 2 vols. (Istanbul: Orhaniye Matbaasi, 1928), 2:707.

[19]*DAI* 10:385, no. 80.

[20]In 1661 the Kalmyks, who were preparing for a campaign against the Crimea, had detained the Crimean envoys (*AMG* 3:461, no. 539). In 1732 Kalmyk khan Donduk-Ombo, who left Russia and was at the time under Ottoman jurisdiction, delayed the Russian envoys for fifty-one days because he suspected that they were spies (Bakunin, "Opisanie," *Krasnyi arkhiv* 5 [1939]: 202).

[21]*Materialy po istorii karakalpakov. Sbornik.* Trudy Instituta vostokovedeniia, vol. 7 (Moscow and Leningrad: Izd-vo Akademii Nauk, 1935), 168.

translated into Tatar and then into Kalmyk or Russian. Typically, the translators were baptized Tatars or cossacks, who learned the language while in Kalmyk captivity. Needless to say, such translators had no professional training and lacked adequate education. Their familiarity with the Kalmyk language was limited to colloquial Kalmyk, and their knowledge of Kalmyk society was at best superficial. In the hierarchy of the Russian bureaucracy, a clear distinction was made between staff translators (*perevodchiki*) and interpreters (*tolmachi*). The interpreters were less competent and usually translated oral messages and speeches, rather than written documents. In 1679, for example, among the employees of the Chancellery of Foreign Affairs in Moscow were listed Taras Ivanov, an interpreter of Tatar and Kalmyk, and Vasilii Martynov, an interpreter of Kalmyk.[22]

It is crucial to understand the problems faced by translators in seventeenth-century Russia. After more than seventy years of Russo-Oirat relations, a 1667 Russian embassy to the Oirat tayishi brought a letter written in Bukharan (Persian). None of the Oirats, however, could read the letter, and there were no Russian interpreters to translate it.[23] In many cases when both the originals and their translations have survived, the translations were often written negligently, and they show numerous mistakes and signs of editing at a later date.

At the time, the authorities had no competent translators into Kalmyk, and Russian officials had to rely on those who claimed to know the languages. Often incapable of translating straightforward texts, they could not hope to understand the subtleties of language. For example, the Mongol Lubsan *tayiji* (an honorable title of a noble) in his letters to the tsar in 1662–63, referred to himself as "*khagan*," which denoted a ruler with the rights of an emperor, while calling the tsar "the white khan," which meant a local ruler.[24] In another example, I. Rossokhin, an experienced translator of Manchu and Chinese in the early eighteenth century, noted that the term *white khan* was used in a disparaging sense with reference to the Russian tsar because in Manchu it was written with a dot at the end, which meant "the khan, who is a subject." The Manchu emperors, referring to their own title, wrote it without a dot, which meant "the autocratic khan." Rossokhin cursed the "stupid frontier interpreters" who, in their ignorance, translated "white khan" as Russian

[22]Iu. N. Rerikh and N. P. Shastina, "Gramota tsaria Petra I k Lubsan taidzhi i ee sostavitel'," *Problemy vostokovedeniia* 4 (1960): 144.

[23]Ibid., 142.

[24]Shastina, *Russko-mongol'skie posol'skie*, 90.

emperor and called the Manchu emperor "bogdo khan," that is, a sacred khan.[25]

In addition to the problem of incompetent translators, there was another, perhaps more important hindrance: translations had to fit the accepted diplomatic terminology, and translators took great pains to avoid precise translations whenever the original phrasing could possibly harm the dignity of the monarch or the Russian state. To this end, watchful Russian officials kept their eyes open and their quills sharpened. Available translations often show numerous signs of editing. The corrections spelled out fully the title of the tsar and introduced such polite expressions as "your royal majesty," "the grand sovereign," and others not mentioned in the original. Often the arrogant tone of a letter was changed, making it more humble and subdued.[26]

When the letters of Lubsan tayiji, in which he referred to the tsar as a local ruler, were delivered to the Russian monarch, they were referred to in Russian terminology as a "petition [chelobit'e] of the Mongol prince." Lubsan offered peace and asked for military assistance, but the government praised him for "seeking the sovereign's favor" and encouraged him "not to violate his oath of allegiance."[27] In its regal arrogance Moscow was quick to confer the status of subject on its nomadic neighbors. When in 1673 the envoys of the well-known and fiercely independent Galdan Boshoktu Khan of the Oirats arrived in Moscow, the first such embassy to Russia, they may have been surprised to be told by Russian officials that their khan was a subject of the tsar.[28]

This attitude of divine supremacy, reflected in the diplomatic practices and mentality of the Russian state, was particularly explicit in the government's attitude toward its nomadic neighbors. It was bluntly expressed by a certain Russian envoy dispatched to the Kazakhs. The Kazakhs, offended by his insistence on their subject status, reproached him, saying that they had sent envoys to Moscow not to become Russian subjects but to have peace with Russia. The envoy angrily replied that it was not befitting the dignity of the Russian monarch to be at peace with

[25]N. P. Shastina, "Perevod I. Rossokhinym istochnika po istorii mongolov 17 veka," Uchenye zapiski Instituta vostokovedeniia 6 (1953): 204.

[26]Examples of Lubsan tayiji's letters of 1661 or Tushetu Khan's of 1675 are found in N. P. Shastina, "Pis'ma Lubsan taidzhi v Moskvu," in Filologiia i istoriia mongol'skikh narodov (Moscow: Izd-vo vostochnoi literatury, 1958), 278. Ayuki Khan was well aware of the mistranslation of his letters and often complained about it (Russko-kitaiskie otnosheniia, 137, no. 83).

[27]Shastina, "Pis'ma," 279–81.

[28]Kychanov, Povestvovanie ob oiratskom, 53.

them because the Kazakhs were steppe animals who were of no use to Russia.[29]

Such attitudes were not unique to the Russian mentality. The Chinese, too, looked at foreign relations from the perspective of a traditional, center-periphery political system. All the foreign embassies that arrived at the "center of civilization" from the periphery were seen as Chinese subjects offering tribute to the emperor. When Ayuki's embassies headed for Tibet, they often sold their herds of horses in China so they could bring lavish presents to the Dalai Lama and obtain precious Chinese tea.[30] This was sufficient to prompt the Qing Emperor Kangxi to mention in his 1683 decree the Torgut Ayuki tayishi as being among those who "paid tribute independently."[31]

The Ottoman sultans were no different. The Kalmyk embassies to the Porte were mentioned in terms similar to those used by the Russians and Chinese. In Ottoman terminology the Kalmyk letters were described as letters of submission, *ubudiyet namesi*, in which the Kalmyks pledged allegiance of servitude and loyalty to the Ottoman Porte.[32]

In an age when symbols not only replaced reality but became a reality in themselves, to understand the symbols meant to understand the reality. A look at surviving Kalmyk letters, or reliable translations of them, makes it obvious that throughout the seventeenth and early eighteenth centuries the Kalmyk tayishis and khans did not regard themselves as Russian subjects. For example, the original of tayishi Daichin's letter of 1661 to the Russian tsar began with these words: "You, the white khan, rule in good health; I am Daichin Khan here, and both of us khans are in good health."[33] The letters of Ayuki Khan and other Kalmyk tayishis to Muscovite provincial governors were essentially imperative directives, while letters to the tsar were addressed to an equal power.[34] Bakunin tells us explicitly what the Kalmyk tayishis thought of their allegiances:

[29]*Kazakhsko-russkie otnosheniia,* 53–54, no. 33.

[30]The tea trade was a firmly controlled monopoly of the Qing government. The importance of tea in the diet of the Tibetans, the Mongols, and the Oirats allowed the Qing to use the tea trade as a political weapon in relations with these peoples. They were permitted to exchange tea for horses under elaborate and stringent provisions of Chinese law (*Taitsin gurun i ukheri koli, to est' vse zakony i ustanovleniia kitaiskogo (a nyne man'chzhurskogo) pravitel'stva,* trans. A. Leont'ev, 3 vols. [St. Petersburg: Imp. Akademiia nauk, 1781–83], 2:29–30, 35; 3:251–53). Similar clauses existed in the laws of the Ming China (*Ustanovleniia o soli i chae,* trans. N. P. Svistunova [Moscow: Nauka, 1975], 67).

[31]*Vneshniia politika gosudarstva Tsin v 17 veke* (Moscow: Nauka, 1977), 183. More about the Qing tribute system may be found in Mark Mancall, *Russia and China: Their Diplomatic Relations to 1728* (Cambridge, Mass.: Harvard University Press, 1971), 3–8.

[32]BA *Nâme-i Hümayun,* 88–89, no. 6; Findiklili, *Silahdar Tarihi,* 2:419.

[33]Kichikov (Ochirov), "K voprosu obrazovaniia," 23.

[34]*Russko-kitaiskie otnosheniia,* 147, 149, nos. 93, 95; *Ocherki istorii Kalmytskoi,* 1:129;

The Kalmyk tayishis never recognized their former allegiances as oaths of allegiance. Its very name, that is, "shert'," is alien not only to the Russian, but to the Kalmyk language as well. They [the tayishis] referred only to the agreement concluded with Prince B. A. Golitsyn. It is obvious that they were not aware of [the contents of] those [previous] "shert'." It is clear from the copies found that the original allegiance records were written in Russian, and were only signed in Kalmyk.[35]

The agreement that Bakunin referred to was dated 1697 and signed by Ayuki Khan and Prince B. A. Golitsyn.[36] The contents and the spirit of this agreement were dramatically different from any former oath of allegiance. Unlike previous treaties, which considered the Kalmyks to be Russian subjects and were limited to exacting obligations from them, this agreement resembled a treaty between two military allies. The Kalmyks were familiar with the contents of this treaty because it was the first document that they recognized as valid. Presumably, this document was either written in Kalmyk or was available in a proper Kalmyk translation.[37]

Bakunin also asserted that the oath of allegiance sworn by Cheren-Donduk Khan in 1724 was the first official Kalmyk oath. It was written in Kalmyk, and before the Kalmyks agreed to it under heavy pressure by the Astrakhan governor Volynskii, they discussed it in numerous meetings among themselves.[38] Even this oath of allegiance, however, contained no clauses expressing submission to Russia, with the exception of a courteous reference to "His Imperial Majesty."

Political Status

Ascertaining the political status of the Kalmyks in their relations with Russia is essential for understanding the substance of Russo-Kalmyk relations, as well as the goals and policies pursued by both sides. The Kalmyks' political status in the seventeenth and eighteenth centuries is a

---

Aleksei G. Sazykin, "An Historical Document in Oirat Script," in *Between the Danube and the Caucasus*, ed. György Kara (Budapest: Akadémiai Kiadó, 1987), 229–33 (for the translation of the latter see Chapter 5); *ODAMM* 2:574, no. 508.

[35]Bakunin, "Opisanie," *Krasnyi arkhiv* 3 (1939): 214–15.

[36]*PSZ* 3:no. 1591.

[37]Not coincidentally, perhaps, Moscow's Chancellery of Foreign Affairs at this time had on its staff P. I. Kul'vinskii—an unusually competent translator of the Kalmyk, Mongol, and Tibetan languages. He was employed by the Chancellery of Foreign Affairs from 1680 to 1683, then from 1688 to March 1706 (Rerikh and Shastina, "Gramota tsaria Petra I," 144).

[38]Bakunin, "Opisanie," *Krasnyi arkhiv* 3 (1939): 214–15.

disputed and confused issue. Were they Russian subjects or free people unfettered by notions of submission? Were they Russia's military ally or a band of mercenaries ready to serve the highest bidder?

Russian historians of the nineteenth century gave different answers to these questions. Some, like N. Ia. Bichurin and A. M. Pozdneev, could not separate themselves from the government's official position. Blinded by Russian chauvinism, they viewed the Kalmyks as Russia's unreliable ally, a band of mischievous nomads always ready to inflict harm. Others, such as M. Novoletov and N. N. Pal'mov, concluded, after having studied Russian archival materials, that the Kalmyks had become Russian subjects by the middle of the seventeenth century.

Soviet historiography also attaches considerable importance to the oaths signed by the Kalmyks in the mid-1650s, regarding them as a turning point in Russo-Kalmyk relations. It alleges that the signing of the first written oath in 1655 marked the Kalmyks' submission and their incorporation into the Muscovite state with the status of subjects. Such a conclusion, however, reflects only the point of view of the Muscovite government, which considered the very first contact with the Kalmyks in 1606 as the date when they submitted to Moscow.[39]

In January 1606, at the very beginning of Kalmyk-Russian relations, the first Muscovite embassy arrived at the Kalmyk ulus with the purpose of convincing the Kalmyks to become Muscovite subjects and to pledge their allegiance (*dat' shert'*) to the Grand tsar.[40] At the time the Muscovites knew very little about the Kalmyks and still confused the tayishi with the mirza—a title used by various Turkic peoples and thus more familiar to Moscow. Muscovy's garrisons in Siberia were small, poorly equipped, and could be easily overrun by the more numerous Kalmyks. Yet from the beginning Moscow insisted on nothing less than the Kalmyks' submission.

The Muscovite government felt that the suzerain-subject relationship between Muscovy and the Kalmyks had to be reaffirmed in various ways. One of them was insisting that the Kalmyks voluntarily select hostages (*amanaty*) from among their nobles and send them to the authorities. The Kalmyks persistently refused to do so, and on one occasion they emphatically replied that they would never give away hostages because

---

[39]*Pamiatniki diplomaticheskikh i torgovykh snoshenii Moskovskoi Rusi s Persiei*, ed. N. I. Veselovskii, 3 vols. (St. Petersburg: Pechatnia P. O. Iablonskogo, 1890–98), 2:259–60; M. L. Kichikov [Ochirov], "K istorii obrazovaniia Kalmytskogo khanstva v sostave Rossii," *Zapiski KNIIaLI* 2 [1962]: 35; *Ocherki istorii Kalmytskoi*, 111–21. The Kalmyks did not consider themselves to be Russia's subjects until September 1724 (see Chapter 5 for details).

[40]*Russko-mongol'skie otnosheniia, 1607–1636*, 28–29, no. 4.

their tayishis were offspring of Chinggis Khan.[41] Yet, two decades later, in 1657, the tayishis Puntsuk and Manjik agreed to send four hostages to Astrakhan. In a letter to Moscow they remarked that although the case was unprecedented for the Kalmyks, the tayishis had decided to comply with the stubborn demands of the Astrakhan governor. On another occasion, Daichin tayishi sought to explain that the Kalmyks had never given hostages, and if he did so he would be disgraced in the eyes of the Crimea, Persia, and the Kalmyk people. Eventually, he too succumbed to the government's demands; the lure of Russian gifts, awards, and trade privileges overcame his fear of disgrace. The Muscovite authorities realized the importance of this concession for the Kalmyks. In a conciliatory gesture, they boarded the Kalmyk hostages not in regular hostage quarters but in a special house and remunerated the hostages with an unusually high compensation.[42]

The symbols of submission were just as important as its tangible manifestations. Thus, upon receiving a letter from His Majesty, the tsar, or when inquiring about his health, the Kalmyk tayishi was expected to stand up and take off his hat. In 1661 Moscow's envoy, d'iak I. S. Gorokhov, arrived at the ulus of Daichin tayishi. During the reception he suggested that Daichin should stand up and take off his hat when the name of the tsar was mentioned. When Daichin replied that the Kalmyks did not have such customs, Gorokhov reproached him, saying that monarchs of all states did so, and for Daichin to remain seated with his hat on was to show dishonor. An embarrassed Daichin explained that he meant no offense. As a compromise, he ordered his interpreter to stand up and continue to translate with his hat off. On this they both agreed.[43]

A proper manifestation of the symbols of honor and respect was always a sensitive issue for Muscovy, which had only recently emerged from obscurity and was struggling to assert its status in relations with other established powers. On two different occasions F. Baikov and I. Perfil'ev, Russian envoys to China in the second half of the seventeenth century, refused to comply with Qing ceremonies and insisted on Russian customs. The Qing, no less stubborn, sent them back home.[44]

---

[41]S. K. Bogoiavlenskii, "Materialy po istorii kalmykov v pervoi polovine 17 veka," *Istoricheskie zapiski* 5 (1939): 73.

[42]Preobrazhenskaia, "Iz istorii," 66–67.

[43]Ibid., 72.

[44]*DRV* 4:120–42; 3:pt. 2:197, 269; Nikolai Bantysh-Kamenskii, *Diplomaticheskoe sobranie del mezhdu Rossiiskim i Kitaiskim gusudarstvami s 1619 po 1792-i god* (Kazan': Tip. Imp. Universiteta, 1882), 10–11; Mancall, *Russia and China,* 44–56. This and other Muscovite missions to the Mongols, Oirats, and Qing China in the seventeenth century are available in

The Russian government sought to underscore the submission of the Kalmyks both in political and diplomatic terms. Throughout the seventeenth century, letters to the Kalmyks were written on a "small Alexander paper" (a fine quality paper of small size) and sealed with either *vorotnaia* or *kormlenaia pechat'* (small seals usually used for decrees meant for internal dissemination).[45]

In some instances the Russian government followed customary tradition and bestowed gifts and symbols of power on the tayishis in yet another attempt to assert authority over its subjects.[46] Thus, when a new oath of allegiance was exacted from the Kalmyks in 1657, the Kalmyk tayishis Daichin and Puntsuk were presented with sable coats and hats—attributes of the suzerain-subject relationship in Moscow's view. In 1664 a Russian military banner was sent to the Kalmyks in an unsubtle move to emphasize that the Kalmyk cavalry had become a part of the Russian army.[47] But the government's failure to secure the Kalmyks' loyalty discouraged further attempts to incorporate Kalmyk military into the Russian army. The necessity of the symbolic gesture was clearly realized later in the eighteenth century. In 1724, when internal rivalry among the Kalmyks was rife, the Astrakhan governor Volynskii suggested to the authorities that a saber, a suit of armor, and a shield be sent to the new khan in the hope that the Kalmyks would regard the gifts as a sign of khanship conferred by Moscow.[48]

In Moscow's view, the most important way to ensure the Kalmyks' submission was to secure an oath of allegiance, and the government constantly insisted on such pledges of allegiance by dispatching a plenipotentiary official who met with the tayishi or khan and secured his written oath. Usually the Muscovite embassies dispatched to the Kalmyks consisted of a middle-rank court official accompanied by several clerks,[49] but at times when securing the Kalmyks' allegiance was of particular importance, such embassies were headed by a high-ranking

---

English translation in John F. Baddeley, *Russia, Mongolia, China*, 2 vols. (London: Macmillan, 1919), 2:130–218.

[45]*DRV* 16:247 (XXIX); E. I. Kamentseva and N. V. Ustiugov, *Russkaia sfragistika i geral'dika* (Moscow: Vysshaia shkola, 1963), 114–19.

[46]According to Robert S. Lopez, customary law demanded a concrete token of every transfer of possession (*The Birth of Europe* [New York: M. Evans, 1967], 163). A. Ia. Gurevich explains that in medieval times it was not enough to sign a document during the transfer of an estate from one person to another. Only upon the performance of ritual, whereby the former owner of an estate publicly handed over a handful of soil to the new owner, was the transaction completed (*Kategorii srednevekovoi kul'tury*, 71).

[47]*Ocherki istorii Kalmytskoi*, 1:118; Preobrazhenskaia, "Iz istorii," 83.

[48]Bakunin, "Opisanie," *Krasnyi arkhiv* 3 (1939): 235.

[49]Kotoshikhin, *O Rossii*, 42.

official. The allegiances had a variety of objectives, the most common of which were to induce the Kalmyks to end their hostile acts against Russia or to ensure their participation in Russia's military campaigns. Although the allegiance was pledged "forever," from Moscow's point of view the death of either party—the tsar or the tayishi—rendered the pledge invalid, and Moscow would insist that the allegiance be renewed.

Yet all the allegiances notwithstanding, the loyalty of the Kalmyks could not be easily secured. An inquisitive foreign observer, Johann Korb, noticed the ambiguous status of the Kalmyks in their relations with Russia. "They do not pay taxes to the tsar, but recognize his supremacy, and in return for annual presents perform military service as allies, rather than subjects."[50] Were they, then, subjects of the tsar or his allies? A careful look at the procedures used by the Kalmyks during the signing of the allegiance may suggest an answer.

Before signing a pledge in 1673, Ayuki tayishi bowed down, kissed an image of Buddha, a book of prayers, and a rosary, and put a saber to his head and throat.[51] This ritual use of religious artifacts was a fairly recent phenomenon, though the saber was a traditional symbolic object. For instance, in the Kalmyk epic "Janggar" and the Oirat epic "Bum-Erdeni" each hero (bagatur), before pledging an oath, draws his saber from its sheath, licks its sharp edge, and then swears allegiance to the other.[52] The intent of such an allegiance, however, was not to establish a suzerain-subject relationship but to consecrate the ties of friendship between two warriors of equal social standing. When the ritual was completed and the allegiance sworn, the heroes became devoted friends, or blood brothers—and.[53]

Clearly, the Kalmyks viewed their relationship with Russia through the prism of the traditional political system of their society. What the Russian government understood to be a suzerain-subject relationship codified in the oath of allegiance, the Kalmyks saw as an alliance between two equal parties, between two brothers, and only later between a father and son. In contrast, when Cheren-Donduk signed the first truly submis-

---

[50]Korb, *Dnevnik puteshestviia*, 139.

[51]*PSZ* 1:924, no. 540.

[52]Todaeva, *Opyt lingvisticheskogo*, 188; "Bum-Erdeni," 99. In 1621, the Oirat envoy to Moscow explained that the Oirats pledged an oath by licking a knife and putting an arrow to their heads and then to their hearts (*Mezhdunarodnye otnosheniia v Tsentral'noi Azii. 17–18 vv. Dokumenty i materialy*, 2 vols. [Moscow: Nauka, 1989], 1:54, no. 11).

[53]This ritual had its roots in the traditional Turko-Mongol institution of *and/ant* (*andhar* in Kalmyk), "an oath." In older times such ties or alliances were forged between men of two different tribes and the ritual was followed by the exchange of gifts (Clauson, *Etymological Dictionary*, 176). It could also denote an adoptive father-son relationship between the two (Vladimirtsov, *Obshchestvennyi*, 60–61).

sive oath of allegiance in 1724, and then another in 1731, he put to his forehead an image of Buddha, not the sword.[54]

When in the eighteenth century the Kalmyks did recognize the supremacy of Russia, they still continued to interpret the suzerain-subject relationship according to the principles of their, not Russia's, political traditions and to view it as a relationship between a father and son. In this relationship it was not only the son-subject who had obligations, such as joining the suzerain on military campaigns. The father-suzerain was obligated to protect his subject and to bestow upon him generous gifts. The suzerain had no right to interfere in his subject's affairs. The suzerain was only a military leader and a bestower of gifts in return for loyalty and military assistance. In short, such a relationship was no different from that between a khan and other tayishis or between the Kalmyk noyon and his nökörs.

Describing the suzerain-subject relationship within Mongol society, Vladimirtsov says:

> They [the subjects] by no means "belong" to their suzerain; they are related to him, usually, as younger kin to elder. The suzerain is only an elder—*akha* for the feudal lords. When displeased with his suzerain, the feudal lord, if he is powerful enough, may undertake a struggle with him; [or] rejecting his submission, he can roam far away from the suzerain. Finally, displeased feudal lords may resort to the help of their kin, [or] seek protection with other suzerains.[55]

Indeed, the Kalmyks used all of these ways to show their displeasure with the Russian government. At various times, the Kalmyks did not hesitate to offer their services to another suzerain, engaging in openly hostile actions against Russia or moving away from their usual pastures.

From the very beginning of Kalmyk-Russian relations the Kalmyks sought payments and access to Russian markets in exchange for providing military assistance. The Russians, however, had a different relationship in mind. They always insisted that the Kalmyks become Russian subjects. The Kalmyks had to sign a written oath of allegiance, to comply with certain demands, and to participate in Russia's military campaigns, for which they received compensation and gifts and were allowed to trade in Russian towns.

For the Kalmyks, Russia remained a military ally as long as the compensation and gifts were regularly supplied. But the promised goods and money often did not arrive because of the financial difficulties of the

[54]*PSZ* 7:353, no. 4576; 8:383, no. 5699.
[55]Vladimirtsov, *Obshchestvennyi*, 159.

Russian treasury. At various times the Russian authorities refused to admit numerous Kalmyk embassies, to expand trade, to supply the Kalmyks with firearms, or to return Kalmyk fugitives. The Don cossacks frequently raided the Kalmyk uluses, contrary to the expectation that the government in Moscow would be able to control such raids by its subjects. The Kalmyks perceived all these events as violations of the written and unwritten conditions of the alliance. According to Kalmyk customary law, such an alliance was in default and could be abrogated.

The difference between Russian and Kalmyk interpretations of the suzerain-subject relationship was rooted in their different traditions of political thinking. In the end, the political conflict between Russia and the Kalmyks reflected a fundamental socioeconomic and cultural gap that separated the two societies.

3

The Arrival of the Kalmyks

The First Encounter

In the second half of the sixteenth century Muscovy continued its rapid expansion prompted by the recent conquest of the cities of Kazan in 1552 and Astrakhan in 1556. Siberia was of particular interest to Moscow. There numerous peoples could easily be subdued by small groups of mercenaries armed with muskets and then forced to pay tribute in furs, a tax in kind known as *yasak*. The conquest not only provided Moscow with an important source of revenue but also enabled the ruler to add to his title the names of the newly vanquished peoples and territories, not an insignificant matter in sixteenth-century Muscovy.

It was during this expansion eastward that the Muscovites first came into contact with the Oirats. Following the example of the neighboring Turkic peoples, Moscow also referred to this newly encountered group as Kalmyks. In 1574 the charter granted by Ivan the Terrible to the merchant family of the Stroganovs declared that the merchants of Bukhara, the Kalmyks, and the Kazakhs should be allowed to trade freely without paying customs in the newly founded Muscovite towns of Siberia.[1] Not until 1606, however, did the Muscovite officials communicate directly with the Oirats.

In the late sixteenth century the Oirats suffered major defeats from the Kazakhs of Tevekkel Khan and the Mongols of Altyn Khan. The pressure exerted by the Mongols in the east and the Kazakhs in the south spurred the Oirats to move in search of new pastures. Thus at the same time the

---

[1]*Sibirskie letopisi* (St. Petersburg: Tip. I. N. Skorokhodova, 1907), 54–55.

Muscovite pioneers were moving farther east and south, building towns and fortresses and laying claims to the new frontiers, the Oirat nomads began moving to the north and west of their traditional pastures in Jungaria.

Cut off by the Kazakhs from their traditional markets in the towns of eastern Turkestan, the Oirats turned their attention to the recently founded Muscovite towns. In September 1606 Kho-Urlük tayishi of the Torgut tribe was the first to explore this opportunity, sending his envoys to the town of Tara on the Irtysh River. According to the contemporary Muscovite source, Kho-Urlük's envoy requested that the grand tsar "favor him [Kho-Urlük], order troops not to be sent against him, and allow him to roam on our [Muscovite] land along the Kamyshlov and Ishim rivers, allow him to come and trade in the town of Tara, and send our envoy to him."[2]

The Muscovite scribes and interpreters were mostly concerned with rendering an event in terms appropriate to exalt the Muscovite ruler's dignity and preeminence. Thus the literary interpretation of passages similar to that mentioned above could and often did mislead scholars.

In fact, Kho-Urlük had no other intention than to solve the border disputes, to offer peace to the Tara residents, to trade with them, and to exchange envoys. Although the offers were meant to secure an alliance between the Kalmyk chief and the town of Tara, Muscovy regarded it as Kho-Urlük's petition to become the subject of the tsar. The Kalmyk tayishi proved that this was not the case shortly thereafter. When the envoys from Tara arrived to meet Kho-Urlük with an ultimatum that he swear allegiance to the Muscovite suzerain and surrender hostages or else vacate the land, Kho-Urlük, insulted by such demands, ordered the Muscovite envoys put to death.[3]

Meanwhile, instructions from Moscow to the Tara governor continued to insist that more envoys be dispatched to the Kalmyks to solicit their oath of allegiance and to confirm their status as Muscovite subjects. Letters from Moscow referred to the Kalmyk tayishis as princes and mirzas—terminology Moscovite officials had learned from years of experience with numerous Turkic peoples, betraying little knowledge of the people they recently encountered.[4]

The years 1607–9 witnessed a lively exchange between the Muscovite and Kalmyk embassies. In January 1607 envoys from Tara left to visit the

[2]*Russko-mongol'skie otnosheniia, 1607–1636. Sbornik dokumentov* (Moscow: Izd-vo vostochnoi literatury, 1959), 28, no. 4.

[3]Ibid., 28–29, no. 4.

[4]Ibid., 21, no. 1.

Kalmyks. This time, however, they arrived at the uluses of the Derbet tribe. Six months later the Muscovite envoys returned to Tara together with representatives of the Derbet tayishis, who agreed to live in peace with the Tara residents. The Kalmyks were interested in political and military alliance with Muscovy against the Mongols of Altyn Khan and the Kazakhs, as well as an opportunity to trade their livestock in the Siberian towns. Some of their embassies were allowed to proceed to Moscow, and even Kho-Urlük tayishi, whose disposition toward the Muscovites was less favorable than that of the Derbet tayishis, once again dispatched his envoys to Tara to agree on terms of peace.

Moscow, however, continued to insist that the Kalmyks submit hostages and pay yasak to reaffirm their status as subjects. If the Kalmyks refused to do so, they had to vacate the pastures along the Irtysh, Om', Ishim, and Kamyshlov rivers, which Moscow considered its territory. The Kalmyk tayishis stated emphatically that they had never paid yasak to anyone and that they were nomadic people who could roam about where they pleased.[5] From 1610 to 1615 the Kalmyks and the garrison of the Siberian town of Tara waged war. Several skirmishes took place, and each time the Muscovite garrison defeated the Kalmyks.[6]

The government intended to deal with the Kalmyks as with many other peoples it previously had confronted. Military governors in Siberia were again ordered to make the Kalmyks pledge fealty to the tsar, to surrender hostages, and to pay annual yasak. Moscow was yet to learn that unlike many peoples of Siberia whose economy was primarily based on hunting, the Kalmyks were organized into an efficient nomadic society of numerous, mobile, warlike, and fiercely independent people not ready to submit to Muscovy.

The Beginning of the Migration

A group of Oirats, whose destination was the Caspian steppes, at first consisted of two tribes, the Torguts and the Derbets. Although contemporary Muscovite sources provide little information about the internal politics and the struggle among the tayishis, the available meager data provide some insight about these two tribes.

The westernmost Oirat pastures were occupied by the Torguts of Kho-Urlük tayishi and the Derbets of Dalay-Bagatur tayishi. After 1604 Kho-Urlük had roamed in the Upper Irtysh River independently from other

[5]Ibid., 39, no. 10.
[6]Ibid., 40, no. 11; 41–42, no. 13.

Oirat tayishis. In the spring of 1608, after having married his sister to Dalay-Bagatur, Kho-Urlük roamed together with Dalay and three thousand people. That summer Kho-Urlük was reported to have had five uluses, a total of four thousand people.[7] The alliance with Kho-Urlük allowed Dalay to wrestle down the rivals in his tribe and to emerge as the chief Derbet tayishi. From that time on Kho-Urlük was mentioned as the sole leader of the Torguts. It was this alliance between the Torguts and the Derbets that enabled them to explore the possibilities of movement farther west.

The course of nomadic migration was always carefully chosen by the leaders of the group. In the beginning of the century the Kalmyks moved northwest to occupy pastures between the Irtysh, Kamyshlov, and Ishim rivers. The Kalmyks were well aware that they would meet no resistance in taking over pastures of Kuchum Khan's recently disintegrated Siberian khanate. It proved to be more difficult, however, to come to an agreement with the Muscovite garrisons they encountered. The Kalmyk tayishis decided to explore another possible route—toward the abundant pastures of the Nogays in the area of the Emba, Yayik, and Volga rivers.[8] As was usual before any major migration occurred, detachments were dispatched to gather intelligence on the situation in the area.

One such detachment was spotted by the Nogays in the vicinity of the Emba River as early as 1608. Five years later, the news that a Kalmyk vanguard of no less than four thousand horsemen had crossed the Yayik forced the Nogays to flee toward the Volga. The Nogays, reinforced by Astrakhan musketeers, returned to confront the Kalmyks, who were already gone.[9]

Typical of nomadic societies, steppe politics involved a frequent reshuffling of political alliances. For some time the new alliances among the Oirat tribes enabled them to gain an upper hand in conflict with Altyn Khan and the Kazakhs. Several campaigns against the Kazakhs,

---

[7]Ibid., 22, no. 2; 29, no. 4; 36, no. 9.

[8]Since the middle of the sixteenth century the Nogays were divided into the Greater Horde with pastures situated east of the Volga and the Lesser Horde roaming the steppes west of the Volga. Among the most important tribes that constituted the Lesser Nogay Horde were the Buchak, Yedichkul, Yedisan, Yamboyluk, and Kuban (Alan Fisher, *The Crimean Tatars* [Stanford, Calif.: Hoover Institution Press, 1978], 24–25). Usually when referring to the Lesser Horde, Russian sources use a specific name of the tribe. For the most comprehensive history of the Nogays see B.-A. B. Kochekaev, *Nogaisko-russkie otnosheniia v 15–18 vv.* (Alma-Ata: Nauka Kazakhskoi SSR, 1988).

[9]Bogoiavlenskii, "Materialy," 56–57. In 1613 the Muscovite embassy dispatched to Persia was warned of a possible encounter with the Kalmyks in the upper Emba and Yayik rivers (N. I. Veselovskii, "Peredovye kalmyki na puti k Volge," *ZVOIRAO* 3 [1888]: 366).

who at the time were caught in the civil strife among different warring parties, were particularly successful, but a renewed threat from the traditional enemies—the Mongols and the Kazakhs—drove the Kalmyks farther northwest, where they once again came into contact with the Muscovite towns.

In the summer of 1615 as many as fifteen thousand Kalmyks were reported to be moving toward the towns of Tara, Tiumen', and Tobol'sk. Two years later the Kalmyks, together with the Bashkir Prince Ishim, raided Ufa province.[10] Greatly concerned with the safety of its small and inadequately protected Siberian towns, the government in Moscow ordered the garrisons reinforced and instructed the governors not to provoke the Kalmyks.[11]

Realization of the Kalmyk military threat to the Muscovite towns and provinces compelled the government to change its attitude and to improve relations between Muscovy and its militant neighbor. In 1616 the government decreed a cessation of relations with China and Altyn Khan but ordered that friendly relations with the Kalmyks should be maintained and that their embassies should be allowed to proceed to Moscow without delay.[12] The insistence that the Kalmyks submit hostages and pay yasak was dropped, although in its official correspondence Moscow continued to address the Kalmyks as its subjects and promised protection in exchange for Kalmyk military assistance.[13]

Meanwhile, continued war with Altyn Khan drove the Oirat tribes farther west. In 1620 the Jungars, who, because of their contiguous pasture lands, bore most of the burden of the war with Altyn Khan, roamed near the town of Tara. The Torguts' and Derbets' pastures were along the Ishim and Tobol rivers, not far from the towns of Tobol'sk and Tiumen.

As in the past, the westernmost pastures were occupied by Kho-Urlük tayishi. In 1619–20 he further strengthened his position by marrying his daughter to Ishim, the son of the deceased Kuchum Khan of the Siberian Tatars. At this time the Kalmyks were reported to have raided the Nogays, whom they found on the Uzen' and Kamysh-Samara rivers between the Yayik and the Volga. In October 1621 Kho-Urlük and the Jungar Chokur (Shukur) tayishi, who roamed with him, dispatched their envoys to Ufa to solve the Kalmyks' disputes with the Bashkirs, who paid yasak to Muscovy.[14]

[10]*Russko-mongol'skie otnosheniia, 1607–1636*, 43, no. 14; N. V. Ustiugov, "Bashkirskoe vosstanie 1662–1664 gg.," *Istoricheske zapiski* 24 (1947): 45–46.

[11]*Russko-mongol'skie otnosheniia, 1607–1636*, 45–50, no. 16.

[12]Ibid., 55, no. 19.

[13]Ibid., 75–76, no. 29.

[14]Ibid., 101, no. 47; 102, no. 48; 120, no. 60; Bogoiavlenskii, "Materialy," 60.

The issue of yasak-paying subjects was always a contentious point between the Muscovites and the Kalmyks. Moscow constantly blamed the Kalmyks for plundering local peoples. The issue was not clear-cut, however, and the Kalmyks also had grievances against Moscow. One example will illustrate the importance of the issue to both parties. The Oirats traditionally relied on the indigenous people of the upper reaches of the Tom' River in the northern Sayan Mountains to supply arms. These people were expert smiths and supplied the Oirats with a variety of iron weapons but not with firearms. Shortly after the fortress of Kuznetsk was founded on the Tom' River, Moscow instructed its governor to make the local people pay yasak to Muscovy. Then, Moscow conjectured, the Oirats would have no place to obtain the arms and would necessarily turn for help to Muscovy.[15]

A new realization of the possibility of the Kalmyk military threat to the Muscovite state brought to the surface Moscow's traditional fears of the nomads and induced the government to order that Kalmyk embassies not be sent to Moscow so that these numerous and warlike people should not learn how to reach the capital. For the time being Moscow gave up the idea of making the Kalmyks pay yasak or enlisting them in military service. Tsar Mikhail Romanov noted that the Kalmyks were of no use, and he scornfully observed that they knew no written language, but he did not want to alarm them and ordered that they be allowed to trade in the Muscovite towns.[16] Several years later, Kalmyk envoys again appeared in Moscow, forcing the government to look for new ways to deal with the threat posed by these militant nomads.

The New Rulers of the Caspian Steppes

In the second decade of the seventeenth century more short-lived alliances between different tribes were formed, to be followed by further rivalries. In the early 1620s several Jungar tayishis joined the alliance of the Derbets and the Torguts—all led by the Derbet Dalay tayishi. A few years later the alliance was joined by another powerful leader, Gushri (Kuisha) tayishi of the Khoshuts. At the same time the Muscovite envoys reported that the Jungar tayishis were squabbling with each other over the ulus of their deceased brother and that Dalay was trying to reconcile them.[17]

In a dispute between the Jungar tayishis, Dalay, the leader of the

[15]*Russko-mongol'skie otnosheniia, 1607–1636*, 115–16, no. 58.
[16]Ibid., 128, no. 65.
[17]Ibid., 136–39, no. 70.

alliance, supported one Jungar group, thus compelling the other group, led by Chokur tayishi, to flee. As usual, the dissident group chose to move in the direction where it would meet the least resistance. When in 1628 news of the war between the Yedisans and the Nogays reached Chokur, he promptly moved toward the Emba and Yayik rivers to take advantage of the situation. The same year several thousand of Chokur's people routed the Nogays on the Yayik River. Shortly thereafter, as many as six thousand Kalmyks were reported to be roaming with Chokur tayishi along the Emba River. Dalay and his allies were determined, however, to bring back the people who had left with Chokur, and an army was dispatched against them. In 1630, on the Yayik, Chokur suffered a crushing defeat at the hands of Dalay and Gushri tayishis.[18]

The beginning of the 1630s set the stage for the steady and irreversible advance of the Kalmyks toward the Caspian steppes. In 1630 another devastating raid was undertaken against the Nogays. Informers reported that this time Kho-Urlük's Kalmyks were responsible for the raid.[19] In 1630–31 as many as ten thousand Kalmyks of Kho-Urlük invaded the steppes in the upper reaches of the Emba and Yayik rivers.[20] A year later Kho-Urlük roamed with his uluses along the Turgay River, between the upper reaches of the Tobol and Ishim rivers, while his son Daichin occupied pastures in the upper reaches of the Yayik, at a distance of a ten-day ride.[21]

In 1630–32 the Nogays were subjected to devastating Kalmyk raids. Unable to resist on their own, some Nogays joined the Kalmyks, but the majority fled to Astrakhan to seek Muscovite protection. A small and ill-equipped Astrakhan garrison could do little, however, in the face of the far more numerous and mobile enemy. Having realized this, some Nogay leaders sought to use Kalmyk military might to their own end. In 1632 a certain Kanabey mirza, who resided in Astrakhan as a hostage of Muscovy, sent a messenger to Kho-Urlük inviting him to march against Astrakhan. Kanabey expected to be released in the winter and promised his assistance in a raid against Astrakhan. The young and anxious Daichin also suggested that his father should wage war against the Muscovite towns.[22]

In spring of 1633 Kho-Urlük's sons Daichin and Louzang (Lauzang, Lubsan), in their raids against the Nogays, reached the vicinity of As-

[18]Bogoiavlenskii, "Materialy," 65–66.

[19]Ibid., 67.

[20]Abul-Ghazi Bahadur Khan, *Rodoslovnaiia turkmen*, ed. and trans. A. N. Kononov (Moscow and Leningrad: AN SSSR, 1958), 44–45.

[21]Bogoiavlenskii, "Materialy," 67–68.

[22]*Russko-mongol'skie otnosheniia, 1607–1636*, 189, no. 94.

trakhan. To stop the Kalmyks, the Astrakhan governor sent a detachment of musketeers to join the embattled Nogays. The Kalmyks emerged victorious from the encounter, which took place at the Bol'shoi Uzen' River between the Volga and the Yayik. Surrounded by the Kalmyks, the Muscovites and the Nogays agreed to peace terms, and the Nogay mirzas promised that they and their uluses would join the Kalmyks. Triumphant Daichin offered his protection to the Nogays. Leaving the Nogays no doubt as to where their loyalty should lie, he mocked the Astrakhan garrison by announcing in an expressive metaphor: "They, the Kalmyks, have such people, who having come to Astrakhan in the midst of summer, will bury the town in snow."[23]

The Nogays, who hoped to find a refuge near Astrakhan, were bitterly disappointed when in 1634 and 1635 they suffered from additional destructive Kalmyk raids. In 1634 the Yedisans and the Yurt Tatars, who resided near Astrakhan, were pillaged by Daichin and his Kalmyks within sight of a small and helpless detachment of Astrakhan musketeers.[24] Some Nogay leaders sent envoys to Daichin to inform him that they would be willing to join the Kalmyks. When they were prevented from doing so by musketeers, the Nogays were left with only one option—to flee farther west. Neither promises nor the use of force by the Astrakhan governor could stop their flight. By 1635 most of the Nogays crossed the Volga in expectation of finding refuge near the Ottoman fortress of Azov. Two years later, the news of an anticipated raid by Daichin against them compelled the Nogays to flee even farther, to cross the Don, and to seek protection of the Crimea.[25]

The numerous Nogays who fled from Astrakhan, eager to avenge the humiliation and abuse they had suffered from the Astrakhan administration, joined the Azov and Crimean Tatars in raiding Muscovite towns.[26] Embroiled in a war with the Polish-Lithuanian Commonwealth in the west, Moscow also found itself facing Nogay and Tatar cavalry along its southern frontier. Devastation of Muscovite towns by the Nogay-Tatar raids and realization of the difficulty of fighting wars on both fronts were among the reasons that forced Moscow to conclude a peace treaty with the Commonwealth in 1634.

After the conclusion of the Polianovka peace treaty with the Poles, Moscow was able to turn its attention to the southern frontier. The

---

[23]*RIB* 2:476–77, no. 138; Bogoiavlenskii, "Materialy," 68–69.

[24]*AI* 2:150, no. 41.

[25]A. A. Novosel'skii, *Bor'ba Moskovskogo gosudarstva s tatarami v pervoi polovine 17 veka* (Moscow and Leningrad: AN SSSR, 1948), 227; Bogoiavlenskii, "Materialy," 76.

[26]The Nogays complained of the Astrakhan governor's corruption and his attempts to turn them into farmers (Novosel'skii, *Bor'ba,* 227).

government's growing concern was reflected in a royal decree ordering that a reinforcement of musketeers be sent to Astrakhan. To correct the mistakes of the past, the decree instructed Astrakhan residents to be friendly to the Nogays and to allow them to use pastures along the Akhtuba River.[27] The government clearly intended to induce the Nogays to return to Astrakhan, but apparently the decree alone was insufficient to dispel the Nogays' doubt that the Muscovites could protect them against the Kalmyks. In Astrakhan, meanwhile, various defensive measures, such as digging moats and building outposts, were taken both to protect those Yurt Tatars and the Yedisans who remained in the vicinity and to prevent them from leaving. No measures were considered inopportune, and the Astrakhan governor did not hesitate to put under arrest those mirzas who were known to have had contacts with the Kalmyks.[28]

The situation was not to be remedied easily, and Moscow was not helped when in 1635 a brittle alliance of the Oirat tribes again burst into a civil war. When Kho-Urlük's growing power became of serious concern to Dalay tayishi, the two former allies turned into rivals, and Kho-Urlük was compelled to move farther west, closer to the Muscovite frontier. In 1633 Kho-Urlük was reported to have an army of twelve thousand horsemen, while his son Daichin had ten thousand. A year later a fugitive from Kalmyk captivity stated that there were twenty thousand horsemen under Kho-Urlük's command. The influx of people could have come either from the incorporation of the newly conquered Nogay tribes or other Kalmyks—fugitives from Dalay and other tayishis. In either case, Dalay perceived the growing power of Kho-Urlük as a challenge to him, and after Kho-Urlük and Daichin refused to surrender some of the Jungars to Dalay, the latter declared war against the two. Under military pressure from Dalay and some of his Kazakh allies, Kho-Urlük moved farther away from the pastures of the Ishim and the Tobol and joined Daichin at the Emba.[29]

In the late 1630s the Kalmyks seemed to be in full control of the wide spaces of the Caspian steppes. They often crossed the Volga in their raids against the Nogays, and their cavalry threatened Astrakhan and other towns along the river as far north as Samara. In 1639 Kho-Urlük was reported to be wintering near Bukhara and summering along the Tobol River. Daichin wintered in the Karakum desert and in summer migrated

[27]*DAI* 2:no. 63. In 1635 the Astrakhan garrison reached a sizable force of 1,000 cavalry musketeers, and 3,000 foot musketeers, 67 gunners, and 2,000 Yurt Tatars in the vicinity of the city (*Knigi razriadnye*, 2 vols. [St. Petersburg: Tip. II Otd. Imper. Kants., 1853–55], 2:818).

[28]Novosel'skii, *Bor'ba*, 228.

[29]*Ocherki istorii Kalmytskoi*, 1:88, 109.

north as far as the Siberian towns, while Kho-Urlük's other son, Louzang, was roaming along the Emba River.[30]

The presence of the Kalmyks in the area was not Moscow's concern alone. Caravans traversing the steppes en route to the khanates of Khiva and Bukhara were increasingly plundered by the Kalmyks. As early as 1633, worried by the disruption of a profitable trade with the Muscovite towns, the khan of Khiva, Isfandiyar, suggested in a letter to the Muscovite tsar that he and the tsar should unite their military efforts against the Kalmyks and force them away from the Emba. Tsar Mikhail gave his consent, but the proposal was not realized and the Kalmyks continued to raid the passing caravans.[31]

A few years later Isfandiyar formed a military alliance against the Kalmyks with the khan of Bukhara, Imam-Kuli, and again invited the Muscovite tsar to join the coalition. In 1640 the khan of Balkh suggested to the tsar that they both send armies against the Kalmyks, whose activities hampered trade between Balkh and Muscovy.[32] Meanwhile, the Kalmyks further established themselves as the major power in the area. In 1639 they routed and conquered the Turkmens of the Mangyshlak peninsula. When a year later the future khan of Khiva, Abul-Ghazi Bahadur, fled to the Turkmens in search of asylum, one Kalmyk tayishi invited him to be his guest of honor. The Kalmyks harbored the fugitive for a year, after which Abul-Ghazi left to launch a successful struggle for the seat of the khan of Khiva.[33]

The arrival of the Kalmyks in the Caspian steppes had a significant impact on Muscovy. During the 1630s to 1640s the Kalmyk plunder of caravans along the land routes connecting Muscovy with the Central Asian khanates and Persia effectively disrupted Muscovy's trade with its neighbors in the east. The merchants were compelled to rely more heavily on the sea route via the Caspian Sea, and the new port was built farther south on the Mangyshlak peninsula. Apparently, the use of the sea route did not compensate for the loss of communications by land, for

---

[30]Bogoiavlenskii, "Materialy," 76–78.

[31]*Materialy po istorii Uzbekskoi,* 141–42, no. 33; 144, no. 35.

[32]Ibid., 152, no. 141; *Istoriia Turkmenskoi SSR,* 2 vols. (Ashkhabad: AN Turkmenskoi SSR, 1957), vol. 1, bk. 1:400.

[33]"Firdaus al-Ikbal," in *Materialy po istorii kazakhskikh khanstv 15–18 vekov* (Alma-Ata: "Nauka" Kazakhskoi SSR, 1969), 451; Abul-Ghazi Bahadur Khan, *Rodoslovnoe drevo tiurkov,* trans. and ed. G. S. Sablukov (Kazan': Tip. Imp. Universiteta, 1914), 33, 283. Kho-Urlük's son Shunkey appears to have been the one Kalmyk tayishi who offered asylum to Abul-Ghazi (M. L. Kichikov [Ochirov], *Istoricheskie korni druzhby russkogo i kalmytskogo narodov* [Elista: Kalmytskoe knizhnoe izd-vo, 1966], 114).

the volume of goods brought through the Astrakhan customhouse declined sharply during this period.[34]

The advance of the Kalmyks and their destructive raids against the
Nogays had also brought about significant changes in the political situation in the south of the country. The sudden departure of the Nogays
from the Volga area left the southern tier of the Muscovite frontier
exposed to nomadic incursions. In the winter of 1636–37, the news of the
Kalmyks' readiness to cross the Volga to strike at the Nogays near Azov
caused the Nogays to flee across the Don and seek refuge in the Crimea.
The Nogays' abandonment of Azov cleared the way for the Don cossacks
to capture the fortress in June 1637. This incident took both the Ottomans and the Muscovites by surprise and brought the two states to the
verge of military confrontation.

The increased danger of the Crimean-Nogay raids, which in 1637 were
expected to reach as far north as the Oka River, impelled the government
to begin repairing the old defense lines and to declare an extensive
mobilization of people and resources. More important, the government
decided to construct a new defense network, known as the Belgorod
line.[35] Fortified lines or *zaseka* had been built in the past. Made of felled
trees, such lines were mostly limited to the forested zones and were
intended not so much to thwart raids as to slow down the advance of the
enemy's cavalry. By the 1630s changes in military technology and in the
Muscovite army enabled the government to undertake construction of
the defense network on a larger scale. New defenses consisted of moats,
palisades, and forts armed with cannons and other firearms. The new
defense network was built farther south than any of the previous *zaseka*
and proved to be an effective safeguard against incursions. Throughout
the seventeenth and eighteenth centuries defense lines served as the
principal mechanism not only in securing the existing frontier but also
in extending it farther south and southeast.

The Death of Kho-Urlük

Tribal warfare among the Oirats was interrupted by a temporary peace in
1640, when the Oirat and Mongol leaders gathered at the *khurultay* in

[34]A. Chuloshnikov, "Torgovlia Moskovskogo gosudarstva so srednei Aziei v 16–17 vv.," in
Materialy po istorii Uzbekskoi, 67, 81.

[35]The seriousness of Moscow's concerns is best attested to by a government decree
ordering that all available weapons be collected from the monasteries for temporary
use (A. I. Iakovlev, *Zasechnaia cherta Moskovskogo gosudarstva v 17 veke* [Moscow: Tip.
I. Lissnera and D. Sobko, 1916], 45–46). For a brief survey of fortified lines, their con-

Jungaria. This year marked the rise of a new coalition of Oirat tribes, the last powerful confederation to emerge in Inner Asia, which endured until the middle of the eighteenth century when it was finally destroyed by the Qing armies. The assembly was an important event in the history of the Oirats, the Kalmyks, and the Mongols. For a time it succeeded in uniting most of the tribes under the banners of Tibetan Buddhism as practiced by the Ge-lug-pa sect.

The *khurultay* demonstrated that the alliance was formed on the conditions offered by the Oirats under the leadership of Erdeni Batur khong tayiji of the Jungar tribe. The Oirat and Mongol representatives adopted a code of law which stipulated severe punishment for those who failed to perform their duties as allies.[36]

Kho-Urlük and two of his sons, Daichin and Elden (Ilden), were also present at the assembly. While in Jungaria Kho-Urlük arranged a marriage between his grandson Puntsuk and one of Erdeni Batur's daughters, and in the spring of 1641 he returned to his ulus braced by an alliance with the powerful Oirat leader. Kho-Urlük's renewed attempts to put many Kalmyks under his sway could not but cause resentment among other tayishis. The alliance with Erdeni Batur did little to save Kho-Urlük and his sons from the raids launched against them by the Derbets and the Khoshuts in 1641–42. Kho-Urlük and his group were finally forced to flee farther west and crossed the Yayik.[37]

Meanwhile, a large group of Nogays left the Crimea and arrived near Astrakhan to seek Muscovy's protection. But many Nogay leaders found that they were less than welcome and were placed under arrest by the Astrakhan governor. The Nogays sent complaints to Moscow about the abuses they suffered and explained that as a result of the mistreatment many of them considered joining the Kalmyks. Indeed, upon the request of the Yedisans, who roamed near Astrakhan, the Kalmyk detachment led by Daichin's son Dayan-Erke tayishi arrived in the vicinity of the city in February 1643 to help the Yedisans escape. The Yedisans, having also seized some of the Nogays, left to join the Kalmyks. The dispatched Astrakhan garrison again proved to be slow and ineffective.[38]

In the summer of 1643 Kho-Urlük was near the town of Samara, while his sons roamed along the Uzen' and the Kamysh-Samara rivers. Several

struction, and functions see Richard Hellie, *Enserfment and Military Change in Muscovy* (Chicago: University of Chicago Press, 1971), 174–80.

[36]*Ikh Tsaas*, 14, nos. 5, 13, 14.

[37]Kichikov (Ochirov), "K istorii obrazovaniia Kalmytskogo," 47; *Mezhdunarodnye*, 1:104, no. 30.

[38]Kichikov (Ochirov), "K istorii obrazovaniia Kalmytskogo," 48; Novosel'skii, *Bor'ba*, 357–58.

times the Kalmyks dispatched envoys to the governor of Samara asking to be allowed to trade with the local inhabitants. The governor, however, refused, and instead demanded that the Kalmyks surrender hostages, return the Yedisans and Nogays, and leave Samara.[39] As a reflection of the government's concern over the increased Kalmyk presence near the Volga, the special Department of Astrakhan Affairs was established in spring 1643, and patrol boats with musketeers were sent to sail up and down the Volga.[40]

In August 1643, preparations for the campaign were in the final stage when five Kalmyk tayishis gathered in Kho-Urlük's camp. A few weeks later, several large Kalmyk detachments crossed the Volga to raid the Nogays along the Terek and Kuban rivers. The Kalmyks were reported to have been joined by the Yedisans, who apparently guided the Kalmyks toward their destination. One detachment, led by Louzang, reached the Kuban, where it defeated a group of Nogays. Another, led by Dayan-Erke, marched toward the Terek River only to find that the Nogays had fled to the mountains. In the winter of 1644 Kho-Urlük himself with an army of more than ten thousand horsemen crossed the Volga. While Dayan-Erke besieged the town of Tersk on the Terek River, Kho-Urlük crossed the Terek and moved farther into the Kabarda. The campaign turned out to be the last one for Kho-Urlük. A combined force of Kabardinians and Nogays decimated his army. Many Kalmyks were taken captive, and Kho-Urlük, with his son Keresan and two grandsons, perished in the battle.[41]

The Ottoman account sheds some light on this event. According to the chronicler Mustafa Naima, a large group of Kalmyks on their way to the Crimea decided to pillage the Kabarda. A force of ten thousand Kabardinians under Prince Alayuk (Alaguk) blocked the mountain pass. Armed with muskets, they engaged the Kalmyks, who were equipped only with sabers and bows. After a fierce day-long battle, when both sides were weary, a detachment of Nogay horsemen, dispatched by the Crimean khan Mehmet Giray IV, arrived to aid the Kabardinians. At the end of the battle, most of the Kalmyks were killed, and the rest returned defeated.[42]

Some of the fleeing Kalmyks were run down by the Kabardinians and Nogays, acting on a tip from the Tersk *voevoda* (military governor). Yet

[39]Kichikov (Ochirov), "K istorii obrazovaniia Kalmytskogo," 49.

[40]Bogoiavlenskii, "Materialy," 81.

[41]*Kabardino-russkie otnosheniia v 16–18 vv. Dokumenty i materialy*, 2 vols. (Moscow: Izd-vo AN SSSR, 1957), 1:243, no. 149; *Russko-mongol'skie otnosheniia, 1634–1654*, 245, no. 66; *Ocherki istorii Kalmytskoi*, 1:110; Kichikov (Ochirov), "K istorii obrazovaniia Kalmytskogo," 49–50; G. F. Miller, *Istoriia Sibiri*, 2 vols. (Moscow and Leningrad: AN SSSR, 1937–41), 2:490, no. 411.

[42]Mustafa Naima, *Tarikh-i Naima*, 6 vols. (Istanbul: N.p., [18–]), 4:104; Evliya Chelebi, *Seyâhatnâme*, 10 vols. (Istanbul: N.p., 1896/97–1928), 7:761–62.

others were later ambushed by the Astrakhan musketeers while crossing the Volga. Out of the army of ten thousand no more than two thousand escaped alive. When four years later the Crimean *kalgay* Krim Giray Sultan alluded to an agreement between the Muscovites and the Crimeans to stop the Kalmyks, he may have meant the 1644 military operation.[43]

That same year the Kalmyks suffered another disastrous defeat at the hands of the Muscovites. *Voevoda* L. Pleshcheev marched from Samara against the group of Dayan-Erke and routed it in the upper reaches of the Yayik.[44] For a short while, Moscow achieved its goal: shaken by stunning military defeats, the Kalmyk uluses rolled back east of the Yayik River.

Daichin Tayishi and the Continuous Advance Westward

In the mid-1640s the Kalmyks roamed along the Ilek, Uil, Sagiz, and Emba rivers, led by several tayishis, Kho-Urlük's sons Louzang and Elden and his grandson Dayan-Erke. At the time, Kho-Urlük's other son Daichin was in Tibet, having left on a pilgrimage in 1642.[45]

Throughout this time the Kalmyks' political fortunes were closely related to the turn of events in Jungaria, and above all with those of their ally Erdeni Batur khong tayiji of the Jungars. In 1643–44 Erdeni Batur launched an unsuccessful campaign against the Kazakhs. Despite his efforts to convince the Derbets and the Khoshuts of Ablay tayiji and Khundelen (Kundelen') tayishi to join him, the Khoshut leaders refused to do so. Erdeni Batur considered them traitors, and upon returning from the campaign he turned his anger against them. To secure his victory, he dispatched an envoy to the Kalmyks of Kho-Urlük and requested their assistance in a war against Ablay and Khundelen. Erdeni's plans, however, were revealed when his envoy to the Kalmyks was intercepted by the Khoshuts.

Upon receiving the news, the Khoshut tayishis acted promptly, and in preparation for war they decided to ally themselves with Muscovy against the Kalmyks. The envoy sent to the governor of Tobol'sk returned to Ablay with good news—the Muscovites would support Ablay and Khundelen in their endeavor and would dispatch a detachment of musketeers to join the Khoshuts against the Kalmyks.[46]

[43] V. V. Vel'iaminov-Zernov, *Materialy dlia istorii Krymskogo khanstva* (St. Petersburg: Tip. Imp. Akademii Nauk, 1864), 423, no. 124.

[44] *AI* 3:398, no. 240; Bogoiavlenskii, "Materialy," 81.

[45] Kichikov (Ochirov), "K istorii obrazovaniia Kalmytskogo," 50; Bogoiavlenskii, "Materialy," 79.

[46] *Russko-mongol'skie otnosheniia, 1634–1654*, 233–35, no. 62.

To discourage a possible Muscovite campaign against them, the Kalmyk leaders chose to negotiate peace with Muscovy and sent their representatives to Moscow. Kalmyk envoys explained that the Kalmyks remained loyal to an agreement with Moscow. The Yedisans, they explained, chose to flee and join the Kalmyks because of the abuses they suffered from the Astrakhan governor, and therefore the Kalmyks were not responsible for their fleeing. In its response the government stipulated that any further progress in the negotiations would depend upon the Kalmyks' offering hostages. At this point the negotiations broke down.[47]

Several military disasters in 1644 and the increased possibility of new campaigns against them in the following year made the Kalmyk tayishis seriously consider returning to Jungaria. Worried by the prospect of being taken to unknown lands against their will, several Yedisan and Nogay mirzas sent their envoys to the Astrakhan governor to inform him that they would flee if such an attempt were undertaken.[48] Whether because of an awareness that the Nogays would not have followed them voluntarily or, more likely, a realization that the Kalmyks would not have been able to pass through the lands controlled by the hostile Khoshuts, the Kalmyk tayishis abandoned their plans to migrate to Jungaria.

Daichin's return from Tibet to his ulus in the upper reaches of the Yayik in 1647 meant a resumption of Kalmyk military campaigns against their neighbors. First, Daichin seized the moment to avenge the death of his father, Kho-Urlük. For the time being Daichin did not have to fear harassment from his rivals, the Khoshuts, who shortly before had submitted to Erdeni Batur in Jungaria.[49] Daichin sent envoys to the Don cossacks inviting them to participate in his campaign against the Nogays and the Crimea. The cossacks' refusal did not change Daichin's plans, and in February 1648 as many as ten thousand Kalmyks led by Daichin, his brother Louzang, and other tayishis crossed the Don River. The movement of the Kalmyk army, however, was hampered by deep snow and frost in the steppes, and lack of grazing for horses soon forced the Kalmyks to return. The objective of the Kalmyk tayishis was not achieved, and their premature campaign caused the Nogays to flee in panic to the Crimea and the Dnieper.[50]

[47]Kichikov (Ochirov), "K istorii obrazovaniia Kalmytskogo," 52.

[48]Russko-mongol'skie otnosheniia, 1634–1654, 263–66, no. 80.

[49]On his return from Tibet Daichin personally witnessed the battle in which Erdeni Batur routed an army of Khundelen tayishi. ("Biografiia Zaya-Pandity," 165; Zlatkin, Istoriia Dzhungarskogo, 132–33).

[50]AMG 2:196, no. 314; 198, no. 318; Le Khanat de Crimée dans les Archives du Musée du Palais de Topkapi (Paris: Mouton, 1978), 185; Kichikov (Ochirov), "K istorii obrazovaniia Kalmytskogo," 55; Novosel'skii, Bor'ba, 394.

More significant than Kalmyk military advances, which continued throughout the following year, was a migration of the Kalmyk uluses farther west. The move was prompted by the arrival in the area of the hostile group of Khoshuts and Derbets led by Khundelen and Dayan-Ombo tayishis. Unable to defeat Erdeni Batur, the leaders of this group decided to leave Jungaria. They moved west, confronted Daichin's Kalmyks, defeated them, and took over their pastures in the upper reaches of the Tobol and Yayik rivers.[51] Daichin together with his displaced people migrated southwest to roam along the Yayik and Sakmara rivers, but insufficient grazing lands forced them to advance farther and to occupy pastures between the Volga and Yayik.

The government in Moscow was not pleased with the Kalmyks' renewed push toward the Volga. Envoys were dispatched to convince Daichin to affirm his status as a Muscovite subject and to move back to his old pastures east of the Yayik. The Kalmyks, pressed by the Khoshuts and the Derbets, however, had little choice but to stay at the pastures between the Yayik and Volga. Negotiations between the Muscovite envoy Ivan Onuchin and Daichin in 1649–50 were fully reported by the envoy. The surviving document is remarkable testimony to the different mentalities of the Muscovite government and the Kalmyk leader (see Appendix).

Throughout the early 1650s Kalmyk raids across the Volga against the Nogays and the Crimeans became more frequent. Some of the Nogays, in search of a safe abode, chose to cross the Dnieper. The Crimeans became increasingly concerned over the emergence of this new and formidable foe near their frontier. The news that the Kalmyks had entered into an alliance with the Don cossacks constrained the movements of the Crimean Tatars and compelled them to turn to the Zaporozhian cossacks for assistance.[52] The Crimean khan blamed the tsar for siding with the Kalmyks and allowing them, together with the Don cossacks, to raid the Crimeans and the Nogays. Considering this a violation of the treaty between Muscovy and the Crimea, the khan demanded that Moscow forbid the Kalmyks to roam along the Volga near Astrakhan and threatened to attack the Muscovite lands unless the tsar severed ties with the Kalmyks.[53]

The Crimea's charges were not completely groundless. In 1650, one of the tsar's decrees sent to the Don cossacks instructed them to dispatch

---

[51]*Russko-mongol'skie otnosheniia, 1634–1654*, 353, no. 112.

[52]*AI* 4:83, no. 32; 195, no. 72; 2:304, no. 493; 313, no. 507; *AIuZR* 8:355, no. 33 (VIII).

[53]Vel'iaminov-Zernov, *Materialy*, 423–24, no. 124; *Reestr delam Krymskogo dvora s 1474 po 1779 goda*, comp. N. N. Bantysh-Kamenskii in 1808 (Simferopol': Tip. Tavricheskogo gub. pravl., 1893), 127.

envoys to the Kalmyks to invite them to march against the Crimea.[54]
During the Kalmyks' numerous crossings of the Volga on the way to
Crimea, they were never reported to have been met and engaged by
Muscovite troops. Moscow did not appear to disapprove of the Kalmyk
raids against the Crimea; but, unwilling to provoke the Crimean khan
into war, it did not dare to encourage the Kalmyks openly.

The situation changed when Moscow's decision to incorporate the
Ukraine in 1654 resulted in a reshuffling of alliances in eastern Europe.
The Crimeans and the Poles, who until then were at war with each other,
now joined together against Muscovy and the Zaporozhian cossacks. In
a desperate search for the new allies, Moscow turned to the Kalmyks for
help. Now the government could openly ally itself with them against the
Crimea. An agreement with the Kalmyks could also free many musketeers stationed in the frontier towns who were now needed on the
western front against the Polish-Lithuanian Commonwealth. To this end
the government began actively to seek an alliance with the Kalmyk
tayishis.

The First Written Russo-Kalmyk Agreements

In February 1655, the first written agreement was reached between the
Kalmyk tayishis and the Muscovite government. Moscow could relate to
the Kalmyks only as a suzerain to a subject, and the agreement was
executed as a Kalmyk oath of allegiance to the tsar. The Kalmyks promised to be loyal to the tsar and to participate in Muscovy's military
campaigns, not to assault Muscovite subjects and to return those who
had been captured in the past, not to insult the Muscovite envoys and to
allow them to return promptly, and to let those Nogays and Yedisans
who wished to return to Astrakhan do so and to turn them back in
future.[55]

Clearly, the document resembled an oath of allegiance of a subject to a
suzerain. Yet the subject status of the Kalmyks, besides the phraseology
of the document, was not reinforced with any terms. Moscow dropped
its demand for hostages and did not demand payments of tax or tribute.
The document signed in Astrakhan by the representatives of the Kalmyk
tayishis, was, in essence, an agreement between allies in which the
Kalmyks promised peace and military cooperation. That was how the
Kalmyk tayishis viewed it, expecting the other side to be similarly obli-

---

[54]Kichikov (Ochirov), *Istoricheskie korni*, 98.
[55]*PSZ* 1:356–57, no. 145.

gated. The government, however, made no promises. It is not surprising that such a one-sided treaty did not last.

Shortly after the treaty with the Kalmyks was signed, the musketeers in the Volga towns were mobilized, and the Kalmyks were instructed to join the Don cossacks and the troops of Bohdan Khmel'nytskyi. Khmel'nytskyi planned a two-pronged attack on the Crimea—the Kalmyks by land and the Don cossacks by sea—to prevent the Crimean army from leaving the peninsula to assist the Poles.[56] On the eve of the spring campaign, further to win the Kalmyks over, the government issued orders to the military governors of the towns and the Bashkirs not to cause any harm to the Kalmyks. Another decree allowed the Kalmyks to roam where they pleased along the Volga and the Akhtuba rivers.[57] Although this decree was a mere post-factum recognition of the current Kalmyk pastures, it was phrased to sound like a benevolent act on the part of the Muscovite suzerain.

The government also gave the Kalmyks permission to trade near Astrakhan. The issue of trade was of crucial importance to the Kalmyks, who persistently asked to be allowed to trade in the Muscovite towns. In the winter of 1654 the Kalmyk tayishis Louzang and Puntsuk, Daichin's son, threatened the Astrakhan governor with war unless he let them trade near Astrakhan on the Volga's west bank.[58]

The Muscovite envoys to Daichin and Louzang were instructed to promise the tayishis that if the Kalmyks marched against the Crimea, they would be permitted to trade in Ufa, Saratov, and other towns. Moscow had learned that by using trade as a weapon it could gain leverage in dealing with the Kalmyks so in 1646 it allowed the Kalmyks to trade near Astrakhan. Three years later, however, the Astrakhan governor refused another of Daichin's requests for trade. When in the same year three thousand horses sent by Louzang for sale were also rejected by the governor, Louzang retaliated by launching raids.[59] Such a cycle was not uncommon. The Kalmyks needed to sell the herds and to acquire goods from the Muscovite towns, and when the government refused, the Kalmyks launched raids in an attempt to impose their conditions by force. Raiding, however, did little to encourage the authorities to open the towns for trade with the Kalmyks.

Despite the government's efforts, the Kalmyks took no part in Mus-

---

[56]*AIuZR* 14:566, no. 19 (IV).

[57]Kichikov (Ochirov), "K istorii obrazovaniia Kalmytskogo," 58.

[58]*DAI* 3:532, no. 126. A specific request to trade on the Volga's west bank was most likely determined by the Kalmyks' need for expeditious sale of the herds captured in the raids against the Nogays.

[59]Preobrazhenskaia, "Iz istorii," 54–56.

covy's campaign of 1655. They remained displeased with Moscow's policies of controlling trade and limiting their pastures. In addition, Moscow's orders failed to stop the Bashkir raids against the Kalmyks, and a constant threat of such raids restrained Kalmyk participation in military campaigns.

In 1656 the Muscovite government insisted that the Kalmyks sign another oath, but the government did not change its position, and this oath, too, proved ineffective. Desperate to enlist the Kalmyks against the Crimea, the government was ready to make new concessions. In the following year another oath was signed in return for which Moscow allowed the Kalmyks' migrations along both sides of the Volga and duty-free trade in the Volga towns of Astrakhan, Chernyi Iar, Tsaritsyn, Saratov, and Samara. A satisfactory solution of the two vital issues—pastures and trade—produced an immediate result. In 1657, the Kalmyks, led by Daichin's son Puntsuk, successfully struck at the Nogays near Azov and brought back one thousand captives and fifteen thousand horses.[60]

Moscow and the Kalmyks continued to interpret such oaths differently. All available contents of the Russo-Kalmyk negotiations, which preceded the signing procedure, clearly indicate that the Kalmyks viewed the oath as an agreement between two military allies, a sort of nonaggression treaty. The Kalmyks were vaguely familiar with the contents of the oaths, whose texts were prepared by the Muscovite government in advance and available only in the Russian language. The Kalmyk representatives merely signed them.[61]

Several surviving documents clearly illustrate that after signing the oaths in the 1650s, Daichin continued to address the tsar as his equal and signed his letters as Daichin Khan.[62] As an independent ruler, Daichin maintained relations with other foreign powers. For three consecutive years after 1655, embassies from Kho-Urlük's sons Daichin, Elden, and Louzang arrived at the Qing court with gifts.[63] In 1655 the Kalmyks sent an envoy to the Persian court of Shah Abbas II, and shortly thereafter the envoy returned with the shah's ambassador. Throughout the late 1650s the Kalmyks continued lively relations with the shah, exchanging embassies and receiving many gifts.[64]

At the time, however, the Kalmyks' relations with the Crimean khan

[60]Kichikov, (Ochirov) *Istoricheskie korni*, 104; Belikov, *Kalmyki*, 18.

[61]Preobrazhenskaia, "Iz istorii," 61.

[62]Kichikov (Ochirov), *Istoricheskie korni*, 118–19.

[63]*Men-gu-iu-mu-tszi. Zapiski o mongol'skikh kochev'iakh*, trans. P. S. Popov, ZIRGOOE 24 (St. Petersburg: N.p., 1895), 144.

[64]Faruk Sümer, *Oguzlar (Türkmenlar)*, 3d ed. (Istanbul: Ana Yayinlari, 1980), 665; *Ocherki istorii Kalmytskoi*, 1:103.

were of greater significance than their relations with Persia. When Moscow tried to enlist the Kalmyks against the Crimea, the Crimean khan spared no efforts to attract them to his side. Even though his envoys did not convince the Kalmyk tayishis to join the Crimeans, the khan's presents and promises did succeed in keeping the Kalmyks at bay throughout the late 1650s. Sketchy records suggest a lively exchange of embassies between the Crimeans and the Kalmyks. In 1658 informers reported to Moscow that another Crimean embassy had visited the Kalmyks and that Daichin and the Crimean khan had agreed on joint military actions against Muscovy. According to the plan, the Crimeans were to attack southern Muscovite provinces at the same time the Kalmyks struck at the provinces of Kazan and Ufa. In a letter to Tsar Aleksei Mikhailovich, the Crimean khan Mehmet Giray IV plainly stated that he now controlled the Kalmyks and that, with God's help, they had become his subjects.[65]

The Kalmyks, to be sure, were no more subjects of the Crimean khanate than of Muscovy. Daichin decided to enter an alliance with the Crimean khan when he realized Moscow's inability to act upon its promises and to stop incursions against him by the Bashkirs and other peoples of the Kazan and Ufa provinces. Fear of the Kalmyks' alliance with the Crimean khan compelled the government to renew its efforts to gain the confidence of the Kalmyks.

The government's changed attitude toward the Kalmyks in 1657 is evident from its major concessions, agreeing to the Kalmyks' demands for more extensive trade and larger pastures. Moscow also learned to provide more tangible rewards and presents that proved convincing to the Kalmyks. After the signing of the 1655 oath, all tayishis received presents worth twenty-four rubles thirty kopecks, and five *vedro* of wine were sent to Daichin. Two years later, when the government realized that it had to match the gifts from the Crimea if it were to attract the Kalmyks to its side, Daichin received a sable coat worth sixty rubles and a fur hat. Other tayishis received similar presents of slightly lesser value.[66] In addition, Moscow promised to pay an annuity to the Kalmyks. Daichin was to receive 200 rubles and Puntsuk 100 rubles, while other tayishis together with their trusted people were to be content with smaller amounts. In total, Kalmyk leaders were promised 810 rubles annually.[67]

In exchange for grants and rewards from Moscow, the Kalmyks were

---

[65]Vel'iaminov-Zernov, *Materialy*, 530, no. 187; *Ocherki istorii Kalmytskoi*, 1:104; *AIuZR* 15:388, no. 9.

[66]Preobrazhenskaia, "Iz istorii," 64, 68.

[67]*Ocherki istorii Kalmytskoi*, 1:121.

expected to cease their relations with the Crimean khanate. The 1657 oath contained a clause prohibiting the Kalmyks from allying with the Ottoman sultan or the Crimean khan. Another important clause secured the Kalmyks' promise to surrender several hostages to Astrakhan.[68] Although the hostages were put up at special quarters and were given larger than usual allowances, agreeing to the government's demand represented a concession on Daichin's part.

Acting upon the oath signed in 1657, the tayishis expeditiously moved against the Nogays near Azov. The new oath, however, had turned out to be short-lived because the Muscovite government failed to keep its promises. In the following years, annuities stopped, and the raids launched against the Kalmyks by the Bashkirs and the Yayik cossacks continued. When in autumn of 1657 the Kalmyk envoy complained to the Ufa governor of the Bashkir raids, the latter, fearful of Kalmyk reprisals, flatly denied them, while at the same time acknowledging their occurrence in his secret report to Moscow.[69] The Kalmyks were disappointed with their Muscovite ally, and the gift-laden embassies from the Crimean khan were making enticing offers.

It appears that during this period the government in Moscow had no consistent policy toward the Kalmyks. Troubled by its own problems, the government seemed unwilling, or more likely unable, to keep its promises. The government could not exercise sufficient authority over its unruly subjects so its orders to live in peace with the Kalmyks were more often ignored than followed by the Bashkirs, the Maris, and the cossacks. Whenever the government found itself in financial straits, as it did frequently, no annuities were sent to the tayishis. More often than not, the government, contemptuous of the idolatrous nomads, attempted to get away with as little as possible. Thus the policy was not based on any consistent effort to maintain relations and to secure the Kalmyks' loyalty but instead was dictated by the necessity of the moment.

After having suffered several defeats from the allied armies of the Zaporozhian cossacks and the Crimean Tatars, and particularly after the 1659 massacre of the Muscovite cavalry near Konotop in the Ukraine, Moscow decided to renew its efforts to seek Kalmyk help. The government's actions clearly illustrate that it was well aware of the Kalmyks' discontent. Before embarking on a new round of negotiations in 1660, Moscow judiciously sent the tayishis two years' worth of annuities. At the same time it took decisive measures to restrain the raids against the

[68]Preobrazhenskaia, "Iz istorii," 67, 69.
[69]Ustiugov, "Bashkirskoe vosstanie," 54–55.

Kalmyks by the Bashkirs and the cossacks and ordered them to release Kalmyk captives in their possession.[70] The seriousness of the government's intentions was also indicated by its choice of a high-ranking official and experienced diplomat, *d'iak* I. S. Gorokhov, to head the embassy. In December 1660 an embassy left Moscow for the Kalmyk uluses.[71] The embassy's goal was clearly stated in the government's instructions to Gorokhov: to secure the Kalmyks' participation in the war against the Crimea. It was not until late May of 1661 that Gorokhov was able to pay a visit to Daichin, whose camp was in the steppe on the Volga's west bank, not far from Astrakhan. Negotiations lasted for several days. To make its case more convincing, the embassy brought lavish presents for Daichin and other Kalmyk tayishis and no-bles—a total of 1,074 rubles worth. Nevertheless, Daichin expressed his displeasure that his annuity was less than that paid by Moscow to the Crimean khan. He then complained of the Bashkir and cossack raids and of the delay of his envoy, who was dispatched to Moscow in 1660. When a few days later Gorokhov met with Daichin's son Puntsuk, the latter brought up similar grievances.[72]

In response to the tayishis' charges, Gorokhov stated that it was not appropriate to bring up the subject of the envoy's delay and to dispute the amount of the annuity. He laid the blame for the Bashkir raids on Daichin, who had failed to release Bashkir captives. Despite these tradi-tional thorny issues, Gorokhov succeeded in persuading Daichin and Puntsuk to take part in the campaign against the Crimea. In addressing the Kalmyks' main concerns, the Muscovite envoy assured the tayishis that the Bashkirs would not strike at them if the Kalmyks joined the campaign. He also promised that the annuities would be paid regularly. Similar promises had been made in the past and were unlikely to con-vince the Kalmyks. In the end, a middleman, the Kabardinian Prince Kaspulat Cherkasskii, whose sister was married to Puntsuk, won the confidence of the tayishis.[73]

On June 8, 1661, Daichin and Puntsuk signed an agreement, whereby in return for annuities and guarantee of the security of the Kalmyk uluses from the raids of Moscow's subjects, the tayishis would dispatch Kalmyk cavalry against the Crimea. Daichin was to send five thousand horsemen, Puntsuk and two other tayishis one thousand each, and four

[70]Preobrazhenskaia, "Iz istorii," 69; *Ocherki istorii Kalmytskoi,* 1:120.

[71]A detailed account of the negotiations between Moscow's ambassador and Kalmyk tayishis is in Preobrazhenskaia, "Iz istorii," 69–77.

[72]Ibid., 71–74; S. M. Solov'ev, *Istoriia Rossii s drevneishikh vremen.* 29 vols. (Moscow: Izd-vo sots.-econ. literatury, 1959–66), bk. 6, vol. 12:576–80.

[73]Preobrazhenskaia, "Iz istorii," 75.

other tayishis five hundred each. Thus a total Kalmyk army of ten thousand was to take part in the campaign.[74]

The Kalmyks also agreed that upon completion of the campaign they would deliver any Muscovite captives released from the Crimea to Astrakhan, capture and send Crimean informers to Moscow, and sell captured people and herds in Muscovite towns instead of returning them to the Crimea for ransom, as was customary.[75] This clause undoubtedly represented another—this time more successful—attempt by the government to limit the political independence of the Kalmyks. Consistent with Moscow's view of the Kalmyks as its subjects, such attempts were made regularly, but usually with little effect. For example, upon Gorokhov's arrival at Puntsuk's camp, he learned that a Crimean envoy was visiting Puntsuk at the same time. Gorokhov's demand that Puntsuk send the Crimean envoy to Moscow was rejected by the tayishi, who explained that after such a violation no one would send an embassy to the Kalmyks in the future.[76] In the signed agreement, however, Daichin and Puntsuk seem to have renounced their right to deal independently with the Crimea. Enticed by an attractive offer to sell their spoils to the Muscovites, they agreed to forsake direct contacts with the Crimea and embarked on the slippery road which in time led to the Kalmyks' growing dependence on Moscow.

Puntsuk Tayishi and His Alliance with Muscovy

Political contacts and trade with Muscovy meant greater economic and political reliance on their neighbor, and Moscow's support came to play an increasingly important role in internal Kalmyk politics. To achieve his own ends, the chief Kalmyk tayishi learned to gain political and economic benefits from his relationship with Moscow. Ordinarily, the opposition was compelled to look for support elsewhere, thus inevitably assuming an anti-Muscovite stance. Increasingly the Kalmyk tayishis found themselves divided into two factions—pro- and anti-Muscovite.

The Kalmyk chief tayishis were clearly exploiting the "Muscovite connection" to aggrandize themselves. In the mid-1650s, in an attempt to augment his power, Daichin deprived his younger brother Elden of several Nogay uluses. Unable to resist, Elden fled back to Jungaria. But Daichin's victory over another possible rival, his brother Louzang, proved

---

[74]Ibid., 76; *PSZ* 1:531–32, no. 300.
[75]*PSZ* 1:532, no. 300.
[76]Preobrazhenskaia, "Iz istorii," 73–74.

to be more difficult. The question of who should control and collect taxes from the various Nogay tribes was at the heart of the dispute between Daichin and Louzang. Using Louzang's raids against the Muscovites as a pretext, Daichin was able to convince Moscow to support him against Louzang. After several years of confrontation, in 1658 Daichin achieved a major victory over Louzang and forced him to flee across the Yayik. The following year Louzang returned seeking revenge but was again defeated and fled. A year later he and his sons perished at the hands of the old enemy, Ablay tayiji of the Khoshuts.[77]

Despite his growing reliance on Moscow's support, Daichin continued to regard Moscow as only one of his allies. In a letter to the tsar in 1661, he left no doubt as to how he viewed his relationship with the Muscovite sovereign:

> May there be prosperity! The white khan and all others, [you] are, probably, in good health there. Daichin khan and all others, we are in good health here. The meaning [of the previous words] is this: to find out (or: to tell) concerning the health of both khans. The meaning of the words that follow is this: in the past both the Crimea and you were an adversary [of ours], but later we became an ally of each of you. After this your envoy Sbon-uulu-yaban [corrupted name of the Muscovite envoy] and Khasbolod brought your decree to us. We acted according to your word. Let us know in future about any action of yours. Send us our envoy soon![78]

When age and poor health caused the proud Kalmyk leader to step aside, he appointed his son Puntsuk the chief tayishi. Only a few months after Daichin and Puntsuk had signed an agreement in June 1661, the government dispatched an embassy to Puntsuk to have him take an oath of allegiance. Moscow, concerned about renewed Crimean attempts to win the Kalmyks over, sought to make sure that Puntsuk would follow his father's policy. In December 1661 Puntsuk pledged loyalty on behalf of himself, his father, Daichin, and his nephew Jalba (Yalba). The document contained a detailed enumeration of the Kalmyks' obligations, all of which reflected Moscow's primary concerns: to prevent the Kalmyks from establishing ties with foreign powers, particularly the Crimea, and to have the new Kalmyk leader reaffirm his loyalty.[79] The government's fears about Puntsuk were unwarranted. Eventually, he forged closer ties with Moscow than any of his predecessors.

[77]Kichikov (Ochirov), *Istoricheskie korni*, 116–17.
[78]This translation is from the available Russian translation of the original letter (György Kara, *Knigi mongol'skikh kochevnikov* [Moscow: Vost. liter-ra., 1972], 159, note 168. A facsimile is in *Ocherki istorii Kalmytskoi*, 1:131).
[79]*PSZ* 1:561–64, no. 316.

Daichin, who used his relationship with Moscow to enhance his position vis-à-vis his brothers, could hardly have suspected that he himself would become a victim of the policies he initiated. Puntsuk also chose to rely on Muscovy to strengthen his position as a Kalmyk chief tayishi against his ailing father. The rift between father and son occurred over Daichin's grandson and Puntsuk's nephew Jalba. To eliminate a potential contender for power, Puntsuk turned against his nephew, using as a pretext Jalba's raids against the towns of Astrakhan and Tersk. Puntsuk, however, went a step further than his father. Unlike Daichin, who was content simply to drive his rivals out, Puntsuk, after having defeated and captured Jalba, turned him over to the Muscovite authorities. Daichin was furious and demanded that the Astrakhan governor release Jalba. When the governor refused, Daichin joined forces with the rebellious Bashkirs.[80]

During the Bashkir uprising of 1662–64, Daichin, together with the Bashkirs, raided the Ufa and Kazan provinces on numerous occasions and often provided refuge for Bashkirs who fled the Muscovite troops. Puntsuk and other Kalmyk tayishis, however, allied with Moscow. The uprising soon subsided and Daichin was compelled to reconcile himself with the authorities.[81]

Puntsuk proved to be a loyal ally of Muscovy. In 1661, the Kalmyks made peace with the Don cossacks and exchanged captives. Throughout the 1660s the Kalmyks became an indispensable ally of the Zaporozhian cossacks, and together they inflicted many defeats on the Crimeans.[82] Until the signing of the 1667 Andrusovo Treaty between Muscovy and the Polish-Lithuanian Commonwealth, Puntsuk continued to take part in the war on Muscovy's side. Kalmyk detachments, sometimes with as many as twenty thousand horsemen, were reported making raids against the Crimean Tatars, the Nogays, and the Poles.[83]

The ultimate test of Puntsuk's loyalty came in 1664, when the Crimeans again approached him with a proposal to join them. The plan was intended to unite the Tatars of the Crimea, Astrakhan, Ufa, and Kazan, together with the Bashkirs, and thus to form a Muslim front against Moscow. Puntsuk refused to join this coalition and warned Moscow of the possible threat.[84]

[80]Kichikov (Ochirov), *Istoricheskie korni*, 129.

[81]*AI* 4:335, no. 175; Ustiugov, "Bashkirskoe vosstanie," 70, 94, 95; *Ocherki istorii Kalmytskoi*, 1:134.

[82]*Krest'ianskaia voina pod predvoditel'stvom Stepana Razina. Sbornik dokumentov*, comp. E. A. Shvetsova, 4 vols. (Moscow: AN SSSR, 1954–76), 1:27, no. 3; *AIuZR* 5:172–73, no. 69; 6:130–31, no. 46.

[83]*AMG* 3:551–52, no. 659; Preobrazhenskaia, "Iz istorii," 81–82; Belikov, *Kalmyki v bor'be*, 23–28.

[84]Kichikov (Ochirov), *Istoricheskie korni*, 130–31.

The government's increased trust of the Kalmyks in the mid-1660s was clearly reflected in its decision to allow Puntsuk to roam along the Don. This decision not only represented another of Moscow's concessions to the Kalmyks but also suited the government's strategic plans. Cooperation between the Don cossacks and the Kalmyks in their raids against the Crimea had allowed Moscow to position the Kalmyks near the Don, closer to the targets of their raids near Azov, Kuban, and the Crimea, thus making such raids more expeditious.

It appears that at this time Puntsuk decided to invest his political fortune in Moscow. In 1664 he requested that the government build new fortresses, one on the Don, another on the Yayik. The fortress on the Don was to have as many as two thousand musketeers to protect and assist Puntsuk against the Crimeans. The fortress on the Yayik was to protect Puntsuk from the incursions of the Oirats of Jungaria.[85]

In recognition of Puntsuk's loyalty, in 1664 Moscow sent him a gilded silver mace, a white banner, and some valuable presents.[86] The political meaning of this gesture was unmistakable. By sending a mace and a banner, Moscow sought to confirm Puntsuk's position as a leader of the Kalmyks. At the same time, the government clearly indicated that it was granting the Kalmyks political status similar to that of the Zaporozhian and the Don cossacks. The Kalmyks were considered Muscovite subjects, albeit with a vestige of administrative autonomy. Moscow believed that it had found a political solution to maintaining relations with the Kalmyks. Once again, however, it did not endure. In 1669, Puntsuk died and his eldest son, Ayuki, emerged as the ruler of the Kalmyks in time to change dramatically the character of Muscovite-Kalmyk relations.

[85]*Ocherki istorii Kalmytskoi*, 1:135.
[86]Kichikov (Ochirov), *Istoricheskie korni*, 131–32.

4

The Rise to Power
of Ayuki Khan

The Rise of Ayuki Tayishi

On Kho-Urlük's visit to the *khurultay* in Jungaria in 1640, he married his
grandson Puntsuk to one of Erdeni Batur's daughters. Shortly thereafter,
a son was born to them. The child was named Ayuki in honor of one of
the gods in the Buddhist pantheon.[1] Later on, Ayuki would pledge his
faithfulness to the canons of the Buddhist faith: "If I ever think of harm-
ing the religion of Buddha and God's laws, then may Nomiin Sakusun
(God the Savior) rip out my heart."[2] Indeed, propagating Buddhist teachings among the Kalmyks and supporting the Buddhist clergy would
become important principles of Ayuki's policies.

Ayuki spent his childhood in Jungaria with his grandfather Erdeni
Batur khong tayiji, who was a learned man and an able politician. Ayuki
must have witnessed Erdeni Batur's striving to achieve his ambitious
projects of uniting the Oirats and the Mongols and of building up a
strong Jungarian khanate. Ayuki was twelve years old when his grandfather died in the winter of 1653.[3] Shortly thereafter, his paternal grandfather, the Kalmyk tayishi Daichin, on the way back from his second
pilgrimage to Tibet, took Ayuki with him.[4]

Growing up at the court of his grandfather Daichin, at the time the
chief Kalmyk tayishi, must have left a strong imprint on the young Ayuki.

[1] John R. Krueger, *Materials for an Oirat-Mongolian to English Citation Dictionary*, 2
vols. (Bloomington, Ind.: Mongolia Society, 1978), 1:45.
[2] Gabang Sharab, "Skazanie ob oiratakh," 147; Batur-Ubashi Tümen, "Skazanie," 32.
[3] "Biografiia Zaya-Pandity," 176.
[4] Lytkin, "Ayuki-Khan kalmytskii," 131–32.

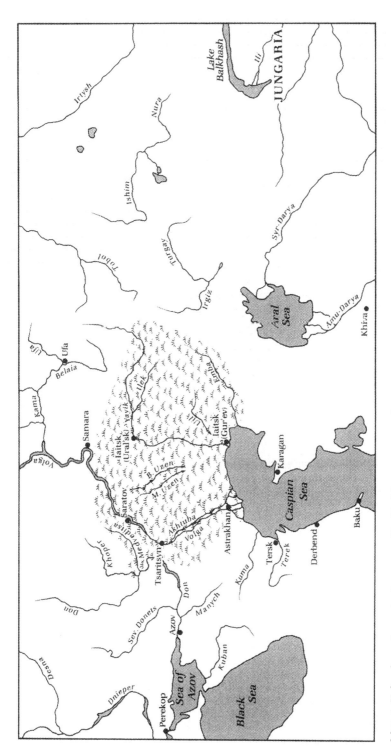

Map 4. Kalmyk pastures in the second half of the seventeenth century.

He saw many dignitaries who came to Daichin to discuss matters of politics and religion, and he heard the words of wisdom of Zaya-Pandita, the inventor of the Oirat script and a most learned man, deeply revered by the Kalmyks and Oirats.[5] Daichin himself was an extraordinary figure, a man of learning who made two pilgrimages to Tibet and was well versed in Tibetan Buddhist literature. Daichin taught his young grandson how to become the ruler of the Kalmyks: "You say that you want to be a noyon—to rule the people. To be a noyon, you must know when to be equal with your subjects, when to rule them, and when to take care of them, as the mother takes care of her child. If you follow these three rules without fail, you will acquire wisdom and become a noyon."[6] Ayuki heeded the advice of his grandfather and followed this path more successfully than his predecessors.

The Russian official Vasilii Bakunin, a contemporary of Ayuki, maintained that before his death the chief tayishi Puntsuk appointed his eldest son, Ayuki, to succeed him. Despite Ayuki's status as official heir apparent, Puntsuk's death brought to the surface old rivalries and new disputes over the position of the chief tayishi. Other tayishis, who perceived themselves more fit to hold the title, defied Ayuki. The new chief tayishi needed to consolidate his position by stopping the feuds and eliminating the challenges.

The main threat to Ayuki came from the east. There, Ablay tayiji of the Khoshuts, pressed by his brother Ochirtu Tsetsen Khan, forcefully moved west toward the Yayik.[7] Together with the Khoshuts of his uncle Khundulen, who joined him in the campaign, Ablay defeated Daichin tayishi and took over his ulus. In open defiance of Ayuki, Ablay then wrote to Moscow demanding that he be given the same annuity previously granted to Puntsuk and Daichin.[8]

In the southern and western parts of the Caspian steppes, Ayuki had to face the rebellious Kalmyk tayishis and the Nogay mirzas. In 1669 Dugar (Duvar) and Bok tayishis moved off to join the Azov Tatars and harassed Ayuki's uluses on the Volga and Don.[9] A year later, when a fight broke out between the Yedisans and the Nogays of Yamgurchi mirza, the

[5]Zaya-Pandita spent the winter of 1656 at Daichin's ulus ("Biografiia Zaya-Pandity," 177).
[6]Batur-Ubashi Tümen, "Skazanie," 31; Gabang Sharab, "Skazanie ob oiratakh," 146–47.
[7]Zlatkin, *Istoriia Dzhungarskogo*, 163.
[8]"Biografiia Zaya-Pandity," 193–94; Lytkin, "Ayuki-Khan kalmytskii," 132; *Ocherki istorii Kalmytskoi*, 1:138.
[9]*Krest'ianskaia voina pod predvoditel'stvom Stepana Razina*, 1:nos. 152, 162, 170. According to one account, Dugar together with his brother and Ayuki's father, Puntsuk, defeated the Torgut tayishi Tsamba, but instead of sharing the spoils, Puntsuk appropriated the entire captured ulus for himself. Dugar, fearing that the same destiny would befall him, fled and found refuge under Crimean protection (*DAI* 6:294, no. 84).

latter rounded up the Astrakhan Yurt Tatars and took them and all his people to the steppes of the Terek River. Since the Kalmyks did not offer adequate protection, fifteen thousand Yedisans defected from the Kalmyks and came to seek refuge near Astrakhan.[10]

The loss of a large number of people and constant military and political challenges from his rivals posed a serious threat to Ayuki. Following the tenets of the diplomatic school of his grandfathers, Ayuki resorted to a familiar stratagem. To regain control of the situation, he decided to ally, albeit temporarily, with some of his adversaries. First, Ayuki was reconciled with Dugar and Bok tayishis, as well as the Don cossacks. He promised to live in peace with the cossacks and requested their assistance against the Nogays of the Malibash and Yamboyluk (Emboluk) tribes, who had deserted him.[11] Ayuki's next move was to strengthen his relations with the influential Kabardinian prince Kaspulat Mutsalovich Cherkasskii, whose younger sister, Abukhan (Abay Khan), was his wife. For many years, the prominent Kabardinian family of the Cherkasskiis had been faithfully representing Russian interests in the area, and Prince Kaspulat Cherkasskii often served as an intermediary between the Russian government and the Kalmyks.[12]

By the summer of 1671 Ayuki's strategy had begun to pay off. Together with Dugar and Bok, the Kabardinians of Kaspulat Cherkasskii, and the Don cossacks, he embarked on a military campaign against the rebellious Nogay tribes of the Malibash and Yamboyluk. The rebels were quickly overwhelmed and forced to return with Ayuki to his pastures.[13]

Ayuki was waiting for an opportune moment to move against his most powerful enemy, Ablay tayiji. When he learned of the squabbles between Ablay and his cousins over the captured uluses, Ayuki wasted no time in attacking Ablay. In the ensuing battle, Ablay's army was defeated and Ablay was forced to flee.[14] A year later, however, in 1672, Ablay returned, this time to triumph. Ayuki suffered a major defeat and lost most of his ulus. He fled, seeking Moscow's protection. At this point, his alliance with Russia became a key factor in deciding Ayuki's destiny. With the remnants of his army reinforced by the Kabardinians of Kaspulat Cherkasskii, as well as the Yayik cossacks and Astrakhan musketeers, Ayuki set out against Ablay. It turned out to be the last battle for Ablay tayiji. His

[10]Bakunin, "Opisanie," *Krasnyi arkhiv* 3 (1939): 195; A. N. Popov, *Materialy dlia istorii vozmushcheniia Sten'ki Razina* (Moscow: Tip. L. Stepanova, 1857), 256.

[11]*Krest'ianskaia voina,* 3:144, no. 134, 112.

[12]Ibid., 134, no. 123; Bakunin, "Opisanie," *Krasnyi arkhiv* 3 (1939): 198; Kichikov (Ochirov), *K voprosu obrazovaniia kalmytskogo,* 18.

[13]*Krest'ianskaia voina,* 3:138, no. 128.

[14]"Biografiia Zaya-Pandity," 194.

army was crushed, and Ablay was taken captive. In acknowledgment and appreciation of Moscow's help, Ayuki handed over Ablay and his family to the Russian authorities. Ayuki was once again in possession of his ulus, and his dignity was restored.[15]

In the next few years, one campaign followed another. Having disposed of his principal rival, Ayuki decided to move against the Nogays, who had fled from him two years earlier and were now roaming the steppes of the upper Kuban River. As a result of a swift campaign against the Nogays, Ayuki regained control over his former subjects and brought many of them back to his Volga pastures. His campaigns succeeded, among other reasons, because of his alliance with his uncle Dugar tayishi. The Kalmyk chronicle emphasized Dugar's important role in Ayuki's early victories, saying that it was Dugar tayishi who made Ayuki a khan.[16]

When the temporary alliance between Ayuki and his uncle Dugar was no longer necessary, Ayuki turned against Dugar and disposed of the last potential contender. To secure Moscow's help, Ayuki slandered his uncle in the eyes of the authorities and, together with Prince Kaspulat Cherkasskii, carried out a military campaign against Dugar. As a result, Dugar and his son Tseren were captured and their uluses taken over by Ayuki. As he had with Ablay tayiji, Ayuki turned Dugar and Tseren over to the Astrakhan authorities. Later, Tseren was sent to Moscow to be baptized and subsequently became known as Prince Vasilii Dugarov.[17]

In a short period of time Ayuki had consolidated his power, and by 1673 he had emerged as the undisputed chief tayishi of the Kalmyks. Showing himself to be an ambitious and crafty politician, he succeeded in eliminating his major rivals and taking over their uluses. His decisive victories over the Nogay tribes of the Yedisan, Malibash, and Yamboyluk, as well as his Kalmyk rivals, brought Ayuki military power, wealth, and the recognition of neighboring peoples.

During the first and most challenging years of Ayuki's rule, he quickly realized the necessity of using Moscow's support to achieve his own goals. Indeed, most of his actions were undertaken on the pretext of serving the interests of the tsar. His alliance with Prince Kaspulat Cherkasskii and the Don cossacks was based on the assumption that all parties involved were serving the Russian sovereign. Ayuki's campaign against the Nogays was also part of Russia's military campaign against the Crimean and Azov Tatars, to whom the Nogays had defected. Finally,

[15]Pal'mov, *Etiudy*, 3:10; *Kabardino-russkie otnosheniia*, 1:341, no. 216.

[16]Batur-Ubashi Tümen, "Skazanie," 36.

[17]Bakunin, "Opisanie," *Krasnyi arkhiv* 3 (1939): 195; *Kabardino-russkie otnosheniia*, 1:340, no. 216.

it was not accidental that Ayuki defeated his rivals Ablay and Dugar on the pretext that they "did many wrongs to the Grand Sovereign His Majesty the Tsar."[18] On Moscow's insistence, Ayuki handed them over as part of his obligations to his beneficent Russian ally.

The government in Moscow also realized the growing importance of Ayuki as the chief Kalmyk tayishi. To secure its ties with Ayuki on the eve of the intended military campaigns in the Ukraine, the government resorted to the familiar device of the written oath of allegiance. Ayuki signed the oath in February 1673, near Astrakhan. The preamble to the oath enumerated the parties on whose behalf Ayuki was signing it—himself, his brothers and nephews and all his people, the Nogay, the Yedisan, the Yamboyluk, the Malibash, and the Kelechin mirzas and their people—clear testimony to Ayuki's increased power. Before signing the oath, Ayuki, in accordance with Kalmyk custom, bowed down, kissed a *burkhan* (one of the Buddha's images), followed by a *bichig* (a prayer book) and prayer beads, and put a saber to his head and throat.

This procedure, along with the general tone and most of the provisions of the oath, call to mind the signing of the oath of 1661 by Ayuki's father, Puntsuk. The following is a summary of Ayuki's promises and obligations as they were set forth in the new oath:

(1) to serve Tsar Aleksei Mikhailovich faithfully and henceforth to be the tsar's obedient subject;

(2) to refrain from pillaging the uluses and herds of the Nogays, the Yedisans, the Yamboyluks, and the Astrakhan Yurt Tatars;

(3) to cease raiding the Russian sovereign's towns and villages and to refrain from bearing arms against, capturing, or plundering the tsar's subjects;

(4) to fight faithfully against the tsar's enemies as commanded by the sovereign and not to betray Russia in its military campaigns;

(5) to refrain from entering into any relations with the Ottoman sultan, the Persian shah, the Crimean khan, the Azov *beys*, the Temriuks, the Tabans, the Besleneys, the Kumyks, and others, and not to assist them with arms, horses, or men;

(6) to prevent the Yedisan, the Nogay, and the Yamboyluk mirzas, who roamed with him, from looting and taking captive the sovereign's subjects and to destroy them without hesitation if they continued to do so;

(7) to allow those Tatar mirzas who in previous years had betrayed the grand sovereign and joined the Kalmyk uluses to leave and return to Astrakhan, not to call on them in the future to join the Kalmyks, and to send those who came of their own free will back to Astrakhan;

---

[18]*PSZ* 1:927, no. 540.

(8) to return, in exchange for appropriate compensation, all Orthodox Christians who wanted to leave for the tsar's towns, while the Russian authorities were to return all those Kalmyks who fled to Russian towns and were unbaptized; those Orthodox Christians who were returning from captivity in Bukhara, Khiva, and Urgench were to be allowed safe passage on their way to the Russian towns;

(9) to refrain from committing any dishonorable act toward envoys of the Russian tsar, such as beating or molesting them, and to let the envoys go without delay; to refrain from sending Kalmyk envoys to the tsar in great numbers;

(10) to trade near Astrakhan without quarreling with the Russian people; as in previous years to send horses for sale to Moscow by the old road via the towns of Tambov, Kasimov, and Vladimir;

(11) to march against the Crimea without any delay on the sovereign's order;

(12) to receive for himself, his brothers, and his nephews an extra compensation (zhalovan'e) for participation in military campaigns, in addition to the annuity (oklad) from the tsar; and

(13) to set out against the Kumyks in the coming spring and, upon defeating them, to move against the Crimean Tatars.[19]

The contents of this oath reveal many contentious issues in Russo-Kalmyk relations and the government's intentions toward the Kalmyks. The commitments on the Russian side were limited to returning unbaptized fugitive Kalmyks and paying annual and additional payments for military services provided. In return, the Russian government expected the Kalmyks to be loyal and obedient subjects. From Russia's point of view, the oath codified the relationship between suzerain and subject and gave the suzerain the right to exercise stringent political control over his subject. Thus it was natural for the Russian government to demand that the Kalmyks sever their relations with other foreign powers. The status of the Kalmyks as subjects also entailed faithful military service to the Russian tsar—one of Moscow's principal goals in its relations with the Kalmyks. Both parties were interested in trade, which was to be conducted at two principal markets, Astrakhan and Moscow.

In contrast to the oath of 1661, the new oath contained two additional clauses. One stipulated that the Russian authorities had to return Kalmyk fugitives who did not convert to Orthodoxy. The issue was of extreme importance to Ayuki, whose growing power caused many malcontents to seek refuge in the Russian towns. The conversion of fugitive

[19]Ibid.

Kalmyks to Christianity was soon to become one of the most contentious issues in Russo-Kalmyk relations.

In another new clause, Ayuki was encouraged by the Russian government to punish those disobedient mirzas who raided and pillaged the sovereign's subjects. It was both a recognition of Ayuki's control over the various Nogay peoples and a realization that it was to Moscow's advantage to strengthen and promote one strong Kalmyk ruler who could curb his people's forays on the Russian frontier.

If the Russian government considered the document an oath of allegiance by the Kalmyks, Ayuki thought of it as an agreement between two allies. In fact, despite its numerous stipulations, the agreement was a clear victory for Ayuki. He needed Russia to help him eliminate his rivals, consolidate his power, secure markets in the Russian towns, and ensure the flow of Russian annuities and gifts. He achieved all of these goals. Most important, in contrast to previous similar documents, he secured the government's promise to return the unbaptized Kalmyk fugitives and recognition that numerous Nogay peoples were under his jurisdiction, not that of the Russian authorities in Astrakhan.

Ayuki assumed, reasonably enough, that his obligations under the alliance, such as providing military service and preventing the raiding of the Russian frontier, would be reciprocated by the Russians. He expected that the Russian tsar would be able to exercise control over the Don and Yayik cossacks and the Bashkirs, whom the tsar claimed as his subjects, and to stop their raids against the Kalmyk uluses. Ayuki also believed that Russian troops would assist him against his own enemies, just as he intended to assist Russia in its military campaigns. Events following the signing of the 1673 oath, however, unfolded differently than both parties expected.

The First Mutual Disillusions

The oath signed in 1673 was prompted by developments on the international scene. The Ukraine in the second half of the seventeenth century was torn apart by warring factions, among them clients of the Polish-Lithuanian Commonwealth, Russia, and the Ottoman empire, each trying to grab a larger piece of territory. In the spring of 1672, sizable Ottoman and Crimean armies invaded the Ukraine to support their ally the hetman Doroshenko in his struggle against the Commonwealth. The initial successes and rapid advances of the Ottomans and Crimeans caused Moscow to fear for the safety of Kiev and the part of the Ukraine controlled by Russia. It was clear to the Russian government that if the Commonwealth were defeated in this war, Russia would have to face the Ottomans and Crimeans alone. Moscow thus sided with the Commonwealth against the Ottomans and mobilized its diplomatic resources to deploy all available military forces on the southern frontier. The Russian authorities then insisted on a new Kalmyk oath of allegiance in an attempt to secure the Kalmyks' participation in the war on Russia's side.

Moscow assigned a significant role to the Kalmyks in its military operations on the southern frontier. The Kalmyk cavalry, with its ability to strike with lightning speed, was invaluable in military operations against the Crimean Tatars and could be used in two different ways. One involved direct confrontations on the battlefield.[20] Another could be characterized as preventive tactics and was concordant with the strategies of nomadic warfare. While the enemy's army was engaged elsewhere, the Kalmyks would launch a raid on the defenseless enemy homeland and its inhabitants, thus forcing the enemy's cavalry to abandon its military campaign and rush back home. Often the mere threat of such raids would stop the Crimean khan from waging war outside the Crimea.[21]

In his 1673 oath Ayuki promised to undertake military campaigns against the Kumyks and the Crimeans in the approaching spring-summer season. Indeed, in August Ayuki and Prince Kaspulat Cherkasskii had marched against the Kumyk Prince Chapolov (Chepolov) and the Nogay Kara-Kasay mirza. Ayuki badly defeated the Kumyks and Nogays and drove off their herds. At the same time he dispatched ten thousand Kalmyks with fifty Kabardinian *uzden'* of Prince Kaspulat Cherkasskii against the Crimean Tatars, while five thousand Kalmyks led by Mazan Batur were sent to join the Russian army of *voevoda* Ivan Khitrovo on the Don.[22] Later, Mazan Batur's military unit tried unsuccessfully to storm the Ottoman fortress of Azov.[23]

---

[20]In 1674 hetman Samoilovich informed the tsar of the Crimeans' intention to march on Kiev and requested the assistance of Russian and Kalmyk troops (*AIuZR* 11:no. 187). Prince Romodanovskii requested their participation in the Crimean campaign of 1675 (*PSZ* 1:1017, no. 614).

[21]When in 1674 the Crimean khan Selim Giray I was urged by the Ottoman sultan to march with his army to aid hetman Doroshenko, the khan replied that he could not do so because of the danger from the Kalmyks and the Zaporozhian cossacks, who would pillage the Crimea during his absence (*AIuZR* 11:405, no. 119). In 1675 Prince Kaspulat Cherkasskii, with the Kalmyks of Ayuki and Solom-Seren, undertook several successful raids against the Crimea, forcing the Ottoman sultan to send some of his troops to assist Selim Giray I instead of concentrating them on the battlefield against the Commonwealth (*PDS* 5:259).

[22]*Kabardino-russkie otnosheniia,* 1:339–40, no. 216.

[23]Solov'ev, *Istoriia Rossii,* bk. 6, vol. 12:457.

When military operations resumed the following year, the Russian government dispatched Prince Kaspulat Cherkasskii to convince Ayuki to march against the Crimeans and the Ottomans. Ayuki declined to participate in the campaign but promised to send in his stead Solom-Seren, a Derbet tayishi who had recently arrived from Jungaria with four thousand tents.[24] In the end, Ayuki chose to place a detachment of seven thousand Kalmyks under the command of Prince Kaspulat Cherkasskii, with orders to raid the Crimean and the Azov Tatars. The military unit, led by Prince Kaspulat Cherkasskii, consisted of five thousand Kalmyks and three thousand Don cossacks, as well as some Russian troops and the Kabardinian nobles. This force set off toward Azov while the remaining two thousand Kalmyks were sent to Perekop (Or-Kapi in Ottoman Turkish).[25]

In the years after the signing of the oath, the number of Kalmyks participating in military campaigns diminished steadily. In contrast to the large cavalry detachments which Ayuki sent during 1673–74, in the following years only small Kalmyk units of several hundred horsemen were reported to have been engaged in combat in various parts of the region. These Kalmyk units fought together with the Zaporozhian and Don cossacks against the Crimean and Azov Tatars, and they joined Prince Kaspulat Cherkasskii against various rival groups on the Terek. The larger Kalmyk units, which were supposed to join the allies, were often reported to have not reached their destination or to have turned back on the eve of battle.[26]

The Russian government interpreted the withdrawal of Kalmyk military assistance as a violation of the oath and ascribed it to the treacherous behavior of its unreliable subjects. While the Russians blamed the Kalmyks for violations, the Kalmyks believed that it was the Russians who were not living up to their part of the agreement. Similarly to the Kalmyks' preying on the Crimea in the absence of the Crimean armies, the seminomadic Bashkirs of the uppermost northern reaches of the Caspian steppes too preyed on the Kalmyks while the latter were waging war elsewhere. During one year, 1675, Ayuki sent two embassies to Moscow to complain about the forays of the Bashkirs and the Don cossacks.[27] When in the same year Ayuki was asked to send the Kalmyks against the Crimean Tatars, he refused to do so on the grounds that he

[24]*Kabardino-russkie otnosheniia,* 1:337, no. 214; Bakunin, "Opisanie," *Krasnyi arkhiv* 3 (1939): 197.

[25]*Kabardino-russkie otnosheniia,* 1:342, no. 217.

[26]*PSZ* 1:1017, no. 614.

[27]*Ocherki istorii Kalmytskoi,* 1:140.

feared the Bashkirs' raids on the Kalmyk uluses.[28] The Kalmyks perceived the continuous raids against them as a failure on the part of Russia to control its subjects, the Bashkirs and the Don cossacks. Ayuki kept his promise and sent the Kalmyk cavalry to assist the Russians, yet Russia could not even protect Ayuki from its own subjects. In Ayuki's view, Moscow had clearly violated the accord.

There were additional reasons for Ayuki's unhappiness with his Russian ally. Although the Russian government had promised to pay annuities to the Kalmyk tayishis and to reward the Kalmyks who participated in the military campaigns, payments were typically delayed, and the increased number of tayishis (owing to recent arrivals from Jungaria) required even larger annuities. Moreover, the rewards received by the Kalmyks were significantly smaller than those given to other groups. For instance, Prince Kaspulat Cherkasskii and his Kabardinian nobles received substantial compensation in furs, hats, silk, and cash after each successful raid, whereas on only one occasion, after the 1675 Crimean campaign, did the Kalmyks receive hats and woolen cloth. Likewise, after successful operations near Azov in 1673, the Don cossacks received 3,000 rubles, 4,200 *chetvert'* of grain, 200 *polovinka* of woolen cloth, 200 *poods* of gunpowder, and 100 *poods* of lead; the Kalmyks received only 300 *vedro* of wine.[29] The same year, the Russian government promised to supply the Zaporozhian cossacks with guns, grenades, and gunners in recognition of their faithful service near Ochakov, yet the Kalmyks were still on the list of the peoples banned from obtaining any firearms.[30]

Such a striking difference in the attitude of the Russian government toward the Kalmyks compared with the cossacks and the Kabardinians should be seen in the context of Moscow's traditional policies toward its Christian and non-Christian subjects. In Moscow's view, the Christian cossacks and the converted Kabardinians were trustworthy, and their loyalty was rewarded in many different ways. But Russia's Muslim subjects could not be trusted and were thus treated differently. The Buddhist Kalmyks, regarded as idol worshipers, were treated in a particularly disparaging fashion.

The alliance with a Russia unable to provide adequate protection and

[28]*Kabardino-russkie otnosheniia,* 1:422, note to no. 392. The fear of raids was mutual. When Russian officials asked the Bashkirs to participate in the Crimean campaign, the Bashkirs replied that if they did so, the Kalmyks of Ayuki would pillage their families, and if they were forced to go, they would rather take their wives and children than leave them alone (*Materialy po istorii Bashkirskoi,* vol. 1: *Bashkirskie vosstania v 17 i pervoi polovine 18 vekov* [Moscow and Leningrad: Izd-vo AN SSSR, 1936], 204–5, no. 71).

[29]*AVD* 1:81, no. 51.

[30]*PSZ* 1:943, no. 557; *DAI* 6:375, no. 126.

to deliver regular and satisfactory annuities and rewards fell short of the expectations of the Kalmyk tayishis. To them, the failure of one party to fulfill its obligations automatically abrogated the agreement. At this point, the Crimean khan's overtures for peace were taken more seriously, and his frequent gift-laden embassies to the Kalmyks made the Crimean offers all the more appealing. The Crimean khan also exercised his influence through his confidants among the Kalmyks, who acted as a kind of a Crimean lobby. A 1676 report by the Zaporozhian cossacks provides a particularly curious insight into the life of the Kalmyk ulus and serves as a clear illustration of the loose political organization of Kalmyk society: "The khan has among them [the Kalmyks] his loyal friend Yusup mirza, who long ago joined the Kalmyks with several thousand of his people, and who lives among them and writes to the khan about everything, and often convinces the Kalmyks to give up their military campaigns; and for this purpose the khan sends him presents every year."[31] The lavish gifts brought from the Crimea were intended to curb the military activity of the Kalmyks in the areas of the Crimea and the Caucasus. For some time the Crimean "gift diplomacy" achieved its goal and caused the Kalmyk raids to shift northward against the Bashkirs and Russian towns.[32]

The 1677 Treaty

On the eve of the renewed military campaign against the Ottomans and the Crimeans in 1677, the Russian government decided to strengthen its relationship with the Kalmyks and ensure their participation in the war on Russia's side. As always, Moscow insisted on an oath of allegiance. Moscow's official motive was to urge the Kalmyks to reaffirm their commitment to the newly enthroned Tsar Feodor Alekseevich.

The oath was signed near Astrakhan on January 15, 1677. It contained several new clauses which reflected the events of the past years and indicated changes in the government's attitude toward the Kalmyks. This time the oath was signed not solely by Ayuki but also by his brother Zamsa (Jamso) tayishi and by Solom-Seren tayishi. By extending responsibility beyond the chief tayishi the government might have been searching for a new way to ensure the loyalty of the Kalmyks.

---

[31]*AluZR* 12:555, no. 156.

[32]Small groups of Kalmyks and Tatars (twenty to one hundred horsemen) were frequently reported to raid small Russian frontier towns and settlements (D. I. Bagalei, *Ocherki iz istorii kolonizatsii stepnoi okrainy Moskovskogo gosudarstva* [Moscow: Imp. ob-vo istorii i drevnostei pri Moskovskom univ., 1887], 257).

To emphasize the submissive status of the Kalmyks, the Russian government attached a new clause to the 1677 oath: "And I, Ayuki tayishi, must receive the decrees of the Grand Sovereign, rising to my feet and taking off my hat, with great respect."[33] The oath also specifically spelled out the Kalmyks' obligations. As before, the Kalmyks were expected to refrain from relations with Russia's adversaries. One clause, however, stipulated in no uncertain terms that any envoys or letters from the Crimea sent to the Kalmyk tayishis must be reported to the Russian tsar. Another clause stated explicitly that the Kalmyk tayishis had to return all the goods their people had pillaged in the years 1675 and 1676, when they had violated their previous oath.

In the oath of 1673, Russian authorities had promised to return unbaptized Kalmyk fugitives. A similar clause in the new oath stated: "And if some of the Kalmyks are baptized by their own will . . . do not petition the Grand Sovereign concerning their return."[34] This marked the beginning of the gradual and persistent efforts of the Russian Orthodox church and the government to convert the "idolatrous" Kalmyks. The new policy of the Russian government eventually had a disastrous effect on Kalmyk society, for the protection offered to the converts induced more Kalmyks to flee to Russian towns and seek conversion.

The new oath stipulated the precise annual payment to Ayuki and other tayishis: 590 rubles in cash. If other tayishis came with their people to join Ayuki, they had to share the same 590 rubles. The number of Kalmyks was constantly increasing because of the influx of Oirats from Jungaria.[35] Ayuki's previous requests that his annuity be increased were perhaps induced by his having to share with the increased number of tayishis. The Russian government decided, nevertheless, that the payments were to remain the same.

The oath of 1677 aimed to reaffirm the Kalmyks' commitments and to ensure their loyalty and military assistance on the eve of the war with the Ottoman empire. Certain clauses of the oath clearly illustrate an attempt to tighten Russia's political control over the Kalmyks. As in previous oaths, the questions of foreign relations and payments remained potential areas of discontent.

---

[33]*PSZ* 2:82, no. 672.

[34]Ibid., 84.

[35]In the period between 1673 and 1677 Ayuki was joined by tayishis Dayan-Ombo (Doyan), Seren, Dol, Bausey, and Ayuki, the son of Sharab. In 1676 Ayuki's sister Dorji-Rabtan (Araptan) arrived with ten thousand tents from Jungaria to join Ayuki ("Istoriia kalmytskikh khanov," 63–64). According to Bakunin, Dorji-Rabtan arrived in 1670 (Bakunin, "Opisanie," *Krasnyi arkhiv* 3 [1939]: 195).

The Role of the Kalmyks in Russo-Ottoman Encounters, 1677–1683

The Russian government was preparing for a direct confrontation with the Ottoman empire. Moscow's strategic plans included the use of the Kalmyks, as well as the Zaporozhian and Don cossacks, all of whom were to serve as a counterforce against the Crimean Tatars. But the efficient use and organization of these allied forces was complicated by Moscow's doubt as to their loyalty. The numerous cossack uprisings and the unreliability of the Kalmyks had taught the Russian government to use caution and to try to keep apart those whom it perceived to be undutiful subjects. The Russian government always insisted that communications between the Zaporozhian and Don cossacks and the Kalmyks were to be conducted through Moscow.[36] Even though such a centralized arrangement made communications less efficient, it gave the authorities better leverage in exercising political control over the cossacks and the Kalmyks and a more efficient means for influencing these different groups for Russia's political ends.

The disloyalty manifested by its subjects was a matter of constant concern to the Russian government. Despite a recent Kalmyk pledge, Moscow was suspicious of the Kalmyks' relations with the Crimea.[37] This overwhelming misgiving on the part of the Russian government was not mere paranoia. Moscow always feared a possible alliance of its unruly Muslim subjects under Crimean and Ottoman auspices. Given the history of Russia's experiences in this area, the very possibility of such an alliance presented a sufficient threat to occupy permanently the minds of the Russian officials. In Moscow's view, the Buddhist Kalmyks in their continued relations with Jungaria and Tibet, as well as the Crimea, were as unreliable as the Muslim peoples.

---

[36]When, on the occasion of the 1675 campaign aganst the Crimea, the Zaporozhian ataman Sirko (Serko) requested that the tsar send him twenty thousand Zaporozhian cossacks under hetman Samoilovich, as well as the Don cossacks and Ayuki's Kalmyks, the tsar replied that the regiment of hetman Samoilovich would join the Russian army of the boyar Romodanovskii; Prince Kaspulat Cherkasskii with the Kalmyks would march against the Crimea; and ataman Sirko would also fight the Crimeans but with his own troops (*AIuZR* 12:102–3, no. 34).

[37]It ordered that a fugitive interpreter sent from the Crimea to the Zaporozhian cossacks be interrogated concerning the intentions of the enemy as well as those of the Kalmyks (ibid., 13:95, no. 21). It had similar concerns about other peoples. Thus Grigorii Ziz'ev, a Kazan musketeer who lived among the Yurt Tatars near Astrakhan, was ordered to keep an eye on them and to find out whether they were in communication with the Crimea, the Kuban Nogays, or the Kalmyks (*DAI* 7:270, no. 52).

Its suspicion and distrust notwithstanding, the Russian government was eager to enlist the Kalmyks in the war against the Ottoman empire and the Crimea. Its attempts to mobilize significant Kalmyk forces during the campaign of 1677 failed, however. A small Kalmyk unit arrived too late at the Ukrainian town of Chigirin, after the Ottoman armies had retreated in August 1677. Instead of providing military help, the Kalmyks caused great damage and laid many areas to waste.

Despite the discouraging reports concerning the Kalmyk cavalry, Russian requests for Kalmyk participation persisted. One account clearly indicates that the Kalmyks were not always entirely to blame for such behavior. The Ukrainian hetman Samoilovich repeatedly requested Kalmyk assistance. A few months after the unhappy experience with the Kalmyks in the summer of 1677, the hetman wrote to the tsar and explained that he nevertheless needed the Kalmyks again. But this time, he insisted that the tsar notify the Kalmyks in sufficient time for them to set out before the spring overflowing of the rivers. On the previous occasion, the Kalmyks had been sent without guides and had ravaged Ukrainian towns because the residents refused them food and drink. To prevent a recurrence of this behavior, the hetman suggested that guides be sent to the Kalmyks from the towns on the way and that food and drink be supplied by the local inhabitants.[38] Clearly, the traditional image of the "savage Kalmyk" was sometimes a function of the inefficiency of the Russian bureaucracy and the poor organization of the campaigns.

In early 1678 the Russian government again tried to convince the Kalmyks to assist the Russian and Ukrainian armies. Ayuki responded that he could not participate in the campaign because of continuous depredations suffered by his people at the hands of the Don and Yayik cossacks.[39] Indeed, there are numerous reports of mutual forays by small groups of Don cossacks, Kalmyks, and Yayik cossacks in the years 1677–78. In a conciliatory gesture, the tsar issued a decree to the cossack towns on the Don, ordering them to stop fighting the Kalmyks and to live with them in peace because the Kalmyks were the tsar's subjects.[40] To reinforce his decree, the tsar ordered 110 musketeers from Astrakhan to go up the Volga River to Chernyi Iar and Tsaritsyn to turn back those Don cossacks who attempted to cross the Volga bent on raiding the Kalmyk uluses.[41] Once again the authorities decided to use Prince Kaspulat Cherkasskii as an intermediary, this time between the Kalmyks and the

[38]AIuZR 13:403, no. 93.
[39]DAI 7:no. 47 (XX).
[40]AVD 1:97–98, no. 61.
[41]DAI 7:no. 47 (XII).

Don cossacks. In 1678 he was dispatched to the Kalmyks in an effort to reconcile the two parties.[42]

To make its case more persuasive, the government sent the Kalmyk tayishis annuities and gifts. In February 1678 *stol'nik* K. P. Kozlov came from Tsaritsyn to Astrakhan to distribute remuneration to Ayuki and Solom-Seren tayishis, who were roaming in the steppes eighty versts from Astrakhan. At the same time the tsar ordered Prince Kaspulat Cherkasskii, Ayuki, and Solom-Seren to join the army in the Ukraine and stipulated that seven *poods* of tobacco be given to the Kalmyks.[43]

In another decree of the same year the tsar ruled that the Kalmyks could fish without any restrictions in the areas of their pastures.[44] Fishing spots on the Volga were the sites of frequent clashes between Kalmyks and Russians. In previous years the government had always protected the exclusive rights of the Russian fishermen. The decision to allow the Kalmyks to fish was yet another measure aimed at winning their favor and ensuring their participation in military campaigns.

This time the efforts proved to be at least partially successful. Ayuki refused to go himself, but he put together a group of horsemen for the *stol'nik* K. P. Kozlov. This group later joined the regiment of the Russian commander in the Ukraine, the boyar Prince G. G. Romodanovskii.[45] Ayuki also placed a Kalmyk detachment at the disposal of Prince Kaspulat Cherkasskii. Cherkasskii's forces consisted of Kabardinians, Kumyks, Nogays, Yedisans, Astrakhan Yurt Tatars, and the Kalmyks of Ayuki and Solom-Seren.[46] In July 1678, a force of 3,800 horsemen under the command of Prince Kaspulat Cherkasskii passed Chuguev en route to Khar'kov and fought near Chigirin in the summer campaign. His detachment was stationed in outposts near Chuguev and Khar'kov until it was disbanded in August 1679.[47]

In a 1678 letter to the tsar, hetman Samoilovich reported his disappointment with the Kalmyks' performance near Chigirin: they had pro-

---

[42]*Putevoditel' po arkhivu Leningradskogo otdeleniia Instituta istorii,* comp. I. L. Valkin (Leningrad: AN SSSR, 1958), 26, Astrakhanskaia prikaznaia palata (f. 178).

[43]*DAI* 8:2–3, nos. 1–2; "Zapisnaia kniga Moskovskogo stola, 1678–79 gg.," *RIB* 11 (1889): 406–7.

[44]*Putevoditel' po arkhivu,* 28, Astrakhanskaia prikaznaia palata (f. 178).

[45]"Spisok saratovskikh i tsaritsynskikh voevod 17 veka," comp. A. A. Geraklitov, *Trudy Saratovskoi uchenoi komissii* 30 (1913): 76.

[46]Mehmed Aga Findiklili mentioned the Kalmyks among forty-four different ethnic and military groups that fought on Russia's side (Findiklili, *Silahdar Tarikhi,* 1:709).

[47]*AIuZR* 13:no. 138; *Kabardino-russkie otnosheniia,* 362–63, nos. 234, 240, 242. According to Bakunin, Ayuki sent three thousand Kalmyks in combat at Chigirin (Bakunin, "Opisanie," *Krasnyi arkhiv* 3 [1939]: 197); Defterdar Mehmed Pasha, *Defterdar Mehmed Pasha Tarikhi,* SK Halet Efendi ilâvesi 189, 100b.

vided him with little help, and following the Ottoman attack they had turned back and left for their homes.[48] Nevertheless, a year later the hetman asked the tsar to order Prince Kaspulat Cherkasskii, together with Ayuki and Solom-Seren, to march to the Ukraine.[49] The persistent requests for the participation of Ayuki or Solom-Seren are understandable, for they would involve significant Kalmyk forces. But the very presence of the Kalmyks in the area was important for hetman Samoilovich. According to reports by spies, even if slightly exaggerated, the Crimean Tatars greatly feared the Kalmyks and fled whenever they learned of their approach.[50]

In the following years, from 1680 to 1683, the anti-Russian feelings of the Kalmyk tayishis became more apparent. There were frequent reports that Ayuki maintained lively relations with the Crimean khan, the pasha of Azov, and the Bashkirs. As early as 1679 the Russian government learned that Ayuki had sent twelve envoys to the pasha of Azov, who then sent them to the Crimean khan Murad Giray I. The envoys related Ayuki's promise to place at the khan's disposal two thousand horsemen for the spring campaign.[51] This was perhaps the same embassy that in August 1680 arrived at the Porte—the first known instance of a Kalmyk embassy to the Ottoman sultan. Turkish records do not reveal the purpose of this Kalmyk embassy, but an early eighteenth-century Ukrainian chronicler and a scribe of the Zaporozhian cossacks, Samiilo Velychko, claimed that the Kalmyks had requested Ottoman protection and pastures east of the Dnieper. On the way home the Kalmyk embassy again stopped in the Crimea, where it was seen by the Russian envoys.[52]

Ayuki's anti-Russian stance in the years 1680–83 cannot be explained solely by the intrigues and the lavish gifts of the Crimean khan. In the past the Crimean khan had continuously attempted to win the Kalmyks over and had sent numerous gifts to the Kalmyk tayishis, a policy that only now was beginning to bear fruit. There were other reasons for Ayuki to reverse his pro-Russian policies. Naturally, Russian records, written in stilted bureaucratic language (intended, more often than not, to please the tsar rather than to report the actual state of affairs), did not register

---

[48]*AIuZR* 13:688, no. 156.

[49]*Kabardino-russkie otnosheniia,* 366, no. 237.

[50]*AIuZR* 13:nos. 34, 50, 116.

[51]*AVD* 1:103, no. 65; *DAI* 8:283–85, no. 77.

[52]The embassy was given an allowance of five hundred *akches* a day, a total of twenty-five hundred *akches* for five days—a modest sum in the Ottoman empire of the late seventeenth century (BA *Ibn ül-Emin Tasnifi, Kharijiye,* no. 30); Samiilo Velychko, *Letopis' sobytii v iugo-zapadnoi Rossii v 17 veke,* 4 vols. (Kiev: Lito-Tip. Iosifa Val'nera, 1848–64), 2:501; "Spisok so stateinogo spiska Velikogo Gosudaria poslannikov: stol'nika V. M. Tiapkina, d'iaka Nikity Zotova k krymskomu khanu Murad-Gireiu v 1681 godu," *ZIOOID* 2 (1850): 608.

any Kalmyk grievances against the Russians. But the expectations and attitude of the Kalmyk tayishis compared with specific Russian policies reveal sensitive issues that probably caused Kalmyk discontent.

Some of the traditional points of contention emerged again in the late 1670s: the cossack raids, which the Russian authorities were not always able to stop, continued to cause great damage to the Kalmyks, and in the period from 1679 to 1682 no payments were received by the Kalmyk tayishis. The Russian treasury was empty as a result of costly wars. The renewed truce with the Polish-Lithuanian Commonwealth and the truce with the Ottoman empire had been signed at great expense. To retain control of Kiev alone, Moscow agreed to pay the Commonwealth two hundred thousand rubles.[53] Yet, despite its financial difficulties, the government found the means to reward Prince Kaspulat Cherkasskii lavishly for his service at Chigirin; the Kalmyk tayishis received no part of this award even though Cherkasskii's forces consisted largely of Ayuki's and Solom-Seren's Kalmyks and Nogays. At the same time the Don cossacks were receiving their payments and rewards, usually much more substantial than those obtained by the Kalmyks.[54]

The distribution of grain and many other commodities was regulated by Moscow so that any item of economic significance was a potential tool of political pressure. Unlike the cossacks, the Kalmyks did not receive any payments in grain. Nor could their limited demand for grain be satisfied by trade because the Russian authorities ordered the Astrakhan Yurt Tatars not to sell or barter grain to the Kalmyks so as not to cause a shortage in the Astrakhan province and thereby inflate prices.[55]

Over the course of many years the Russian authorities had been agitating among numerous Nogay, Yedisan, and other Turkic tribes that roamed with Ayuki in an attempt to convince them to abandon the Kalmyks and to roam in the vicinity of Astrakhan. Using the Yurt Tatars as intermediaries, the authorities promised protection to the leaders of the tribes, hoping that in return the presence of these nomads would better safeguard Astrakhan from hostile raids. Previous experience had also taught that these nomads would shortly grow dependent on Astrakhan, settle down, and become as meek and harmless as the Yurt Tatars. In 1678, several Nogay mirzas with their people left the Kalmyks and came to settle near Astrakhan.[56]

---

[53]Solov'ev, *Istoriia Rossii*, bk. 7, vol. 13:222.

[54]The usual annual payment to the Don cossacks in the late seventeenth century consisted of three thousand rubles, woolens, ammunition, grain, and wine, as well as tangible rewards for each military campaign. See details in *DAI* 10:211–13, no. 60 (III).

[55]*DAI* 7:268, no. 52.

[56]*DAI* 8:no. 7.

Ayuki regarded such actions by the Russian government as openly hostile. In nomadic societies a conquered tribe, if not closely related to the tribe of the conquerors, usually retained its separate identity and functioned as an autonomous economic and political entity. A conquered people was expected to participate in the Kalmyks' military expeditions and pay a tax.[57] The loss of such people damaged Ayuki's power and prestige. He saw such Russian policies as directed against his interests and incompatible with his status as an ally.

In his campaigns against Russia and in his effort to create an anti-Russian coalition, Ayuki showed more zeal than in his collaboration with Russia. In 1680, one thousand Kalmyks, Azov Tatars, and Nogays marched up the Don to ravage the settlements of the Don cossacks. Later that same year, the Crimean Tatars, the Azov Tatars, and the Kalmyks—three thousand horsemen altogether—looted the Russian town of Penza.[58]

On January 2, 1681, another embassy from the Crimea arrived at Ayuki's ulus. The Crimean embassy offered sumptuous gifts to Ayuki and Solom-Seren and tried to convince them to march with the Crimeans against the Ukrainian towns.[59] Upon learning this, the Russian government promptly dispatched Prince Kaspulat Cherkasskii to the Kalmyks. Shortly thereafter, Prince Cherkasskii reported to the tsar that he had conducted secret negotiations with Ayuki and succeeded in convincing him to resist being tempted by the gifts of the Crimean khan and instead to serve the Russian tsar faithfully.[60]

Instead, in summer 1682, Ayuki waged an outright war against Russia. The moment could not have been more opportune. In Moscow the government was preoccupied with an uprising of infantry soldiers and musketeers, and in the Volga provinces the natives—the Bashkirs, the Maris, and the Chuvashs—had rebelled against Russian domination. According to Russian sources based on Bashkir reports, Ayuki mustered an army of forty thousand Kalmyk, Nogay, Yedisan, and Kabardinian horsemen armed with three cannons and four thousand muskets.[61] The figure of forty thousand seems to be exaggerated, but it does indicate that

---

[57]The Yedisans among the Kalmyks were taxed a measure of cloth (kumach) from each household (Bakunin, "Opisanie," Krasnyi arkhiv 3 [1939]: 195).

[58]DAI 8:286, no. 77; Vel'iaminov-Zernov, Materialy dlia istorii Krymskogo, 650, no. 251; Ocherki istorii Kalmytskoi, 1:141.

[59]Ocherki istorii Kalmytskoi, 1:141; AVD 1:106, no. 67.

[60]Kabardino-russkie otnosheniia, 376, no. 246.

[61]AI 5:138, no. 87 (V); DAI 10:69, no. 25 (I); I. G. Akhmanov, Bashkirskie vosstaniia 17-pervoi treti 18 vekov (Ufa: BGU, 1978), 49. The most comprehensive discussion of the middle Volga region is in Andreas Kappeler, Russlands Erste Nationalitäten. Das Zarenreich und die Völker der Mittleren Wolga vom 16. bis 19. Jahrhundert (Cologne and Vienna: Böhlau Verlag, 1982).

Ayuki managed to assemble a sizable army for his venture. Ayuki's army entered Kazan and Ufa provinces and was joined by many rebellious Bashkirs. Those who had entered into alliance with Russia were taken captive or killed, and the entire area from Kazan to Ufa was reported to have been ravaged.[62] Continuous Kalmyk raids along the Volga in 1681–83 seriously disrupted communications between the towns of Tsaritsyn and Astrakhan.[63]

The Russian government responded by ordering the Don cossacks to set out against the Kalmyks. The cossacks stated that they would be happy to do so but that their ability to act was limited. If the Kalmyks moved to distant parts of the steppe, the cossacks would not be able to reach them because of the lack of water. But if in autumn the Kalmyks came closer to the Volga, the cossacks would prey on them.[64]

At the same time that Moscow was planning to unleash the Don cossacks against the Kalmyks, it also attempted to divide the Kalmyks and the Bashkirs. The authorities called upon the Bashkirs, the Maris, and the Chuvashs to abandon Ayuki and join the Russian troops.[65] By the end of 1682 Russian troops had succeeded in crushing the main forces of the insurgent Bashkirs, and many of them abandoned Ayuki and returned to their old pastures near Ufa. Ayuki then sent six hundred horsemen to besiege the small Russian town of Krasnyi Iar, situated not far from Saratov, and to find out whether the Russians were willing to have peace again. If his peace offer was rejected, Ayuki threatened to plunder the towns on the Volga.[66] The Russian government was eager to negotiate peace, and although Ayuki's offer looked more like an ultimatum, a new document resulted from the truce, defined in Russian parlance as an oath of allegiance.

On January 24, 1683, Ayuki, Solom-Seren, and Zamsa tayishis signed the oath in the presence of the boyar, *voevoda* Prince Andrei Golitsyn. The new document differed from the one of 1677 only in one paragraph, which mentioned the Bashkir revolt. In this paragraph Ayuki recognized that he and other tayishis had violated the previous pledge by raiding the Kazan and Ufa provinces, assisting the rebellious Bashkirs, pillaging Ukrainian towns and villages, and capturing Russians, Bashkirs, and Maris. Ayuki promised to return the captives and not to violate the oath again.[67]

The new oath did not have much effect on Kalmyk-Russian relations,

[62]*DAI* 10:70, no. 25 (I); *Materialy po istorii Bashkirskoi*, 1:210, no. 76.
[63]Bakunin, "Opisanie," *Krasnyi arkhiv* 3 (1939): 197.
[64]*DAI* 10:no. 26.
[65]*Ocherki istorii Kalmytskoi*, 1:142.
[66]*DAI* 10:155, no. 49.
[67]*PSZ* 2:496, no. 990.

which continued to totter on the brink of a direct confrontation for several more years until new political winds changed the direction of the Kalmyk arrows.

The Anti-Russian Policies of Ayuki Khan, 1683–1697

Despite the recent oath, Ayuki's Kalmyks resumed their raids on the Russian towns a few months later, in the spring of 1683. They looted Bashkir settlements, Russian towns on the Volga, and cossack settlements on the Don. The Russian government encouraged the Don cossacks to launch attacks against the Kalmyks, and numerous skirmishes between the Kalmyks and the cossacks ensued.[68]

A year later, when the Bashkir uprising had been suppressed, Ayuki signed another oath in the presence of Prince Andrei Golitsyn.[69] After the signing, the government ordered the Don cossacks to stop raiding the Kalmyk uluses because the Kalmyks were loyal subjects again.[70] The loyalty the Russian government expected from the Kalmyks would remain a matter of doubt for many years to come, but Ayuki did modify his policies to some extent.

At the beginning of 1685 Ayuki sent his envoy to the Don cossacks and suggested that they join him in his campaign against the khan of Khiva (Dar'inskii khan). Ayuki explained that he was organizing this campaign because "in previous years the khan of Khiva paid tribute to Ayuki, but now has ceased to do so, and does not allow people from the Kalmyk uluses to trade in Khiva."[71] According to Ayuki's scheme, the Don cossacks were to go down the Volga to the Caspian by boat, then by sea to the Yayik River, and by horse from the Yayik to the Amu-Darya, to the khanate of Khiva. The ataman of the Don cossacks, Frol Minaev, requested Moscow's permission to join the Kalmyks. Such permission was denied on the grounds that Ayuki was undertaking this expedition of his own free will and had not petitioned Moscow regarding it. The failure to enlist the Don cossacks for the Turkestan campaign did not immediately discourage Ayuki. The following year he sent twice to *voevoda* I. F. Volynskii to find out whether he would dispatch Russian musketeers to assist him against Turkestan.[72]

[68]*AVD* 1:nos. 73, 75.

[69]I. I. Iorish, *Materialy o mongolakh, kalmykakh i buriatakh v arkhivakh Leningrada. Istoriia, pravo, ekonomika* (Moscow: Nauka, 1966), 135, no. 420; Bakunin, "Opisanie," *Krasnyi arkhiv* 3 (1939): 198.

[70]*DAI* 11:134, no. 45.

[71]Ibid., 264, no. 99; *AVD* 1:122–23, no. 79.

[72]Ibid.; Iorish, *Materialy o mongolakh, kalmykakh i buriatakh*, 137, no. 426.

In the same years, 1683–84, the Oirat Galdan Boshoktu Khan undertook successful campaigns against western Turkestan and the Kazakhs.[73] The arguments between Ayuki and Galdan over the Oirats who had left Jungaria and joined Ayuki did not turn into open hostility, and such action may have been coordinated, although there is no evidence to confirm such an assumption. It is more likely, however, that both saw this as an opportune time to raid the wealthy provinces of Turkestan. Weakened by internal wars among the various khanates and the restless Karakalpak, Uzbek, and Kazakh tribes, Turkestan presented an attractive target, as Kalmyk intelligence sources were quick to report. But Ayuki received no military support from the Russians or cossacks and could not launch a large-scale military campaign on his own against distant and well-fortified Khiva. He had to wait for a more favorable opportunity.

Meanwhile, the possibility of obtaining abundant booty appeared elsewhere on the horizon. In 1684–86 the Kalmyks found themselves subject to the intrigues of Jan III Sobieski. The Polish king hoped to enlist the Kalmyks and the Zaporozhian and Don cossacks in his war with the Ottoman empire. At the beginning of 1684 he sent his envoys with a letter to Ayuki, inviting him to become a subject of the Polish crown and assuring him that the lands between the Bug and the Dnieper would be given to the Kalmyks for pastures. Should the Kalmyks refuse the offer but were willing to dispatch their horsemen, the king promised to reward them generously.[74]

The king's message came a little too late. Shortly before, in 1683, envoys from the Ottoman sultan and the Crimean khan arrived at the Kalmyk uluses intent on convincing them to set out against the Commonwealth.[75] Perhaps it was for this reason that Jan Sobieski made such an extraordinary offer in an attempt to swing the Kalmyks to his favor.

When the news of the efforts of the Polish king to enlist the cossacks and the Kalmyks reached Moscow, the Russian government immediately sent decrees to the Don cossacks and the Kalmyks ordering them "to take part in no war without the tsar's permission."[76] But the inducements of action and plentiful booty were more compelling than decrees from Moscow. In the two years since the signing of the truce between the Ottomans and Russians in 1681, the Don cossacks had submitted numerous petitions to Moscow requesting more money and supplies. They complained that now that the war was over, they found it difficult to live

---

[73]Kychanov, *Povestvovanie ob oiratskom*, 83.

[74]O. Makhatka, "Diplomaticheskaia deiatel'nost' 'Sviashchennoi ligi' sredi kazachestva i kalmykov v 1683–86 gg.," *Vestnik LGU, seriia istorii, iazyka i literatury* 14 (March 1958): 38; *DAI* 10:no. 103 (III).

[75]*DAI* 11:265, no. 99.

[76]Ibid., 175, no. 58.

within the constraints of the tsar's annual payments, which had not been increased.[77] These requests fell on deaf ears. The government forbade the cossacks to violate the truce by raiding Ottoman subjects and saw no reason to increase the cossacks' annuity. It is not surprising that the cossacks, like the Kalmyks heavily dependent on booty, were eager to serve anyone under the right circumstances. The Polish king, subsidized by the pope, offered generous rewards, and warfare offered the possibility of spoils. Several groups of Don cossacks and Kalmyks thereupon went to war on the Commonwealth's side.[78]

In March 1685, Jan Sobieski sent another embassy to the Kalmyks inviting them to take part in the spring campaign. The interests of the Polish crown did not coincide with those of the Russian state. Although Russia had signed truces with the Commonwealth in 1667 and the Ottoman empire in 1681, it had no firm peace treaty with either. Moscow had no intentions either of strengthening the Commonwealth at the expense of its own subjects or of provoking the Ottomans into a new war. In the worst possible scenario, a massive departure of cossacks and Kalmyks could expose Russia's southern frontier and make it extremely vulnerable to Tatar raids. Accordingly, in his diplomatic correspondence with the Polish king, the Russian tsar objected to the overtures of the Polish government to the cossacks and the Kalmyks and claimed that they violated the Andrusovo Treaty.[79]

At the same time, Moscow continued to try to persuade the cossacks and the Kalmyks not to assist the Polish king. The Russian government had learned that payments and gifts were more eloquent than words. The Don cossacks received the promise of substantially increased payments, and, at least for the next two years, these were delivered in full. A more permanent solution came later the same year, when Russia signed an "eternal peace" with the Polish-Lithuanian Commonwealth, joined the anti-Ottoman coalition, and enlisted the cossacks and the Kalmyks in the war against the Ottoman empire. According to Moscow's plans, the Kalmyks were to contribute twenty-four thousand horsemen to a large-scale campaign against the Crimea in the spring of 1687.[80] Moscow's expectations were not realized. In contrast to the cossacks, there is no suggestion that the Kalmyks had received any payments, just as there is no evidence of any participation by Kalmyk cavalry in this campaign.

For years the Kalmyks had maintained close ties with the Crimean

[77]AVD 1:no. 80.
[78]DAI 11:nos. 2, 11, 93 (III); AVD 1:no. 84.
[79]AVD 1:131, no. 86; DAI 11:no. 13; 12:no. 22 (IV).
[80]PDS 7:58–59.

khan, the *bey* of Azov, and the Nogays of the Kuban. Throughout the late 1680s and 1690s these relations became particularly active. In 1686 the ataman of the Don cossacks, Frol Minaev, complained that the Kalmyks had continued to maintain ties with Azov, where they drove their cattle for sale. He claimed that, had they not done so, the inhabitants of Azov would have abandoned the fortress long ago out of starvation. The tsar ruled that an order should be sent to Ayuki from the Kazan Chancellery to the effect that Ayuki should not drive cattle to Azov or the Crimea and that he should buy and sell whatever he needed in the Russian towns. Those of Ayuki's people who violated this decree and continued to do business with Azov or the Crimea would be captured and hanged and the merchandise and the earnings from this trade would be confiscated for the tsar's treasury.[81]

Treating the Kalmyks as it did the rest of its subjects, the Russian government made another unambiguous attempt to gain complete control over the Kalmyks' trading and diplomatic relations. The general tone of this decree was harsh and varied from insistence on following the oath of allegiance to naked intimidation. By threatening to hang those who violated this decree, the government intended to apply to the Kalmyks capital punishment as provided by Russian law. Throughout the years the Russian authorities gradually increased their demands on the Kalmyk tayishis to apply harsh measures to those Kalmyks who violated the oaths. In the 1673 and 1677 oaths the authorities insisted that the Kalmyk tayishis bring to ruin any Kalmyks who continued to raid Russian towns. In the oath of 1683 this insistence was replaced by an even stronger exhortation "to punish and ruin them without any excuses."[82] The decree of 1686 left no doubt that the Russian authorities had decided to exercise the full severity of Russian law and to apply capital punishment if necessary. The heaviest possible penalty under Kalmyk law, however, was limited to a large fine paid in cattle and arms. Such open and unequivocal interference with and disregard for the Kalmyk legal code could only further irritate Ayuki and inevitably made him seek closer ties with the Crimea and the Ottoman Porte.

Thenceforth until the end of the 1690s, the exchange of Kalmyk and Crimean embassies took place virtually every year. Ottoman records for 1686 state concisely that provisions were given to three Kalmyk embassies to the Porte. One Kalmyk envoy arrived in March and was given prayer beads made from coral—a symbolic present he was expected to bring back home. Another envoy came to the Porte in August. He was

[81]*DAI* 12:317–18, no. 33.
[82]*PSZ* 2:496, no. 990.

accompanied by a certain Mehmed-Aga and received 5,800 *akche* as a subsistence allowance. The provisions given to the third Kalmyk embassy were recorded in December of the same year. Kalmyk envoys arrived again in July of the following year.[83]

More information is available about the Kalmyk embassy that arrived at the Porte a year later, in July 1688.[84] The Kalmyk envoy brought a letter from Ayuki. The available Ottoman translation of this letter abounds with terms and expressions emphasizing the subject status of the Kalmyks in a style similar to Russian translations of Kalmyk letters. Just as the arrogance of the Russian state, imbued with the principles of Russian Orthodoxy, could not conceive of various neighboring peoples as other than Russia's subjects, so the supremacy of Islam in the Ottoman empire did not allow it to place itself on a par with non-Muslim peoples. The Kalmyk envoy was received together with the Uzbek envoy in the Audience Hall (Arz Odasi). While the Uzbeks' relationship to the Porte was characterized as one of brotherhood (*karindashlik*), the status of the Kalmyks was reaffirmed as one of servitude (*kullugunuzda*).[85]

In the letter delivered by the Kalmyk envoy, Ayuki stated that despite the differences in religion the Kalmyks were prepared to live in peace with all Muslim peoples and to provide service to the Ottoman sultan. Such was the written message; the rest of the communication was meant to be related orally by the envoy. A written response was given to the envoy by the Ottoman grand vizier. Curiously, the grand vizier addressed Ayuki as a commander in chief of the Kalmyk people (*umde-i umera-i tawa'if-i Kalmak*), not as a khan, as Ayuki referred to himself. The vizier's response does not appear to be overenthusiastic about the Kalmyks' offer but is rather reserved. It stated that Ayuki's letter expressing love and mutual friedship had been received and, God willing, the friendship between the Crimean khan and Ayuki would grow day by day.[86]

The restrained tone of the Ottoman response was perhaps caused by the Porte's disenchantment with the Kalmyks. It is possible that the gift of prayer beads, sent with the Kalmyk envoy two years before, had been a symbolic invitation to the Kalmyks to join the world of Islam and become Muslims. Ayuki's reply had been only an offer of peace "despite the differences in faith."

A similar attitude was displayed by the Crimean khan, who also treated the Kalmyks as a people outside the realm of Islam. The Kalmyk

[83]BA *Ibn ül-Emin Tasnifi, Kharijiye*, nos. 123, 117, 79, 55, 137.

[84]The envoy was given 7,000 *akches* upon his arrival at the end of July and in August an allowance in kind worth 4,160 *akches* (ibid., nos. 120, 155, 169).

[85]Findiklili, *Silahdar Tarikhi*, 2:419.

[86]BA *Nâme-i Hümayun*, no. 5, p. 59.

embassies en route to the Porte always passed through the Crimea. Embassies to the Porte were relatively infrequent, however, and the palace of the Crimean khan was the ultimate destination for most such Kalmyk embassies. In 1688 the Kalmyk envoy to the Porte made his first stop at the Crimea and informed khan Selim Giray I that if he desired military assistance, Ayuki would send him many horsemen. The khan replied that he was in no need of an army of foreigners (*bir gayri adamle askera ihtiyajimiz yok*). The Crimean khan too considered the Kalmyks to be his subjects and instructed them to affirm their loyalty by protecting the Crimean borders, for which service they would be rewarded.[87]

The Crimean khan placed little trust in Ayuki's promises. In the same year of 1688, when the Porte requested Crimean help in its war against the Hapsburgs, Selim Giray wrote to the Uzbek khan Subhan Kulu Mehmed asking him to assist the padishah in the war against his enemies. He explained that this assistance did not entail sending troops to the theater of war in the Balkans, but rather stopping the Kalmyks from launching a raid against the Crimea at a time when Crimean troops were off on campaign. This time, however, the Kalmyks did not attempt any such raid.[88]

By the end of the 1680s Ayuki's power was based not only on his prestige, personal qualities, and political status but also on the significant amount of material wealth he had managed to accumulate over the years. In August 1688 a herd of six thousand horses belonging to Ayuki was driven to Moscow for sale. In contrast, the Kalmyk Chagan Batur tayishi was able to send only four hundred horses.[89] These appear to be the largest known parties of horses driven to Moscow by the Kalmyks. From this time on, the authorities preferred that the Kalmyks sell their horses in the Volga towns, or else the Russians dispatched officials to purchase horses and camels in the Kalmyk uluses. The reasons for this were not hard to guess—to limit the Kalmyks' access to Moscow and to reduce the damage done to the local inhabitants along the route of such trading parties.[90]

[87]Findiklili, *Silahdar Tarikhi*, 2:419.

[88]Akdes Nimet Kurat, *IV–XVIII Yüzyillarda Karadeniz Kuzeyindeki Türk Kavimleri ve Devletleri* (Ankara: Türk Tarikh Kurumu Basimevi, 1972), 256–57.

[89]*DAI* 12:222, no. 17.

[90]The Kalmyks' presence in the Russian capital was a nuisance for the authorities. In 1688, for instance, a decree was issued concerning the Kalmyks, who smoked tobacco and started fires in the courtyards of the residencies (*ODB* 16 [1910]: no. 1116). The passage of Ayuki's *tabun* in August 1688 near Saratov triggered complaints from the local residents of the trampled meadow lands and other significant damages caused by the Kalmyks ("K istorii Saratovskogo kraia iz Donskikh del," *Trudy Saratovskoi uchenoi arkhivnoi komissii* 4, pt. 1 [1893]: 51).

The concentration of power in Ayuki's hands was the culmination of an ongoing process of active trade and diplomatic relations with foreign powers and successful raids on neighboring peoples. Not the least important was the constant flow of Oirats from troubled Jungaria, torn by internal and external conflicts. Thus Chagan Batur tayishi, who belonged to the Khoshut tribe, also left Jungaria with his ulus and in 1687 reached the Volga steppes.[91]

Ayuki's increased power and prestige needed to be expressed and reinforced by new symbols. In his 1688 letter to the Ottoman sultan, Ayuki had already referred to himself as a khan. Official confirmation of this title arrived from Tibet in 1690, in a special decree of the Dalai Lama which conferred the title of khan on Ayuki.[92] Considering Ayuki its subject, the Russian government did not wish to recognize the title bestowed on him from Tibet. The records continued to mention Ayuki tayishi until 1708, when for the first time official Russian documents referred to Ayuki Khan.[93] The Ottomans referred to Ayuki in a variety of ways, using such titles as the ruler (hâkim) of the Kalmyks,[94] commander in chief (umde-i umera),[95] the Kalmyk king (Kalmak krali)[96] and as early as 1704, khan.[97] The Crimean khan Selim Giray I was one of the first to accept Ayuki's new title. In his 1695 letter to the Russian tsars, the Crimean khan referred to "the Kalmyk khan Ayuki Khan." For Selim Giray I to recognize Ayuki as a khan was not a mere formality. It was a diplomatic act of considerable political significance, for it meant that for

[91]*PSZ* 2:no. 1245. But just as some Oirats, dissatisfied with their leaders, were leaving Jungaria, others were leaving Ayuki for the same reasons. In 1690 two Kalmyk tayishis, Cheter (Seter) and Batur, with their uluses numbering three hundred and five hundred fighters, respectively, left Ayuki and joined the Don cossacks. Explaining his reasons, Cheter said that Ayuki intended to ruin him because he, Cheter, had helped the cossacks against the Nogays. Batur explained that he left because Ayuki had raided his ulus several times and because of Ayuki's oppression (*DAI* 12:276, no. 17 [XX]); Ayuki's raids on Batur's ulus, perhaps, were not totally groundless, as the Kalmyk chronicler Gabang Sharab informs us that Batur and Solom-Seren were known to have plotted against Ayuki (Gabang Sharab, "Skazanie ob oiratakh," 155).

[92]"Istoriia kalmytskikh khanov," 70; Bakunin, "Opisanie," *Krasnyi arkhiv* 3 (1939): 198. The decree did come from Tibet but was not from the true Dalai Lama V, who had been dead since 1682. His death, however, was not revealed for political reasons until the late 1690s (Tsepon W. D. Shakabpa, *Tibet: A Political History* [New Haven: Yale University Press, 1967], 123–28; *The World of Buddhism*, 265; Kychanov and Savitskii, *Liudi i bogi strany snegov,* 89–90).

[93]*PSZ* 3:no. 2207; *Materialy po istorii Bashkirskoi,* 1:no. 104.

[94]BA *Nâme-i Hümayun,* no. 6, pp. 89, 520.

[95]Ibid., no. 5, p. 59.

[96]Findiklili, *Silahdar Tarikhi,* 2:419, 670, 707.

[97]BA *Nâme-i Hümayun,* no. 6, p. 89.

the first time the Kalmyk khan was seen as equal to the Crimean khan. The usual reference to Ayuki as one in the service of the Crimea was replaced by a new formula mentioning Ayuki as the Crimean khan's firm friend and brother (*muhkem dost ve kardeshimizdir*).[98]

In the following years Ayuki continued to mantain good relations with the Crimeans and the Ottomans and to dispatch his embassies to Azov, the Crimea, and the Porte.[99] One such embassy consisted of ten people and arrived at the Porte in August 1692. Among the presents it brought were a bow the size of a carder's bow, ten arrows the size of a spear, a quiver, and a riding horse. The padishah personally placed a robe of honor on each of the ten envoys and assured them that he would grant all their wishes if the Kalmyks continued to be loyal to the Porte and kept up good relations with the Crimean khan.[100] Another Kalmyk embassy arrived at the Porte in August 1693, bringing a letter and gifts consisting of nine riding horses and a falcon. The envoy explained that the Kalmyks had shown the sincerity of their relations toward the Porte by supplying the Crimean army with forty thousand horses, three thousand warlike Nogays, and one thousand Kalmyks. In return the envoy was given assurances of mutual friendship, granted a robe of honor, and allowed to leave for home without delay.[101]

In the early 1690s Kalmyk-Crimean relations reached their highest point. Kalmyk trade with Azov and the Crimea grew to immense proportions. A 1693 Kalmyk embassy to the Porte boasted of forty thousand horses delivered to the Crimea. Russian sources corroborate the arrival of at least one such group of ten thousand horses in 1691. Another large herd of twenty thousand horses arrived for sale in Bakhchesaray in March 1695.[102] It was at this exact time that the Crimean khan recognized Ayuki Khan as an independent ruler and ally. Selim Giray I was so confident of his relationship with Ayuki that he announced to Peter I that, if the Russian tsar wished to become a brother and a friend of the Crimean khan and the Kalmyk khan Ayuki, all three countries (*yurt*) would live in peace.[103]

---

[98]Vel'iaminov-Zernov, *Materialy dlia istorii Krymskogo*, 768, no. 296.

[99]*DAI* 12:266, no. 17 (XIII), 278, no. 17 (XX); *AVD* 1:153, no. 101; BA *Ibn ül-Emin Tasnifi, Kharijiye*, no. 261; Vel'iaminov-Zernov, *Materialy dlia istorii Krymskogo*, 764, no. 293.

[100]Findiklili, *Silahdar Tarikhi*, 2:670.

[101]Ibid., 707. This was probably the same embassy that was earlier reported to be in the Crimea in May 1693 ("Spisok s stateinogo spiska Vasiliia Aitemireva, poslannogo v Krym s predlozheniem mirnykh dogovorov, 1692–95," *ZIOOID* 18 [1895]: 31).

[102]"Spisok s stateinogo spiska Vasiliia Aitemireva," *ZIOOID* 18 (1895): 13, 75; 19 (1896): 26.

[103]Vel'iaminov-Zernov, *Materialy dlia istorii Krymskogo khanstva*, 768, no. 296.

The Azov Affair

Throughout the late 1680s and early 1690s, Ottoman-Crimean efforts to win over the Kalmyks, or at least to neutralize them, were quite successful. During this period, the Kalmyks' relations with Russia declined significantly. The Kalmyks provided no military assistance for the ill-fated Russian campaigns against the Crimea in 1687 and 1689. Nor did any Kalmyk cavalry participate in the first siege of Azov in 1695. Conversely, according to Don cossack reports, the Kalmyks passed information to officials in Azov indicating that preparations to besiege the fortress were under way. In gratitude, the Ottoman military governor—pasha of Azov—sent Ayuki numerous gifts, including armor and muskets, and requested his assistance in anticipation of Ayuki's sending him a Yedisan cavalry unit.[104] In a slightly different account of this event, an eighteenth-century Crimean historian, Sayyid Riza, relates that Merdan Ali Aga, the influential vizier of the Crimean khan,[105] who was sent with an embassy to the Kalmyks in early 1695, brought back with him to the Crimea news of the expected Russian siege of Azov and possible invasion of the Crimea.[106] Thus the information disclosed by Ayuki provided enough time for the Azov garrison to prepare for the siege and for the Crimean khan to dispatch his cavalry promptly to aid Azov.[107] Inevitably, Ayuki's role in transmitting intelligence and supplying food for the inhabitants of Azov, along with other factors, contributed to the failure of the 1695 Russian campaign against Azov.

The Russians were fully aware throughout this period of the Kalmyks' ties with the Crimea and Azov and tried to take measures, ranging from the confrontational to the conciliatory, to disrupt them. Moscow's main concern at the moment was Ayuki's trade with Azov. In 1686 the cossacks complained that the Kalmyks' supplying cattle and horses to Azov contributed largely to the survival of that Ottoman fortress. Two years later they again reported that the lively trade between the Kalmyks and Azov persisted.[108] Preparing for the decisive siege of this Ottoman fortress, the

---

[104]*AVD* 1:173, no. 112.

[105]Smirnov, *Krymskoe khanstvo*, 675.

[106]Sayyid Riza Efendi, *Al-Sab' al-Sayyâr fî akhbâr Mulûk al-Tâtar*, SK Hamidiye 950, 111b. A copy of the only known publication of the original is also in SK Esad Efendi 2298 (Sayyid Muhammed Riza, *Asseb o-Sseyar ili sem' planet soderzhashchii istoriiu krymskikh khanov* [Kazan': Universitetskaia tipografiia, 1832], 224).

[107]The Crimean khan sent a sizable army assembled from various Tatar, Nogay, and Kabardinian (Circassian) tribes led by his son Kaplan Giray (Mehmed Rashid, *Tarikh-i Rashid*, 6 vols. [Istanbul: Matbaa-i Amire, (1865)], 2:352).

[108]The exact volume of this trade was not known. The cossacks explained that it was difficult to capture Kalmyk informants and learn about their intentions because the

authorities wanted to make sure that no food supply would reach Azov from the mainland. Since appeals to Ayuki proved ineffective, Moscow resorted to other measures. It ordered the Don cossacks to position small detachments along the routes that the Kalmyks used for driving their cattle to Azov to interdict such drives. The government continued to encourage the Kalmyks to trade in the Russian towns.[109]

The final siege of Azov came in 1696. On the eve of renewed military operations the two opposing powers, the Russian and the Ottoman empires, both made a bid for Kalmyk support. At the end of 1695 envoys of the Ottoman sultan came to Ayuki. They offered many gifts and asked for military assistance. Ayuki accepted the gifts, presenting in return five hundred horses, but refused to provide any troops.[110]

Realization of the approaching downfall of Azov made Ayuki reconsider his pro-Ottoman and Crimean policies. By the end of 1695 Ayuki was well aware that Azov could not withstand another Russian siege. While still remaining on good terms with the Ottomans, he began to make overtures to the Russian government and sent his envoy to the Russians informing them that Azov was about to fall. Ottoman intelligence reported that Ayuki received the tsar's envoy and that he reached an agreement with the Russians to strike against the Ottoman frontiers. Kadir Shah Mirza, who provided this information to the Ottomans, confirmed that Ayuki had spread false rumors about his animosity toward his own son Chakdorjab to conceal his agreement with the Russians. He warned that Ayuki was not to be trusted. The Ottomans, well aware of Ayuki's maneuvering, nevertheless expected him to remain neutral in the conflict. In fact, Ayuki did dispatch 3,000 horsemen to join the forces of the boyar and *voevoda* A. S. Shein and 1,172 horsemen to join Prince Cherkasskii.[111]

Another important event effectively brought an end to relations be-

---

Kalmyks had five hundred horsemen stationed as scouts all along the way (*DAI* 12:250, no. 17).

[109]For instance, the town of Iaitsk (Iaitskii gorodok, Gur'ev), situated in the estuary of the Yayik, was an important center for trade with the Kalmyks from the early 1680s. The town had a permanent customhouse and a designated place where Kalmyks brought their goods for bartering. To provide a further incentive, the government often exempted the Kalmyks from customs duties. In 1691 the customs official of Iaitsk was ordered not to collect customs duties on horses, sheep, or cows brought for sale or barter by the Kalmyks and Tatars (V. N. Darienko, "Osnovanie goroda Gur'eva," *Voprosy istorii*, Alma-Ata 5 [1973]: 195; *AI* 5:361–62, no. 210).

[110]*DAI* 10:385, no. 80 (XIII).

[111]Findiklili, *Nusretnâme*, 1:220–21, 229; *Sbornik vypisok iz arkhivnykh bumag o Petre Velikom*, comp. G. V. Esipov, 2 vols. (Moscow: Univ. tip., 1872), 1:327–28, 334; *PB* 1:594, note to no. 109.

tween the Kalmyks and the Crimeans. In April 1696 a large group from among the various Nogay tribes that roamed with the Kalmyks departed to join their coreligionists on the Kuban. In his letter to the Porte, the Crimean khan explained that the Kalmyks, in violation of their previous agreements, had entered into an alliance with Russia. The Kalmyks had thereupon begun to oppress (*jevr*) the Nogays who lived among them, and as a result ten thousand nomadic Nogays with all their families, property, and cattle slipped away from the Kalmyks and fled to the Kuban. The Crimean *kalgay* Devlet Giray Sultan, who was in the area, welcomed the Nogays and accompanied them to safety at the place where Achu fortress was to be founded.[112] Ayuki then threatened to kill the remaining four thousand Kazan (sic) Nogays because they had killed his son. The Nogays requested help from the Crimean *kalgay*, suggesting that if he attacked the Kalmyks from without, the Nogays would strike a blow from within. In the end, the Nogays fled with the Kalmyks in pursuit, but the three-thousand-man force of the *kalgay* bravely confronted the Kalmyk advance detachment of four thousand, routed them, and successfully brought the Nogays to the Kuban.[113]

One witness to this event, Ali Mirza, retold the story in credible detail. According to Ali Mirza, the Yedisan tribe had requested the *kalgay*'s help. The *kalgay* set out from the Kabarda to the Volga with a three-thousand-man army made up of his own warriors and the Crimean *sekban* soldiers, as well as two thousand brave Yamansadaks (Yamansadak—literally strong, firm quiver, was the name of one of the Tatar tribes). Then the Yedisans, joined by the *kalgay*'s force, left behind their families and property, and together with the newcomers pillaged the area up to Astrakhan, including the suburbs of the town. When Ayuki learned of this raid he and his sons set off in pursuit. Ayuki divided his force in three groups of four thousand horsemen each and placed them at distances of a three-hour ride from each other. He himself was at the head of the rear-guard group. The Kalmyks attacked furiously. At one point during the battle, as the Kalmyks mounted another attack, the Crimeans began to withdraw, which caused their front line to break rank. The Kalmyks rushed ahead and suddenly confronted a line of the *sekban* soldiers, who discharged their muskets at the Kalmyks and then counterattacked with swords. The Kalmyk vanguard group was forced to flee. The second group of Kalmyks was also routed, and Ayuki with his horsemen chose to escape from the battlefield. The victorious *kalgay* arrived in Kabarda with the Yedisan and the Yamboyluk Nogays.[114]

[112]Findiklili, *Nusretnâme*, 1:251; Rashid, *Tarikh-i Rashid*, 2:398.
[113]Findiklili, *Nusretnâme*, 1:252–53.
[114]Ibid., 253.

In the past the Nogays had been known to desert the Kalmyks whenever the opportunity presented itself, and Ayuki brought them back in 1672. Another desertion of the Nogays, in 1696, was not a spontaneous occurrence but a carefully prepared event. Before this incident, the Crimean khan sent to the Porte to obtain permission for the Nogays to come and roam on the Kuban. When such permission was granted, the Nogays were notified.[115] In the end, the loyalty of the Ottomans and the Crimeans lay with their Muslim brothers, the Nogays, and not with the idolatrous Kalmyks.

The fall of the Ottoman fortress of Azov had a fundamental impact on the steppe area between the Caspian and Azov seas. For centuries this Ottoman stronghold had served as a vital communication link between the numerous Muslim Tatar and Nogay tribes of these steppes and their brothers in Islam from the Crimea and the Ottoman empire. Russia's capture of Azov threatened to sever these ties. Both the Russians and the Ottomans clearly realized the strategic importance of Azov as a communication point linking the inland routes to the steppes with the sea routes to the Crimea and Istanbul. To compensate for the loss of Azov, the Ottomans hastily began to build another fortress, which they named Achu (modern Achuevo).[116] Meanwhile, the Russian government was eager to consolidate its victory. The fortifications, which had been severely damaged during the siege, had to be rebuilt. The people of Azov had either fled or been taken captive, and consequently the fortress town had to be resettled. Along with three thousand infantry troops, four hundred Kalmyk horsemen were assigned to stay near Azov at an annual salary of five rubles per person.[117]

The loss of his people, the duplicity of the Crimeans, and his humiliating defeat forced Ayuki to change his pro-Ottoman policies. In April 1697 he sent an envoy to the Don cossacks to tell them that he wanted to end his friendship with the Crimean khan. He wished to roam along the Volga, Don, Khoper, and Medveditsa rivers and soon intended to attack the Nogays on the Kuban.[118] Moscow was prompt to respond. It dispatched Boyar Prince B. A. Golitsyn, who met Ayuki on the Kamyshenka River in July 1697. According to the Kalmyk account, Peter the Great, before leaving for Holland, sent Prince B. A. Golitsyn to relay to the Kalmyk khan the tsar's special request for protection of the Russian

[115]Ibid., 251.

[116]The new fortress was founded at a location a ten-hour riding distance (around forty miles) north of the older Ottoman fortress of Temrek (Temriuk) near the estuary of the Kuban River (Findiklili, *Nusretnâme*, 1:251–52; Rashid, *Tarikh-i Rashid*, 2:498).

[117]*PB* 1:111, no. 125.

[118]*AVD* 1:183, no. 117.

southern frontier.[119] Perhaps such a request was related orally, but more likely it is a mere product of fancy, for it can be found nowhere in the Russian sources.

After short negotiations Prince Golitsyn and Ayuki Khan produced a document remarkably different both in letter and in spirit from all previous ones concluded between Russia and the Kalmyks. The new document was an agreement between two equal powers. Unlike previous oaths, the document did not emphasize the submissive status of the Kalmyks and did not seek to exact any obligations from them.

Instead, all six clauses of the agreement contained commitments made by the Russian government. Briefly, the contents of the clauses were as follows:

(1) In case of war with the Bukharans, the Karakalpaks, or the Kazakhs (Kazakhov *kirgizskikh*) Ayuki would be given two light cannons and three mortars with cannonballs and bombs, gunners and grenadiers, and twenty *poods* of gunpowder in addition to the twenty *poods* of powder and ten *poods* of bullets that he would receive annually.

(2) Ayuki would be allowed to roam freely and safely near the grand sovereign's towns.

(3) If the Kalmyks, while participating in the sovereign's military campaigns, were to flee from the enemy, they should be given refuge in the Russian towns as well as military assistance. When sending his people on such campaigns, Ayuki should always give them an accompanying letter signed by himself which they should present to the *voevodas* in the towns.

(4) Those Kalmyks who fled from Ayuki to seek refuge in the Russian towns should neither be given refuge there nor be baptized. *Voevodas* who forced baptism on the refugees would pay Ayuki a penalty of thirty rubles per person.

(5) Ayuki's people were to be transported across the Volga anywhere between the towns of Chernyi Iar and Saratov without delay or harassment.

(6) Orders would be sent to Ufa, to the Yayik and the Don towns, that neither the Bashkirs nor the cossacks should start any quarrels, but rather must live with the Kalmyks in peace and friendship.[120]

This agreement reveals a drastic change in the policy of the Russian government. For the first time, instead of demanding another oath of allegiance, the Russian government was prepared to make its own commitments and to deal with long-standing Kalmyk grievances. In the past,

---

[119]Pozdneev, "Astrakhanskie kalmyki," 151–52.
[120]*PSZ* 3:no. 1591.

the inability of the Russian government to protect the Kalmyks and to provide them with military aid, to transport them across the Volga, to allow free trade in the Russian towns, and to return the Kalmyk runaways all had been seen by Ayuki as a failure on the part of the tsar to fulfill his obligations as an ally. After the humiliating defeat at the hands of the Crimeans, Ayuki once again painfully realized the ever-growing importance of firearms in the new style of warfare and particularly the devastating power of cannon. For the moment, the Russian government chose to assume certain responsibilities in meeting Ayuki's requests, and the first written agreement between the two as equal parties had been signed.

5

Uneasy Alliance:
Ayuki Khan and Russia, 1697–1722

Rebellion of the Sons

Shortly before the Russo-Kalmyk agreement was signed in July 1697, another important event in Oirat history occurred elsewhere. After a long and relentless struggle with China, the khan of Jungaria, Galdan Boshoktu, died in a remote part of western Mongolia.[1]

The Kalmyk tayishis always maintained close relations with the Jungar khans. The course of events in Jungaria often affected the Kalmyk tayishis' own political calculations and diplomatic maneuvers. When Ayuki learned of Galdan Boshoktu's death, he moved promptly to strengthen his ties with Tsevang-Rabtan, Galdan's former rival and now the new khan of Jungaria.

Traditionally, political brotherhood was best forged by matrimonial alliances. In 1697–98 Ayuki gave his daughter Seterjab in marriage to Tsevang-Rabtan and himself took as a wife Tsevang-Rabtan's cousin Darma-Bala, who had arrived in the Caspian steppes to marry Ayuki's youngest son, Gundelek. This was Ayuki's fourth marriage.[2]

---

[1]Zlatkin puts the date of Galdan's death at March 13, 1697 (Zlatkin, *Istoriia Dzhungarskogo*, 208), but Kychanov and B. P. Gurevich point to early May 1697 (Kychanov, *Povestvovanie ob oiratskom*, 172; B. P. Gurevich, *Mezhdunarodnye otnosheniia v Tsentral'noi Azii v 17-pervoi polovine 19 v.* [Moscow: Nauka, 1979], 55).

[2]Ayuki's first wife, Erentsen, bore him three sons: Chakdorjab, Sanjib, and Gundelek. Upon the death of his father, Puntsuk, Ayuki married his stepmother Uanjal, who bore him a son, Gunjib. At the time of Ayuki's fourth marriage, his wives, Erentsen and Uanjal, were both deceased. Ayuki had abandoned his third wife, the Kabardinian Abukhan. She spent the rest of her days residing near Astrakhan, living off the allowance she received from Ayuki. Ayuki's fourth wife, Darma-Bala, was to become an influential figure in Kalmyk society. She bore him three sons: Cheren-Donduk, Galdan Danjin, and Barang. After Ayuki's

It is reasonable to assume that the death of Galdan Boshoktu Khan in Jungaria, which came when Ayuki had accumulated power unparalleled by any previous Kalmyk tayishi, once again inflated Ayuki's ambition. The new khan of Jungaria, Tsevang-Rabtan, was still in the process of consolidating his power. At the moment, Ayuki felt himself strong enough to challenge Tsevang-Rabtan and make his bid for the title and position of paramount importance—the khan of all the Oirats.

Ayuki's Pan-Oirat design could be accomplished only with the blessing of the Dalai Lama, that is, only if Tibet could be convinced that Ayuki would serve its interests better than Tsevang-Rabtan. In 1698, for these or other purposes, Ayuki sent a large embassy to Tibet. The embassy was headed by Ayuki's nephew Arabjur, who was accompanied by his mother and five hundred other people.[3] At the same time, realizing that he would not succeed in his plans unless he reached an understanding with the government in Beijing, Ayuki sent his envoy Erke-Getsul to the Manchu emperor.[4]

While making his plans Ayuki did not forget his more immediate goals. Strengthened by Russian military support, Ayuki directed his rage against the Nogays, who had fled from him to the Kuban two years previously. This Kalmyk raid was devastating to the Nogays. In a brief and deliberately cryptic note to Peter I, Prince B. A. Golitsyn mentioned the event but felt ashamed and embarrassed to write about it in detail. In an apparent massacre many Nogays were butchered and their herds taken away. After the raid the price of horses in Astrakhan fell as low as five *altyn* each, indicating the magnitude of the disaster.[5]

Having punished the Nogays, Ayuki again turned his eyes toward Jungaria. Though still hesitant, Ayuki decided to move cautiously toward his new objective. In 1699 worried Russian officials reported that for unknown reasons, Ayuki and all his people had crossed the Yayik.[6] At this time Ayuki's son Sanjib left his father together with fifteen thousand tents. He arrived in Jungaria the following year.[7]

There are several contradictory accounts of this important event. The

---

death in 1724, she would play an important role in the ensuing power struggle (Bakunin, "Opisanie," *Krasnyi arkhiv* 3 [1939]: 195, 198; Zlatkin, *Istoriia Dzhungarskogo*, 220).

[3] Bantysh-Kamenskii, *Diplomaticheskoe sobranie del*, 75.

[4] The envoy is reported to have arrived at the Qing court the following year, 1699, and presented the emperor with a large gray horse. Erke-Getsul was generously rewarded and sent back, but he never returned to Ayuki and was presumed to have died on the way back ("Zapiski Tulishenia o ego poezdke v sostave tsinskogo posol'stva k kalmytskomu khanu Aiuke v 1712–1715 gg.," in *Russko-kitaiskie otnosheniia v 18 veke. Materialy i dokumenty*, vol. 1: *1700–1725* [Moscow: Nauka, 1978], 471).

[5] *PB* 1:698, note to no. 228.

[6] Ibid., 278–79, no. 265.

[7] Gabang Sharab, "Skazanie ob oiratakh," 150.

Russian envoy to Jungaria in 1722–24, artillery captain Ivan Unkovskii, relates the Jungars' view of this event. Two other accounts—one by the Russian official Vasilii Bakunin, the other by Donduk-Ombo, the Kalmyk khan from 1735 to 1741—tell the story from the Kalmyk point of view.

The two latter accounts indicate that Ayuki's sons Chakdorjab, Sanjib, and Gundelek were at odds with their father because he favored Gunjib, the son by his second wife.[8] Seeking justice, the three brothers rebelled against Ayuki by leaving him and taking all their people. Moscow promptly dispatched Prince B. A. Golitsyn, who solved the crisis by reconciling the sons with their father. Only Sanjib refused and decided to migrate to Jungaria together with his fifteen thousand tents. Upon his arrival there, the Jungar khan Tsevang-Rabtan seized Sanjib's people and then sent Sanjib and his family back to Ayuki. Such is the story told by Bakunin and Donduk-Ombo.[9]

Unkovskii's more detailed account says that when Sanjib reached Jungaria, Tsevang-Rabtan invited Sanjib to visit him. Sanjib refused and instead requested that his envoy be allowed to pass through on his way to Tibet. The Jungars then discovered that in the collar of the envoy's robe there was a secret letter to the Dalai Lama, requesting permission to kill Tsevang-Rabtan. The envoy was detained, and Tsevang-Rabtan, having beguiled Sanjib with splendid feasts and offers of friendship, captured and annexed his people.[10]

One can venture to reconstruct the course of events by viewing the available accounts in the existing political context. In 1699 Ayuki cautiously began to move toward Jungaria. He positioned himself to the east of the Yayik River, keeping an eye on Jungaria. Since his embassies from Tibet and China had not yet returned and the situation in Jungaria remained uncertain, Ayuki judiciously decided to wait. Perhaps Sanjib disagreed with his father's tactics and saw an opportune moment for his own ambition in a bid for power. He must have been aware of Ayuki's plans to unseat Tsevang-Rabtan and decided to make such an attempt on his own. The results of this departure were tragic for Sanjib and disastrous for Ayuki. Sanjib, who had left his father with fifteen thousand tents, returned home with seven people. The loss of such a large group of

---

[8]According to the Kalmyk chronicler Gabang Sharab, Ayuki indeed intended to give all of his uluses to Gunjib (ibid., 152).

[9]Bakunin, "Opisanie," *Krasnyi arkhiv* 3 (1939): 198–99. Donduk-Ombo's account is in A. M. Pozdneev, "K istorii ziungarskikh kalmykov. Pis'mo," in *Posol'stvo k ziungarskomu khuntaichzhi Tsevan-Rabtanu kapitana ot artillerii Ivana Unkovskogo i putevoi zhurnal ego za 1722–1724 gody, ZIRGOOE,* vol. 10, pt. 2 (St. Petersburg: Tip. V. F. Kirshbauma, 1887), 255. Ayuki's reaction to Sanjib's departure was only a puzzling remark: "The one who sleeps cannot help the one who does not" (Gabang Sharab, "Skazanie ob oiratakh," 149).

[10]*Posol'stvo k ziungarskomu,* 187–89.

people and herds significantly undermined Ayuki's might. For the time being, he had to abandon his grandiose designs because the acquisition of the fifteen thousand Kalmyk tents, or more than sixty thousand people, decisively tipped the scale of military and political power in Tsevang-Rabtan's favor.

Tsevang-Rabtan was probably aware of Ayuki's plans, and when the opportunity presented itself, he decided to strike a heavy blow at his potential rival. When he succeeded, Tsevang-Rabtan left no chance for his new subjects to escape. Contrary to common practice among nomadic peoples, whereby the newly incorporated group continues to exist as a separate and independent unit, Tsevang-Rabtan chose to divide the captives and disperse them among various Jungar uluses. Ayuki's first embassy to Jungaria, requesting the return of the Kalmyks, arrrived in 1703.[11] It ended unsuccessfully, as did many subsequent embassies.

In China, watchful Qing officials were quick to notice and indicate to the emperor the political importance of Tsevang-Rabtan's action for all of Central Asia. In 1704 the Emperor Kangxi stated that in the past Tsevang-Rabtan had displayed respect and obedience, but after Galdan's death and his own victories over the Kazakhs, Tsevang-Rabtan began to change. After taking over the Torguts, he was becoming more and more arrogant.[12]

Sanjib's departure was only the first in the series of misfortunes that befell Ayuki at the turn of the new century. The rebellion of his eldest son, Chakdorjab, in 1701 almost succeeded in deposing Ayuki. Apparently, when Chakdorjab found one of his wives with Ayuki, he wanted to kill his father but was prevented from doing so. Learning of such outrageous behavior on the part of their khan, the Kalmyk tayishis decided to join Chakdorjab and left Ayuki. In the meantime, Ayuki's favorite son, Gunjib, sent an assassin to murder Chakdorjab. The assassin shot at Chakdorjab but only wounded him. After this failed assassination attempt, Gunjib fled and took refuge in Saratov, while Ayuki fled to the town of Iaitsk with his remaining one hundred tents. To salvage the situation, Moscow promptly dispatched Prince B. A. Golitsyn, who shortly thereafter arrived at Samara, a town on the Volga River. Golitsyn sent his representatives to Chakdorjab and secured Chakdorjab's return by promising to reconcile him with Ayuki.[13]

---

[11]Pozdneev, "K istorii ziungarskikh kalmykov," 256.

[12]Ibid., 257.

[13]Bakunin, "Opisanie," *Krasnyi arkhiv* 3 (1939): 198–99. According to Donduk-Ombo, the reconciliation did not take place in Samara but in a little town of the Orenburg region called Samur-Khala (Pozdneev, "K istorii ziungarskikh kalmykov," 255).

In the absence of more reliable data and precise chronology, it is impossible to establish the validity of this account. It is clear, however, that Chakdorjab rebelled against his father, who had chosen to bypass him in favor of his fourth son, Gunjib, as the heir apparent. Gunjib's sudden death and Ayuki's promise to reinstate Chakdorjab as his legitimate heir might have been among the reasons that secured the return of the prodigal son. Perhaps the news of his brother Sanjib's fate in Jungaria also made Chakdorjab more willing to negotiate. The ultimate result was that Ayuki again, as many times in the past, was restored to power by the Russians.

Moscow's concern and mediation were not motivated by altruistic reasons alone. The Kalmyks' departure exposed southern Russian towns to Nogay and Tatar raids, which endangered vital communications and exacted a toll in life and property. Russia also needed the Kalmyk cavalry for its renewed military campaigns, this time against Sweden. In August 1700, one day after a thirty-year truce with the Ottoman empire had been announced, Peter I declared war on Sweden—a costly war that would last for twenty-two years.[14]

Ayuki Khan was considering ways to repair the damage caused by Sanjib's departure and to regain the prestige he had lost through his rift with Chakdorjab. After his return in 1703 to the pastures along the Volga, Ayuki first undertook to convince Munko-Temir tayishi of the Derbets to join him there.[15] A marriage between Ayuki's daughter Buntar and Munko-Temir's son Cheter was a tangible symbol of an agreement previously reached between Ayuki and the Derbet tayishis. Ayuki's task of winning over the Derbets was facilitated by their own desire to leave the Don to avoid constant clashes with the cossacks. In the summer of 1704 Munko-Temir, together with most of his people, joined Ayuki.[16]

[14]Small Kalmyk contingents are reported to have participated in the campaigns near Lake Ladoga in northern Russia during the first years of the war. These Kalmyk contingents usually were part of a larger cavalry unit of cossacks, Tatars, Bashkirs, and others. This motley unit assembled from various peoples was known as "the lower Volga cavalry" (*nizovaia konnitsa*) (PB 2:60, no. 429; 235, no. 572; 333, note to no. 416; 355, note to no. 429).

[15]Approximately four thousand Kalmyk tents of the Derbets, led by Solom-Seren tayishi, had first arrived from Jungaria in the early 1670s. Solom-Seren joined Ayuki's Torguts but in acccordance with the customs of nomadic society remained politically and economically independent. It was Solom-Seren and his Derbets who more often than other Kalmyks performed military service for Russia. The three-thousand-man Kalmyk contingent near Azov also consisted of Derbets under the command of Munko-Temir, a son of Solom-Seren. The Derbet Kalmyks of Munko-Temir and his son Cheter were the only ones who refused to join Ayuki in his move toward Jungaria and remained on their pastures along the Don (PB 1:278–79, no. 265).

[16]Some of the minor Derbet tayishis such as Bolchak, Kichikey, Dedial, Adiak, and Kadi chose to stay on the Don and near Azov (Bakunin, "Opisanie," *Krasnyi arkhiv* 3 [1939]: 199; AVD 1:218, no. 139; 237, no. 153).

In early 1704 the Kuban Nogays and the Crimean Tatars were preparing to raid the Kalmyks to avenge their tribesmen who had been butchered by the Kalmyks.[17] It was perhaps with the purpose of preventing
such raids and patching up his friendship with the Crimeans and the
Ottomans that Ayuki made another overture to the Ottoman sultan. The
moment could not have been better, as a year had passed since a new
sultan, Ahmet III, had ascended the Ottoman throne. It was time for
relations to be renewed. Ayuki's embassy arrived at the Porte in late
September or early October 1704. The embassy was headed by the es-
teemed and trusted Ish Mehmed Aga, described as one of Ayuki's Muslim subjects. The envoy bore the honorable title of equerry (kütelji/
kötelji)[18]—a confidant of the Kalmyk khan. Ish Mehmed Aga brought
with him a short letter, which, according to the Ottoman translation,
emphasized Ayuki's faithfulness and allegiance in the past and indicated
his present promise to implement the padishah's orders to the best of
his ability.[19] The letter also stated that "the sincerity of Ayuki's convic-
tions and the rest of the message were to be delivered by the envoy
orally." In other words, Ayuki wanted to confirm his intentions with
some appreciable practical plans, which his envoys were to deliver in
confidence.

The Ottoman response, delivered in a letter from the grand vizier,
was circumspect and restrained. The vizier welcomed Ayuki's renewed
pledges of submission with the guarded remark that the extent of the
padishah's rewards and the benefits of his protection would equal the
extent of Ayuki's obedience. Ayuki was also instructed to confirm his
sincerity by deeds, namely, by living in peace with his Muslim neighbors,
most of all with the Crimean khan Selim Giray. The letter mentioned that
the Porte had also been pleased to receive a missive from Ayuki's eldest
son "with a sincere protestation of loyalty." It ended on a cautious but
hopeful note: "Let God Almighty grant you success in the service of the
Ottoman state."[20]

Whether because of the power of this divine invocation or the force of
political circumstances, the following years were not marked by any

---

[17]AVD 1:236, no. 152; Vel'iaminov-Zernov, Materialy dlia istorii Krymskogo, 770, no. 298.

[18]In the available French translation of this document this important title is left out
(Chantal Lemercier-Quelquejay, "Les Kalmuks de la Volga entre l'empire Russe et l'empire
Ottoman sous le règne de Pierre le Grand," Cahiers du Monde Russe et Soviétique, 7 [1966]:
73). Kütelji of the original document (see also kütel in Mehmet Zeki Pakalin, Osmanli Tarih
Deyimleri ve Terimleri Sözlügü, 3 vols. [Istanbul: Milli Egitim Basimevi, 1971], 2:345) is
derived from the Mongol köteji (Vladimirtsov, Obshchestvennyi, 162; Gerhard Dörfer, Tür-
kische und mongolische Elemente im Neupersischen, vol. 1: Mongolische Elemente im
Neupersischen [Wiesbaden: F. Steiner, 1963], 459–60).

[19]BA Nâme-i Hümayun, no. 6, pp. 88–89; Rashid, Tarikh-i Rashid, 3:149.

[20]BA Nâme-i Hümayun, no. 6, pp. 89–90.

serious hostilities between the Kalmyks and the sultan's Muslim subjects. The tsar and the sultan exercised their influence over the neighboring peoples to maintain the peace they both needed. The Russian government tried to harness the fierce energy of the Kalmyk raids and rechannel it against its adversaries abroad and at home.

The Astrakhan Uprising of 1705–1706

In 1705–6 the lower Volga region was in the throes of an uprising. Old and traditional Russia, irritated and angered by Peter I's reforms and introduction of alien customs, took arms in its remote steppe corner, Astrakhan. Situated in the estuary of the Volga, the city was surrounded by deserts and steppes sparsely inhabited by nomadic Kalmyks and Tatars. Astrakhan's garrison was small, and the fate of the city often depended on the goodwill of the neighboring Yayik and Don cossacks. It is not surprising, therefore, that one of the first acts of the rebels was to send delegations to Ayuki, Chakdorjab, and the Yayik cossacks. Dispatched in early August 1705, the delegations were well received in the Kalmyk uluses, and the delegates returned with promises of peace. The small Volga towns of Chernyi Iar and Krasnyi Iar swiftly joined in the uprising, and the rebels decided to march on Tsaritsyn. Ayuki's son Chemet informed the Tsaritsyn *voevoda* of the approaching army of rebels, and the city prepared for a siege. In the ensuing battle, the participation of the Kalmyks on the government's side was crucial in defeating the rebels.[21]

The Kalmyk cavalry near Tsaritsyn consisted of the Derbet Kalmyks of the tayishis Munko-Temir, Cherkes, Chemet, Cheter, and others. The leaders of the uprising were well aware of this fact and instructed their followers to engage only the Derbet Kalmyks, and not those of Ayuki and Chakdorjab. For its part, Moscow tried not to antagonize Ayuki's Kalmyks. It explicitly ordered the Don cossacks not to avenge their previous quarrels with the Kalmyks and thus furnish them with a reason to join the rebels.[22]

From the beginning of the rebellion, Ayuki had maintained a position of neutrality and on occasion played the role of mediator between Astrakhan and Moscow. The situation changed in the spring of 1706, when the government troops led by General Field Marshal B. P. Sheremet'ev approached Astrakhan. On the eve of this decisive campaign,

[21]N. B. Golikova, *Astrakhanskoe vosstanie 1705–06 g.* (Moscow: Izd-vo Moskovskogo univ-ta, 1975), 130–33, 174.

[22]Ibid., 175–76, 197; *AVD* 1:250, no. 160.

the government sent presents to Ayuki accompanied by the request that he dispatch the Kalmyk cavalry.[23] The presents, however, were very modest when compared with the favors conferred on the Don cossacks. In addition to their annual payment and supply of arms, the cossacks also received twenty rubles per person for not joining the rebels.[24] Ayuki's request that he be supplied with four cannons, gunpowder, and bullets was turned down, and Moscow instructed the local authorities to find a suitable and respectful pretext for the refusal.[25]

Nevertheless, Ayuki decided to join the government troops because the arrival of the regular Russian army would mean a quick end to the uprising and hence the promise of good spoils. Ayuki provided the Russian commander with information about the rebels' possible alliance with the Kuban Nogays and Karakalpaks and sent his Kalmyks to join the Russian army. Describing the successful siege of Astrakhan, official reports mentioned that the Kalmyks were not skilled in siege warfare but were, nevertheless, of great help to the Russian army.[26] Unlike the well-known Razin uprising in the 1670s, or the Pugachev uprising a century later, the Astrakhan uprising of 1705–6 failed to gain the support of the cossacks and was therefore doomed to be swiftly extinguished. The participation of the Kalmyks on the government's side condemned the uprising to an even earlier end.

The role of the Kalmyks in quelling the uprising and the destruction they wrought in Astrakhan dominated the news of the day. Echoed in the reports of foreigners stationed in Moscow, the news reached the West that the rebellion has been put out single-handedly by the Kalmyk Ayuki Khan. Even the desperate Polish king, August II, in an attempt to secure his crown from the pretender, requested from Russia eight regiments of cavalry and four thousand Kalmyks.[27]

The Russo-Swedish war continued to make new demands on the Russian military. Among other problems, the military experienced a severe shortage of cavalry. In 1705–6 the government issued decrees obliging every eighty—later one hundred—households to provide one armed horseman.[28] According to Moscow's plans, the Kalmyks were to provide from ten to fifteen thousand horsemen. Taught by unfortunate

[23]Golikova, *Astrakhanskoe vosstanie*, 231, 284.

[24]*AVD* 1:252, no. 162.

[25]*Perepiska fel'dmarshalov F. A. Golovina i B. P. Sheremet'eva v 1705–6 gg.* (Moscow: Tip. V. Got'e, 1851), 59–60; *PB* 4, pt. 1:221, no. 1203.

[26]*PB* 4, pt. 2:822, note to no. 1202; *Perepiska fel'dmarshalov*, 42; Golikova, *Astrakhanskoe vosstanie*, 238–39, 300.

[27]Golikova, *Astrakhanskoe vosstanie*, 204; *PB* 4, pt. 1:293, no. 1272; 337, no. 1321.

[28]*PSZ* 4:313, 350, no. 2065. The need for horses was met by purchasing them from Ayuki, as well as from the areas of the Kuban and Kabarda (*PB* 4, pt. 2:825, note to no. 1203; *Perepiska fel'dmarshalov*, 50).

previous experience, this time the Russian officials requested the Kalmyks to arrive at the pastures near the Dnieper River and spend the winter there so that in the spring they would be ready to set out immediately on campaign.[29] Contrary to expectations, no more than three thousand Kalmyks left to join the Russian army against Swedish troops. Shortly before these Kalmyks reached Moscow, they suddenly turned around and went home, plundering a few Russian villages on the way.[30]

The Bashkir Uprising

Attempts to employ the Kalmyks in the battles of two regular armies proved unsuccessful once again. The Kalmyks were much more effective in launching raids against the irregular armies of their neighbors, and the following years provided numerous opportunities to do so. Peter I's reforms were causing widespread discontent. In many areas, accumulated vexations were ready to spill over into violent uprisings. This time again it happened in a remote part of Russia where the control of central authorities was weaker and the abuses by local officials exacted a heavier toll. At the end of 1708 the peoples of the middle Volga area rose against the new taxes imposed on them by the government to subsidize the continuing war. Although numerous other peoples participated in this uprising, it is usually referred to as the Bashkir uprising.[31]

The final spark that ignited the uprising in the middle Volga area was the tsar's order to execute a certain Murad Sultan, who fell captive near the town of Tersk while trying to capture it with a group of Nogays.[32] The Bashkir uprising occurred at the same time that the army of the Swedish king, Charles XII, entered the Ukraine. In this situation Peter I could not afford to send sufficient Russian troops to quell the rebellion so that the Kalmyks were to become the main force in the ensuing punitive expedition. This time Ayuki was easily persuaded to march against the Bashkirs. The Bashkirs were his old foes, and the campaign offered abundant booty. In contrast to his previous contributions to the Russian military, for this campaign Ayuki promised to send twenty thousand Kalmyks, eight thousand armed with muskets.[33]

The Bashkir uprising was only one in a series of revolts against the

[29]*PB* 4, pt. 2:397, note to no. 1523.

[30]Bakunin, "Opisanie," *Krasnyi arkhiv* 3 (1939): 200; *PB* 6:337, note to no. 1950.

[31]The detailed course of the events is outlined in V. I. Lebedev, "Bashkirskoe vosstanie 1705–11 gg.," *Istoricheskie zapiski* 1 (1937): 81–102.

[32]For a detailed account of Murad Sultan's adventures see Michael Khodarkovsky, "Uneasy Alliance: Peter the Great and Ayuki Khan," *Central Asian Survey* 7, no. 4 (1988): 10–11.

[33]*PB* 7, pt. 1:635, note to no. 2347; *Materialy po istorii Bashkirskoi,* 1:235, no. 101.

Russian authorities. Discontent among the Don cossacks, which had been growing for some time, finally burst forth. After the conquest of Azov, Moscow felt that it could tighten its grip on the Don cossacks. One restrictive order followed another, further encroaching on cossack independence. Various decrees required the cossacks' relocation closer to Azov, the demolition of new cossack settlements, and the return of Russian fugitives who had recently joined the cossacks.[34] The tone of the decrees became increasingly imperative and the punishments applied extremely harsh. In 1708 the Don cossacks rebelled against the loss of their traditional liberties.

The Russian government asked Ayuki to send his people against the cossacks. Ayuki replied that he had sent all his horsemen to campaign against the Bashkirs and he had only a few people left to protect his uluses and to gather intelligence.[35] Instead, four thousand Kalmyks of Munko-Temir tayishi crossed the Volga and moved against the cossacks. Apparently, this force was insufficient, and it was decided to split twenty thousand of Ayuki's Kalmyks into two groups, sending ten thousand against the Bashkirs and ten thousand against the cossacks.[36] In the end, seven thousand Kalmyks led by Chakdorjab, together with five hundred Russian troops of Ivan Bakhmet'ev, pillaged the Bashkir villages and took many captives.[37]

The Kalmyks played a crucial role in quelling the Bashkir and cossack uprisings, as the Russian officials on the scene explicitly stated in their reports to Moscow. Prince P. I. Khovanskii reported that the Kalmyks were the main fighting force in the area and that they had saved Saratov from the rebellious cossacks. The Astrakhan governor Petr Matveevich Apraksin went even further in his appreciation of Ayuki's Kalmyks. He noted that it was difficult to exist in this part of the country without Ayuki's assistance.[38]

The Russo-Kalmyk Treaties of 1708 and 1710

For the time being, the roles traditionally ascribed to the Don cossacks and the Kalmyks were reversed; the cossacks proved to be unreliable, while the Kalmyks performed valuable service. Newly strengthened Kal-

[34]Solov'ev, *Istoriia Rossii*, bk. 8, vol. 15:176–77.

[35]Ibid., 175. After the departure of Ayuki's Tatar and Nogay subjects to the Kuban and those of Sanjib to Jungaria, it seems that the Kalmyk army of twenty thousand horsemen was indeed the maximum Ayuki could muster.

[36]*PB* 7, pt. 1:626–27, note to no. 2340; 8, pt. 2:956, note to no. 2842.

[37]*Materialy po istorii Bashkirskoi*, 1:266, no. 119.

[38]*PB* 7, pt. 2:892–93, note to no. 2438; 750–51, note to no. 2386.

myk-Russian relations culminated in the signing of another treaty between Ayuki and Petr Apraksin, who had just been appointed governor of all the middle and lower Volga region, including the towns of Tersk, Astrakhan, Ufa, and Kazan. On September 30, 1708, while on his way to Kazan to assume the new responsibilities, Apraksin met Ayuki on the Akhtuba River, two hundred versts from Astrakhan. There they signed a document in which the government found a new diplomatic formula for dealing with the Kalmyks and determining their political status. In all seventeenth-century oaths, the government blatantly sought to enforce the Kalmyks' subject status to the Russian crown. The 1708 agreement was meant to achieve the same goal but in a different fashion. Ayuki was now officially referred to as a khan. The agreement was signed between two equal parties—the minister and Governor P. M. Apraksin and Ayuki Khan—who shook hands and promised to be sincere friends and foster brothers. Both of them, however, were supposed to serve His Majesty, the tsar.

It would appear that by the early eighteenth century the Russian authorities had learned more about their Kalmyk nomadic neighbors. The government finally realized that the Kalmyk khan never perceived his relationship to the Russian tsar as one of subject and suzerain, but rather as between two brothers. In the kinship-based political language of Kalmyk society it meant friendship and cooperation between two allies. Russian imperial dignity could not fully recognize this, much less express it officially. Hence Moscow found a more subtle way of dealing with the Kalmyks. The logic was simple but effective: power was delegated to a local governor, and Ayuki was recognized on a par with him, but both remained the subjects of the tsar. Ayuki's lack of awareness of these subtleties can be clearly discerned from his ensuing correspondence with Apraksin in which Ayuki referred to the governor as "my minor, younger brother"[39]—in Kalmyk diplomatic language an explicit statement of Apraksin's inferior position.

The 1708 agreement consisted of eight articles. The Russian government recognized in the usual terms Ayuki's faithful service to the tsar and encouraged him to perform similar services in the future whenever the sovereign might need them. The agreement stipulated that payment would be provided only upon the performance of military service. Ayuki Khan was not to leave the banks of the Volga and should not let the tayishis cross the Volga westward to plunder Russian towns and settlements. Those tayishis who had done so in the past, particularly Chemet and Munko-Temir, were to be restrained from such activities. Ayuki

[39]*Russko-kitaiskie otnosheniia,* 1:111, no. 53.

promised to do so but explained that these tayishis' pastures were far away from his and that he was not always aware of their plans and actions. He also promised to send five thousand Kalmyks against the Nogays and the Kabardinians, who had besieged the town of Tersk in the past and were constantly raiding its suburbs. In return for Ayuki's promises, the Russian government made a commitment to protect Ayuki from his enemies and to supply him with Russian troops and cannons, if needed.[40]

The contents of the agreement reveal that it was yet another attempt to secure military cooperation and the cessation of hostilities between the two parties. This is precisely how Ayuki viewed it. But the phrasing of the agreement and its terminology were intended to emphasize Ayuki's status as a subject and conveyed this impression to future historians.

In the wake of the agreement, the rewards and payments received by the Kalmyks were more substantial than ever. For their participation in the Bashkir campaign of 1708 the Kalmyk tayishis received seven thousand rubles, although Prince B. A. Golitsyn requested that Moscow send ten thousand rubles for this purpose. The following year, with a request to provide three thousand Kalmyks for the approaching decisive confrontation with the Swedish army, Governor Apraksin sent Ayuki one thousand ducats, two falcons, and four thousand rubles' worth of furs.[41]

In June 1709 Ayuki dispatched a contingent of 3,300 horsemen against the Swedish army in the Ukraine. Led by Chakdorjab, they proceeded toward Khar'kov and then Poltava. The rumors, perhaps deliberately spread, that Ayuki was approaching with a force of forty thousand Kalmyks caused panic in the Swedish camp. In fact, the Kalmyk contingent arrived at Poltava on July 4, a few days after the battle of Poltava had been fought.[42]

The small size of the contingent and Ayuki's lack of enthusiasm for campaigns against Sweden clearly indicate that his interests and concerns were different from those of the Russian government. The rebellion in the middle Volga region gained even more strength when Kaziy, a newly chosen khan from among the Karakalpaks, arrived in the region in the early 1709 to lead the revolt.[43] In addition to the continuous depredations from the cossacks, the Kalmyks increasingly became a target of more daring raids by the Karakalpaks and Kazakhs. There were further rumors that the rebellious cossacks, Karakalpaks, Bashkirs, Kazakhs, and

---

[40]*PSZ* 4:419–22, no. 2207.

[41]*PB* 8, pt. 2:956, note to no. 2842; 9, pt. 2:793–94, note to no. 3145.

[42]*PB* 9, pt. 2:932, note to no. 3218; 9, pt. 2:970, note to no. 3242.

[43]Lebedev, "Bashkirskoe vosstanie 1705–11 gg.," 98. (The name *Khazei* mentioned in the Russian account is a corruption of the Nogay and Karakalpak *Kaziy*.)

Kuban Nogays had reached an agreement to unite against Russia.[44] The prospect of facing such a powerful alliance was not appealing to Ayuki.

Having little trust in the Russian government's promises of support, Ayuki began to search for ways to conclude peace agreements with his adversaries. In winter 1709, before military activities resumed in the spring-summer season, he sent a letter to the Bashkirs with an offer of peace. The Bashkirs showed complete confidence in Ayuki's promises, and when Governor Apraksin threatened the Bashkirs with unleashing Ayuki against them, they replied that Ayuki had offered them peace and would not lie about it.[45] In the following two years Ayuki indeed sent no troops against the Bashkirs.

To reaffirm his good intentions and the present alliance with the Muslim peoples, Ayuki in 1709 sent to the Porte Mehmed Salih Beg, the envoy from among Ayuki's Nogay subjects. Mehmed Salih Beg arrived at the Porte in August 1709 and delivered a letter, the contents of which are not known. The envoy was accorded many imperial favors and was sent back with an Ottoman letter. This written response to Ayuki's message was similar to previous ones. It encouraged Ayuki "to be firm on his path of loyalty and friendship," admonished him to show respect to the Crimea, and praised him for not having joined the rebellion of the Circassian khan against the Crimea.[46]

Reassured by the warm reception given to Mehmed Salih Beg, the following year Ayuki sent another embassy to the Porte to report his deeds. The Kalmyk embassy, led by Pehlivan Kuli Beg, arrived at the Porte at the end of July 1710. This time Ayuki's letter was addressed to the grand vizier and contained similar affirmations of friendship. For the first time, however, the Ottoman officials recorded the oral message of the Kalmyk envoy, which is significant.

The envoy mentioned the events that led to the capture and execution of Murad Sultan and explained that the Russians wanted Ayuki to send his Kalmyks against the Ishteks.[47] Ayuki refused twice, having told the Russians: "You murdered the Ishtek Sultan, and they [the Ishteks] are still in a blood feud [*kan dâvasi*] with you, and I cannot and will not stop

---

[44]*PB* 9, pt. 2:850–51, note to no. 3174; Solov'ev, *Istoriia Rossii*, bk. 8, vol. 15:175.

[45]*Materialy po istorii Bashkirskoi*, 1:256, no. 116.

[46]BA *Nâme-i Hümayun*, no. 6, pp. 201, 520.

[47]Ishtek is usually assumed to be the name the Kazakhs and Nogays used for the Bashkirs. The peoples of the Volga area, however, clearly distinguished between the Bashkirs (Bashkurt) and the Ishteks (Kurat, *VI–XVIII Yüzyillarda Karadeniz*, 376–77). Most likely, the Ishteks were nomadic and seminomadic people of the eastern and southern regions of the Bashkiriia and different from the Bashkirs of the more agricultural northern region.

them. We are in agreement with each other, [because] we are all descendants of Chinggis [Khan] and originated from the same clan."[48] The envoy then related an event that had occurred the previous winter. When forty thousand Russian troops marched against the Ishteks, Ayuki assisted the Ishteks, who counterattacked, forcing the Russians to withdraw onto the ice at a place where the Volga was frozen. The Ishteks then cut the ice above and below the Russians' position, and the Russian army with its horses and baggage train sank. The envoy added that at the time of his departure from the Kalmyk ulus, the envoys of the Ishteks, Karakalpaks, and Kazakhs were visiting Ayuki Khan.[49]

One cannot fail to observe that the true facts in the account are mixed with nonsensical allegations, such as the exaggerated size of the Russian army and Ayuki's preposterous claim to be a descendant of Chinggis Khan. All of them, however, served one purpose—to underscore Ayuki's loyalty and the valuable service he had performed to the Porte and to present himself as an ally of the Muslim peoples, with whom Ayuki could more easily find a common ground in ties of kinship, rather than religious affinity.

Meanwhile, the Russian government approached Ayuki again. In September 1710 Governor Apraksin and Ayuki Khan met and signed a new agreement providing Ayuki with an annuity of one thousand rubles and increased amounts of gunpowder and bullets in exchange for military cooperation.[50] The tsar personally requested that Ayuki and all his people move to the Don and spend the winter there. The strategic plans of the Russian government called for the Kalmyks to assume temporarily the role traditionally played by the Don cossacks, who were still in revolt. Roaming along two tributaries of the Don—the Sal and Manych rivers— the Kalmyks were to form a mobile defense line to stop the cossack and the Nogay raids and to prevent the Crimean Tatars and the Kuban Nogays from uniting their forces.

Ayuki Khan and the tayishis Chemet, Cheter, and Donduk-Ombo all signed the agreement and promised to meet the Russian requests. The following year ten thousand of Ayuki's Kalmyks were campaigning

---

[48]BA *Nâme-i Hümayun*, no. 6, p. 201.

[49]Ibid., 201–2. Two Ottoman chronicles also briefly describe the mission of the Kalmyk envoy to the Porte (Rashid, *Tarikh-i Rashid*, 3:326–27; Findiklili, *Nusretnâme*, 2:262). The chronicles differ slightly in the time of embassy's arrival and in presentation of the events. The account presented above is by far the most reliable.

[50]*PSZ* 4:547–50, no. 2291. An annual salary of one thousand rubles equaled that of a Russian major general (a foreign officer of the same rank usually received almost twice as much as his Russian counterpart). For annual salaries of the Russian army officers in the early eighteenth century see *PSZ* 4:590, no. 2319.

against the Bashkirs.[51] Another ten thousand spent the winter on the Don and apparently saw no action. In spring 1711 Ayuki asked for instructions because no one seemed to know what these Kalmyks were supposed to do.[52] The answer came when war, which broke out anew between the Ottoman and Russian empires, provided employment for the Kalmyks.

Among the Ottomans' numerous grievances against the Russians was a recent raid on the Crimea by a band of Kalmyks and Russians, who killed twenty Muslims, pillaged their property, and drove away seventeen hundred head of cattle.[53] In November 1710 the thirty-year truce between the Russians and Ottomans was abrogated.

The Kuban Campaign of 1711

Never had the victorious Russian tsar been so confident of his military success and convinced of his destiny than after his triumph over the Swedish king at Poltava. Throughout the winter, Peter made preparations for the approaching encounter with the Ottoman army. In his plans the Kalmyks were to be employed as the counterforce against the Kuban Nogays. The Kalmyks proved to be more than a mere counterforce, and their campaign against the Kuban Nogays brought devastation of immense proportions to the region.

In early March 1711, Peter wrote to Ayuki promising him plentiful rewards if he set out with his people against the Kuban. P. M. Apraksin was supposed to join Ayuki later with Russian troops. Ayuki promised to send the Kalmyks and reassured the Russian authorities that the Kuban Nogays would not be able to withstand his assault. One of Ayuki's confidants secretly informed the Russians that Ayuki had his own reasons for raiding the Kuban, where those Yedisans and Yamboyluks who had deserted him in the past had taken refuge.[54]

Despite his enthusiastic promises, Ayuki was slow to act. One dramatic event, however, made Ayuki step up his campaign preparations. Returning from one of their raids in the Saratov-Penza area, the Kuban Nogays together with a group of rebellious cossacks encountered a small Kalmyk contingent led by Chemet tayishi. In the ensuing skirmish the Kalmyks were defeated and Chemet tayishi was captured and beheaded.[55] Or-

[51]*Materialy po istorii Bashkirskoi*, 1:276, no. 127.
[52]*PB* 10:677–78, note to no. 3885.
[53]Rashid, *Tarikh-i Rashid*, 3:340; Findiklili, *Nusretnâme*, 2:266.
[54]*PB* 11, pt. 1:94–95, no. 4281; 123–24, no. 4313; 134, no. 4324.
[55]Ibid., 495–96, note to no. 4443.

dinarily, prisoners of war were exchanged or ransomed. The execution of such a prisoner, particularly one of noble descent, was an act of dishonor and deliberate humiliation and invariably provoked a vendetta. The killing of Chemet tayishi infuriated Ayuki, who immediately turned his rage against the Kuban.

The movement of the Kalmyks had an immediate effect on the military situation in the area. Rumors of the Kalmyks' intended campaign against the Kuban induced ten thousand Kuban Nogays, who had already crossed the Don to join the Crimean army, to return home.[56] A Kalmyk army of 20,474 horsemen reportedly took part in this campaign. At the end of June, the Kalmyk army joined a unit of Governor Apraksin, 4,100 strong. The combined army of the Kalmyks, Russians, and Kabardinians arrived at Azov in the middle of August, and after a fifteen-day march through the steppes it reached the Kuban River. On the same day the vanguard of the expeditionary force, which consisted of 14,000 Kalmyks and 1,500 Russians, completely routed the Kuban Nogays. Two days later, joined by the rest of his army, Apraksin moved up the Kuban, burned numerous villages, and destroyed the Kuban town of Kopyl (Kopich in Turkish), the residence of the Kuban sultans.

The Kalmyks are reported to have slaughtered the male population, taking women and children captive. During the four days of the campaign, the Kuban area lost 38,540 of its residents. Out of this formidable number, 11,460 Kubans were killed, 5,060 drowned in the river, and 22,100 were taken captive, among them only 700 males, the rest being women and children. The Kalmyks also captured 2,000 camels, 39,200 horses, 190,000 cattle, and 220,000 sheep. The value of this enormous booty was enough to capitalize more than 11,000 families. The disaster was immense but still not complete, as fortune stubbornly refused to show any signs of favor to the Kubans. On the way home, the Russian commander Apraksin learned that a group of 3,000 Kuban Nogays was returning to the Kuban after successful raids deep in Russia. A promptly dispatched Kalmyk contingent intercepted and defeated the Kubans, and as a result 2,000 Russian captives obtained freedom. An army of 7,000 people led by the Crimean *nureddin* (the third most important office in the Crimea), who was dispatched to help the Kubans, was also routed by the Kalmyks.[57]

---

[56]Ibid., 134, no. 4324.

[57]N. E. Brandenburg, "Kubanskii pokhod 1711 g.," *Voennyi sbornik* 54 (1867): 29–42; *PB* 11, pt. 2:397, note to no. 4657; Akdes Nimet Kurat, *Prut Seferi ve Barişi 1123 (1711)*, 2 vols. (Ankara: Türk Tarihi Kurumu Basimevi, 1951–53), 2:578–82; Kirimi al-Hâj 'Abd al-Ghaffâr, *'Umdat al-Tawârikh*, ed. Necib Asim, *TOEM*, supplement 11 (Istanbul: Matbaa-i Amire, 1924), 154.

In November 1711 Peter I wrote to Apraksin from Riga thanking him for the destruction he had wrought upon the Kuban.[58] After the disastrous Prut campaign, when the tsar himself almost fell captive to the Ottomans and was forced to sign a humiliating treaty, the Kuban massacre or, to use a contemporary expression, "the successful campaign in the Kuban," served Peter as perhaps the only consolation in a year that otherwise was miserable for him.

Upon completion of the Kuban campaign, the Russian government, instead of increasing rewards, increased its demands on the Kalmyk military. In the spring of 1712 Ayuki was supposed to send no less than fifteen thousand Kalmyks to take up a position in the Ukraine, between the towns of Izium and Khar'kov, in case the Ottomans resumed military operations. At the same time, Governor Apraksin sent his representatives to Ayuki to ask for twenty thousand horses free of charge.[59]

The envoy Ayuki dispatched to Moscow brought a letter addressed to Chancellor G. I. Golovkin, in which Ayuki stated his grievances in no uncertain terms. He complained about bureaucratic procedures set up by the government to prevent his embassies from going directly to Moscow by rerouting them to Saratov and then to Kazan. He complained about the customs duties his trade representatives had to pay in To-bol'sk, about the unheard-of request for twenty thousand horses free of charge, about the constant demands for the Kalmyk cavalry, and about other issues. Ayuki vaguely promised to send fifteen thousand Kalmyks but explained that to do so was risky because of expected Kuban raids against his uluses.[60]

The presence of the Kalmyks in the Ukraine was an important part of Peter I's strategic plans. To encourage Ayuki, the tsar ordered that the grievances be addressed and that apart from the fifty thousand rubles appropriated for paying fifteen thousand Kalmyk and five thousand cossack troops, an additional five thousand rubles be immediately delivered to Ayuki.[61] In the face of the Kuban raids, even such an attractive payment could not persuade Ayuki to send a significant part of his cavalry to the Ukraine. The issue disappeared altogether when the good news of a renewed peace treaty arrived from Istanbul. For the time being, the Kalmyk cavalry was no longer needed in the Ukraine.[62]

---

[58]*PB* 11, pt. 2:599, note to no. 4953.

[59]Ibid., pt. 1:433, 435, note to no. 5184.

[60]The Kuban Nogays, demanding the return of their prisoners, had been about to set out the previous year but aborted the campaign when they learned that the Russian detachment had been sent to assist Ayuki (*PB* 11, pt. 1:435–36).

[61]Ibid., 436–39; *SRIO* 11:227, no. 55; 25:355, no. 311.

[62]*PB* 12, pt. 1:527, note to no. 5274.

Ayuki under Siege

Both the Ottomans and the Russians were aware of the disastrous effect the full-fledged participation of the Kalmyks in the war would have on the opposite side. When in June 1711 the Ottomans and the Russians finally concluded a peace treaty—which remained in effect for twenty-five years—one of its eleven clauses was devoted solely to the Kalmyk raids. Clause nine stipulated:

> No Muscovites or subjects of Muscovy are to be found among the Kalmyks who show any hostility and cause any harm to the Crimean people, who are the subjects of the Sublime Porte, or to the Circassians and Nogays, who are the subjects of the Crimea; and the Crimeans or other Tatar peoples shall not use the Kalmyks as an excuse to cause any harm to the Muscovites or Muscovy. When damage has been caused by either side, then the disobedient ones shall be firmly seized and punished; captured people and cattle shall be returned.[63]

This provison of the treaty is a good illustration of the Porte's equivocal attitude toward the Kalmyks. On one hand, the document recognized their political independence from Russia and, in a way, the inevitability of their raids. On the other hand, Russia was encouraged to exercise the political and military means available to restrain such raids against Ottoman subjects. Apparently, after the devastation the Kalmyks had inflicted on the Kuban, the Porte realized that even such moderate goals of its policies toward the Kalmyks as keeping them at peace with the Muslim peoples could not be easily attained.

To avenge the Kuban massacre the Porte intended to send troops against the Kalmyks in 1712 and to direct that the Kazakhs attack the Kalmyks from the east. A letter containing the outline of this plan was sent to Kazakh khan Gayib Mehmed with a returning Muslim pilgrim. The pilgrim, however, after leaving Astrakhan, was captured by the Kalmyks, and only rumors of such a letter reached the Kazakh khan. Uncertain that the letter had indeed been dispatched, Gayib Mehmed decided to attack the Kalmyks and launched two raids against them. Later, the Kazakh khan sent his envoy to the Porte to report his deeds and his intention to proceed with more raids against the Kalmyks, who were not faithful servants of the Ottoman sultan.[64]

A similar letter was brought to the Porte from the khan of Bukhara Abul

---

[63]BA *Nâme-i Hümayun*, no. 6, p. 286; *Muahedat Mejmuasi*, 5 vols. (Istanbul: Jerede-i Askeriye Matbaasi [1878–82]), 3:227.

[64]BA *Nâme-i Hümayun*, no. 6, pp. 292–93.

Fayiz Sayid Mehmed Bahadur Khan. The khan also wanted to know whether the news was true that the Kalmyks, who had previously been the khan's friends, were now allied with Russia and had turned against the people of Islam. If it was true, the khan suggested that he should attack the Kalmyks from one side, while the Ottoman-Crimean forces would attack from the other.[65] One can safely assume that both embassies returned home with the sultan's approval of the campaign against the Kalmyks because vigorous Karakalpak and Kazakh raids were conducted the next year, 1714.[66]

Daring Kazakh and Karakalpak raids were motivated not only by fervent religious zeal and a sense of Islamic solidarity. Nomadic societies are more often guided by their customary, unwritten rules and their own sense of security than by any ideological premise. One such unwritten rule implies that, when dissent and rivalry break out among the leaders of one nomadic group, this action necessarily invites the predatory activity of other nomadic groups. At the time, further discord between Ayuki and his eldest son, Chakdorjab, made the Kalmyks a convenient raiding target. In his letter to the sultan, Kazakh khan Gayib Mehmed explicitly stated that he intended to take advantage of the division among the Kalmyks.[67]

The new conflict between Ayuki and Chakdorjab occurred over the issue of inheritance of Chemet tayishi's ulus. After Chemet was killed by the Kubans, Chakdorjab seized Chemet's two wives and his entire ulus. Ayuki insisted that since Chemet had no sons, the ulus should pass into the possession of Chemet's nephew Abasha (corrupted Ubashi?). Unable to force Chakdorjab to return the ulus, Ayuki wrote to the tsar requesting that a special envoy be sent to Saratov to arbitrate the case; only then, he added, would Chakdorjab agree to return the ulus. A Russian official was thereupon dispatched to Saratov.[68] Perhaps he helped to reconcile the old and wise father with his mutinous son, or perhaps the increasing number of Kazakh raids was even more compelling than the arguments of the Russian official. In any event, the two were reconciled in the summer of 1714, when in the presence of eminent Qing envoys and numerous Kalmyk nobles and clergy, Ayuki declared Chakdorjab to be his legitimate heir. As an act of confirmation, Ayuki handed Chakdorjab the khan's seal, which he had received from Tibet in 1690.[69]

The increased Kazakh and Karakalpak raids from the east and the

[65]Ibid., 296–97.
[66]*Materialy po istorii karakalpakov*, 164.
[67]BA *Nâme-i Hümayun*, no. 6, p. 292.
[68]*Russko-kitaiskie otnosheniia*, 1:145, no. 91.
[69]Bakunin, "Opisanie," *Krasnyi arkhiv* 3 (1939): 205; Pal'mov, *Etiudy*, 3–4:47–49.

constant threat of Kuban-Crimean raids from the southwest compelled the Kalmyks to seek even closer ties with Russia. In time, the Kalmyk military grew more dependent on Russian supplies of firearms, gunpowder, and bullets, and the Kalmyk tayishis became more accustomed to the Russian way of life. They became more conscious of luxury goods such as furs, woolens, silks, and even such wonders as watches—all of which were important status symbols.[70] The ordinary Kalmyks grew accustomed to those little pieces of metal called money, which they could exchange for certain goods.

Likewise, the Russian residents of the Volga towns were dependent on the Kalmyks' supplies of horses and cattle, and the government needed Kalmyk horses and, even more, Kalmyk horsemen. In times of war, the Kalmyk cavalry was invaluable in harassing the enemy's rear, providing intelligence, and neutralizing the enemy's cavalry. In times of peace, the Kalmyks served as a mobile defense line against possible incursions. As the events of 1711–14 showed, both goals could be achieved with increased payments and rewards and with more lenient and receptive policies. There was another factor, however, that made Russia's attitude toward the Kalmyks particularly accommodating during 1712–14. This factor was a high-ranking embassy dispatched by the Manchu emperor to Ayuki Khan.

The Qing Embassy Visits Ayuki

In November 1712 the embassy from China entered Russian Siberia. Russian officials reported that it consisted of seven senior envoys and twenty-six other people. It was presumed to be on an important mission. Moscow instructed the border officials to let the embassy through but to try to learn its goals.[71] Fearful that the embassy had been sent to enlist Ayuki against the Jungar khan Tsevang-Rabtan, the government, during the years when the embassy was traversing Russian territory, tried to placate Ayuki and assumed a conciliatory attitude toward the Kalmyks.[72] Moscow's fears were confirmed by the news dispatches from Siberia, where Russian officials had heard rumors to this effect. It was perhaps

---

[70]On the occasion of the arrival of the Qing embassy, Ayuki and Chakdorjab requested numerous items from Astrakhan, as well as one hundred dragoons with cannons and flutes to greet the Qing officials (*Russko-kitaiskie otnosheniia*, 1:nos. 94–96, 99).

[71]Ibid., 130–32, nos. 74, 76.

[72]Shortly before the arrival of the embassy to the Kalmyks, Ayuki sent his envoy to Moscow with several requests, which were immediately acted upon (*Russko-kitaiskie otnosheniia*, 1:145–46, nos. 91, 92).

on this basis that future historians believed that the Qing embassy attempted to recruit Ayuki.[73]

If the event is considered in the context of the political situation in Inner Asia as well as Sino-Russian and Sino-Kalmyk relations, the story will appear to be quite different from that which has been ordinarily assumed. The official pretext of the 1714 Qing embassy to Ayuki was to settle the issue of return of Ayuki's nephew Arabjur, who in 1698 made a pilgrimage to Tibet and remained there for five years. The subsequent hostility between Ayuki and Tsevang-Rabtan over Sanjib's ulus prevented Arabjur from returning via the traditional route through Jungaria. Awaiting more favorable conditions, Arabjur went to China, where he was welcomed by the emperor.[74]

In May 1709 the Kalmyk embassy went to China via a new route through Russian Siberia. The embassy consisted of five envoys from Ayuki and three from Chakdorjab. At Ayuki's request, the embassy was accompanied by a Russian officer and other military personnel. Later the same year the embassy arrived in China.[75] Its ostensible goal was to scout a new route for Arabjur's return.

Such lively Sino-Kalmyk relations cannot be explained only by concern over Arabjur's return. There is little doubt that the embassies had other political goals as well. The evidence suggests that Ayuki was interested in an alliance with China to take revenge on Tsevang-Rabtan and recover the lost uluses. The Qing envoys were explicitly instructed to promise no action against Tsevang-Rabtan if Ayuki mentioned the issue.[76] It is reasonable to assume that Ayuki, aware of the growing tensions between Tsevang-Rabtan and the Qing government, sent his own embassy to China in 1709 to suggest joint action against the Jungar khan. The 1714 Qing embassy to Ayuki came to find out more about the Kalmyks and their military capabilities.

This was not the sole goal of the Qing mission, however, nor was it the most important one. Only a small part of the written instructions to the Qing envoys was devoted to the Kalmyks. A far more significant part of the memorandum was concerned with Russia. The envoys were instructed on how to behave and what to answer, when and if they met the

---

[73]Zlatkin, *Istoriia Dzhungarskogo,* 224–25. Although the emperor's written instructions to the embassy are in total contradition with the above-mentioned assumption of the embassy's goals, Bantysh-Kamenskii presumed that there must have been a secret oral message to Ayuki (Bantysh-Kamenskii, *Diplomaticheskoe sobranie del,* 76). Pal'mov has agreed with him (Pal'mov, *Etiudy,* 1:19).

[74]Bantysh-Kamenskii, *Diplomaticheskoe sobranie del,* 75.

[75]*Russko-kitaiskie otnosheniia,* 1:111–13, nos. 53–54.

[76]"Zapiski Tulishenia," 439.

Russian tsar. They were to find out about the Russo-Swedish war, Siberian garrisons, Russian customs and morals, and the Russian people—to gather and bring home information regarding Russia's military, political, and social conditions.[77] Apparently, the Manchu emperor, ready to start a war with Tsevang-Rabtan, was concerned about the possibility of Russia's military assistance and its alliance with the Jungar khan. Thus the desire to learn more about its rapidly expanding neighbor to the north and west prompted the Manchu government to take the extraordinary step of sending an embassy to the barbaric lands. The pretext of sending it to the Kalmyk khan could not have been more convenient.

A detailed account of the embassy's two-year travels through Russia was written shortly afterward by one of the embassy's envoys, a Manchu named Tulishen.[78] After a long journey and many delays, the Qing embassy finally arrived in July 1714 at a place called Muntokhay,[79] where Ayuki was awaiting his eminent guests. The embassy was received with much pomp and the next day was given its first audience. During their fourteen-day stay with the Kalmyks, the envoys were received several times by Ayuki and were entertained with feasts and tournaments. In the course of the discussions, Ayuki displayed a good knowledge of the current state of Qing political affairs and bombarded the envoys with many questions about China's geography, climate, military, ethnic composition, and the emperor's life-style.[80] Neither side raised the issue of a war against Tsevang-Rabtan. As far as Arabjur's return was concerned, it

[77]Ibid., 440, 443.

[78]This fascinating account was first published in Manchurian in 1723 and later the same year translated into Chinese. It has since been translated into many languages, including Russian (the latest among several translations is "Zapiski Tulishenia," 437–83), French (Paul Le Gaubil, "Relation chinoise contenant un itinéraire de Peking à Tobol, et de Tobol au pays des Tourgouts," Observations mathématiques, astronomiques, géographiques, chronologiques et physiques, vol. 1 [Paris and Rollin: N.p., 1729]), English (Sir George Thomas Staunton, Narrative of the Chinese Embassy to the Khan of the Tourgouth Tatars, in the Years 1712, 13, 14, and 15 by the Chinese Embassador [London: J. Murray, 1821]), German (Giovanni Stary, Chinas erste Gesandte in Russland [Wiesbaden: Otto Harrassowitz, 1976]), and Japanese (Shunju Imanishi, Tulishen's I-yü-lu [Nara, Japan: Tenri Daigaku, 1964]).

[79]The location of Muntokhay is a disputed issue. I believe Pallas was correct in designating it as an area between the Volga and Akhtuba rivers extending from Tsaritsyn to Chernyi Iar (Pallas, Travels through the Southern Provinces, 199). Tulishen's map and description of the place also point to the same locale ("Zapiski Tulishenia," 473–74). The name is derived from the Kalmyk men tokho, which literally means correct bend, and indicates the area where both rivers bend to form one of the richest grasslands in the Caspian steppes and a traditional pasture of many nomadic peoples (cf. Golstunskii, Mongolo-oiratskie zakony, 102; Pal'mov, Etiudy, 1:25). Curiously, Edward Keenan traced the etymology of Kazan' to the Iranian origins also meaning bend, hook (Keenan, "Kazan'—The Bend," Harvard Ukrainian Studies 3–4 [1979–80]: 484–96).

[80]"Zapiski Tulishenia," 467–72.

was agreed that Ayuki should petition the tsar to allow Arabjur to pass through Siberia.

Moscow was not particularly happy about Ayuki's relations with China. When the Qing requested that the embassy be allowed to pass through Siberia, the Russian government, reluctant to jeopardize Sino-Russian relations and the hard-won Nerchinsk Treaty of 1689, did not dare to deny its passage. It was easier instead to bar the Kalmyks from reaching China. At the end of 1714, even before the Qing embassy returned to Beijing, Ayuki dispatched his envoys to China. This time, however, the order from Moscow to the governor of the Siberian town of Tobol'sk commanded him to detain the Kalmyk envoys.

Ayuki wrote to the tsar explaining that he had sent the envoys with only one purpose, to buy tea and silks in China.[81] Since any political message he wanted to deliver to the Manchu emperor could have been carried by the recently departed Qing embassy, it is likely that Ayuki was telling the truth. The Kalmyks' interest in trade with China was to grow of necessity. Since the route to Tibet via Jungaria had become inaccessible, China remained the only place where the Kalmyks could procure such essentials as tea and Tibetan medicines, as well as various luxury goods.

The Russian government, nevertheless, was determined not to let Sino-Kalmyk relations flower. In his letter to Ayuki, Peter I vaguely explained that the envoys could not be allowed through because of the situation in the region. To soften the effect of this reply, however, the tsar ordered that Ayuki was to receive 2,500 *chetvert'* of grain and 3,000 rubles, with which he could purchase goods in Tobol'sk duty free. Meanwhile, the tsar's decree stipulated that Ayuki's relations with foreign powers were not to be discussed in the senate but handled in secret by the Chancellery of Foreign Affairs and supervised personally by Chancellor G. I. Golovkin. Special care was to be taken not to anger Ayuki.[82]

In April 1715 the Qing embassy returned safely to Beijing, bringing news of Russian preoccupation with the war against Sweden, the insignificance of the Russian garrisons in Siberia, and the tensions between the tsar and the Jungar khan. The emperor decided to act upon this intelligence immediately. He decreed that troops were to set out against Tsevang-Rabtan and that the Russian government was to be informed of this action.[83] As far as the Qing were concerned, the embassy had successfully accomplished its mission.

[81]*Russo-kitaiskie otnosheniia,* 1:155, no. 107.

[82]Ibid., 156–59, nos. 109–11; 168, no. 121.

[83]"Zapiski Tulishenia," 481.

Prince Bekovich-Cherkasskii's Expedition
and Its Consequences

In the history of Russia, the first quarter of the eighteenth century was a period of rapid modernization. The reforms inaugurated by Peter I shook the foundations of the old Muscovite state and, despite resistance from many quarters, had a dramatic impact on the society. A new capital rose on the shores of the Baltic Sea, newly built factories produced arms for the modernized Russian army, the bureaucracy was reorganized, and unfamiliar fashions and ideas from the West stirred up new aspirations among many Russians.

To subsidize his far-reaching changes and to pay for his military adventures, Peter sought new sources of revenue. In 1714 he organized two expeditions to search for mineral resources and, in particular, for gold. One was sent to the town of Yarkand (Erket), deep in Jungaria, to investigate the widespread rumors of gold sands there. Another expedition, led by Prince Aleksandr Bekovich-Cherkasskii, set out for the khanate of Khiva to learn more about the gold that was rumored to be found in the dried-up estuary of the Amu-Darya.[84]

Even though finding gold was the primary purpose of both expeditions, their agenda also included political goals. The leaders of the expeditionary forces were instructed to build fortresses along the way and to attempt to bring the local peoples into the Russian dominions. In particular, Bekovich-Cherkasskii's expedition was assigned such political and military tasks as winning over the Kumyk and Kabardinian people of the Caucasus, building a fortress on the Mangyshlak peninsula, and turning the khan of Khiva into a Russian subject.

Without adequate knowledge of the areas or any inkling of the extreme difficulties involved in such enterprises, both expeditions were doomed to failure. The Jungar expedition, led by Lieutenant Colonel Ivan Bukhgolts, was soon surrounded by a large Jungarian force. With their supplies cut off and troops consumed by such deadly diseases as the Siberian pest and scurvy, the remnants of the expeditionary force returned home.[85] An even more tragic fate befell Bekovich-Cherkasskii's expedition, and Ayuki Khan appears to have been one of the principal contributors to the expedition's unfortunate end.

[84]*PSZ* 5:105–6, no. 2811; 108–10, no. 2815. For a brief discussion of Russia's relations with Bukhara and Khiva see Edward A. Allworth, *The Modern Uzbeks, from the Fourteenth Century to the Present: A Cultural History* (Stanford: Hoover Institution Press, 1990), 90–100.

[85]A. N. Popov, "Snosheniia Rossii s Khivoi i Bukharoi pri Petre Velikom," *ZIRGO* 9 (1853): 248–51; A. I. Maksheev, "Karta Dzhungarii, sostavlennaia shvedom Renatom, vo vremia ego plena u kalmykov s 1716 po 1733 god," *ZIRGOOG* 11 (1888): 114.

In 1715–16 Prince Bekovich-Cherkasskii, in search of the old estuary of the Amu-Darya, explored the eastern shores of the Caspian Sea and founded two fortresses there: one, which he named St. Peter, was located on the Mangyshlak peninsula; the foundations of the other were laid on the shores of the Krasnovodsk Bay.[86] In the mid-1670s, the khan of Khiva in his correspondence with the Russian tsar, had suggested that the Russians should build a port on the Mangyshlak to secure the trade route to Khiva from the depredations of Kalmyk raids.[87] Now the initiative belonged to the Russian tsar.

Having reported his achievements to Peter I, Bekovich-Cherkasskii shortly thereafter received new instructions. He was to march toward Khiva with an expeditionary force of four thousand men to convince the khan of Khiva to accept Russian suzerainty. He was then to send people to find out about the route to Yarkand and India via the Amu-Darya and Syr-Darya rivers.[88]

Shortly before the expedition was ready to set forth, Ayuki sent letters to Bekovich-Cherkasskii's headquarters warning that the khan's troops were gathering in Khiva and of the difficulties entailed in marching through a desert region lacking water and fodder.[89] Ayuki's warnings did not seem to cause much concern in the Russian camp, and in summer 1717 Bekovich-Cherkasskii and his troops were on the way to Khiva. The expeditionary force now numbered only half of its planned strength because Bekovich-Cherkasskii had to leave some of his troops in the new fortresses to replace those who had perished from diseases. Bekovich-Cherkasskii wrote to Ayuki in the hope that he would send Turkmen reinforcements. Ayuki refused to provide any assistance, citing the excessive heat. Instead, he sent one Turkmen guide with ten other Kalmyks and Turkmen. Shortly thereafter, when Bekovich-Cherkasskii's force was camping at a place called Childan, about halfway to Khiva, the Turkmen guide together with other people sent by Ayuki fled. Some of them returned to the Kalmyks, others arrived in Khiva.[90] According to some reports, it was after these Kalmyk and Turkmen spies had arrived in Khiva that the khan ordered the arrest of Bekovich-Cherkasskii's envoys present in Khiva and began to assemble his army.[91]

---

[86]Popov, *Snosheniia Rossii s Khivoi i Bukharoi*, 242–43, 57.

[87]*Materialy po istorii Uzbekskoi*, 225, no. 87; 232, no. 93; 235, no. 95.

[88]*PSZ* 5:no. 2993.

[89]*Materialy po istorii karakalpakov*, 167, 293.

[90]Popov, *Snosheniia Rossii s Khivoi i Bukharoi*, 259–61; V. Illeretskii, "Ekspeditsiia kniazia Cherkasskogo v Khivu," *Istoricheskii zhurnal* 7 (1940): 47–49.

[91]Popov, *Snosheniia Rossii s Khivoi i Bukharoi*, 330; *Russko-turkmenskie otnosheniia v 18–19 vv. do prisoedineniia Turkmenii k Rossii. Sbornik arkhivnykh dokumentov* (Ashkhabad: Izd-vo AN Turkmenskoi SSR, 1963), 49, no. 24.

Soon an army of Khivans, Karakalpaks, Uzbeks, and Kazakhs had surrounded Bekovich-Cherkasskii's group. Helpless against the firepower of Russian cannons and muskets, however, the khan of Khiva, after a few unsuccessful attempts, gave up his plans for taking the Russian camp by force. Instead, the khan succeeded in convincing Bekovich-Cherkasskii of his good intentions and advised the Russian commander to divide his force in five different groups under the pretext that all the Russian troops could not be provisioned in one place. When the Russians, following Bekovich-Cherkasskii's order, left the camp and split in separate groups, they were immediately surrounded by the khan's troops, who killed some of them and took the rest captive. Prince Bekovich-Cherkasskii and his two assistants were killed. Their heads were cut off, stuffed with grass, and exhibited near one of the gates of Khiva.[92]

The blame for the annihilation of Prince Bekovich-Cherkasskii and his force was laid on Ayuki Khan. Ayuki had informed the khan of Khiva that Bekovich-Cherkasskii was simply posing as an envoy while his real intention was the conquest of the khanate. A few years later, the Bukharan envoy to Russia confirmed that he had personally seen a letter to this effect from Ayuki to the khan of Khiva.[93] At the same time, we must recall, Ayuki sent letters to Bekovich-Cherkasskii and other Russian officials warning of the dangers of such a campaign. By weaving a complex web of intrigues, Ayuki thought to protect himself from any unexpected turn of events.

A look at the events precededing the expedition reveals that Ayuki had his own reasons for playing such a game with Prince Bekovich-Cherkasskii. Despite the peace treaty between Russia and the Ottoman empire, which obliged both sides to restrain the Kalmyks and the Nogays respectively, clashes between the two nomadic peoples persisted. In 1714 the Kalmyk tayishis Cheter and Solom-Dorji led four or five thousand Kalmyks in a raid against the Kuban.[94] The Kubans responded with small raids until finally a long-awaited Kuban campaign against the Kalmyks took place in the spring and summer of 1715.

Aware that Bakhti Giray Sultan's sizable army of Kubans and Crimeans was about to launch a campaign, Ayuki and Chakdorjab sent numerous requests to Astrakhan for arms and soldiers. Yet Astrakhan was silent.

---

[92]Popov, *Snosheniia Rossii s Khivoi i Bukharoi*, 266–67; *Russko-turkmenskie otnosheniia*, 33–34, no. 13.

[93]Popov, *Snosheniia Rossii s Khivoi i Bukharoi*, 270; Bakunin, "Opisanie," *Krasnyi arkhiv* 3 (1939): 202. Ts. K. Korsunkiev believes that the Khiva khan was attempting to lay unjustified blame on Ayuki (Korsunkiev, "K voprosu o gibeli otriada Bekovicha-Cherkasskogo v Khive v 1717 godu," *KNIIaLI, Uchenye zapiski, seriia istorii* 8 [1969]: 83–84).

[94]*Russko-kitaiskie otnosheniia*, 157–58, no. 110.

The Kuban-Crimean force delivered a heavy blow to the Kalmyks and took back to the Kuban many of the Yedisans and Yamboyluks.[95] Ayuki had to abandon his tent and hastily flee to Astrakhan. After finding refuge there, Ayuki requested help from Prince Bekovich-Cherkasskii, who was in Astrakhan with his troops. Bekovich-Cherkasskii's troops came out of the city and faced the army of Bakhti Giray Sultan, but despite Ayuki's requests, Bekovich-Cherkasskii refused to order his troops to open fire at the numerically superior adversary. Bakhti Giray, too, did not dare to attack the Russians and soon retreated.[96] Ayuki, who had lost many people and much of his own property, was infuriated and never forgave Bekovich-Cherkasskii for his failure to assist him and to protect the Kalmyks. When, two years later, the opportunity presented itself, Ayuki did not hesitate to take revenge on Bekovich-Cherkasskii.

Concerned over the safety of the Kalmyks, the Russian government raised the question of the Kuban raids with the Porte. The Ottomans, however, intended to place the Kalmyk issue outside the realm of Russo-Ottoman relations. In a letter to the tsar in April 1716, the grand vizier stressed that Ayuki Khan was not a subject of any state, that he alone could receive the envoys of the foreign states and dispatch his own, and that he never stayed in one place. The grand vizier tried to make clear that because of the Kalmyks' independent status, the Kubans' vengeful attack against them should not be construed as a violation of the peace treaty with Russia. The vizier admitted that the Yamboyluks were subjects of Ayuki Khan, thus implicitly recognizing the necessity of their return to the Kalmyks. He further stated that, in the future, Russia would be notified if the Kubans came to Astrakhan to raid the Kalmyks, Yamboyluks, or Russians.[97]

Under pressure from virtually every direction—the Kubans in the south, the Bashkirs in the north, the Kazakhs in the east—and mistrusting his Russian ally, Ayuki chose to make peace with his most powerful adversaries—the Kubans. For this purpose he sent an envoy to the *kalgay* Bakhti Giray Sultan.[98] Bakhti Giray (also known as Deli Sultan—the crazy sultan) was embroiled in the uprising against the newly appointed Crimean khan, who replaced Bakhti Giray's father, Kara Devlet Giray Khan. Bakhti Giray welcomed an alliance with Ayuki.

---

[95]In 1737, while enumerating accumulated Russian grievances against the Porte, Russian Chancellor A. I. Ostermann mentioned that as many as 10,300 of Ayuki's people had been taken to the Kuban (BA *Nâme-i Hümayun*, no. 7, p. 461).

[96]Bakunin, "Opisanie," *Krasnyi arkhiv* 3 (1939): 201. Pal'mov believed that there might have been personal animosity between Ayuki and Prince Bekovich-Cherkasskii (Pal'mov, *Etiudy*, 3–4:29).

[97]BA *Nâme-i Hümayun*, no. 6, pp. 368, 370.

[98]Ibid., 370.

The agreement reached between Ayuki and Bakhti Giray provided that Ayuki would assist Bakhti Giray against his rivals in the Kuban in exchange for the return of the recently captured Yamboyluks and Yedisans. In the winter of 1717 the Kalmyks, led by Chakdorjab, inflicted substantial damage on those Kubans who did not join Bakhti Giray. In the end, the Kalmyks returned home with fifteen thousand of the Yedisan and Yamboyluk tents.[99]

Upon completion of the Kuban campaign, Chakdorjab left 170 Kalmyks with Bakhti Giray to serve as guides through the Russian provinces. Bakhti Giray's forces devastated the Russian provinces of Kazan and Voronezh, particularly Penza and Simbirsk counties. As a result of the campaign, 12,107 Russians fell captive and material damages were estimated at 622,657 rubles.[100] When the commanders of the Russian towns requested the Kalmyks' help against the Kubans, Ayuki replied that he could not do so without a special decree. Ayuki reminded the Russian officials that he had received the same answer from Prince Bekovich-Cherkasskii, who in 1715 refused to fire at the Kubans.[101] Ayuki's revenge was complete, both on Prince Bekovich-Cherkasskii and on the Russian authorities.

The Changing Character of
Russo-Kalmyk Relations, 1718–1722

The fundamental social changes that Kalmyk society was undergoing became particularly pronounced during Ayuki Khan's last years. The Kalmyks enjoyed great economic prosperity. The taste the Kalmyk tayishis developed for Russian goods and the increased payments and special rewards they received for occasional military service contributed to a larger accumulation of Russian money and goods in the hands of the Kalmyk nobility.

This process of accumulation of riches in the hands of the Kalmyk nobility was threatening the old social edifice of Kalmyk society. The growing demand for Russian products and money contributed to increased competition among the different tayishis and exerted additional pressure on the established rules and laws of a society still guided by traditional customs. Under the circumstances, the tayishis could resort to two different ways of increasing their herds—stepping up raids against their neighbors or raising taxes on their subjects. Raids could be

[99]Pal'mov, *Etiudy*, 3–4:36, 38.
[100]A. A. Geraklitov, *Istoriia Saratovskogo kraia v 16–18 vv.* (Saratov: Drukar', 1923): 322.
[101]Bakunin, "Opisanie," *Krasnyi arkhiv* 3 (1939): 202; *AVD* 1:278, no. 177.

launched only under favorable circumstances. Raising taxes seemed more expedient to the tayishis but eventually led to a growing social polarization within Kalmyk society and to an increased number of Kalmyk fugitives to Russia.

The increasing demand for and accumulation of riches had another severe repercussion for Kalmyk society. As the Kalmyk tayishis became more discriminating in their tastes for foreign goods, they began to see the advantages of obtaining specific goods by trade, rather than taking the potluck that could be acquired through raiding. Such a redirection of energies slowly led to the decreased militancy of the Kalmyks and in turn invited upon them the destructive raids of the poorer and more violent nomadic peoples in the area. The Kazakh and Karakalpak raids against the Kalmyks became more frequent and detrimental than they had been previously.[102]

After the unfortunate episode of 1715 involving Bekovich-Cherkasskii and Ayuki, the Russian government took some measures to improve relations with the Kalmyks. Several decrees allowed the Kalmyks to drive horses to Moscow for sale without the payment of bridge tolls and guaranteed the Kalmyk envoys in Moscow an allowance of three hundred rubles a year.[103] In 1719 the senate issued a decree stipulating that, if Ayuki sent his envoys through Astrakhan or any Siberian towns with the knowledge of the Chancellery of Foreign Affairs, custom duties were not to be exacted on goods worth up to three thousand rubles. If, however, the worth of the goods exceeded three thousand rubles, or if the envoys were sent without the knowledge of the Chancellery of Foreign Affairs, custom duties were to be exacted.[104] This decree was intended to please Ayuki but, more important, to give him an incentive for informing the authorities of his trade and political contacts with foreign powers.

This decree also signaled that the Russian government had chosen a new way to control the Kalmyks' political ties with other states. Unable in the past to control the Kalmyks either by legislative decrees or by military power, the authorities now attempted to do so by providing the Kalmyk khan with an economic incentive to report on his foreign relations. The new attitude of the government was in accord with the new forms of economic and political thought which began to take root after Peter I's reforms.

---

[102]Numerous raids against the Kalmyks occurred throughout 1718–21 (*Materialy po istorii karakalpakov*, 168–69).

[103]*PSZ* 5:nos. 2598, 3046.

[104]Ibid., no. 3314.

Every aspect of life in early eighteenth-century Russia was affected by Peter the Great's reforms. The restless tsar, full of grand designs, had more plans than he could carry out in his lifetime. One major project was the fortification of the southern frontier; defensive lines were to be constructed and the frontier moved farther south and east. As early as 1694 Peter ordered the construction of the Tsaritsyn fortified line. During the many years that the work took, the authorities ran into many problems because of inadequate supplies of labor and materials.[105] When the Tsaritsyn line was completed in 1718, it stretched from the Volga to the Don and consisted of a moat and an earthen rampart topped with a wooden palisade, as well as twenty-five outposts and four fortresses.[106]

The completion of the Tsaritsyn fortified line had significant strategic importance and political implications. The new defense line effectively checked nomadic raids from penetrating deep inside the country via the previously least-defensible inland route. Underscoring the importance of this fact, the government decided to designate Astrakhan as a separate province, comprising the towns of Simbirsk, Samara, Syzransk, Kashkar, Saratov, Petrovskii, Dmitrovskii, Tsaritsyn, Chernyi Iar, Krasnyi Iar, Gur'ev (on the Yayik), and Tersk.[107]

Artemii Volynskii was appointed governor of the newly formed province in the south.[108] A favorite of Peter's, Volynskii was perhaps one of the most typical representatives of the new generation of Russian bureaucrats, a faithful servant of the state and an embodiment of that arrogance of power which reflected the new confidence of an expanding and modernizing Russia.

The creation of the Tsaritsyn line, the designation of Astrakhan province as a separate administrative unit, and the arrival on the scene of Governor Volynskii all became visible landmarks of the increasingly restrictive Russian policies toward the Kalmyks. These policies were not directed against the Kalmyks alone but were symptomatic of more aggressive Russian plans in the entire Caucasus and Caspian Sea area.

---

[105]When the labor shortage was particularly acute, Peter I did not mind using slaves, for which purpose several thousand Kuban prisoners were bought from the Kalmyks (*PB* 10:436, no. 4153).

[106]F. M. Preobrazhenskii, "Volga v Saratovskoi gubernii," in *Saratovskii sbornik. Materialy dlia izucheniia Saratovskoi gubernii*, vol. 1, pt. 1 (Saratov: Tip. gubernskogo upravleniia, 1881): 318; Geraklitov, *Istoriia Saratovskogo kraia v 16–18 vv.*, 324.

[107]*PSZ* 5:no. 3119.

[108]Some information concerning the controversial life of this Russian statesman can be found in "Zapiska ob Artemii Volynskom," *ChOIDR* 2 (April–June 1858): 135–70; "Artemii Petrovich Volynskii. Materialy dlia biografii," *Russkaia starina* 5 (June 1872): 934–51; I. I. Shishkin, "Artemii Volynskii," *Otechestvennye zapiski* 128–30 (1860); Ernst German, "Zhizn' Volynskogo, ego zagovor i smert'," *Russkii arkhiv* 4 (1866): 1351–74.

These plans were adopted largely under the influence of one man—
Governor Volynskii. Upon his return with the embassy from Persia, Volynskii tried to convince the tsar of the need to take advantage of the
political turmoil in Persia and move determinedly into the Caucasus to
take over the southern Caspian shores.

The policies of the previous Astrakhan administration toward the
Kalmyks were not acceptable to Volynskii. He intended to govern the
Kalmyks with an iron fist and expected their obedience and loyalty.[109]
The new governor decided to replace *stol'nik* D. E. Bakhmet'ev, whom
he considered too lenient with the Kalmyks, with his own appointee,
Captain Vasilii Beklemishev. We may recall that after Ayuki's defeat by the
Kubans in 1715, the government had finally heeded his requests and
provided him with six hundred Russian and cossack cavalry under the
command of Bakhmet'ev. Although this detachment was to function as
Ayuki's personal guard, its other mission was to spy on Ayuki and gain
knowledge of his contacts with foreign powers.[110] Presumably, the spy-
ing of the Russian officer soon annoyed Ayuki, for he requested that
Bakhmet'ev be transferred to Saratov and provide military assistance
from there if the need should arise.[111]

In reorganizing the Astrakhan administration, Volynskii hired a competent translator and interpreter for the Kalmyks. The translator's name
was Vasilii Bakunin, whose invaluable account we are already familiar
with. Bakunin was the first translator of the Kalmyk language in Astrakhan. Previously, the local authorities relied on interpreters (*tolmachi*), who would render the text in general terms from Kalmyk into
Tatar. Perhaps the precision and competency of the new translations
made Volynskii acutely aware of the imperative tone of Ayuki's letters to
the governor. The furious Volynskii indignantly returned such letters to
Ayuki.[112]

[109]One incident may serve as an illustration of the mood and attitude of Volynskii and his
followers toward the Kalmyks. The story was told by the Russian ambassador Flori Beneveni, head of the Oriental department of Russia's Chancellery of Foreign Affairs. During his
visit to Shemakha, Beneveni learned of the outrageous behavior of Volynskii's envoy, the
Greek Dimitraki. Dimitraki invited to his place of residence Ayuki Khan's envoy, who was
also present in the city. When the Kalmyk envoy arrived, Dimitraki began to yell at him and
to berate both the envoy and Ayuki Khan. When the Kalmyk objected to such behavior,
Dimitraki declared that he could do to him whatever he wanted because his master was
the Astrakhan governor Artemii Volynskii. In a rage, Dimitraki ordered that the Kalmyk
envoy be given 150 blows (Popov, *Snosheniia Rossii s Khivoi i Bukharoi*, 348–49).

[110]Such were Bakhmet'ev's secret instructions (Pal'mov, *Etiudy*, 3–4:41–42, 47; Bakunin,
"Opisanie," *Krasnyi arkhiv* 3 [1939]: 202).

[111]*PSZ* 5:486, no. 3062.

[112]Pal'mov, *Etiudy*, 3–4:45; Bakunin, "Opisanie," *Krasnyi arkhiv* 3 (1939): 207.

With the new administration in Astrakhan and its heavy-handed approach toward the Kalmyks, the differences between Russian and Kalmyk interests became more pronounced and the disputes more frequent. In the past, too, the Russian government had repeatedly attempted to enforce its policies upon the Kalmyks, but lacking sufficient means to carry out such a policy, the government often had to compromise. Now, the military and economic power of the Russian state was great enough that it could afford to apply more rigorous policies toward the Kalmyks. Perhaps no person could have done it in a more confrontational way than Governor Volynskii. The government's instructions were to prevent the Kalmyks' ties with foreign powers, while still treating them respectfully and amicably, but the overzealous governor had his own interpretation of them.[113] He regarded the Kalmyks simply as mutinous and spoiled Russian subjects and referred to them even in official correspondence as "my children."[114] These children had to be restrained and their submission enforced through the strict application of Russian laws and regulations.

The first meeting between Volynskii and Chakdorjab took place in September 1721, at which time both promised to be friends and brothers. One month later, Chakdorjab was complaining bitterly about the new governor and numerous abuses to the Kalmyk people in Astrakhan. Volynskii's replies stated that if Kalmyks were captured by the Russians, there were good reasons, and he referred to damage caused by the Kalmyks.[115]

The complaints were warranted on both sides. Some of the cases clearly reveal that the Russians and the Kalmyks had little knowledge of each other's societies and the ways they functioned. Coupled with the new Astrakhan administration's insensitivity and disrespect toward Kalmyk laws and customs, this led to mounting conflicts between the two sides. In 1721, for example, Volynskii demanded that the Yamboyluks and Yedisans be scattered around the Kalmyk uluses. Volynskii, hoping to prevent any future defection of these tribes, failed to understand that this would be contrary to the common practice of Kalmyk society and inconsistent with its social organization. Needless to say, the Kalmyk tayishis strongly objected, particularly Chakdorjab, who alone exercised power over these tribes.[116]

In another incident, a group of Kalmyks from Ayuki's ulus crossed the

---

[113]*PSZ* 6:228–29, no. 3622.
[114]Pal'mov, *Etiudy*, 3–4:87.
[115]Ibid., 54, 58, 60, 63–69.
[116]Bakunin, "Opisanie," *Krasnyi arkhiv* 3 (1939): 203.

Volga above the Tsaritsyn fortified line to take payment of a debt from the Kalmyks of Chakdorjab's ulus. When the debtors refused to pay, Ayuki's Kalmyks seized some of their horses according to the customary law of barimta. On the way home, this group of Kalmyks was attacked by Russian soldiers, who captured two people and seventeen horses. The Russians considered the horses to be unlawfully seized and were determined to stop the thieves.[117]

These and similar cases were numerous. Volynskii and his administration intended to apply Russian laws in all their severity to the Kalmyks, including the imposition of various penalties, frequent beating and torturing of the Kalmyks, and on occcasion their arbitrary execution. Considering such actions cruel and unjustified, both Ayuki and Chakdorjab complained of the Astrakhan authorities' refusal to solve Kalmyk-Russian disputes in a more favorable manner.

The Persian Campaign of 1722–1723

The news of the rapid disintegration of the Persian empire under the weight of its internal problems and fierce attacks by Afghan armies hastened preparations for the campaign in Persia. Volynskii insisted on a large-scale campaign, and as soon as the war with Sweden was over Russian troops under the personal command of the tsar set out from Moscow in May 1722. Avenging wrongs done to Russian merchants in Shemakha served as the pretext for the campaign, although an official note informed the Persian shah of Russia's sincere intentions to help him clear the area of rebels. None of these statements reflected the real goals of this military undertaking, which aimed at strengthening the Russian position in the strategic area of the Caucasus. Some of the immediate goals were to capture the cities of Shemakha and Derbent, to gain control of the silk routes to Persia, to annex the area of the southern Caspian Sea and Azerbaijan, and to establish Russia firmly in the Caucasus with the ultimate purpose of winning over the Georgian and Armenian subjects of the Ottoman empire.

According to Peter I's plans, the Kalmyks were to play a role in the campaign. To underscore the importance of Russia's ties with the Kalmyks and to ensure their participation in the campaign, Peter, who had newly proclaimed himself emperor of all Russia, decided to meet the Kalmyk khan. In early summer of 1722, when Peter was on his way to Astrakhan, the two rulers met near Saratov. According to the accounts of

---

[117]Pal'mov, *Etiudy,* 3–4:61–62.

eyewitnesses, Ayuki arrived on horseback with his two sons and fifty other people. He alighted twenty yards from the Volga bank, where he was received by a privy counselor. The emperor then went on shore, saluted Ayuki, and invited him aboard the galley. Ayuki's wife, Darma-Bala, was similarly received by the empress.

During the meeting, Peter asked Ayuki to supply a force of ten thousand Kalmyk cavalrymen. Ayuki promised to send five thousand, diplomatically explaining that even five thousand of his brave horsemen would suffice for Peter's purposes. Ayuki then presented the tsar with eighty camels and the tsarina with fifty pregnant mares.[118] The emperor seemed to be delighted, and the empress gave Ayuki's wife a golden watch studded with diamonds, as well as brocades and silks. A treaty between the "two mighty monarchs" was concluded in a short time.[119]

The five-thousand-man Kalmyk detachment promised to the tsar turned out to number only 3,727 horsemen. It was led by Ayuki's grandson and Chakdorjab's son Batu.[120] This Kalmyk detachment did not seem to be of much use to the Russian army. Ayuki was determined not to commit himself fully to one side but to maintain relations with all. Taking sides with one party would invite attack by the other. This was too risky in a situation in which Ayuki saw no reliable ally who could effectively shield him from his numerous adversaries. His policies were to sustain a delicate balance that would keep him from being fully involved in the conflict of the warring parties. Several episodes illustrate his policies.

Throughout all these years Ayuki maintained friendly relations with Bakhti Giray. In 1721 Ayuki notified Bakhti Giray of Volynskii's return to Astrakhan and thus facilitated Bakhti Giray's attack on the Russians.[121] The following year, to support Bakhti Giray Sultan against his rivals, Ayuki together with the Don cossacks launched a large-scale raid against the Crimea and caused substantial damage.[122] On yet another occasion, shortly before the meeting with Peter near Saratov, Ayuki informed the

---

[118]SRIO 3:351, no. 29.

[119]Such is the account of a contemporary, John Bell (Staunton, Narrative of the Chinese Embassy, 156–58). Bakunin described the event in terms befitting a Russian official. According to him, Ayuki came to see Peter the Great to show his respect and partake of the great honor of being received by His Majesty (Bakunin, "Opisanie," Krasnyi arkhiv 3 [1939]: 205). Yet another account says that Ayuki received from the tsar a sword studded with diamonds (Pal'mov, Etiudy, 1:55).

[120]Batu was born of a concubine but nevertheless was regarded as a noyon and Chakdorjab's son (Bakunin, "Opisanie," Krasnyi arkhiv 3 [1939]: 204).

[121]V. P. Lystsov, Persidskii pokhod Petra I, 1722–23 (Moscow: Izd-vo Moskovskogo universiteta, 1951), 96.

[122]BA Nâme-i Hümayun, no. 7, pp. 58–59.

Khiva khan of the arrival of the Russian troops and their possible march on Khiva the following winter.[123]

Having asked for the Kalmyk cavalry, Peter specifically requested Ayuki not to send any Tatars for this campaign. Later on, a Kuban Nogay disguised in Kalmyk dress was discovered among the Kalmyks participating in the campaign. According to Ayuki's scheme, the Nogay spy was supposed to keep an eye on the Russian troops and at a certain point to report their location to Bakhti Giray Sultan.[124]

The campaign on the Caspian shores brought initial success. Russian troops captured the city of Derbent and approached Baku. After the first successful advances, however, the campaign faced the same problems that Russian armies encountered in all major distant expeditions—poor organization of the rear and inadequate supply of food and ammunition.[125] A decision was made to send part of the army back to Astrakhan. Peter chose to return with some of his troops. On the way from Astrakhan to Moscow, the tsar once again met with Ayuki Khan, near the town of Chernyi Iar on the Volga. This time the meeting was requested by Ayuki, who had probably learned of the government's intention to make Ayuki's nephew Dorji-Nazar the khan's successor. The letter sent by Ayuki stated: "The cause of sending [this] letter by Ayuki-khan to [His] Brilliance, the Great Emperor, having the destiny, [presented] by Great Heavens: hearing that you prepare to depart, [we have] sent [this letter] in order that [You] should depart after [that is, should not go away without] being treated to [our] tea. [Our] envoy [is] Danzin [?]."[126] According to Bakunin, the seventy-five-year-old Ayuki asked the tsar to support his son by Darma-Bala, Cheren-Donduk, whom he had chosen to be his successor. Peter agreed to do so.[127]

There is an indication, however, that, despite his promise to Ayuki, Peter continued to favor Dorji-Nazar as the candidate who would best serve Russian interests.[128] Here were grounds for potential clashes between the Russian and the Kalmyk candidates. Earlier, in February 1722, Chakdorjab's death from alcoholic intoxication had brought forward yet another candidate, Chakdorjab's eldest son, Dosang.[129]

[123]Popov, Snosheniia Rossii s Khivoi i Bukharoi, 382.

[124]Bakunin, "Opisanie," Krasnyi arkhiv 3 (1939): 206.

[125]SRIO 3:352–53, no. 33; Pavel Sheremet'ev, Vladimir Petrovich Sheremet'ev, 1668–1737, 2 vols. (Moscow: Sinodal'naia tip., 1913–14), 1:255–56.

[126]This letter has been published and translated by Aleksei Sazykin, "An Historical Document," 231.

[127]Bakunin, "Opisanie," Krasnyi arkhiv 3 (1939): 205–6.

[128]According to Pal'mov, a secret tsar's decree designated Dorji-Nazar the Kalmyk khan upon Ayuki's death (Pal'mov, Etiudy, 3–4:222, 373).

[129]Ibid., 57, 119; Bakunin, "Opisanie," Krasnyi arkhiv 3 (1939): 203.

Ayuki's old age and the death of his popular heir apparent, Chakdor-jab, awoke among the Kalmyk tayishis the envy and hostilities which for some time had lain dormant. The impending vacancy of the prestigious title of Kalmyk khan and the uncertainty as to who would come to power suddenly exposed the belligerence and antagonisms that permeated Kalmyk society. In their bids for power and prestige, the various warring factions were soon to cause Kalmyk society to enter into a long period marked by internal discord, squabbles, and wars.

6

Succession Crisis, 1722–1735

The Struggle for Succession

Chakdorjab's death on February 19, 1722, brought his son Dosang an ulus of seven thousand tents and leadership in the family. Because his father had been designated the heir to Ayuki Khan, Dosang assumed that the right to the title of khan belonged to him. Aware of Ayuki's old age, Dosang was unwilling to wait. He promptly sent letters to the Astrakhan governor promising faithful service in return for the governor's support of his candidacy.[1] Governor Volynskii was quick to respond positively to Dosang's appeal, which he saw as a welcome opportunity to gain leverage against Ayuki and to create legitimate opposition to the khan.

Dosang's ambition was resented not only by Ayuki but also by Dosang's brothers, whose tents Dosang seized forcibly.[2] After attempts to convince Dosang to distribute the tents from Chakdorjab's former ulus among the brothers had failed, Ayuki ordered a formidable army of twenty thousand horsemen to wage war against Dosang. The commander of these Kalmyk troops was Ayuki's grandson and Gunjib's son Donduk-Ombo. At the same time, Ayuki wrote to Governor Volynskii asking him to stop the hostilities between the brothers. Aware of the governor's support for Dosang, Ayuki made a last effort to prevent bloodshed, implying that reconciliation was possible if the governor withdrew

---

[1]Pal'mov, *Etiudy*, 3–4:120.

[2]According to Chakdorjab's will, although Dosang was to receive the largest share of one thousand tents, the ulus was to be distributed among all his sons (Bakunin, "Opisanie," *Krasnyi arkhiv* 3 [1939]: 204–8; Pal'mov, *Etiudy*, 3–4:119).

his support from Dosang. The size of the assembled Kalmyk army and the earnestness of the enterprise, however, clearly indicate that Ayuki did not have reason to hope for a peaceful outcome.

Dosang wrote to Volynskii, requesting assistance and explaining that his people were scattered among different pastures and there was no time to assemble them to confront such a large force. Dosang requested arms, troops, and boats to ferry his Kalmyks across the Akhtuba. Volynskii supplied Dosang with firearms but could send only a small detachment of troops. In November 1723, Donduk-Ombo, avoiding confrontation with nearby Russian troops, attacked Dosang at a location near the Akhtuba, about fifty versts from Astrakhan.

In the ensuing battle, a total of one hundred were killed and many more wounded. Even the arrival of Governor Volynskii could not salvage the situation. Donduk-Ombo, with thirteen thousand Kalmyks, formed a semicircle in front of Volynskii and his troops and blocked their further advance. In a message to the governor, Donduk-Ombo stated that if Russian troops moved any further, they would be treated as an adversary. Volynskii chose to halt the movement. Donduk-Ombo then sent several detachments which captured from Dosang six thousand Kalmyk tents. Helpless, Volynskii returned to Astrakhan, where he met Dosang, who had fled there with the remaining three thousand troops and two thousand tents.[3]

The apparent success of Donduk-Ombo and Ayuki's party appeared to solve the succession crisis, which was to sap the very foundations of Kalmyk society in the years to come. The solution, however, was only temporary, as the internal war of 1723 only exacerbated the crisis by further factionalizing Kalmyk society and weakening the political and military power of the Kalmyk khan.

By the 1720s Kalmyk society was torn apart by warring factions. Taking advantage of this internal dissension, fifteen thousand Nogay tents again fled to the Kuban, never to return to the Volga. The Derbet tayishi Cheter moved away with most of his people to the Don. Dorji-Nazar and his ulus roamed near the Yayik. Victorious Donduk-Ombo, supported by his mistress, Ayuki's wife, Darma-Bala, laid claim to the khan's title. Ayuki placed the authority of his power behind his son Cheren-Donduk. Dosang continued to claim his legitimate right to the title and, although deprived of many tents, was still a strong candidate because he had the support of the Astrakhan administration. One of the most influential figures, the chief Kalmyk lama Shakur-Lama, was an adherent of the pro-

---

[3]Bakunin, "Opisanie," *Krasnyi arkhiv* 3 (1939): 208–9; Pal'mov, *Etiudy*, 3–4:124–26, 129–32, 134.

Russian coalition and apparently supported Dosang.[4] Moreover, Dosang's youngest brother, Baksaday-Dorji, sought to become a khan by different means. He converted to Christianity and assumed the Christian name Petr in honor of his godfather, the Russian tsar Peter I. He was given the surname of Taishin and became known as Petr Taishin.

Each faction advanced a candidate with claims to the title of khan. Which of the pretenders had a legitimate right to the title? In 1731, Petr Taishin, perhaps having his own interests in mind, claimed:

> According to our Kalmyk customs, a khan's successor should be his eldest son. Our grandfather Ayuki Khan was married to three wives. My father was the eldest son of the first wife. The eldest son of my father was my brother Dosang, but he died and now I am the eldest. The eldest son of the second wife was Donduk-Ombo's father. The eldest son of the third wife was Cheren-Donduk. And according to our Kalmyk customs the son of the first wife was supposed to be a khan, but not the son of the third wife.[5]

According to the highest Kalmyk religious authority, Shakur-Lama, the successor to the khan could be any member of the khan's family—his sons, grandsons, and nephews—and Cheren-Donduk, Dosang, and Donduk-Ombo were all possible candidates. On another occasion, Shakur-Lama noted that if Dosang tried to solve the case in the Kalmyk court, zargo, he would lose because he had disobeyed Ayuki's decision, thus clearly implying that a khan had the right to choose his own successor. Another influential figure among the Kalmyks, zayisang Yaman, also confirmed that in accordance with Kalmyk law either Cheren-Donduk or Dosang could assume the title of khan.[6]

In the absence of strict rules of succession, both Cheren-Donduk and Dosang had legitimate claims to leadership. Military power and political influence were often more important factors than the force of an ill-defined law. Thus Donduk-Ombo and Dorji-Nazar, who were even more remote in the genealogical line, were also regarded as potential candidates. The problem was that no candidate could boast clear military and political superiority, and the feuds continued.

This was not the first time the Kalmyks experienced turmoil and the pains of self-inflicted wounds caused by internal wars. Ayuki, too, had had to fight to consolidate his power in the position of the chief Kalmyk tayishi. But the consequences and the intensity of the present succes-

---

[4]Shakur-Lama secretly warned Dosang that Ayuki, if he found it necessary, was prepared to attack Dosang (Bakunin, "Opisanie," *Krasnyi arkhiv* 3 [1939]: 208).

[5]Pal'mov, *Etiudy*, 3–4:121. For a theoretical discussion of the succession issue see the section "Succession" in Chapter 1.

[6]Pal'mov, *Etiudy*, 3–4:290, 294–95, 316.

sion struggle were far more severe than in the past. To understand the peculiarities of the situation, it is necessary to have a closer look at Kalmyk society. Earlier, I observed that one could achieve the position of chief tayishi and later that of khan either by a persuasive claim or by the use of force. In most cases, the victorious successor had more people and herds and larger armies than any other single tayishi. Only the alliance of the dissenting tayishis and their combined military force could threaten his position. Thus every new chief tayishi or khan had to consolidate his power either by lobbying some tayishis or, when necessary, by undertaking military actions against the others. Losing this delicate margin of superiority meant that the chief tayishi had to yield to a more powerful and popular leader, usually his eldest son. This happened to Ayuki's grandfather Daichin, who because of his old age had to step aside in favor of his more energetic eldest son, Puntsuk. Several times Ayuki, too, was almost compelled to resign his position to his eldest son, Chakdorjab, but each time the interference and support of the Russian government enabled him to retain his title.

The goal of Russian policies toward the Kalmyks in the seventeenth and early eighteenth centuries was to promote one strong leader who could control the other tayishis. Russian policy makers thought that by having one person in charge of the Kalmyks they would be able to hold him responsible and thus prevent Kalmyk raids along the Russian frontier. Such policies, however, had an inherent drawback. They could create too powerful a leader, one capable of uniting the Kalmyks and pursuing his own independent goals. Indeed, Ayuki's tenure was marked by his ever-growing accumulation of power and was a direct result of the Russian policies.

The appointment of Artemii Volynskii as governor of Astrakhan reversed the traditional Russian approach toward the Kalmyks. The goal of the Russian government remained the same—to turn the Kalmyks into obedient Russian subjects. Previously, however, the government had attempted to achieve this goal by fostering a central authority among the Kalmyks. Such Russian policies were intended to curb raids and were dictated by Russia's weakness and the vulnerability of its frontier. Now, with improved defenses and a modernized army, the Russian government felt more secure. As the fear of raids began to subside, the same goal could be achieved by undermining the power of the khan and promoting civil strife among the Kalmyks. The maturing Russian empire was now armed with truly imperial policies of divide and rule.[7]

[7]Volynskii made his case clear in a letter to the Chancellery of Foreign Affairs. He explained that it was in Russia's interest to create opposition among the Kalmyks by supporting Dosang against Ayuki, and thus, by letting the tayishis quarrel, to curb Ayuki's autocratic power (ibid., 123).

Volynskii's policies were not guided solely by national interests. His eagerness to implement them was often stimulated by the prospect of personal gain. On numerous occasions Volynskii was accused of taking bribes. In one such instance, Ayuki complained that Volynskii supported Dosang because the governor received a bribe of one hundred horses. In his own account to his superiors in St. Petersburg, Volynskii vehemently denied such accusations, but similar complaints from different quarters indicate that Volynskii did not shun bribes to support his life-style.[8]

Paradoxically, as Russian authorities began to implement the new policy of dividing the Kalmyks, the previous policy of supporting a single leader made the office of the khan more appealing than ever. The traditional role of the khan in Kalmyk society had been limited to several major functions. The khan was, first of all, commander in chief in large military campaigns. He also had significant political influence over Kalmyk affairs through the privilege of appointing his own zayisangs to the Kalmyk court of justice, the zargo. Previous Russian policies toward the Kalmyk khan gave the holder of the office other privileges, including the right to send more frequent embassies to the capital and to receive larger payments and luxury goods. Russia's military support gave a khan authorization for bolder actions against recalcitrant tayishis, or at least those portrayed as such by the khan. Clearly, relations with Russia transformed the position of the Kalmyk khan from the traditional one with limited military and political functions into a much more centralized and powerful office.

Both the more attractive position of the Kalmyk khan and the increased intensity of the succession struggle were results of Russian policies. Yet the unexpected severity and persistence of the conflict aroused concern in the Russian government. The news of a forty-thousand-strong Kazakh and Karakalpak army ready to raid the Kalmyks and the Russian provinces spurred the government to action.[9] In January 1724, the government sent Ayuki a letter urging him to stop the feuds among the Kalmyks,[10] but the letter did not arrive in time. On February 19, 1724, Ayuki Khan died at the age of seventy-seven. Although the old khan's death was not unexpected, it brought new concerns and anxieties to the Russian authorities.

The administration feared that Ayuki's wife, Darma-Bala, who temporarily replaced the deceased khan, together with her lover Donduk-Ombo, her son Cheren-Donduk, and other tayishis, would enter into an

---

[8]Ibid., 129.

[9]*Materialy po istorii karakalpakov*, 174–75.

[10]Pal'mov, *Etiudy*, 3–4:149–50.

alliance with the Crimeans and the Kubans. As Dosang continued to enjoy Russian support and Donduk-Ombo was known for his pro-Crimean and pro-Kuban tendencies, such worries were not unwarranted. The prospect of such an alliance was particularly threatening at this time, when Russia was involved in negotiations with the Ottomans over conquered territories near the Caspian Sea and war between the two empires could break out at any moment.

At the time, most of the Kalmyks of Ayuki's uluses were situated on the west bank of the Volga, gradually moving up the river with the approach of warmer spring days. Dosang with his ulus was roaming in the vicinity of Astrakhan. Dorji-Nazar occupied the easternmost pastures of the Kalmyks, where more than twenty thousand of his tents were roaming between the Volga and Yayik.

Volynskii, who had just returned from St. Petersburg, brought with him confirmation of the authorities' plans to declare Dorji-Nazar the new Kalmyk khan. The candidacy of Dosang was dismissed because the governor considered him to be stupid and a drunk. Donduk-Ombo could not be trusted. Cheren-Donduk was regarded as a young and weak tayishi, who, if he were to become khan, would necessarily find himself under Donduk-Ombo's influence. Thus the candidacy of a powerful Kalmyk tayishi, Dorji-Nazar, the son of Ayuki's cousin Nazar, seemed to be the most suitable. In return, Dorji-Nazar was obliged to give his son as a hostage to the Russian authorities and to pledge his allegiance.[11]

Once again Volynskii showed little understanding of Kalmyk society and a total disregard for Kalmyk laws. Firmly believing in the power of Russian arms and the weight of his own authority, he thought Dorji-Nazar would serve Russian interests better that anyone else. Dorji-Nazar's acceptance by the Kalmyk tayishis was of secondary concern to the governor.

Nevertheless, precautionary plans were made in case the Russian candidacy met with strong opposition from the Kalmyk tayishis. Volynskii was instructed to befriend Darma-Bala, Cheren-Donduk, and other tayishis by offering them gifts, for which purpose he was given one thousand rubles, a sum he later found insufficient. Volynskii was also allowed to use military force if the gifts were not persuasive enough and the opposition to Dorji-Nazar continued.[12] The situation, however, developed differently than the authorities had anticipated.

An embittered Dosang, abandoned by the Russians in his struggle for the title of khan and anxious to recover the tents he had lost to his

---

[11]Bakunin, "Opisanie," *Krasnyi arkhiv* 3 (1939): 210; Pal'mov, *Etiudy*, 3–4:221–25.
[12]Bakunin, "Opisanie," *Krasnyi arkhiv* 3 (1939): 211; Pal'mov, *Etiudy*, 3–4:226.

brothers, entered into a relationship with the Crimea. Soon rumors spread that a large force of Crimeans and Yedisans, who recently had deserted the Kalmyks, was preparing to launch an attack on the Volga's west bank against the Kalmyks of Darma-Bala, Cheren-Donduk, and other tayishis, all formerly comprising a pro-Ayuki party.

Even within this group united by hostility toward Dosang and refusal to accept Dorji-Nazar as the Kalmyk khan, there was no consensus on what action to take. Anticipating a Crimean raid against them and unable to repel such an attack, the Kalmyk tayishis had only two options. One was to move north, where they faced the Tsaritsyn defense line; another was to cross the Volga to the east. The latter choice was made impossible by the spring overflow of the Volga, and most of the tayishis agreed to ask the Russian authorities to let them cross the Tsaritsyn line. This request was dictated by desperation, for the tayishis realized that if they crossed the line they would be submitting to Russian control and placing themselves at the mercy of the Russian administration.

Donduk-Ombo, the leader of the pro-Kuban coalition among the Kalmyks, suggested that the Kalmyks go to the Kuban and join Bakhti Giray Sultan. But such influential Kalmyks as Shakur-Lama and the zayisang Yaman, staunch supporters of pro-Russian policies, succeeded in convincing Darma-Bala and Cheren-Donduk to seek Russian protection, and their uluses began to cross the line. Reluctantly, Donduk-Ombo joined them.

Fears of a Crimean raid were now replaced by new anxieties. The Kalmyks found themselves confined to an area they could not easily abandon. Behind them, to the south, was the Tsaritsyn line; in the west there were the cossack posts along the Don; by the Volga there were Russian posts in the east; and in the north lay the densely populated Russian provinces. Rumors spread that Volynskii would come to the Kalmyk uluses to seek retribution for their previous quarrels and to seize the tents claimed by Dosang.

Darma-Bala summoned the council of tayishis and zayisangs, which decided not to accept Volynskii's resolutions but to send envoys to the capital to complain about the governor and to request his dismissal. In a remarkably revealing statement, the council blamed Volynskii for the present troubles among the Kalmyks, saying that "were it not for his protection of Dosang, the Kalmyk tayishis would have ruined Dosang, and there would have been no internal dispute."[13]

Although overzealous and unpopular among the Kalmyks, Volynskii usually followed the orders of his superiors. The Russian government

[13]Pal'mov, *Etiudy*, 3–4:174.

decided to use the situation to make a new attempt at inducing the Kalmyk tayishis to convert to Christianity. Volynskii was instructed to make the tayishis return the tents that belonged to the newly converted Petr Taishin. Dosang was also supposed to receive his tents, but only if he chose to convert. In the beginning of 1724 decrees were issued to translate the Bible into the Kalmyk language and to find people who could serve as missionaries.[14]

On September 1, 1724, Volynskii and Dorji-Nazar met near Saratov. The negotiations were short and did not produce the desired outcome. Dorji-Nazar declined to accept the title of khan, explaining that he was less powerful than others, and referred to possible legitimate successors such as Ayuki's son Cheren-Donduk and grandsons Donduk-Ombo and Dosang. When Volynskii continued to press his case, Dorji-Nazar made it clear that he would not be accepted by the tayishis as their khan and that even though they might agree to it now, they would later betray him and seize his tents. Even Volynskii's promise to give him two thousand Don cossacks for his protection did not convince Dorji-Nazar to change his mind.[15]

The growing pressure from the Russian authorities was felt by all Kalmyk leaders. Unwilling to accept the Russian terms and unable to enforce their own, the Kalmyk tayishis entertained their last available option—moving away. To avoid losing the nearly ten thousand tents seized from Darma-Bala, Cheren-Donduk, and Dosang during the feuds, Dorji-Nazar considered leaving for Jungaria, but increased Kazakh raids against him and the difficulties of such a journey made him give up his plans. Darma-Bala with her Kalmyks, confined by the Tsaritsyn line, also considered returning to Jungaria and sent her envoy to the Jungar khan to explore the possibility. Donduk-Ombo, meanwhile, tried to convince others to join him in an attempt to cross the Don and seek refuge in the Crimea.[16]

Volynskii was looking for ways to defuse this explosive situation. At the beginning of September he began to confer with the Kalmyk tayishis, whom he invited to gather near Saratov to attempt to resolve the crisis. After long and delicate negotiations, the Russian governor and the tayishis agreed on Cheren-Donduk's candidacy. On September 19, 1724, Cheren-Donduk was proclaimed Kalmyk viceroy and signed the oath.[17]

---

[14]*PSZ* 7:nos. 4427, 4492.

[15]Bakunin, "Opisanie," *Krasnyi arkhiv* 3 (1939): 212–13; Pal'mov, *Etiudy*, 3–4:284–87.

[16]Pal'mov, *Etiudy*, 3–4:263; Bakunin, "Opisanie," *Krasnyi arkhiv* 3 (1939): 213.

[17]Several prominent Kalmyks were instrumental in bringing about this settlement. They were zayisang Yaman, Shakur-Lama, and Darma-Bala's Tibetan doctor, emchi—all, for different reasons, strong adherents of pro-Russian policies. Yaman's interest in furthering

Volynskii was determined to take full advantage of the Kalmyks' desperate situation to achieve his long-sought goals. One demand followed another. In addition to Cheren-Donduk, Volynskii insisted that other major Kalmyk tayishis and zayisangs also sign oaths. At first, this demand caused an uproar among the Kalmyks, but, with little recourse, they soon agreed to sign. Apart from a 1697 agreement with Russia, the Kalmyks regarded the present oath as the only valid document because it was the first one written in Kalmyk, discussed by the tayishis, and then signed by them, even though not entirely of their own volition.[18]

The oaths signed by Cheren-Donduk and other tayishis and zayisangs contained promises similar to those made in the past. One clause secured the tayishis' promise to scatter the Nogays among the Kalmyk uluses should the Nogays return to the Volga. It served as another indication of Volynskii's success in enforcing the conditions he had long demanded from the Kalmyks.[19]

Faithful to the principle of divide and rule, Volynskii further demanded that the Kalmyk tayishis return tents to Dosang. Constant interference in Kalmyk affairs by the Russian governor could only result in protracted Kalmyk feuds, and the appointment of Cheren-Donduk as viceroy did little to stop the internal upheavals.

The Rule of Cheren-Donduk, 1724–1735

Meanwhile, the weather added force to the governor's demands. The arrival of cold autumn days and the exhausted pastures between the Volga and Don forced the Kalmyks to start their movement south to the warmer steppes by the Caspian Sea. Volynskii continued to insist on the tayishis' return of Dosang's tents before they were let through the Tsaritsyn line. Shakur-Lama explained to Volynskii that the reconciliation could not be achieved quickly because of the compexity of the dispute, and cold weather required that the Kalmyks begin moving south as soon as possible. But even the assurance of his loyalist, Shakur-Lama, that the tayishis promised reconciliation and that they would start searching for Dosang's tents after crossing the line could not dissuade Volynskii. He

---

Russia's cause was determined chiefly by his personal ties to Russian officials and desire for riches. The emchi was more concerned with bringing an end to the Kalmyk discords, while Shakur-Lama seemed to combine both the interest of the Kalmyks and his personal gain. For an account of these complex negotiations see Pal'mov, *Etiudy*, 3–4:288–323.

[18]Bakunin, "Opisanie," *Krasnyi arkhiv* 3 (1939): 215.

[19]*PSZ* 7:352–54, no. 4576.

knew that once the Kalmyks were outside the line, it would be hard to control them and to bring about the desired result.

Returning the tents to Dosang meant more to Volynskii than just implementing the government's policies. The show of Russian force and Volynskii's personal appearance had not stopped Donduk-Ombo from seizing Dosang's uluses. Given Donduk-Ombo's treatment of Volynskii and his troops, the governor regarded the incident not only as a military failure but a personal humiliation.

Despite instructions from General Field Marshal Mikhail Golitsyn to follow the government's orders strictly, Volynskii chose to disregard two decrees from the senate instructing him to let the Kalmyks pass to their winter pastures. Volynskii also intercepted Golitsyn's letters to the Kalmyks, trying to gain time and keep the Kalmyk tayishis unaware of the orders.

During these turbulent months the Kalmyk tayishis launched a major effort to vilify Volynskii in the eyes of his superiors. They insisted that envoys be allowed to reach the capital to complain about the governor. The energies put into the effort to achieve Volynskii's dismissal from above were unprecedented and attest not only to Volynskii's rough handling of Russo-Kalmyk relations but also to the Kalmyks' growing familiarity with the ways of the centralized Russian bureaucracy.

Pressures on Volynskii were building up. The commanders from the Volga towns reported increased Kalmyk raids and clashes with Russian residents. General Field Marshal Golitsyn gave direct orders to let the Kalmyks through, and the commander of the Tsaritsyn line, General Ia. S. Shamordin, was not sympathetic to Volynskii's policies. Rumors spread that the Kalmyks might try to cross the Don, and an impatient Donduk-Ombo was ready to force his way through if necessary. On October 16, 1724, Volynskii, hard-pressed, gave an order to let the Kalmyks through the line.[20]

The Kalmyk tayishis kept their promises. After having crossed the line, Dosang was able to recover his tents, and the tayishis seemed to have reconciled their differences. Although not all of Volynskii's terms were met, he had good reason to be satisfied with the outcome because the crisis temporarily subsided. This time, however, the Russian government assumed a hard-line policy and continued to press the governor to impose more demands on the Kalmyks. The senate ordered Volynskii to declare Dorji-Nazar the Kalmyk khan. After Volynskii's objection that there was no hope of making Dorji-Nazar a khan, he was ordered to

[20]Pal'mov, *Etiudy*, 3–4:306, 314, 329, 330, 341, 342, 348.

take one of Cheren-Donduk's brothers hostage and to secure Cheren-Donduk's pledge to surrender one of his sons as a hostage.[21]

Even Volynskii felt compelled to explain to his superiors that a demand for hostages would endanger the precarious balance of power among different Kalmyk interest groups. Such a move threatened to ruin the fragile agreement reached by the tayishis. Volynskii suggested that it would be wiser to wait and to impose more restrictions on the Kalmyks the next time they were within the Tsaritsyn line.[22]

Apparently Volynskii made a convincing case, for in February 1725, the newly enthroned Empress Catherine I granted Cheren-Donduk the official title of Kalmyk viceroy and promised imperial favors and rewards for his loyal service.[23] In reality, the new viceroy's rewards amounted to only half those received by his father, Ayuki. A special senate decree stipulated that the late Ayuki Khan's annuity of one thousand rubles and two thousand *chetvert'* of rye flour be divided equally between the viceroy and Ayuki's widow, Darma-Bala.[24]

A decrease in payments to the Kalmyk tayishis was not only a sign of the diminishing political importance of the Kalmyks and other nomadic and seminomadic peoples in the face of rapidly growing Russian military predominance. It was also part of the Russian government's search for fiscal prudence in an attempt to ease the burden of Russia's heavily taxed peasants. The curtailments were easier made in a budget for Russia's non-Orthodox clients because the country's growing military might was accompanied by the government's growing intolerance and new proselytizing efforts among non-Orthodox peoples. The 1724 budget of the Chancellery of Foreign Affairs, approved by Peter I, allowed an annual sum of forty-two thousand rubles for the Kalmyk tayishis, as well as the nobles and envoys of other peoples. A year later, Catherine I's budget provided for the same purpose only seven thousand rubles.[25]

True imperial favor went to those who chose to convert to Christianity. Upon his conversion, Petr Taishin was given an annuity of one thousand rubles and five hundred *chetvert'* of flour. Moreover, the senate's decrees obliged the Astrakhan governor to give Taishin twenty-four dragoons for his personal protection and to offer military assistance if any of the

---

[21]Bakunin, "Opisanie," *Krasnyi arkhiv* 3 (1939): 216–17; Pal'mov, *Etiudy,* 3–4:370–72.

[22]Bakunin, "Opisanie," *Krasnyi arkhiv* 3 (1939): 216; Pal'mov, *Etiudy,* 3–4:371–73.

[23]*PSZ* 7:423, no. 4660.

[24]Bakunin, "Opisanie," *Krasnyi arkhiv* 3 (1939): 217. In contrast to this modest sum for the khan's family, the Georgian Tsar Vakhtang and his family were allotted substantial amounts of flour, oats, hay, and firewood in addition to the annual payment of twenty-four thousand rubles (*PSZ* 7:no. 4818).

[25]*PSZ* 7:no. 4696.

5. Iconostasis of a mobile church presented by Peter I to Petr Taishin, the grandson of Ayuki Khan (from Vitevskii, V. N. *I. I. Nepliuev i Orenburgskii krai v prezhnem ego sostave do 1758 goda.* 3 vols. Kazan': Tipo-Litografiia V. M. Kliuchnikova, 1897).

tayishis threatened to attack him. A special officer was appointed to keep an eye on Taishin and to serve as a liaison between him and the authorities.[26]

Shortly after his conversion, Taishin returned to roam between the Volga and Don not far from Tsaritsyn with his ulus of 334 tents. To take advantage of disarray among the Kalmyks and to build on its initial success, the government ordered the Holy Synod to launch a major effort to convert the Kalmyks. A special mobile church, which was personally

[26]This position went to the Saratov *dvorianin* Luka Shakhmatov, who spent six years at the post (Bakunin, "Opisanie," *Krasnyi arkhiv* 3 [1939]: 217; E. N. Kusheva, "Khoziaistvo saratovskikh dvorian Shakhmatovykh v 18 veke," *Izvestiia AN SSSR*, ser. 7, no. 7 [1929]: 582).

donated by Peter I to Petr Taishin, was consecrated and, together with religious items and books, sent to Taishin's ulus.[27]

To teach the newly "enlightened" in the lexicon of the Orthodox church and to convert the infidels, the Holy Synod sent to Taishin Father Nikodim Linkeevich of Alexander Nevsky Monastery and three pupils to study the Kalmyk language and later become priests and deacons. Nikodim, who knew the Kalmyks well, was supposed to replace a lower-ranking priest previously sent to Taishin. Before his departure, Nikodim received instructions consisting of twelve points. Realizing the difficulties of his mission, the synod instructed him to avoid long daily prayers. He was to give only short morning and evening prayers, which were commonly used by the Russian military. He was also warned to guard against the "seductive nets" of heresy on the part of "traitors," Old Believers who resided near the Don and Kuban. Nikodim was to restrain the Kalmyks from using alcohol and idol worshiping, but most important, he was to spread God's teachings and serve as a personal example to the Kalmyks.[28]

Conversion was the most certain way to win the support of Russia, but not the only one. Collaborators who served well in promoting Russian interests were also appropriately rewarded. Some traditional Russian loyalists, such as the head of the Kalmyk clergy, Shakur-Lama, whom the authorities would have found difficult to convert, also received generous compensation for their efforts.[29]

The reconciliation of the tayishis, achieved with great difficulty, proved to be short-lived. At the end of February 1725, Dosang and his brother Nitr-Dorji violated the truce by raiding and seizing some of the tents of their brothers. The attack spurred retaliation against Dosang and his allies. When Cheren-Donduk and his party agreed with the Kuban Bakhti Giray to attack Dosang's party, Dosang faced the same uneasy choice as Cheren-Donduk had in the previous year: to stand up to an attack by superior forces or to seek Russian protection behind the Tsaritsyn line. Petr Taishin's arrival from Moscow in Tsaritsyn did not make the choice any easier. Taishin boasted that the tsar had promised to build a town

---

[27]*PSPR* 4 (1876): nos. 1245, 1292, 1321, 1407, 1413, 1439, 1449; *ODD* 5 (1897): 100. A picture and a detailed description of the church's iconostasis is in V. N. Vitevskii, *I. I. Nepliuev i Orenburgskii krai v prezhnem ego sostave do 1758 goda,* 3 vols. (Kazan', Tipo-Litografiia V. M. Kliuchnikova, 1897), 2:505–7.

[28]Vitevskii, *Nepliuev,* 2:II, III, 507; *PSZ* 7:437–38, no. 4683.

[29]Volynskii requested that generous rewards be sent with Shakur-Lama's envoy to Moscow for the lama's crucial role in achieving the reconciliation between the tayishis (Pal'mov, *Etiudy,* 3–4:373–74). The government sent Shakur two hundred gold coins, *chervonets* (each *chervonets* amounted to three silver rubles, i.e., six hundred rubles in total) and six hundred rubles worth of furs (Bakunin, "Opisanie," *Krasnyi arkhiv* 3 [1939]: 218).

near Astrakhan for him and his baptized Kalmyks and that he would be able to reside there in winter, while roaming with his herds in summer. Praising the benefits of conversion, Taishin tried to convince Dosang and others to move behind the line.

Taishin's assurances, however, achieved the opposite effect. Most of the tayishis expressed their strong opposition to crossing the line, by bringing up fears of being forcibly baptized by the Russians. Some tayishis stated resolutely that they were ready to die in their own faith; others suggested moving westward toward the Manych River and spending the summer on the pastures along the six small rivers there and perhaps moving away from Russia altogether. Dosang himself was mistrustful of Petr Taishin's intentions. He suspected that Taishin, relying on Russian support, might take over his ulus. Only the arrival of the Russian translator Bakunin and his assurances of the Kalmyks' safety dispelled these apprehensions, and Dosang with his people and other tayishis chose to cross the line.[30]

Crossing the Tsaritsyn line might have temporarily saved Dosang and other tayishis belonging to his party from the attacks of Cheren-Donduk, but it could not save them from internal hostilities. Unable to stop these warring rivalries, the tayishis decided to send their best zayisangs to Volynskii. They explained that peace among the Kalmyks was impossible because there were too many pretenders. They wanted to cross the Volga in winter to join Cheren-Donduk and let one person rule the Kalmyks.

Another opportunity to end Kalmyk internal dissension passed by. Volynskii decided that it was not in Russia's interests to see the Kalmyks united under one ruler. The governor forbade Dosang and others to cross the Volga and instead allowed them to move westward, to cross the Don and join the ulus of Cheter tayishi. Thus the Kalmyks were split again. Fourteen thousand tents were reported to be near the Don and twenty thousand near the Volga.[31]

Volynskii, explaining his policies to the empress, referred to Peter I, who inaugurated the policy of dividing the Kalmyks into two groups, and added that it was necessary "to restrain the ungrateful Kalmyk people."[32] Meanwhile, in St. Petersburg the realization was growing that Volynskii's policies had gone so far as to harm Russian interests. Incessant internal wars had significantly undermined Kalmyk economic and military power, which prevented the Kalmyks from serving the objectives of the

[30]Bakunin, "Opisanie," *Krasnyi arkhiv* 3 (1939): 218–20.

[31]Ibid., 223. The numbers seem contradictory. Dosang and General Field Marshal Mikhail Golitsyn reported that there were as many as thirty thousand tents near the Don, excluding the tents belonging to Cheter tayishi (*SRIO* 55:182, 196).

[32]Bakunin, "Opisanie," *Krasnyi arkhiv* 3 (1939): 223.

Russian government. In a reply to the government's request to send six thousand Kalmyks to the fortress of St. Peter, Volynskii admitted that the request could not be fulfilled because of internal Kalmyk feuds.[33]

Constant Kalmyk complaints and the growing confrontation between Volynskii and General Field Marshal Mikhail Golitsyn over the Kalmyk policies also added to the government's dissatisfaction. In October 1725, an imperial decree instructed Volynskii to surrender his governorship in Astrakhan and to assume the post of governor in Kazan. One month later, supervision of Kalmyk affairs was transferred to General Field Marshal Golitsyn, and Volynskii was put under his command.[34] During this period of transition, Volynskii's coarse and boorish personality again manifested itself. Golitsyn complained that, despite his orders, Volynskii had not arrived to report to him on Kalmyk affairs and had not sent an interpreter so that there was no one to send to the Kalmyks or to translate Kalmyk letters. Volynskii was ordered to St. Petersburg.[35]

At the end of winter of 1726 the Kalmyk uluses were spread along the pastures on the Volga's west bank and the Caspian shores. The largest group, consisting of the Kalmyks of the viceroy Cheren-Donduk, Darma-Bala, Donduk-Ombo, and other tayishis, had their pastures stretching from Chernyi Iar on the Volga to the Kuma River. Dosang and his group were near the Don. The Kalmyks' westernmost flank was occupied by the Derbet ulus of Cheter tayishi, and Dorji-Nazar and his ulus between the Volga and Yayik were holding the easternmost flank against the advancing Kazakhs.

With the arrival of spring, the largest group of Kalmyks, led by Cheren-Donduk, found itself in a desperate situation. The nomadic cycle required the Kalmyks to leave the exhausted winter pastures and move toward new pastures farther north, and the Kalmyk tayishis were reduced to two options. One was to cross the Tsaritsyn line, but given the experience of the past this option was dismissed because the tayishis refused to submit to unlimited Russian authority. Another option was to cross the Volga toward its east-bank pastures, but increasing Kazakh raids did not make that decision easy. Until this time Dorji-Nazar had been able to resist Kazakh pressure. News of internal turmoil among the Kalmyks invited renewed Kazakh raids.

So they could roam safely on the east bank of the Volga, the Kalmyk tayishis requested arms and ammunition from Russian authorities. The

[33]Ibid., 221.
[34]Pal'mov, *Etiudy*, 1:71; *SRIO* 55:244. The information from this and some other volumes of *SRIO* is based on the published protocols, journals, and decrees of the Supreme Privy Council (Verkhovnyi Tainyi Sovet) from 1726 to 1730.
[35]*SRIO* 55:229, 244.

requests were denied.[36] Even Shakur-Lama added his voice to the complainers. He pointed out that the Russian troops did not protect the Kalmyks and the authorities refused to supply arms at a time when thirty thousand Kazakhs were camped two days' distance from the Yayik. The authorities in Astrakhan replied only that they had no orders to help the Kalmyks and that it was impossible to give them cannons without Russian personnel.[37] In contrast to this reply, similar requests of the Yayik cossacks prompted by the same need met a generous response from the government, and the cossacks' supply of gunpowder, bullets, cannonballs, and cannons was greatly increased.[38]

By refusing Kalmyk requests, the Russian government may have sought to prevent the Kalmyks from crossing the Volga. Fearing a Kalmyk departure for Jungaria, Russian authorities tried to encourage them to cross the Tsaritsyn line. Russian officials in Astrakhan may have been caught in a transitional period, with Volynskii already gone and the new supervisor of Kalmyk affairs, General Field Marshal Golitsyn, not yet fully in charge. The remoteness from the Astrakhan region of Golitsyn's residence in Khar'kov, Volynskii's obstructions, and the absence of interpreters indicate that the transition of power did not occur smoothly. It is also possible that the government tried to capitalize on the continuing dissent among the Kalmyks and to demonstrate to the tayishis the advantages of conversion. At the same time that they were denied Russian protection, the new convert, Petr Taishin, was promised all possible military assistance.

The majority of the Kalmyks led by Cheren-Donduk, Darma-Bala, and Donduk-Ombo seriously considered leaving Russia. At first, the viceroy and the tayishis intended to move to the Kuban. This initiative must have come from Donduk-Ombo. Informants to the Russians, known as "well-wishing Kalmyks" in official Russian terminology, reported frequent exchanges of envoys between Bakhti Giray Sultan and the Kalmyks. Bakhti Giray invited the Kalmyk tayishis to send troops and to take back their Yedisans and Yamboyluks. The tayishis, however, having had most of their troops on constant guard first against Dosang and later against the Kazakhs, could not spare more than two thousand horsemen for such an expedition. Moving to the Kuban at this time did not appear to be a good idea because the Kuban region itself was caught in internal wars, and Bakhti Giray soon had to flee in fear of the Ottoman troops sent against him.[39]

[36]Materialy po istorii karakalpakov, 187; SRIO 57:205.
[37]SRIO 55:235.
[38]PSZ 7:no. 4686.
[39]SRIO 55:232–34, 236.

The only possible escape route from increasing Russian control was toward Jungaria. Previously Darma-Bala had entertained this idea and shortly after Ayuki's death sent her envoy to the Jungar khan, Tsevang-Rabtan. The envoy failed to return, and the following year Darma-Bala sent another envoy to Jungaria, but he was seized by the Kazakhs before reaching his destination. The goal of these envoys was to find out about the possibilities of a political alliance with Tsevang-Rabtan and securing such an alliance by arranging the marriage of one of Tsevang-Rabtan's daughters to Cheren-Donduk.[40]

Darma-Bala's plans encountered significant opposition. Cheren-Donduk feared ending like his brother Sanjib, whom the Jungar khan had deprived of all his people. Shakur-Lama and the influential Yaman and Samtan zayisangs insisted on staying near the Volga. Referring to their experience in many lands, they claimed that from Tibet to Jungaria and from the Don to the Kuban no pastures were better and richer than those near the Volga, and to stay here they were willing to accept Russian protection.[41]

At the end of 1726 or the beginning of 1727 Donduk-Ombo sent his envoys to Tsevang-Rabtan. This was the last Kalmyk embassy to Jungaria for some years. Shortly after the envoys' arrival, the Jungar khan died unexpectedly and mysteriously. Evidently he was found to be poisoned, and a cloud of suspicion was cast over many players in this medieval steppe mystery.[42] Whoever was responsible for his death, the result was the same for the Kalmyk tayishis—it meant the end of their plans to move to Jungaria and the resumption of another cycle of open hostilities between the Kalmyks and their relatives in Jungaria.

[40]Pal'mov, *Etiudy*, 1:63–65. Some reports mentioned that Tsevang-Rabtan and his army were expected to arrive from Jungaria to take the Kalmyks under his protection (*SRIO* 56:241–42).

[41]Pal'mov, *Etiudy*, 3–4:369; Bakunin, "Opisanie," *Krasnyi arkhiv* 3 (1939): 224.

[42]Galdan-Cheren, who inherited his father's title, found the Kalmyk envoys guilty of poisoning the khan and ordered their execution. Whether Tsevang-Rabtan was indeed poisoned by the Kalmyk envoys is not known. Pal'mov suggested that it may have been done by Darma-Bala, who wanted to get rid of Tsevang-Rabtan for political and personal reasons, but what she would have gained by doing this is not at all clear. Tsevang-Rabtan's successor, Galdan-Cheren, claimed that Donduk-Ombo had sent poison to Galdan-Cheren's stepmother to poison Galdan, but she instead chose to poison her husband. In the absence of any definitive evidence, it is also possible to assume that Galdan-Cheren, having first gotten rid of his brother and rival Louzang-Shuno, who later found refuge among the Volga Kalmyks, saw an occasion to murder his father and to lay the blame on a Kalmyk plot (Zlatkin, *Istoriia Dzhungarskogo*, 235–36; Pal'mov, *Etiudy*, 1:68–70).

Change in Russian Policies

During all this time the Russian government was well aware of the Kalmyks' intentions to leave for Jungaria. After Volynskii's dismissal, government officials continued to use restrictive measures to prevent the Kalmyks from leaving. Despite the Kalmyks' requests, the government denied them military assistance and ammunition supplies and delayed its annual payment.[43]

Such measures did not succeed, however, and the Russian government was forced to resort to more conciliatory tactics. Two occurrences were of particular significance in convincing the authorities of the need to change their policies toward the Kalmyks. The first event was the arrival of large groups of Kazakhs at the Yayik and the anticipation of their raids against the Kalmyks and the Russian provinces. The emergence of a new and formidable enemy along the Russian frontier immediately raised the strategic importance of the Kalmyks in the eyes of the Russian government. The second important event was a temporary cessation of internal wars and the unification of the Kalmyks into one group under the nominal leadership of Cheren-Donduk. In July 1726, Cheren-Donduk defeated Dosang's ally, the Khoshut Lekbey tayishi. Cheren-Donduk's explanation of the event to Russian officials provides another insight into the tribal organization of Kalmyk society. Cheren-Donduk described the custom that prevailed among the Torguts (the majority of the Kalmyks under Ayuki and his family), the Derbets (under Cheter tayishi), and the Khoshuts (under Lekbey tayishi): "If there was a quarrel between the Derbets and the Khoshuts, then our khan reconciles them. If there was a quarrel among the Torguts, then the Derbets and the Khoshut should remain neutral and stay with the khan. And the Derbets behaved according to the custom, but Lekbey tayishi roamed away from us, contrary to custom."[44]

Poor pastures along the Don and raids against his ulus from both the Crimea and his Kalmyk rivals convinced Dosang to give himself up to the protection of Cheren-Donduk. Soon his ulus crossed the Don and joined the Kalmyks near the Volga. This time the Russian authorities did not try to prevent Kalmyk unification. In a revealing statement General Field Marshal Golitsyn explained to the empress that if she wished to have the Kalmyks divided, this could have been better accomplished by gifts and

---

[43]*SRIO* 56:188, 205, 206.
[44]Ibid., 230.

persuasion. But dividing their uluses could well result in destruction of Kalmyk society.[45]

To improve relations with the Kalmyks and to assist them in the face of the Kazakh threat, the Russian government decided to meet the Kalmyk requests, but not without taking precautions. The Russian authorities consented to give the Kalmyks irregular cossack troops. According to Golitsyn's disposition, sending regular troops would have been unwise because of their lack of mobility and general ineffectiveness on a distant campaign in the arid steppe. To these tactical concerns he added his fears that the Kalmyks and the Kazakhs might strike a secret deal and attack the Russian contingent.[46]

The Kalmyks were to be provided with ammunition and cannons, but the latter were to be given only with Russian personnel. The official pretext for such a strict regulation was concern that the cannons might fall into enemy hands.[47] It is obvious, however, that leaving the cannons in Kalmyk hands worried the government just as much as their being captured by enemy forces. Also as part of the effort to improve Russo-Kalmyk relations, a special decree ordered that overdue payments be sent immediately to Cheren-Donduk and Darma-Bala.[48]

Meanwhile, informants reported that Bashkir envoys had arrived at the Kalmyk uluses to offer an alliance against the Kazakhs. At this same time, Kazakh envoys were involved in negotiations with the Kalmyks. Rumors quickly spread that negotiations concerning a Kazakh-Kalmyk alliance against Russia were being held. The Kalmyks warned the Russians that the Kazakhs were considering actions against Russia together with the Kubans.[49]

The growing Russian concern over the arrival of the Kazakhs and its possible impact on the shifting alliances in the area made the change in Russian policies toward the Kalmyks more apparent. The government feared a possible alliance along the Muslim axis of the Kazakhs, Kubans, and Crimeans, who together might present a serious challenge on Russia's southern frontier. To prevent the Kalmyks from joining such an

---

[45]Bakunin, "Opisanie," *Krasnyi arkhiv* 3 (1939): 225; *SRIO* 55:447; 56:182. Previously, Shakur-Lama indicated to Golitsyn that both the Kalmyks and the Russians would gain from such unification (*SRIO* 56:207, 215).

[46]Ibid., 55:344–46; 56:181, 470–71.

[47]Ibid., 56:215, 231.

[48]Following financial and legal arguments in the government over these monies, the Chancellery of Foreign Affairs promptly submitted to the empress a memorandum concerning payments to the tayishis in previous years. The memorandum demonstrated that, according to tradition, the present payment had to be given from sources other than the seven thousand rubles allotted for gifts and the upkeep of envoys (ibid., 178–80, 245–49).

[49]Ibid., 187, 198.

alliance and to use them as a vanguard force against the Kazakhs, the Russian government chose to arm and help them.

In autumn 1726, an army of ten thousand Kazakhs of Shemiaka Khan and Barak Sultan of the Middle Horde, together with Abul Khayir Khan and Ishim Sultan of the Lesser Horde, crossed the Yayik and attacked the Kalmyks. As in the past, the main thrust of the Kazakh force fell upon the ulus of Lubji, the son of Dorji-Nazar. When news of this attack reached Cheren-Donduk, Donduk-Ombo, and other tayishis, they gathered an army of twenty thousand to pursue the Kazakhs. The Kalmyks caught up with the Kazakhs near the Yayik and engaged them. The tired Kazakhs decided to encamp on the steppe, and having slaughtered many horses and cattle, they created a wall out of the carcasses. After a four-day siege the two sides agreed to a peace. The Kazakhs returned their spoils and surrendered sixty hostages. The leaders on both sides—the Kalmyk tayishis and the Kazakh khans and sultans—swore an oath to be at peace for "as many years as it takes a newborn to grow up and to be able to ride a horse and to shoot from a bow."[50] Peace with the Kazakhs for the time being relieved pressure on the Kalmyks from the east. They could now turn their eyes toward the Kuban, which itself was in the flames of an uprising.

The Rise of Donduk-Ombo

Donduk-Ombo, perhaps more than any other tayishi, benefited from the unification of the Kalmyks. His ulus grew larger because some of the tents ended up in his possession. Most important, he exhibited the qualities of a gifted military leader and a politician and thus commanded more power and respect among the Kalmyks than the official viceroy Cheren-Donduk. Always supported in his actions by Darma-Bala, his stepmother and lover, Donduk-Ombo became the de facto leader of the Kalmyks.

His position was further reinforced by his alliance with the Kuban rebel Bakhti Giray Sultan. Bakhti Giray, who found refuge among the Kalmyks, asked the Kalmyk tayishis for help in return for those Nogay tribes who had fled the Kalmyks but now wanted to rejoin them. Donduk-Ombo decided to provide Bakhti Giray with Kalmyk horsemen, despite the warnings of Russian authorities not to do so because such an act could be considered by the Porte as a violation of the treaty. At the end of 1726 seven thousand Kalmyk troops led by Bakhti Giray were

---

[50]Bakunin, "Opisanie," *Krasnyi arkhiv* 3 (1939): 225–26.

reported pillaging the Kubans and the Tatars near Azov.[51] Kalmyk support of Bakhti Giray and raids against the Kubans and the Tatars reached such proportions that the Ottomans submitted an official complaint to the Russian envoy in Istanbul, Ivan Nepliuev, warning that if the Russians did not take action against the Kalmyks, the Porte would allow the Crimeans to cross the Russian border to put an end to Kalmyk raids.[52]

At first the government in St. Petersburg tried to turn the situation to its own advantage. The Supreme Privy Council made a covert decision to try to induce Bakhti Giray to become a Russian subject. In return, the Russians would offer Bakhti Giray protection and make Russian troops available to him for use against his enemies. If this was not enough, Bakhti Giray could be promised the Crimean khanate. Such an offer, however, should be made in secret. To avoid the suspicions of the Ottomans, Major Beklemishev would arrange the offer so it would appear as if Bakhti Giray had been caught and brought to Russia by force.[53]

This elaborately contrived plot was destined not to materialize. Bakhti Giray had no interest in Russian protection. Neither did his friend and ally, Donduk-Ombo. He did not limit his targets to the Ottoman provinces but extended them well into Russian territory. During the years 1727–28, damage caused by Kalmyk raids within Russia amounted to 34,446 rubles, excluding the cost of seized cattle and captives.[54] Russian authorities reported that an angry Donduk-Ombo tried to avenge himself for the Russians' refusal to allow him to marry Darma-Bala.[55]

The authorities made it clear that if the Kalmyks continued to assist Bakhti Giray, the Crimeans would soon retaliate, and Russia would not protect the Kalmyks. But the raids persisted, and the threat of an Ottoman-Crimean reprisal increased. In early 1728 Ottoman troops were reported arriving at Azov, where they were joined by the Crimean cavalry.[56]

In response to the growing possibility of another round of hostilities on its southern frontier, the Russian government began to reinforce its troops in the area. Upon the news of the Bashkir envoys' arrival at the Kalmyks' camp and their possible preparations to raid Russian prov-

---

[51]BA Nâme-i Hümayun, no. 7, pp. 131–33. At this time the Kuban region was inhabited by four major Nogay tribes: the Yamboyluk, Yedisan, Yedichkul, and Kazayakli (Kasay oglu). The Yedisans and Yamboyluks, who had recently fled from the Kalmyks, had arrived at the Kuban and subsequently rebelled, wishing to return to the Volga (Rashid, Tarikh-i Rashid, 6:573; SRIO 5:504).

[52]SRIO 56:610; Bakunin, "Opisanie," Krasnyi arkhiv 3 (1939): 227.

[53]SRIO 63:789, no. 387.

[54]Bakunin, "Opisanie," Krasnyi arkhiv 3 (1939): 227.

[55]SRIO 63:10, no. 5.

[56]Ibid., 69:227, no. 125; 75:191, no. 70.

inces, Golitsyn immediately requested more troops. If the Bashkirs and Kalmyks united, he expected the Karakalpaks and Kazakhs to join them. He hastened to add that with only three dragoon regiments he would not be able to hold out against these four hordes. The government ordered six or seven thousand regular troops to be stationed near Tsaritsyn together with two thousand Don cossacks.[57]

The Kalmyks were warned again not to go to the Kuban to try to recover the Yedisan and Yamboyluk uluses, but this time the warning was followed by punitive measures. The government ordered annual payments to the Kalmyks withheld, and the decree of January 1728 forbade the residents of Volga towns from trading arms to the Kalmyks under threat of death. In anticipation of increased Kalmyk raids against the Russian population, authorities took preventive steps. Each town on the Volga from Astrakhan to Saratov was given twenty boats for water patrols, and any Kalmyks who were caught engaging in hostile actions were to be hanged. To remove the source of their troubles, the authorities also offered a reward of five thousand rubles for Bakhti-Giray's head.[58]

Apparently, these measures did not prevent the Kalmyks from embarking on their Kuban campaign. Even some of the staunchest Russian advocates such as Shakur-Lama and Yaman and Samtan zayisangs replied to the Russian demands with the simple logic that they would be guilty if they attacked Russian provinces, but the government could not forbid them from going to the Kuban. The Kuban campaign, however, bore no fruit because the Ottomans took prudent measures to prevent the return of the Yedisans and Yamboyluks. They moved them first to the Crimea and finally relocated them in the vicinity of the town of Belgorod (Akkerman in Ottoman) not far from the Dnestr River.[59]

The Russian government was aware that Donduk-Ombo championed the Kalmyks' anti-Russian policies. Diplomatic efforts to restrain Donduk-Ombo were only partially successful. The convened council of the Kalmyk tayishis decided not to engage in hostile actions against Russia, and even Donduk-Ombo's intimate and loyal friend Darma-Bala found it difficult to support him. Donduk-Ombo found himself at war with the viceroy Cheren-Donduk and his supporters.

When it became known that Donduk-Ombo intended to attack towns on the Don and then flee to the Crimea to seek Ottoman protection, the

---

[57]Ibid., 79:73–76, no. 40; 79:265–66, no. 141.

[58]Bakunin, "Opisanie," *Krasnyi arkhiv* 3 (1939): 228–29.

[59]Ibid., 229–30. According to the Ottoman chronicler, the Yedisans and Yamboyluks decided to flee the Kuban to avoid being taken to the Volga again and requested to go to the Crimea (Rashid, *Tarikh-i Rashid*, 6:575).

government decided to resort to a different course of action. The Supreme Privy Council ordered that Donduk-Ombo be captured or, if this was not possible, that he be killed.[60] With the help of Shakur-Lama, the government contrived a plan to capture Donduk-Ombo. According to the plan, when Donduk-Ombo was to cross the Volga to its east bank, Cheren-Donduk, Darma-Bala, and Shakur-Lama would request Donduk-Ombo's troops, reportedly numbering from seven to eight thousand horsemen, for the war against the Kazakhs. Two regular regiments and irregular cossack troops were also to be brought to the east bank of the Volga under the same pretext, and after having warned the tayishis not to intervene, these troops would destroy Donduk-Ombo's ulus. The action would be taken when the Volga was in full flood so that Donduk-Ombo could not cross it and flee to the Kuban. In case Donduk-Ombo chose not to cross the Volga but to spend the summer on its west bank, he would be attacked by the troops from the Tsaritsyn line, the Don cossacks, and other tayishis.

As with Bakhti Giray, such plans were easier made than accomplished. After year-long attempts to entrap Donduk-Ombo, the Russian officials gave up the idea. They reported that Donduk-Ombo was too clever, cautious, and tough. He always had no less than five hundred people guarding him, and other tayishis, afraid of his revenge, refused to collaborate.[61]

With the disappearance from the scene of two Crimean rebels, Bakhti Giray and Jan-Timur (the latter found refuge among the Kalmyks), the tumultuous Kuban affairs became temporarily calm. Bakunin relates that Bakhti Giray was reinstated in the Kuban by the Kalmyks and in 1729, when campaigning in the Kabarda, was ambushed and killed by the Kabardinians in a narrow mountain gorge.[62] Thus ended the uprising in the Kuban, bringing another temporary truce among the Kalmyks.

---

[60]Bakunin, "Opisanie," *Krasnyi arkhiv* 3 (1939): 231.

[61]*SRIO* 94:543–47. We are told that Donduk-Ombo enforced his authority among his own people with the help of a clan called Tomut. The Tomuts were the people born into mixed marriages between Kalmyk women and the Kazakhs and Bashkirs who had joined the Kalmyks in the past. Later, the offspring of such marriages developed into a distinct group. They dressed like the Kalmyks, but most of them practiced Islam and spoke both Kalmyk and Tatar languages. Donduk-Ombo favored the Tomuts and kept them as his personal guards (Bakunin, "Opisanie," *Krasnyi arkhiv* 5 [1939]: 201).

[62]Bakunin, "Opisanie," *Krasnyi arkhiv* 3 (1939): 231–32. The Ottoman chronicler in his contradictory account of these events claimed that Bakhti Giray fled to the mountains while escaping the Crimean army of Selamet Giray Sultan. Standing no chance on his own, Jan-Timur repented and was forgiven by the Crimean khan (Rashid, *Tarikh-i Rashid*, 6:574–76).

Another Round of Relations with China and Tibet

With the death of the Jungar khan Tsevang-Rabtan, Kalmyk plans to join the Oirats of Jungaria had collapsed, but Darma-Bala and Dorji-Nazar— two principal proponents of this plan—did not give up their hopes entirely. When reconciliation with the Jungars proved to be impossible, they decided to resort to other means.

At the end of 1729 the Kalmyk viceroy and the tayishis dispatched their envoys to the capital to obtain permission to send a Kalmyk embassy to Tibet. Cheren-Donduk, Shakur-Lama, and Dorji-Nazar expressed their wish to participate in such a pilgrimage. The goal of the trip, they explained, was to eulogize Ayuki's ashes in Tibet. The government con- sented to allow such an embassy to pass through Siberia but ruled out Cheren-Donduk's and Shakur-Lama's participation, fearing that their absence would undermine the influence of the pro-Russian party among the Kalmyks. To soften the refusal, the government sent gifts to the viceroy and two hundred gold coins to Shakur-Lama.[63]

The authorities trimmed the size of the embassy from approximately one hundred members to twenty or thirty. Shakur-Lama argued that this number was too low. He insisted that the size of the embassy had to be increased because of the large volume of goods it would carry, but most important because a small embassy would not command sufficient respect from other peoples. A compromise was reached when all major Kalmyk tayishis, except Donduk-Ombo, were allowed to appoint their own envoys with servants on the embassy. In the end, a Kalmyk embassy of thirty-six people left the Volga steppes for Tibet, carrying with it three thousand rubles worth of goods free from custom duties.[64]

It turned out later that on the way to Tibet the embassy stopped in Beijing. The envoys spent two months there, after which four of the envoys turned back, while the rest continued their journey to Tibet. Suspicious of changes in the originally planned route, Russian officials detained the four returning envoys and subjected them to lengthy inter- rogations. The authorities found 128 books and personal letters which the envoys carried from China to the Kalmyk tayishis. The contents of some of these letters, as well as the following events, clearly demonstrate that eulogizing Ayuki's ashes was not the principal goal of the Kalmyk

[63]Bakunin, "Opisanie," *Krasnyi arkhiv* 3 (1939): 232.

[64]Ibid., 233; Pal'mov, *Etiudy*, 1:76–78. According to other sources, this embassy numbered more than three hundred people (Luciano Petech, *China and Tibet in the Early 18th Century*, 2d ed. [Leiden: E. J. Brill, 1972], 165–66).

embassy. In fact, the embassy's main objective was to suggest to the Qing government the possibility of a Kalmyk-Qing alliance against the Jungars. It appears that only one Kalmyk envoy, sent by Darma-Bala, was entrusted to relate the message to the Qing; the rest of the envoys were not told about the embassy's secret goal.[65]

More Kalmyk envoys were aware of another political goal of the embassy—to achieve the removal of the present viceroy, Cheren-Donduk. He was recognized by the Kalmyks as a weak and incapable leader, and there was a consensus among the tayishis on this issue. Darma-Bala's group had found a possible candidate who would be willing to take the initiative and implement the cherished idea of moving back to Jungaria— Galdan-Danjin, another of Darma-Bala's sons and Cheren-Donduk's younger brother. Darma-Bala's envoy mentioned to the Qing officials that the Kalmyks had not regarded Cheren-Donduk as a legitimate khan because the title of khan had not been conferred on him by the Dalai Lama. To secure such confirmation for Galdan-Danjin was another goal of the Kalmyk embassy.[66]

The Qing government was interested in the Kalmyks' proposal and sent its own embassy to the Kalmyks in 1731. This embassy was later to split in two; one section went to Moscow, and the other proceeded with the original mission to the Kalmyks. The Qing made no secret of their plans. The envoys informed Russian officials that they had arrived with the emperor's decree to invite the Kalmyks to participate in combined Qing-Kalmyk military actions against Jungaria. They also made it clear that they intended to invite Louzang-Shuno, who resided among the Kalmyks and was a legitimate pretender to the title of Jungar khan, to accept Qing protection in return for the promise of becoming the Jungar khan.[67]

For the sake of Sino-Russian relations, the Russian government did not consider it prudent to hinder the embassy's visit to the Kalmyks. It insisted, however, that the Kalmyks were Russian subjects and could not meet Qing requests without the consent of the Russian empress. The government also feared that the Qing emperor's decree might have contained a declaration conferring on Cheren-Donduk the title of khan. To forestall such an event and to gain the Kalmyks' favor, the government rushed an envoy to declare Cheren-Donduk the Kalmyk khan and to bring lavish gifts to the tayishis. The matter was so urgent that Vasilii

[65]Pal'mov, Etiudy, 1:81–82, 87–88.
[66]Ibid., 89–90. For a well-informed and detailed discussion of these events see Pal'mov, Etiudy, 1:76–116.
[67]Bantysh-Kamenskii, Diplomaticheskoe sobranie del, 165–66; Bakunin, "Opisanie," Krasnyi arkhiv 3 (1939): 234; Pal'mov, Etiudy, 1:119–23.

Bakunin, who was assigned as a guide to the Qing embassy, was instructed to delay it for as long as possible. Only on May 1, 1731, when Cheren-Donduk was able to reach the vicinity of the town of Dmitrievsk, was he declared the Kalmyk khan. In the presence of Shakur-Lama, other members of clergy, and many Kalmyk nobles, the Astrakhan governor I. P. Izmailov conferred on Cheren-Donduk the title of khan and bestowed on him the symbols of the khan's authority—armor, a sable fur coat, and a hat. Cheren-Donduk swore allegiance by putting an image of Buddha to his forehead and affixing his seal to the written oath.[68] Vasilii Bakunin was running out of excuses to explain the delay of the Qing-Kalmyk meeting and was relieved to find out that the delicate matter was over. The meeting between the Qing envoys and the Kalmyks could now take place, and a few days later the embasssy set out for the Kalmyk uluses.

On June 5, 1731, the embassy was given an audience by Cheren-Donduk, Darma-Bala, Shakur-Lama, and other prominent Kalmyks. To avoid any surprises, the government instructed Cheren-Donduk as to what his answers should be and appointed the Saratov governor, Lieutenant Colonel Vasilii Beklemishev, to be present during the reception of the embassy.

Everything went as the Russian authorities had planned. The Qing officials announced that they had come to congratulate both Cheren-Donduk and Darma-Bala, who succeeded Ayuki Khan, and brought gifts from the emperor. The Qing made it clear that they were interested in the Kalmyks' participation in a war with Jungaria. Following Russian instructions, Cheren-Donduk replied that he could not send any troops without the Russian empress's order because he was her loyal subject. The request that Louzang-Shuno join the Qing met with a similar response. The Russian officials kept a close eye on the course of negotiations, and Beklemishev took particular pains to see that Cheren-Donduk's written reply to the Qing emperor was carefully worded in accordance with the Russian memorandum.

On June 18 the embassy left the Kalmyks and set out for home. The efforts of the Russian officials and the Kalmyk replies apparently succeeded in convincing the Qing envoys that the Kalmyks indeed were under Russian control. Shortly after the embassy's return to Beijing, the Qing emperor sent a letter to St. Petersburg requesting that a few thousand Kalmyks be permitted to march against Jungaria. The Qing believed that if the Kalmyks set out, they would be joined by the Kazakhs, Kirgiz, and other tribes and would defeat the Jungars.

[68]*PSZ* 8:382–83, no. 5699.

The Russian government diplomatically declined to meet such a request and referred to the friendly relations between Russia and Jungaria. This crushed Qing hopes for the creation of a coalition of various nomadic peoples to engage the Jungars in the west.[69]

Cheren-Donduk's Last Years, 1731–1735

The nomination of Cheren-Donduk as Kalmyk khan had little effect on other tayishis who sought to exploit the weakness of the khan's power. After successfully handling the Qing embassy's mission, Vasilii Beklemishev was promoted to the rank of colonel. He had reported that, despite his efforts, it was impossible to stop the wrangling among the tayishis because they had become too numerous. He hastened to add that as long as the tayishis argued about hierarchy of power, pastures, and other issues, civil war among them was inevitable unless someone chose to behave like Ayuki and kill his relatives to seize their uluses.[70]

Beklemishev's observation clearly underscored the importance of having one strong leader able to unite the Kalmyks. The Russian government's support for Cheren-Donduk was intended to create such a strong leader, faithful to Russian interests. But because Cheren-Donduk enjoyed no great popularity among the Kalmyks, his nomination as khan resulted only in increasingly bitter Kalmyk feuds.

The old grievances surfaced again. Petr Taishin complained that, as a legitimate successor to Ayuki, he ought to be the khan. Donduk-Ombo's hostility toward Cheren-Donduk and the pro-Russian party among the Kalmyks had never ceased. Now the two disgruntled tayishis, united by a common interest, waged war against Cheren-Donduk. In the east, Dorji-Nazar and his son made frequent raids against Cheren-Donduk's ulus. For some time Dorji-Nazar had been nurturing plans for an alliance with Abul Khayir Khan, the ruler of the Kazakh Lesser Horde, against Cheren-Donduk and Russia. During the years 1731–32, Dorji-Nazar and his son sent frequent embassies trying to convince the khan to reject the advances of the Russians and instead turn against them, but the envoys of Cheren-Donduk, and in particular a Russian envoy, Mamet Tevkelev, succeeded in convincing Abul Khayir of the advantages of a Russian protectorate.[71]

[69]This information is based on the work of Pal'mov, *Etiudy*, 1:117–200.

[70]Bakunin, "Opisanie," *Krasnyi arkhiv* 3 (1939): 237–38.

[71]*Kazakhsko-russkie otnosheniia,* 73, 79, no. 33; 90, no. 37. For the origins and location of the Lesser, Middle, and Greater Kazakh hordes see Martha Brill Olcott, *The Kazakhs* (Stanford, Calif.: Hoover Institution Press, 1987), 10–12.

It was only the raw power of the Russian military that kept Cheren-Donduk in his office. Nevertheless, neither a sense of gratitude nor the fear of losing Russia's support stopped him from maintaining relations with other foreign powers. Kalmyk envoys were known to visit the Persian shah, and an Ottoman envoy was sighted in the Kalmyk uluses.[72] Perhaps the best evidence of such ambassadorial exchanges lies in the origin of the items presented by the Kalmyks to the Qing embassy in 1731. Among the gifts were Ottoman muskets and a bow, as well as Persian silks, brocades, and garments.[73]

Cheren-Donduk's relations with the Crimea in the early 1730s involved more than exchange of envoys and gifts. In 1730, the Crimean Kaplan Giray Khan suggested a meeting with Cheren-Donduk and Darma-Bala. The meeting did not take place because the Kalmyk khan and his mother were closely watched by Russian officials. Nonetheless, some agreement must have been reached because one thousand Kalmyks participated in the Crimean campaign against the Kabarda. The Crimean khan particularly favored these "bloodthirsty and wild Kalmyks" and rewarded each one of them with garments.[74] The "reward" of the Russian government was a harsh decree ordering Cheren-Donduk to stop sending troops against the Kabarda.[75]

The issue of Kalmyk fugitives, traditionally a point of contention between the Kalmyk tayishis and Russian authorities, also stood in the way of Cheren-Donduk's good relations with the administration. In six years of missionary activity among the Kalmyks, Father Nikodim Linkeevich had converted 59 men and 135 women. Most of the new conversions were superficial and, though receiving the benefits due them, the converts continued to adhere to their old Buddhist practices. Father Nikodim recommended that the baptized Kalmyks be separated from other nonbelievers and sent to Ukrainian towns to learn Christian ways. Nikodim complained of the hardships he had experienced among the Kalmyks, particularly referring to the difficulties of the nomadic life-style in winter at his advanced age. His younger pupils, assigned to learn the language, voiced similar complaints about the nomadic life-style, which prevented them from learning Kalmyk properly.[76]

Dissatisfied with the progress of conversion, the Russian government decided to intensify its efforts at proselytizing among the Kalmyks. In

---

[72]Bakunin, "Opisanie," *Krasnyi arkhiv* 3 (1939): 236.

[73]Pal'mov, *Etiudy*, 1:188, 190.

[74]'Abd al-Ghaffâr, *'Umdat al-Tawârikh*, 170–72.

[75]*Kabardino-russkie otnosheniia*, 2:70–76, nos. 58, 61.

[76]*ODD* 10 (1901): 579, no. 346; 583, no. 347. For a list of the converts by name see Appendix XXV to no. 347.

1732 the senate ordered that a school be organized at the Ivanov monastery in Astrakhan to teach the children of the baptized Kalmyks both Russian and Kalmyk grammar.[77] The expectations of both the government and the new converts were not realized. Petr Taishin, for example, felt disappointed because his hope to become the Kalmyk khan, the primary reason for his conversion, did not materialize. The authorities were disillusioned by the lack of serious Christian intentions on the part of Taishin and other new converts. Father Nikodim wrote that Taishin discouraged his Kalmyks from being baptized and continued to worship idols.[78]

The fate of ordinary Kalmyks who chose to convert was not always a happy one. Most of the newly converted Kalmyks knew nothing of Russian language, laws, or customs and were frequently abused.[79] Many Kalmyks died soon after their conversion, if not from abuse and the dramatic change of life-style, then from diseases to which they had not been previously exposed.

All the efforts to reconcile the Kalmyk tayishis during this time and to make them recognize Cheren-Donduk as their khan had failed. Donduk-Ombo and Petr Taishin were preparing to attack the Kalmyk khan. In October 1731, Cheren-Donduk, whose ulus was near the Chernyi Iar on the Volga, learned that Donduk-Ombo's army had set out against him. To forestall an attack on his ulus, Cheren-Donduk hastily gathered two thousand horsemen and decided to strike first.

In the meantime, imperial decrees from the capital reached Cheren-Donduk and Donduk-Ombo, urging them not to engage each other. Donduk-Ombo was ready to cease hostilities, but Cheren-Donduk replied that once they mounted their horses a clash was inevitable. With his army of two thousand he attacked Donduk-Ombo's superior force of no less than ten thousand horsemen. After initial success, Cheren-Donduk's troops had to turn around and flee. Donduk-Ombo's victory was complete. Cheren-Donduk with twenty-five people fled to Tsaritsyn; Darma-Bala and Galdan-Danjin, with a few others, found refuge in Saratov; and Shakur-Lama, after wandering in the steppes, found his way to

---

[77]*PSZ* 8:no. 5960.

[78]*ODD* 10 (1901): 330–31, no. 178.

[79]In one such case, a Kalmyk known as Kharam fled to Saratov with his wife and daughter and appeared at the desk of Stepan Shakhmatov, who was in charge of Kalmyk affairs in Saratov. Upon Kharam's conversion, Shakhmatov convinced the Kalmyk to work for his cousin Luka in return for a house and some cattle. Luka, however, listed Kharam as his serf in the 1723 census. When Kharam complained to the local authorities, he was beaten with rods, put in chains, and then delivered to Luka Shakhmatov's winter residence. In the next census of 1732 Kharam was listed as dead (Kusheva, *Khoziaistvo*, 595). See also Nil Popov, *V. N. Tatishchev i ego vremia* (Moscow: Tip. V. Gracheva, 1861), 325–27.

Tsaritsyn. Donduk-Ombo acquired about fifteen thousand tents, some of which he generously gave to his allies Petr Taishin and other tayishis as rewards for their assistance.[80]

Russia's concern grew when Darma-Bala warned authorities that the strengthened Donduk-Ombo would seek to leave the Volga and Yayik pastures. At a time when disputes between Russia and the Ottoman empire over annexed Persian territory and the Caucasus were threatening to turn into another military confrontation, the prospect of the Kalmyks' departure or, worse, their alliance with the Ottomans, was fraught with serious consequences for Russian strategic interests.

Top government officials convened in the capital to discuss the critical situation. They resolved to dispatch Lieutenant General Prince Ivan Bariatinskii with instructions to try to convince Donduk-Ombo not to leave. If peaceful means failed, Bariatinskii was to use military force. If Donduk-Ombo chose to move to the Kuban, Bariatinskii was to station troops along the Volga to prevent him from crossing it. In case Donduk-Ombo intended to cross the Yayik and move east, the tayishis loyal to the government, together with the cossacks, were to pursue him.[81]

These orders, however, were not easy to implement. Along the 412-verst stretch of the Volga from Astrakhan to Tsaritsyn there were no other centers of population, except for the small town of Chernyi Iar and the fortress of Enotaevsk. In winter, when the river was frozen, it was almost impossible to prevent the Kalmyks from crossing it on the ice. Should Donduk-Ombo move toward the Kuban, the option of pursuit was limited because Bariatinskii was instructed not to enter Ottoman territory and not to provoke the Porte.

The final and most important Russian disadvantage was a lack of sufficient mobility and endurance, necessary for steppe warfare. Well aware of this failing, Donduk-Ombo scorned the Russians when he learned of their troop movement. He boldly stated that he was not afraid of the Russians because they needed three years to start moving, and even when they had moved, they stayed for three months at one place. As if to demonstrate Russia's helplessness, on December 18, 1731, he and his ulus crossed the Volga to the west bank.[82]

In anticipation of Donduk-Ombo's movement toward the Kuban, the Russian government began to implement its measures. Prince Bariatinskii ordered six dragoon regiments to leave their winter quarters and take up positions along the Don. He feared that Donduk-Ombo might

---

[80]Bakunin, "Opisanie," *Krasnyi arkhiv* 3 (1939): 238–40.
[81]Ibid., 241–42.
[82]Ibid., 243–44.

force his way across the river, after which nothing could prevent him from moving on to the Crimea. Later, some of these regiments, together with three thousand cossacks, were ordered to move to the Kuma and Kuban rivers to block Donduk-Ombo's movement in that direction.

After familiarizing himself with the situation in the field, Prince Bariatinskii realized that the military force at his disposal was inadequate to confront an army of twenty thousand Kalmyks under Donduk-Ombo. Winter conditions and the problem of supplies presented additional difficulties. To win time and to prepare for a spring campaign, Bariatinskii wrote to Donduk-Ombo and offered to meet him. Donduk-Ombo agreed to a meeting sometime in the spring when the weather improved but insisted that first Bariatinskii should arrest Shakur-Lama, whom Donduk-Ombo considered a source of many Kalmyk troubles.

While negotiations with Donduk-Ombo continued, the news reached the government that the Kalmyk khan Cheren-Donduk, never popular among the Kalmyks, had lost almost all his support. Bariatinskii was ordered to inquire confidentially about a possible candidate to replace Cheren-Donduk and to comply with Donduk-Ombo's preconditions for a reconciliation if they included the removal of one of the tayishis Donduk-Ombo found offensive. If Donduk-Ombo insisted on Shakur-Lama's dismissal, Bariatinskii was to consider such a move carefully because Shakur-Lama had been loyal to Russia through the years.[83]

The government, eager to see the Kalmyks reconciled, was prepared to sacrifice even its strongest supporter, Shakur-Lama. It may be, however, that the desire of the government for a peaceful solution to the crisis was not related forcefully enough to the officials below. Or perhaps Prince Bariatinskii persisted in his belief that only the sound of Russian cannons could halt Donduk-Ombo's aggressive intentions.

On February 3, 1732, Bariatinskii set out from the Don with several dragoon and infantry regiments numbering 4,619 Russians, 4,692 cossacks, and 5,000 Kalmyks. Having been informed that Donduk-Ombo intended to move toward the Yayik, Bariatinskii decided to take a direct route through the steppes and to march toward Astrakhan to prevent Donduk-Ombo from crossing the Volga. A three-week march through the waterless and cold steppes brought the expeditionary force the miseries so often experienced by Russian troops on similar campaigns. While already on the march, Bariatinskii learned that Donduk-Ombo had moved in another direction, along the Kuma toward the Kuban. By this

---

[83]Ibid., 248–49.

time the march through the unfriendly winter steppes had begun to take its toll, and pursuit would have been suicidal.[84]

The military campaign, unsuccessful as it was, was not a total failure. Petr Taishin, his brother Batu, and some other tayishis who had roamed with Donduk-Ombo fled to the Volga when they heard of the approaching Russian troops. Some of them crossed the river and joined Dorji-Nazar, but Petr Taishin was arrested in Krasnyi Iar.[85]

Once again Cheren-Donduk was reinstated in the position of khan by Russian military force. Although this was against the will of the majority of Kalmyks, they were divided by quarrels and different interests and unable to resist Russian military might. Only one tayishi, Donduk-Ombo, was determined to fight to the end. Unable to counter the Russian threat, he sought refuge in the Kuban, bringing with him more than eleven thousand Kalmyk tents.

Donduk-Ombo's Challenge

After Donduk-Ombo found refuge in the Kuban, the main concern of Russian policies in the region was to achieve his return. Russian officials were instructed to make every effort to convince Donduk-Ombo to return peacefully and to promise to reconcile him with Cheren-Donduk. At the same time, the Russian resident in Istanbul, Ivan Nepliuev, tried to press the Ottomans to have Donduk-Ombo expelled. His message to the Porte made it clear that Russia was prepared to organize a military campaign to catch and return Donduk-Ombo, even though it might mean entering Ottoman territory.[86]

Meanwhile, Donduk-Ombo and his Kalmyks experienced extreme hardships in the Kuban. Donduk-Ombo's pastures were situated in the steppes, a two-day ride from Azov along the rivers Egorlyk, Kalaus, and Manych, and the upper reaches of the Kuma. This part of the Kuban steppes proved to be less hospitable than the Volga ones, and many Kalmyk herds perished because of the lack of sufficiently large pastures, water, and grass. Impoverished Kalmyks, who had no herds of their own, found little fish in the river, and to save themselves from starvation they often had to sell their children to the Kubans in exchange for millet.[87]

---

[84]When the expedition reached Astrakhan it was short some 2,883 horses, 45 people were dead, many more were sick, and the army was exhausted (ibid., 249–51).

[85]Ibid., 252–54.

[86]Bakunin, "Opisanie," Krasnyi arkhiv 5 (1939): 198.

[87]Ibid., 201.

The Kalmyks' stay in the Kuban was further aggravated by the traditional hostility between the Kubans and Kalmyks. This hostility had formed gradually over the years, fueled by mutual raids and religious differences. The Kubans openly despised the Kalmyk as infidels, explaining succinctly to the Russian envoy that a wolf and a sheep could not live together on the same island.[88]

Nonetheless, even such adverse conditions could not bend the will and determination of Donduk-Ombo. He continued to resist pressures from both Russia and the Crimea. On one occasion, when Donduk-Ombo requested the Crimean khan's permission to cross the Don, the khan demanded one hundred Kalmyk children. To clarify relations between himself and the Crimean khan, Donduk-Ombo replied that he would consider this only if the khan intended it as a sign of friendship, not as tribute or hostage taking. One month later, the Crimean khan informed Donduk-Ombo that he would not be allowed to cross the Don.[89]

Donduk-Ombo did not rush to accept Russia's conditions. He made an attempt to mend differences with the Kalmyk khan and sent his envoy to Cheren-Donduk to suggest a meeting near the Volga to resolve their grievances without Russian participation. In a letter to the empress, Donduk-Ombo made it plain that the present problems stemmed from Russian interference in Kalmyk affairs, and he demanded that the Russians leave the Kalmyks to iron out their differences among themselves. If this condition was met, Donduk-Ombo was willing to return to the Volga.[90]

The Russian government knew that to satisfy Donduk-Ombo's demand meant agreeing to his dominance over the Kalmyks, which the government was not yet ready to accept. Constant interference in Kalmyk affairs continued to exact a heavy toll on Kalmyk society. Growing Russian encroachment had a devastating effect on the Kalmyk people and their herds. Donduk-Ombo lost many herds trying to escape Russian arms and found himself confined to small and insufficient pastures. Cheren-Donduk, following Russian orders, was caught in a similar situation. To make sure that the Kalmyk tayishis would not attempt to join Donduk-Ombo, the authorities insisted that Cheren-Donduk and his people winter on the Volga's east bank. There they could not find shelter for their herds similar to that offered by the marshes of the Caspian Sea on the west bank, and a deep snow together with frost caused many Kalmyk herds to perish.[91]

[88]Ibid., 197, 198.
[89]Ibid., 201.
[90]Ibid., 203.
[91]Ibid., 205.

The loss of their herds pushed many Kalmyk paupers into Russian towns, where, if they were to stay, they had to convert to Christianity. The tayishis attributed this directly to Russian policies, which they had protested unsuccessfully. Complaints from the Kalmyk khan to Russian officials were also in vain. Such a situation ultimately contributed to the erosion of both the prestige of the khan and the Kalmyks' relations with Russia.

Squabbles among the Kalmyk tayishis on the east bank of the Volga persisted, and Cheren-Donduk could do little to stop them. Dorji-Nazar's Kalmyks, in search of Russian protection from the Kazakhs, moved closer to the Volga and frequently raided Cheren-Donduk's Kalmyks.[92] On the other side of the Volga, Donduk-Ombo, though making demands on the government, did not expect Russian goodwill. In numerous sorties his Kalmyks harassed the Russians near the Volga and the cossacks along the Don. Together with the Crimeans and Kubans, they twice defeated Russian and Don cossack expeditionary forces. Prince Bariatinskii again recommended military action against Donduk-Ombo. In time, the government found Bariatinskii incapable of dealing with the situation adequately and ordered him to surrender control over Kalmyk affairs to the commander of the Tsaritsyn troops, Major General Tarakanov.[93]

This change in command had no effect. Donduk-Ombo kept pressing his grievances against the authorities, conditioning his return to the Volga upon their satisfaction. Donduk-Ombo demanded the release of Petr Taishin and the return of the baptized Kalmyks and those bought as slaves by the Russians for a small sum. He also insisted that uluses be given to his former allies Batu and Donduk and that he be treated equally with his other brothers.[94]

While the Russian government weighed these options, Donduk-Ombo grew stronger, and his prestige among the Kalmyks increased both because of his own bold actions and Cheren-Donduk's ineptitude. In

[92]In a complaint to the Russian authorities concerning Dorji-Nazar's actions, Cheren-Donduk drew an intense picture of the brutality committed by Dorji-Nazar's Kalmyks. In one raid against Cheren-Donduk's ulus, Dorji-Nazar's Kalmyks pillaged forty-three tents and slaughtered many men and women. The raiders brought back with them seven captives who were then lashed with whips. The victors subsequently drank their victims' blood until they died. While still alive, some of the captives had their stomachs cut open, and their bile was used for treatment of camels diseased with scab. On another occasion, Dorji-Nazar's Kalmyks cut off the heels and toes of their Kalmyk captives before they released them (ibid., 207).

[93]Despite all the measures Bariatinskii took, some of the Kalmyks continued to flee Cheren-Donduk to join Donduk-Ombo. Thus Danjin-Dorji tayishi with two hundred tents successfully made his way to Donduk-Ombo, and many other small groups were reported joining him as well (ibid., 203–6, 208–9).

[94]Ibid., 210.

February 1734, he defeated Donduk-Dashi tayishi near Astrakhan and captured about two thousand tents. Shortly thereafter, three thousand tents from the ulus of the Erketen zayisangs made their way toward the Kuban and joined Donduk-Ombo.

The Russian military commander Tarakanov and the Astrakhan governor Izmailov both reported their inability to protect the Kalmyks on the Volga's west bank. The adverse conditions of the arid steppes combined with the nature of the Kalmyk nomads, constantly on the move and widely scattered, made protection impossible. Vasilii Bakunin, asked by the government to prepare a memorandum on the situation among the Kalmyks, stated that military action against Donduk-Ombo could not be undertaken because of inadequate number of troops available and recommended trying again to convince Donduk-Ombo to come to terms peacefully.[95]

In August 1734, the government dispatched a Don cossack officer, Danil Efremov, to deliver another message to Donduk-Ombo. In the message, the Russian Vice-Chancellor Andrew Ostermann first rebuked Donduk-Ombo for his actions. In response to Donduk-Ombo's accusation that the Kalmyks' troubles were the result of Russian interference, Ostermann referred to the events of 1701, when a reconciliation between Ayuki and Chakdorjab had been reached as a result of Russian mediation. Ostermann made vague promises to meet Donduk-Ombo's demands but brushed aside the question of returning Kalmyk converts to their original uluses.[96]

Notes of reconciliation were also sent to Dorji-Nazar as well as some Kabardinian nobles who were Donduk-Ombo's relatives and supported him. All these efforts, however, failed to impress Donduk-Ombo. The news soon reached the authorities that Cheren-Donduk, Darma-Bala, and other tayishis were considering joining Donduk-Ombo in the Kuban because the Russian administration refused to return their fugitives. To prevent this from happening, the khan's ulus, which at the time was behind the Tsaritsyn line, had been transferred on the government's order to the Don.[97]

Despite all its efforts to save Cheren-Donduk's khanship, the Russian government finally realized the futility of such attempts, and Russia's preparations for war with the Ottoman empire made finding a solution all the more urgent. In March 1735, an imperial decree laid the blame for the Kalmyk feuds on Cheren-Donduk, calling him a drunkard and a khan

[95]Ibid., 212, 215–16.
[96]Ibid., 217–18.
[97]Ibid., 220. Vasilii Bakunin's account ends here.

with no power. He was dismissed and called to St. Petersburg. In his stead, Empress Anna declared Donduk-Ombo the chief governor of the Kalmyks and decreed a general reconciliation among the Kalmyks with no retribution.[98]

The victory of Donduk-Ombo and the concessions he secured from the Russian government were an eloquent tribute to his remarkable determination. With clear objectives in mind, Donduk-Ombo showed that he could be prudent, cautious, or merciless as events demanded. Donduk-Ombo's skills as a crafty politician were complemented by his military valor. A careful and brave commander, he early appreciated the use of muskets and cannons, and in encounters with the enemy he suffered few defeats.[99] For the first time since Ayuki's death, the Kalmyks were united under capable leadership, although years of civil war had exacted a great price from Kalmyk society.

The government's support of the unpopular Kalmyk khan Cheren-Donduk, whose authority was based solely on Russian military might, had perpetuated internal wars among the Kalmyks. Numerous herds and people were lost in the process. The fragmentation of power among the Kalmyk tayishis made their uluses attractive prey for their neighbors and resulted in further loss of herds and people—the principal capital in nomadic society.[100] Inadequate government payments to the Kalmyk tayishis throughout these years failed to provide substantial relief.

Moreover, the Russian government, guided by its strategic interests rather than the necessities of the Kalmyks, frequently prescribed to the tayishis their pasture locations. The result was a forced redistribution of grazing areas and abandonment of traditional seasonal nomadic routes, which often meant a substantial loss of herds from cold or drought.

Bereft of their herds, many Kalmyks were unable to sustain their way of life and were compelled to turn to fishing or to flee to Russian towns to convert. The growing number of Kalmyk runaways and their conversion continually figured in the complaints of the tayishis. The extent of this growing problem for the Kalmyks can be seen from the following figures: during his tenure among the Kalmyks, from 1725 until 1731, Father

---

[98]*PSZ* 9:no. 6705.

[99]Bakunin, "Opisanie," *Krasnyi arkhiv* 5 [1939]: 208; *Materialy po istorii Rossii. Sbornik ukazov i drugikh dokumentov, kasaiushchikhsia upravleniia i ustroistva Orenburgskogo kraia,* comp. A. I. Dobromyslov, 2 vols. (Orenburg: Tipo-Litografiia F. B. Skachkova, 1900), 2:17–22.

[100]Curiously, the Jungar khan, as remote as he was from the Kalmyks, was also successful in draining Kalmyk human resources. During his war with the Kazakhs, he declined any form of ransom for the Kazakh prisoners in his possession, insisting that they be exchanged for the Kalmyk prisoners of the Kazakhs on a one-to-one basis (*Materialy po istorii Rossii,* 1:104).

Nikodim succeeded in converting 200 Kalmyks. In the following period, from 1731 to 1735, more than 2,600 Kalmyks were reported to have accepted Christianity—a significant outflow of people prompted by the disastrous civil war and the weakened Kalmyk economy.[101]

Many other Kalmyks chose to sell their children as a way to deal with poverty. The demand for Kalmyk children was great, but adult Kalmyk men and women were also of value to the Russians. In the early 1720s the government introduced laws prohibiting slavery among the Russians, but it tacitly permitted the purchase of Kalmyks and Tatars and instructed Governor Volynskii to allow such transactions to proceed.[102] In 1737 this policy finally culminated in a manifesto declaring that the Kalmyks and peoples of other ethnic groups who were baptized or purchased at a young age did not have to be put on the tax rolls. This allowed Russians to purchase, baptize, and keep such chattel without paying tax on them. Kalmyks who complained and requested to be set free were beaten with rods and turned over to their masters. The law, however, extended only to the first generation of the converts, and their children were to be put on the tax roll.[103]

Russian officials found unlimited uses for Kalmyk slaves. Thus the Astrakhan governor Vasilii Tatishchev suggested that Russians should be allowed to purchase Kalmyks and should then sell them to Russian commanders in cities to be used as recruits for military service.[104] Not satisfied with existing legal provisions, the Russians often abused the Kalmyks and captured some illegally or paid a small sum for others.

The protracted civil war among the Kalmyks was a direct result of the Russian government's interference in Kalmyk affairs. Such policies of the Russian government, primarily concerned with exercising better control over the Kalmyks, brought to Kalmyk society a severe economic impoverishment. It also resulted in the Kalmyks' weakened military might. The years of civil war were only part of a larger ongoing drama which eventually altered the way of life of the Kalmyk nomads forever.

[101]*ODD* 14 (1910): 537–39, no. 414.

[102]Most of the purchased and baptized Kalmyk children were twelve or thirteen years old (ibid., 20:nos. 23, 116, 163, 176, 213, 224). *PSZ* 6:226, no. 3622. For an extensive discussion of slavery in Russia see Richard Hellie, *Slavery in Russia, 1450–1725* (Chicago: University of Chicago Press, 1982).

[103]*PSZ* 10:no. 7438 (6); 12:nos. 8941, 9193.

[104]N. N. Pal'mov, "K astrakhanskomu periodu zhizni V. N. Tatishcheva," *Izvestiia AN SSSR*, ser. 7 (1928): 330.

7

Russian Colonization and
the Kalmyks' Decline and Exodus

The Rule of Donduk-Ombo, 1735–1741

After an imperial decree declared Donduk-Ombo "the chief governor of the Kalmyk people" in March 1735, the Russian government adopted a more conciliatory approach to the Kalmyks. The resumption of war with the Ottoman empire made Donduk-Ombo's cooperation extremely important. Urgent military needs left no time for bargaining and compelled the government to make concessions to the new Kalmyk ruler.

During the ensuing years, imperial decrees conceded one issue after another to Donduk-Ombo. Among the first was granting permission for the Kalmyk embassy, which had returned from Tibet and was being detained in Moscow, to come back to the uluses. This conciliatory gesture was followed by another, more important step—the removal of Shakur-Lama, Donduk-Ombo's chief opponent, from the Kalmyk political scene. Shakur-Lama was sent to St. Petersburg, where he soon died.[1]

In comparison to Cheren-Donduk's annuity of 500 rubles and 1,000 *chetvert'* of flour, Donduk-Ombo was to receive 3,000 rubles and 2,000 *chetvert'* of flour every year. Other tayishis were to share an annual sum of 2,000 rubles.[2] The Kalmyks were also generously rewarded for their successful military operations. In March–April 1737, as an incentive for another campaign against the Kubans, Donduk-Ombo received 7,730 rubles for himself and 70,120 rubles to be distributed among the Kalmyk

[1] *Materialy po istorii Rossii*, 2:39–41, 261–63.
[2] *PSZ* 9:nos. 7027, 7103.

troops led by the tayishis and some Kabardinian nobles. Two years later, ten thousand Kalmyk troops received 98,750 rubles.[3]

The extent of Russian concessions to Donduk-Ombo is best seen in the issue of conversion to Christianity. Always a stumbling block in Kalmyk-Russian relations, the question of conversion was resolved in the khan's favor. The government instructed Russian residents along the Volga, Don, and Yayik not to accept Kalmyk runaways in the future and to send them back to their uluses.[4] The government sought to assemble those who had been baptized in previous years in one ulus headed by Petr Taishin's widow, Princess Anna Taishina. The government developed a plan according to which all baptized Kalmyks residing along the Volga from Astrakhan to Tsaritsyn were to be gathered under the command of Colonel Zmeev. They were to build a fortress at the place where the Tok River discharges into the Samara River. Princess Taishina was to reside in the fortress with her zayisangs, while the rest of the Kalmyks were to roam in the vicinity until they grew accustomed to a more sedentary lifestyle and learned to till the land. Garrison members drafted from the peasants were supposed to teach the Kalmyks basic agricultural skills, and the government would provide money and tax exemptions as an additional incentive.[5]

In 1739 such a town was founded, but, in anticipation of possible Kazakh or Kalmyk raids against the settlement, the government chose a different location deeper inside the Russian provinces. The town was built near the Volga above the city of Samara and appropriately named Stavropol' (in Greek, the town of the cross), presently known as Tol'iatti. The town had three churches and one school. The Kalmyks were put on the government's payroll and given military ranks and a hierarchy similar to that of the cossacks.[6]

[3]*SRIO* 117:176, 196; 126:366.

[4]*AVD* 2:163, no. 160.

[5]*PSZ* 10:nos. 7228, 7335, 7733; *SRIO* 124:464–67. The realization of this project was entrusted to Vasilii Tatishchev and his assistants (Popov, *V. N. Tatishchev*, 620–30). In the past, to ensure that the baptized Kalmyks could not easily flee or be returned by force, the authorities had sent the fugitives further away and assigned them residence in the Ukrainian town of Chuguev, located near Khar'kov. Kalmyks had resided in Chuguev since 1696, when, upon the conquest of Azov, some of them had arrived at Chuguev to settle there. From fifty families in 1712 the Kalmyk population of Chuguev grew substantially so that by 1740 it could sustain four Kalmyk cavalry companies—a total of 214 horsemen (*Istoricheskaia khronologiia Khar'kovskoi gubernii*, comp. K. P. Shchelkov [Khar'kov: Univ. tipografiia, 1882]: 60; Filaret, Archbishop of Chernigov, *Istoriko-statisticheskoe opisanie Khar'kovskoi eparkhii*, otdelenie 4, *Chuguevskie okrugi voennogo poseleniia* [Khar'kov: Univ. tip., 1858]: 74, 75; K. P. Shovunov, "Kalmytskie kazach'i poseleniia i ikh voennaia organizatsiia v 18 veke," in *Issledovaniia po istoricheskoi geografii Kalmytskoi ASSR* [Elista: N.p., 1981], 19–22).

[6]*PSZ* 10:nos. 7549, 7800; *Topografiia Orenburgskoi gubernii*, comp. P. I. Rychkov in 1762 (Orenburg: Tip. B. Breslina, 1887), 81–85.

The Russian government made an earnest effort to make this project succeed. The official reports told of some Kalmyks learning crafts and trades, teaching their children Russian, and observing Christian laws. Stavropol' served as a safe repository for newly converted Kalmyk fugitives, and its population rapidly grew from a few hundred converts to almost eight thousand Kalmyks a quarter of a century later. On one occasion, in 1765, authorities were compelled to relocate some of the Kalmyks to Orenburg because Stavropol' was overpopulated.[7] The project, however, never took root. In the early 1770s Pallas observed that the Russian influence had no lasting effect on the town's Kalmyks, with the exception of some nobles and those who were employed in the town's administration. Aside from this small group, most of the Kalmyk residents remained Buddhists. They preferred to roam with their herds and forgot how to till the land.[8]

Russia's generous policies toward Donduk-Ombo bore fruit as the Kalmyk khan performed an extremely valuable service to the government. While Field Marshal Peter Lacy was besieging Azov and the armies of Field Marshal Burkhard Münnich were marching through the Crimea, it was essential to prevent the Kubans from rendering any assistance to either Azov or the Crimea. Assigned to contain the Kubans within their own area, the Kalmyks did not just arrest the Kubans' activities but brought utter destruction to the entire Kuban region.

During a campaign in November–December of 1736, twenty thousand Kalmyks of Donduk-Ombo, together with five thousand Don cossacks, ravaged the Kuban. They reduced to the ground the major city of the Kuban—Kopyl. Thousands of Kubans were slaughtered, drowned in the river, or taken captive. The campaign took place when the Kuban herds were being brought back from the mountains to winter in the valleys, and tens of thousands of sheep, horses, and cattle ended up in Kalmyk hands.[9]

Over the next few years Donduk-Ombo continued his depredations in the Kuban. He defeated and captured many and spared only those who chose to surrender and give hostages.[10] The Kuban, however, was not the only theater of military activities in which the Kalmyks were involved. Smaller Kalmyk detachments took part in the siege of Azov and the invasion of the Crimea. The Kalmyks harassed and pillaged the enemy, and in one especially noteworthy raid brought back to the Russian camp

[7]*PSZ* 12:nos. 9110, 9444; 17:no. 12,317.

[8]Pallas, *Reise*, 1:114–15.

[9]*SRIO* 80:90–92, no. 40; K. H. Manstein, *Zapiski Manshteina o Rossii, 1727–44* (St. Petersburg: Tip. R. S. Balasheva, 1875), 94–95, 104–5; Belikov, *Kalmyki v bor'be*, 76–83.

[10]*SRIO* 80:297–98, no. 150; 313–14, no. 154; 476, no. 238.

more than a thousand Crimean captives.[11] Apparently, Kalmyk acts of aggression in the Kuban and Crimea greatly annoyed the Ottomans and provoked the sultan to order the Crimean khan "to raid the Volga Kalmyks in such a manner that it will be no longer necessary to attack them again."[12]

When the Kalmyk troops were participating in the war against the Ottomans, the Kazakhs attempted several raids against the vulnerable Kalmyk uluses. In some of the more successful raids the Kazakhs took significant numbers of Kalmyk herds and captives.[13] The Russian government learned to manipulate the raids that different nomadic peoples carried out against each other and to use them to its own advantage. Thus the Kazakhs of Abul Khayir Khan were encouraged to attack the mutinous Bashkirs, or Dorji-Nazar's Kalmyks, when they rebelled. The Kalmyks and Bashkirs were often used to restrain the Kazakhs.[14] This time, however, the Kazakh raids against the Kalmyks were unwelcome by the Russians, and the government ordered local authorities to protect the Kalmyks because "the Kalmyks were needed in the war against the Tatars."[15]

The government sought to win Donduk-Ombo's goodwill by bestowing on him the title of khan and the appropriate insignia—a banner, a saber, a fur coat, and a fur hat.[16] Earlier only extreme circumstances had impelled the Russian government to grant the title of Kalmyk khan. The unquestionable prestige and importance of Ayuki, made a khan by the Dalai Lama, had forced the Russian government to recognize and address him as such. In another case, Cheren-Donduk was hastily granted the title of khan in an attempt to forestall a similar action by the Qing embassy. Donduk-Ombo became the third Kalmyk khan recognized by the Russians—the ultimate tribute to his power and a manifestation of Russia's urgent need for his military service.[17]

Even such a high honor, when it came from the Russians, did not impress Donduk-Ombo. To become a real khan in his eyes and those of the Kalmyks, he needed to be confirmed by the Dalai Lama and to receive

---

[11]'Abd al-Ghaffâr, 'Umdat al-Tawârikh, 174, 182, 206; SRIO 120:306; Manstein, Zapiski Manshteina, 124, 127.

[12]BA Nâme-i Hümayun, no. 2, pp. 24–25.

[13]Vitevskii, Nepliuev, 1:251–53.

[14]The imperial order of 1734 specifically instructed Russian officials to play nomadic hordes against each other (Kazakhsko-russkie otnosheniia, 115, no. 51); Materialy po istorii Rossii, 1:37, 38; 2:69.

[15]SRIO 117:82; 130:652.

[16]PSZ 10:no. 7191.

[17]In 1740, in another unprecedented gesture to the Kalmyk khan, Donduk-Ombo was presented with a gold medal worth fifty gold coins (SRIO 146:490).

the khan's seal from Tibet. Interestingly, Donduk-Ombo referred to himself as a khan only in correspondence with Russian authorities. In his letters to Tibet and the Mongol nobles, he continued to use the title of tayishi. To receive the title from the Dalai Lama, Donduk-Ombo decided to dispatch an embassy to Tibet and in 1737 notified the government of his intention.[18]

In another sign of respect for Donduk-Ombo's wishes, the government agreed that the embassy to Tibet would number seventy people and carry with it ten thousand rubles' worth of goods, far more people and goods than had been allowed the previous Kalmyk embassy of 1729. Like the previous embassies, this one also had goals that were intended to be kept secret from the Russian government.

Besides securing the title of khan for himself, Donduk-Ombo's other wish was to ensure that his son, Randul, become his successor. The forty-five-year-old khan's seemingly premature concern over his heir was not accidental because it had been known for some time that Donduk-Ombo was infected with a deadly disease, syphilis. To seek the Dalai Lama's approval of Donduk-Ombo's choice was one of the embassy's goals. The embassy, however, was not destined to reach Tibet. The Qing, eager to avenge the Russian government's refusal to allow the Kalmyks to take part in the war with Jungaria, balked and declined to grant the embassy passage through China. Unwilling to provoke Donduk-Ombo's anger, Russian authorities continued to insist on the embassy's passage. Only the Kalmyk khan's death in 1741 broke the impasse, and the authorities ordered the embassy's return.[19]

In the past Ayuki Khan's favoritism of his son Gunjib at the expense of the legitimate successor, his eldest son, Chakdorjab, had triggered the latter's revolt. An almost identical turn of events unfolded when Donduk-Ombo's eldest son, Galdan-Normo, realized that his father intended to bypass him and instead declare his brother Randul the successor. The rebellion erupted in the summer of 1738, when Galdan-Normo was campaigning against the Kazakhs. Donduk-Ombo notified Astrakhan that Galdan-Normo had rebelled and had been joined by other tayishis. Galdan-Normo's army, which at first numbered two thousand Kalmyks, soon embraced half of the Kalmyk troops.[20]

Such rapid growth of the rebellion was not accidental. If Cheren-Donduk was too weak a leader, Donduk-Ombo represented the opposite extreme. His harsh rule was strongly resented by many tayishis. The next

---

[18]Pal'mov, *Etiudy*, 1:238–39.
[19]For a detailed discussion of this embassy see Pal'mov, *Etiudy*, 1:238–52.
[20]Pal'mov, *Etiudy*, 2:3–4; *SRIO* 124:235.

Kalmyk viceroy, Donduk-Dashi, characterized his predecessor's repressive rule: "Making no distinction between the tayishis, nobles or commoners, [laymen] or clergy, men or women, Donduk-Ombo had some murdered, others arrested, yet others [whole families] uprooted, and then denounced them, as if they were conspiring against the Russian government."[21] Less concerned with the welfare of his subjects than with his own riches, Donduk-Ombo also charged the Kalmyks interest on the flour allowance he received from the government and later lent to his people.[22]

In response to Donduk-Ombo's request, the Astrakhan governor promptly dispatched a detachment of regular and irregular troops to join Donduk-Ombo. The arrival of the Russian troops, combined with the government's diplomatic efforts, may have convinced Galdan-Normo to back down. At any rate, Galdan-Normo did not seem to inherit the determination and stubbornness of his father, and the rebellion soon lost its momentum.[23]

Just as Russia's role during the rebellion against Ayuki in 1701 had secured Ayuki in his position as khan, so Russia's interference through diplomatic and police actions during the 1738 rebellion resolved the issue in favor of Donduk-Ombo Khan. This time, however, the rebellion was suppressed more quickly and easily because of several new factors. First, the increased Russian military presence in the area and supremacy of Russian firearms made Russia's diplomatic language much more persuasive. Second, Russia's control over the Kazakh Lesser Horde allowed the government to use the Kazakhs to limit the Kalmyks' mobility and to prevent them from moving to Jungaria. Finally, the Kalmyks themselves, weakened by internal wars, grew more dependent on Russian products and services and thus were more amenable to Russian political advances.

In March 1741, Donduk-Ombo died. His death unleashed another cycle of violence, bitter disputes, and internal wars among the Kalmyks. As usual, hostilities spilled over against the Russians as well. To pacify the Kalmyks and to name a new Kalmyk viceroy, the government dispatched Vasilii Tatishchev. A capable administrator and also, incidentally, the first Russian historian, Tatishchev was at the time under investigation on charges of bribery and corruption as the head of the

---

[21]Pal'mov, *Etiudy*, 2:1.

[22]Popov, *V. N. Tatishchev*, 305.

[23]Other tayishis resisted a little longer until they too were persuaded to rejoin Donduk-Ombo. Most of the mutinous tayishis and zayisangs were later arrested and sent to Russian towns where many died shortly thereafter from diseases. A detailed description of the rebellion is found in Pal'mov, *Etiudy*, 2:1–35.

Orenburg region. The government transferred Tatishchev to Astrakhan and conditioned dismissal of the charges against him on the success of his mission. The arrival of Vasilii Tatishchev in Astrakhan in 1741 marked an important juncture in Kalmyk history.

The Rule of Donduk-Dashi, 1741–1761

Donduk-Ombo's death almost immediately resulted in a renewed internal war among several Kalmyk factions. Donduk-Ombo's widow, Jan, wanted to see her son Randul become the khan. She was opposed by a group led by Darma-Bala, Dorji-Nazar, and others who wanted to install Ayuki's son Galdan-Danjin.[24] The Russian government was no less determined to place in office its own candidate, Chakdorjab's son Donduk-Dashi, a powerful tayishi who had long been loyal to Russian interests.[25]

Tatishchev was instructed to invite eleven major tayishis to meet at a specified location and in their presence to declare Donduk-Dashi the Kalmyk viceroy. Tatishchev then was to administer the oath of the tayishis to the new viceroy and to distribute annual payments among those present. If the Kalmyks of Jan's group refused to take an oath, Tatishchev was allowed to convince them by the use of force, but not to destroy their uluses.[26]

On September 4, 1741, Donduk-Dashi was declared the Kalmyk viceroy in a ceremony followed by a big feast. The Russians imposed strict conditions on the new ruler: he could not engage in relations with foreign powers; he could not request or take back any Kalmyk converts; and he had to give his son as a hostage. Jan was conspicuous by her absence at the ceremony. News soon reached Russian authorites that Jan, fearful of reprisals, had fled.

Jan crossed the Volga, where she intended to spend the winter on the Kuma. Donduk-Dashi's raids against her and the desertion of many

[24]Jan accused the opposition of disrespect toward the khan's widow because of her Kabardinian origin and Muslim religion. Jan's people eventually killed the pretender of the opposition, Galdan-Danjin, and rumors spread that Jan was also determined to get rid of Darma-Bala and Donduk-Dashi (*Kabardino-russkie otnosheniia,* 2:106, no. 84; *Ocherki istorii Kalmytskoi,* 1:193–94; Popov, *V. N. Tatishchev,* 277–78).

[25]In 1739, Donduk-Dashi's disagreements with Donduk-Ombo had compelled the former to request Russian permission to settle together with Princess Taishina in Stavropol'. For security reasons, the government chose to settle Donduk-Dashi in the Krasnoiarsk fortress situated on the Kama defense line. There he and his zayisangs were given payments in cash and grain, as well as additional allowances for the purchase of hay, candles, and firewood (*PSZ* 10:no. 7774).

[26]Popov, *V. N. Tatishchev,* 265–66.

people from her ulus, however, compelled her to move farther south with her remaining one thousand tents and to seek refuge in her native Kabarda. The government's fears became particularly acute when it learned that Jan had requested help from the Kubans and the ruler of Persia, Nadir Shah, who at the time was on a campaign in southern Dagestan. To prevent Kabarda from becoming another center of Kalmyk rebellion, the government instructed Tatishchev to act immediately.[27]

To meet with Jan and convince her to return, Tatishchev dispatched his son Evgraf, an officer in the Russian army. The lack of forthcoming aid from the Persian shah or the Kuban, the neutrality of her Kabardinian relatives, and concern that all of her uluses, which she had left behind, might end up in Donduk-Dashi's hands were some of the considerations that finally moved Jan to accept the Russian proposition. No less compelling was the small but well-armed force that Evgraf Tatishchev brought with him.[28]

To halt unrest among the Kalmyks, the Astrakhan governor Vasilii Tatishchev decided to take more decisive measures. Having declared to the Kalmyk tayishis that their present trouble stemmed from Jan's conspiracy against Donduk-Dashi, he had her arrested and sent to Saratov and later to Moscow.[29]

Tatishchev's tougher policies applied not only to the rebellious Jan and her supporters but to the Kalmyk viceroy as well. After repeated clashes with the Astrakhan governor, Donduk-Dashi decided to leave for St. Petersburg to relate his numerous complaints and requests in person. They included the right to send an embassy to Tibet, composing a code to regulate Kalmyk-Russian disputes, permitting unrestricted fishing on the Volga, and building two fortresses, one on the Yayik to prevent the Kazakhs from crossing the river and another on the Volga to serve as his winter headquarters.[30] Among these issues, two were of particular im-

---

[27]Ibid., 280–81, 286, 297–98, 308; *Kabardino-russkie otnosheniia*, 2:106, no. 84; Pal'mov, "K astrakhanskomu periodu," 333.

[28]Popov, V. N. *Tatishchev*, 295–303; *Kabardino-russkie otnosheniia*, 2:103, no. 82.

[29]The government initially intended to keep Jan under arrest, but persistent requests from her Kabardinian relatives to release her made the authorities change their mind because it was more important to win Kabarda's loyalty at this crucial time when troops of Nadir Shah were approaching the area. In 1744, Jan and her two sons and four daughters were converted from Islam to Christianity. After that she became known under her Christian name as Princess Vera Dondukova. She received a house in Moscow and an annual salary, while her sons joined the military and were assigned to a prestigious cadet corp (AKV 4:269, 271; 6:157; *Ocherki istorii Kalmytskoi*, 1:194–95; Solov'ev, *Istoriia Rossii*, bk. 11, vol. 22:338; Popov, V. N. *Tatishchev*, 315, 351, 352).

[30]Popov, V. N. *Tatishchev*, 311–13.

portance to the Kalmyks: fishing rights on the Volga and the resolution of the numerous disputes between the Kalmyks and the Russians.

Seeds of Discontent

Throughout the 1730s and 1740s the Russian population along the Volga was constantly growing. To reinforce the Tsaritsyn line, the government launched a program of resettling the Don cossacks along the Volga. By 1743 the total number of cossacks residing in Volga towns and settlements between Astrakhan and Saratov reached 2,779 men.[31] Along with the cossacks, the population of the Volga towns grew significantly because of an influx of people attracted by the local trades and industries. The increased number of town residents together with stepped-up Russian military presence in the area provided relative safety for the towns and enabled its inhabitants to expand their activities by putting to use nearby meadows and engaging in more intensive fishing in the river. Tatishchev's plans envisaged further colonization of the Volga and building more towns and fortresses along the river.[32]

At a time when the Russian population and industries were rapidly growing in the Volga area, the Kalmyk economy, severely undermined by the internal wars, showed further dramatic signs of decline. In the 1740s as many as ten thousand Kalmyk tents were listed as poor (*ubogie*, or *skudnye*), that is, families without any herds or with herds insufficient to sustain life.[33] An increasing number of these Kalmyks had to turn to fishing. The government, however, was concerned with protecting its fishing rights monopoly and required that the Kalmyks fish only at certain times and locations and not market their fish to anyone. Tatishchev suggested that Kalmyk-Russsian tensions over fishing could be defused by hiring Kalmyk laborers to work with Russian fishing teams. In 1742, 6,400 Kalmyk tents, having no other means of survival, found employment at Russian fisheries.[34]

---

[31]*PSZ* 9:no. 6496; Popov, *V. N. Tatishchev*, 647.

[32]Popov, *V. N. Tatishchev*, 640–48. Tatishchev had similar plans for the colonization of the Yayik, but the Orenburg governor Ivan Nepliuev objected to them, insisting that such a process would ruin the Yayik cossacks. The government's attitude toward the plight of the cossacks on the Yayik proved to be remarkably different from that toward the Kalmyks on the Volga. The government agreed with Nepliuev's argument and the empress's decree granted the Yayik cossacks exclusive fishing privileges (Vitevskii, *Nepliuev*, 1:254–56).

[33]Popov, *V. N. Tatishchev*, 637.

[34]Ibid., 635–40; Pal'mov, *Etiudy*, 5:2–3.

Fishing sites and grazing lands, formerly used by the Kalmyk herds and now turned by the Russians into hayfields, were the sites of frequent clashes between dispossessed Kalmyks and Russians. The Kalmyks often fell victim to Russian vigilantes and reciprocated with violence of their own. Donduk-Ombo's request for a special law code in the 1730s had been prompted by the necessity to solve these mounting Kalmyk-Russian disputes, which in the 1740s grew in both number and intensity.

While in the Russian capital, Donduk-Dashi succeeded in making his case clear, and the government apparently had faith in him and was willing to meet most of his requests. Referring to Donduk-Dashi's loyalty in the past, the government instructed Tatishchev to change his confrontational policies toward the Kalmyks. Donduk-Dashi's arrival in the capital in person and concession that his son would reside in Astrakhan as a hostage seemed to convince the government of his good intentions.[35]

Among other concessions, Donduk-Dashi was granted permission to dispatch an embassy to Tibet. His request to place the Derbet Kalmyks under his supervision was also met, and in 1743 the Derbets were transferred from the Don to the Volga.[36] The onerous task of compiling a new law code for the Kalmyks was entrusted to Tatishchev. The government sent him a Russian translation of the 1640 Kalmyk law code to serve as a basis for the new one. Some important changes, however, had to be made, and Tatishchev was instructed to replace the fines provided in Kalmyk law for murder and theft by appropriate punishments based on Russian law.[37]

Russian policies were now directed toward strengthening the new viceroy's position. As in the past, concessions to the viceroy were prompted less by Russia's goodwill than by the immediate necessity of the situation. This time, a threat from Persia compelled the Russian government to adopt a more accommodating attitude toward the Kalmyks.

Throughout the late 1730s and 1740s the name of the Persian ruler, Nadir Shah, inspired awe among peoples from the eastern frontiers of the Ottoman empire and Caucasus to Central Asia and India. Having defeated the Moguls of India and left in ruins the khanates of Khiva and Bukhara, Nadir Shah turned his victorious armies against the Caucasus and rapidly approached the Russian frontier. The alarmed Russian authorities began a buildup of their troops in the fortress of Kizlar. Russian

[35]Popov, V. N. Tatishchev, 314.
[36]AVD 2:303–4, no. 334; Kazakhsko-russkie otnosheniia, 300, no. 118.
[37]Popov, V. N. Tatishchev, 315.

concessions to Donduk-Dashi were directed at securing his loyalty and Kalmyk participation in a possible military conflict.

Despite the government's orders, tensions between the Astrakhan governor and the Kalmyk viceroy were growing. The disputes were numerous, and all the requests and complaints on both sides notwithstanding, most of them remained unresolved. While Donduk-Dashi continued submitting his complaints, Tatishchev was determined to execute justice according to his notions and Russian laws. Tatishchev accused the tayishis of selling Kalmyk children to the Crimea and Kuban, but Donduk-Dashi found this justifiable because the tayishis were desperately poor. In his turn, Donduk-Dashi accused the Russians of continuing to convert Kalmyks. Tatishchev replied that those Kalmyks had embraced Christianity voluntarily. Tatishchev complained that the Kalmyks were destroying the Volga fishing industry by fishing with forbidden fishing tackle, wasting many fish, and often pillaging Russian fishermen. Donduk-Dashi explained that poor Kalmyks had no other means to survive, that they suffered from the Russian ban on the sale of fish and salt, and that the Russians frequently abused them physically. Tatishchev pointed out that Kalmyks employed at the fisheries were earning enough money to buy themselves a horse and some cattle and return to their ulus, but they could never save enough money because tayishis and zayisangs mercilessly deprived them of most of their earnings by cheating them and exacting various taxes. Tatishchev also blamed the Kalmyk clergy, whom he said received large endowments at a time when many Kalmyks were starving.[38]

These and numerous other contentious issues were deeply rooted in the competing character of two different economies: one based on extensive nomadism and becoming increasingly destitute, the other that of a centralized bureaucratic Russian state marked by rapid growth and prosperity. The clash between the two societies assumed the shape of a personal confrontation between Donduk-Dashi and Tatishchev.

Donduk-Dashi sent one complaint after another to St. Petersburg, implicating Tatishchev in taking bribes, failing to follow the government's orders, lawlessly acquiring property, and obstructing justice.[39] To be sure, some of the charges were meant to slander the governor and

---

[38]On one occasion Donduk-Dashi intended to build a Buddhist temple in Astrakhan. Unable to make a decision on his own, Tatishchev referred the matter to St. Petersburg. The response from the capital said that it was not appropriate to build a temple for idol worshiping in the empire of Her Majesty, particularly with the government's money. In his answer to Donduk-Dashi, Tatishchev was told to find a more diplomatic excuse but to refuse permission just the same (ibid., 305–6, 319, 328–36).

[39]Ibid., 336–38; Pal'mov, "K astrakhanskomu periodu," 338.

achieve his dismissal. Most of them, however, were not totally groundless, as throughout his administrative career Tatishchev had been known
to supplement his income by numerous other means. In his turn, Tatishchev reported that Donduk-Dashi was considering leaving for the
Crimea or Kuban and was conducting a lively correspondence with the
Persian shah.[40]

Tired of his administrative duties and anxious to devote more time to
his literary labors, Tatishchev, citing his advanced age, poor health, and
Donduk-Dashi's hostility toward him, petitioned the government to re-
lieve him from his post.[41] The government, concerned about a confrontation between Tatishchev and the Kalmyk viceroy and the latter's possible
plans to leave Russia, acted favorably on the governor's request. In June
1745, a decree relieved Tatishchev of his command and appointed Lieutenant General D. F. Eropkin to take charge of Kalmyk affairs.[42]

A New Approach: A Look at Russo-Kazakh Relations

The expansion of the Russian frontier to the southeast and the creation
of the Orenburg defense line increasingly brought the Russians into
contact with their populous nomadic neighbors, the Kazakhs. In the
past the government's principal goal was to prevent the Kazakhs from
advancing toward the Volga and to use the Kalmyks as a buffer to
preclude the formation of a threatening alliance of the Crimeans and
Kubans with their numerous coreligionists, the Kazakhs. In time, however, realization of the Kalmyks' declining economic and military power
lent more importance to Russia's relations with the Kazakhs. By the mid-
eighteenth century such Russian towns as Orenburg and Troitsk became
major trading centers with the Kazakhs, and the possibility of turning
the Kazakhs into Russia's loyal subjects became more realistic.

In this situation, continued mutual raids between the Kalmyks and
the Kazakhs were not in Russia's interests, save for instances when the
government chose to unleash one to restrain the other. Russia's attempts
to keep peace between these two peoples were only partially successful.
The government did succeed in preventing massive Kazakh migration
west of the Yayik and thus certainly saved the Kalmyks from being swept
away by the more numerous and vigorous Kazakh nomads. The Russian
government did not want the Kalmyks to be obliterated by the Kazakhs

[40]SA 6:371, 431, 462, 477.
[41]Pal'mov, "K astrakhanskomu periodu," 340.
[42]Popov, V. N. Tatishchev, 655–57.

in the same way the Nogays had been destroyed by the Kalmyks a century earlier. But scattered settlements of Yayik cossacks and inadequate Russian troops could not stop the incessant Kalmyk-Kazakh raids.

At first, in dealing with the Kazakhs the government resorted to the old and familiar policies of co-opting the Kazakh elite. Thus to strengthen a friendly Kazakh khan, the government was ready to put a detachment of Russian troops at his disposal, to build him a fortress to serve as winter quarters, and to provide monetary compensation to the khan and his possible heirs.[43] In time, however, the government began to emphasize a different strategy suggested by the Orenburg governor Ivan Nepliuev. According to Nepliuev, the best way to pacify the Kazakhs was not by the use of force but by allowing them to trade with Russian towns. Indeed, as the number of Kalmyk herds sharply declined, the supply of Kazakh horses and sheep increased so dramatically that Russian merchants often bought Kazakh herds and sold them for profit in Astrakhan.[44]

Such Russian policies brought remarkable success. In 1759, almost one thousand Kazakhs traded daily at the Orenburg market, where they exchanged their herds for grain. They are reported to have grown accustomed to storing hay and grain for the winter, and the governor expected them to settle in a permanent community and discard their nomadic life-style.[45] A secret commission of the Siberian governor went even further in its recommendations. It suggested that indulging the Kazakhs was the best way to pacify them. The commission explained that if the Kazakhs were permitted to roam near the Russian frontier and the Kazakh nobles had houses built for them, the Kazakhs then would learn how to cut and store hay and realize the advantages of a sedentary life-style. Then the people and herds would forget how to roam in winter, grow dependent on houses and storage, and eventually cease their raids.[46]

The question of whether to allow the Kazakhs to roam near the Russian frontier had long been debated in the government. The Orenburg governor Nepliuev favored the Kazakhs' proximity to the Orenburg defense line. He argued that since the construction of the line, the danger of a Kazakh-Bashkir alliance had disappeared, and the Kazakhs, like the Kalmyks and Bashkirs, could be used against Russia's enemies.[47]

---

[43]*Kazakhsko-russkie otnosheniia*, 495, no. 190; 533–34, no. 206; 577, 584–85, no. 225.

[44]Ibid., 346–47, no. 135.

[45]Ibid., 576, no. 225.

[46]Ibid., 630, no. 246.

[47]Ibid., 574, no. 225; *SA* 9:407. The government's major concern was preventing any contact between the Kazakhs and their Muslim coreligionists in the Crimea and the Kuban (Kraft, *Turgaiskii*, 52, no. 172; 114, no. 306).

Playing different peoples against each other to quell rebellion or subdue opposition became an established principle of Russian policies. The government often enlisted the Kalmyks against the Bashkirs, Kazakhs, and Don and Yayik cossacks. Ivan Nepliuev related in his memoirs how he had used the Kalmyks against the Kazakhs and the Kazakhs against the Bashkirs. In 1755, during the Bashkir uprising, his cynical policies resulted in the Bashkirs and Kazakhs massacring each other.[48]

The goals of Russian policies toward the Kazakhs in the middle of the eighteenth century were similar to those toward the Kalmyks, that is, to eliminate raiding activities, to reduce a nomadic people to the status of faithful subjects, and to use them for Russia's military and political ends. Taught by its previous experience with the Kalmyks, the government realized that these goals could be achieved more effectively by fostering the nomads' dependency on the products of Russian society and promoting a sedentary life-style.

The relative safety of the Russian frontiers girded by extensive defense lines, the unquestionable superiority of the Russian military, and the full coffers of the Russian treasury, able to dispense gifts and compensation with relative ease, all permitted the Russian government to engage in a policy of promoting the economic dependency of the nomads. Not the least important, a new generation of government officials had emerged in Russia. These pragmatic statesmen were brought up and educated on Western ideas which they brought with them to govern the country.

Growing Russo-Kalmyk Disputes, 1741–1765

Colonization of the Volga area and the colonists' encroachment on the Kalmyk pastures resulted in more Russo-Kalmyk disputes, many of which could not be resolved and which further escalated the confrontation between the two groups. In 1747 the government learned that Donduk-Dashi was considering leaving Russia. The departure route was uncertain although some tayishis suggested crossing the Yayik to head for Persia via Bukhara while others were in favor of moving in the opposite direction toward the Kuban.[49]

Disturbing news of the Kalmyks' possible departure prompted the authorites to act. The government ordered the Volga and Don cossacks to avoid clashes with the Kalmyks. As for the thorny issue of the Kalmyk

[48]I. I. Nepliuev, *Zapiski Ivana Ivanovicha Nepliueva (1693–1773)* (St. Petersburg: Izd-vo A. S. Suvorina, 1893), 147–48, 155–61.

[49]Pal'mov, *Etiudy*, 2:86; *AVD* 2:437–38, no. 432.

converts, the decree specified a penalty of twenty rubles for those who were captured by force. If they were not baptized, they had to be turned back; if baptized, the offender was fined another thirty rubles. Some of the baptized were to join the Russian fishermen, others were sent to Stavropol'.[50]

Short-term concessions, however, could not address the fundamental issues of Russo-Kalmyk relations. Russian expansion in the area caused increased impoverishment among the Kalmyks and inevitably led to  further confrontation. By 1744, according to the Kalmyks' own accounts, ten thousand tents, or one-third of the total Kalmyk population, were listed as poor.[51] Donduk-Dashi claimed that these impoverished Kalmyks were responsible for the growing number of raids and pillaging. The viceroy suggested that all such poor Kalmyks should be assembled in one group and be moved farther away from Russian towns and villages. The local authorities declined the proposition, however, on the grounds that there was no confirming order from the capital.[52]

Some years before, Donduk-Ombo had recognized the seriousness of the problem and requested the authorities to compile a law that would help resolve some of the disputes constantly arising between the Kalmyks and the Russians. When the request remained unanswered, Donduk-Dashi also approached the government on this issue several times. Tatishchev, who had been entrusted with compiling such a law, had not done so. A principal difficulty was reconciling Kalmyk and Russian laws in a manner acceptable to both sides.

The main legal debate centered around murder cases. Russian law provided capital punishment for murder, while the most severe punishment meted out by Kalmyk law was a fine paid in cattle or other valuable goods. The Russians insisted that a Kalmyk who had murdered a Russian be executed. The Kalmyks strongly objected to this and were satisfied when a Russian charged with murder of a Kalmyk simply paid a fine.[53]

---

[50]Vitevskii, *Nepliuev*, 2:601–2; *AVD* 2:450, no. 437; 474, no. 443.

[51]Pal'mov, *Etiudy*, 2:125.

[52]Ibid., 128–29.

[53]One case illustrates particularly well the different legal principles that guided Russian and Kalmyk societies. Three Kalmyks were murdered by Russians. Under interrogation, one of the defendants explained how this had happened. A group of Russians were mowing grass when a few Kalmyk tents came to graze their herds. The Kalmyks let the herds loose, and a great deal of hay was eaten or trampled. The ensuing argument turned into a fight in which three Kalmyks were beaten to death. The Russians involved in the murder received life sentences at saltpeter works and had their nostrils torn out, but Donduk-Dashi was not happy with this outcome. He did not care what happened to the perpetrators of the crime. According to Kalmyk law, all offenses were punished by a fine,

Other legal issues revealed differences in attitudes and mentality between the two cultures. For example, the Russians considered stealing
horses and cattle a serious offense, while the Kalmyks, more often than
not, viewed it as a show of a warrior's courage and skill. The Russians
tried to find an offender and punish him, usually by beating with rods.
The Kalmyks resorted to their customary law of barimta, avenging the
offender by recapturing the stolen goods and seizing some of the offender's herds as well. In one such case the Kalmyks captured more than
a thousand horses from the Kazakhs. Abul Khayir Khan requested that
the government allow him a barimta against the Kalmyks. To persuade
the reluctant Russian authorities, Abul Khayir explained that the barimta
was a law among the nomads and that even the Kalmyk Ayuki Khan, who
had ruled almost as an autocrat, had resorted to it.[54]

Another source of contention was Russian demands for Kalmyk cavalry, which, at the time of the Kalmyks' economic decline, imposed an
additional burden on the Kalmyk herds and people. The Kalmyks were
usually easily convinced to join military campaigns that promised abundant booty, as against the Nogays in the Kuban. Russian military campaigns in more remote areas and against regular armies did not offer
significant spoils and, despite cash payments to the participants, enjoyed little popularity among the Kalmyks.

Throughout the 1740s relatively small Kalmyk detachments of about
one thousand horsemen are known to have set out for various military
campaigns at Russian request.[55] The expanding Russian empire, however, required more troops to engage in new wars and to contain the
various peoples within its borders. The troops were needed to quell
rebellious peasants who suffered from high taxes; to control the Old
Believers, who refused to accept the new Russian way of life; to pacify
mutinous Bashkirs, demanding freedom to practice Islam; to restrain
restless nomads along the southern and eastern frontiers; and to engage
in wars in Europe. In addition, the government perceived that an abating

---

and he expected to receive fifty rubles for each murdered Kalmyk. Although he was told
that such a verdict was worse than a death sentence, he continued to insist on monetary
compensation for the victims (Popov, V. N. Tatishchev, 339–40). Pal'mov cites several other
such cases (Etiudy, 2:128, 139, 142). For more about the use of Russian laws as a mean of
social integration of non-Russian peoples see Marc Raeff, "Patterns of Russian Imperial
Policy towards the Nationalities," in Soviet Nationality Problems, ed. Edward Allworth
(New York: Columbia University Press, 1971), 36–37.

[54]Vitevskii, Nepliuev, 3:794.

[55]In 1741–42 Kalmyk detachments took part in the Russo-Swedish war. Five years later,
they were in the Baltic area, but much more frequently they were cited in the campaigns
against the Bashkirs and Kazakhs (Ocherki istorii Kalmytskoi, 1:211; SRIO 136:107, no. 32; SA
6:44–45; Kazakhsko-russkie otnosheniia, 294).

of the Kalmyk civil war would make them better able to contribute to the Russian military effort.

In 1756, preparing for the Prussian campaign, the government ordered four thousand Kalmyk horsemen, each with two horses, to be sent to the Ukraine, while another four thousand Kalmyks were assembled and made ready to set out on short notice.[56] Donduk-Dashi, assembling the required force, pointed out to the authorities that compliance with the order entailed significant costs and risks for the Kalmyks. The Kalmyk viceroy raised concerns over possible Kuban or Kazakh raids while Kalmyk troops were away on a distant campaign. He also reminded the authorities that even at the time of Kalmyk prosperity under Ayuki Khan, the Kalmyks had never sent more than five thousand cavalry on a distant campaign and that supplying eight thousand horsemen now, at a time of privation, put an extremely heavy burden on the Kalmyks.[57]

The government responded favorably to Donduk-Dashi's complaints. In a symbolic gesture intended to mollify the Kalmyks, it ordered that white and red wool, which the Kalmyks were supposed to receive for their hats and clothing, be dyed yellow because the Kalmyk religion did not allow them to wear hats of any other color. (Indeed, the ruling sect in Tibet was known as the Yellow Caps, from the color of the caps worn by the monks.) More significantly, however, the government agreed to reduce the number of required Kalmyk troops to five thousand.[58]

Donduk-Dashi, who had been ill for some time, had previously requested that the government confirm his only son, thirteen-year-old Ubashi, as heir apparent. To secure the Kalmyks' participation in the campaign of the following year and seeking to legitimize Donduk-Dashi's successor to prevent another round of Kalmyk internal wars, the government decreed Donduk-Dashi the Kalmyk khan and Ubashi his successor.[59] Four years later, Donduk-Dashi Khan died, yielding his place to Ubashi.

During the two decades of Donduk-Dashi's rule, Kalmyk society slid into further decline. Growing impoverishment led some Kalmyks to sell their children, and many adults sought earnings from fishing or fled to Russian towns in search of a better life. Others chose to join the ranks of the Kalmyk clergy. But even the uluses of the Kalmyk lamas, always generously rewarded by both rich and poor, could not offer sanctuary to aid the destitute. In 1756, to illustrate the Kalmyk privation, Donduk-

[56]*SRIO* 136:97–100, no. 31; 219–20, no. 74.
[57]Ibid., 100–104, no. 31.
[58]Ibid., 559–61, no. 237.
[59]Ibid., 562–64, no. 237.

Dashi pointed out that during prosperous times, the ulus of the chief Kalmyk lama had consisted of 3,000 to 4,000 tents of the *shabinars*, but it now numbered only 1,040.[60]

Kalmyk destitution was not only a result of the protracted civil war among the tayishis. Creation of the Tsaritsyn line and the capture of Azov in 1736 gave an enormous impetus to colonization of the Don-Volga area and brought the Kalmyks into conflict with Russian residents over grazing lands, fishing rights, and forced conversion. In the period from 1741 to 1763 almost two hundred villages were built in the lower Don region. The new residents turned the adjacent steppes into cultivated fields, and the Don cossacks extended their control as far as the Manych River and Lake.[61] In the mid-1750s, three thousand new colonists with their wives and children came to settle along the Akhtuba, and two thousand came to Astrakhan. Growing economic enterprises, such as the state-run vineyards, the silk factories of Tsaritsyn, and the exploitation of salt mines near Elton Lake, attracted numerous Ukrainian and Russian colonists.[62] The government had little concern for Kalmyk needs and was interested only in protecting its monopoly on fishing and salt mining.

Throughout this period, despondent Kalmyks continually entertained the idea of leaving the Volga steppes. But having no good options, the Kalmyk tayishis were always cajoled by Russian concessions and promises. It would be another ten years before Russia's political and economic interference became so intolerable that the tayishis, in a desperate move, sanctioned a mass exodus back to Jungaria.

Imminence of the Crisis under Ubashi

Ubashi's succession was no different from previous ones; it was accompanied by an outburst of hostilities among the tayishis. This time, however, the issue of the heir's inexperience and young age—Ubashi was only seventeen—made it easier for pretenders to lay claim to the khan's seat.

The first to rebel against the young heir was Donduk-Ombo's grandson Tsebek-Dorji, but his attempt to convince the government that he was a more suitable candidate to be Kalmyk khan met with no success. There

---

[60]Ibid., 104, no. 31.

[61]*Don i stepnoe Predkavkaz'e. 18—pervaia polovina 19 veka: zaselenie i khoziaistvo* (Rostov-na-Donu: Izd-vo Rostovskogo universiteta, 1977), 33, 81–85, 136.

[62]Solov'ev, *Istoriia Rossii*, bk. 12, vol. 24:496; A. N. Minkh, "K istorii pereseleniia malorossiian v Saratovskii krai," *Trudy Saratovskoi uchenoi arkhivnoi komissii* 4, pt. 1 (1893): 17–18.

were also disturbances in connection with the late Donduk-Dombo's wife, Jan (now baptized and known as Princess Vera Dondukova), who had recently settled in the fortress of Enotaevsk. Shortly after her arrival at Enotaevsk, rumors spread that the government had sent Princess Dondukova with the intention of installing her as ruler of the Kalmyks and declaring her son the Kalmyk khan. Fears that the authorities were planning a forced baptism of the Kalmyk people fed more more fuel to the fire. Decrees were sent to the tayishis to allay their apprehensions and assure them that the government did not intend mass conversions and did not wish to force a ruler upon the tayishis against their will. The government strongly supported the legitimate successor, Ubashi, and to dispell any doubts, it conferred upon him the title of Kalmyk viceroy in October 1762.[63]

At the same time, the government aimed subtly to extend its power over the ancient Kalmyk institution of the zargo—the khan's judicial and legislative council. Traditionally the zargo had consisted of eight zayisangs, all from the khan's ulus. Russian authorities decided to change this by allowing the zayisangs of other uluses to be elected and represented in the zargo according to their uluses' population. Decisions were now made by a majority vote.[64] This change fundamentally altered the balance of power in Kalmyk society by reducing the khan's influence. A modified zargo or "Kalmyk government," in official Russian parlance, was a sophisticated attempt to prevent a Kalmyk ruler from accumulating too much power. Such a goal was now to be achieved through a legislative body rather than by means of military threat or fostering political divisions—policies the government had employed in the past.

Among the strongest opponents of the new viceroy was Zamyan, tayishi of the Khoshuts. In a dispute with Donduk-Dashi in 1756–59, Zamyan had lost many of his tents to the viceroy. Now Ubashi refused to return the tents Zamyan considered to be his own. Frustrated and alienated, Zamyan turned to the Russian authorities, asking for permission to settle down. For Zamyan this meant construction of a settlement, increased annual payments, and the authorities' protection.

The Astrakhan governor N. A. Beketov personally presented Zamyan's request to the Chancellery of Foreign Affairs. The request raised the wider issue of settling the Kalmyk people in fixed residences. Upon deliberation, the commission of the chancellery decided that the wide-scale settling of the Kalmyks would not be in Russia's interests. First, the Kalmyks served to protect Russia's frontier. Because of their constant

---

[63]SRIO 48:450, no. 495; nos. 501–6; Solov'ev, *Istoriia Rossii*, bk. 13, vol. 25:240–41.
[64]SRIO 48:459, no. 504; Pal'mov, *Etiudy*, 5:25.

migrations, hostile raiding parties did not know their whereabouts and were afraid of running into them. A second factor against the Kalmyks' settling was that it would leave the steppes vacant. The Kazakhs could then press from behind the Yayik toward the Volga and form an alliance with their coreligionists in the Kuban and Crimea, as well as some peoples of the Caucasus. Finally, the commission felt that it was always useful to have mobile troops that could be quickly deployed in wars with the Ottoman empire.[65]

The commission also pointed out some difficulties that would arise should the Kalmyks be settled. The Kalmyks were strongly attached to their old customs, and settling some of them along the Volga must be done with extreme caution to avoid stirring the suspicions of others. Seeing Zamyan's request as an experimental case, the government did allow him to settle down.[66]

The fears expressed by the commission turned out to be fully justified. The decision to allow Zamyan to settle down caused widespread dissatisfaction among the Kalmyk tayishis, the viceroy, and the zargo, who perceived the government's action as favoring Zamyan against them and Zamyan's permission to settle as an attempt to extricate him from the authority of the viceroy and the zargo. The tayishis saw it as a bad example to others who might be encouraged to follow in Zamyan's footsteps. The government's explanation that Zamyan would remain under the authority of the viceroy did little to alter this perception. In retaliation Ubashi confiscated Zamyan's ulus, and Zamyan's life was reported to have been in danger.[67]

It is possible that Zamyan's case would not have caused such a strong Kalmyk reaction had it been an isolated incident. New policies of Catherine II, however, prompted rapid colonization of the Volga region, and the government's handling of the Zamyan affair further increased the frustrations of the Kalmyks. In September 1765, Ubashi complained to the Astrakhan governor Beketov over numerous settlements that were springing up along the Greater Irgiz and other Volga tributaries. He noted that these lands had never been settled before and had always been used by the Kalmyks for pastures. Ubashi warned the governor that if the

---

[65]*PSZ* 16:827–29, no. 12,198; *SRIO* 48:406–13, no. 964.

[66]It ordered that a settlement be built for Zamyan on the west bank of the Volga, sixty verst north of Astrakhan, where he was to reside together with 250 cossacks. Construction proceeded slowly, and Zamyan was able to move into his house in the newly founded settlement only six years later, in 1770. Today, a small, isolated town on the west bank of the Volga, Zamiany, still bears the name of the person for whom it was built (*PSZ* 16:829–32, no. 12,198; Pal'mov, *Etiudy*, 5:31–32).

[67]Pal'mov, *Etiudy*, 5:27–28, 31.

number of settlements continued to grow, Kalmyk herds would soon be hard-pressed for fodder and would perish.[68]

A year later, Ubashi again wrote to Beketov and officials in the Russian capital complaining of growing Russian settlements along the Volga and the spread of German colonies to the steppes south of the Tsaritsyn line. In 1765 a Kalmyk raid inflicted substantial damage on a settlement of German colonists on the Sarpa River near Tsaritsyn. This attack attracted the empress's attention, and in her decree to Ubashi she reprimanded him for such an act of violence. In response to Kalmyk grievances, Catherine II stated that they had sufficient pastures on both banks of the Volga and that growing settlements could only bring them increased trade and refuge from adversarial raids.[69]

Catherine II did not intend to abandon her plans for Volga colonization because of Kalmyk complaints. Concomitantly, colonization of the area grew at a faster pace after 1765, when the government issued a decree allowing the state lands to be sold on the condition that the new owners would bring their peasants and settle them on this land.[70] From 1764 to 1768 more than one hundred foreign settlements mushroomed in the lower Volga area. Catherine II considered Kalmyk complaints a slight nuisance to Russian interests in the area. Far from the Kalmyk steppes, in her palace cabinet, looking at her maps, which showed large, unpopulated lands in the Volga and Caspian region, the empress was convinced that there was plenty of room for the Kalmyks to roam. Their complaints, she felt, were unjustifiable. How little she understood the nature of nomadic society is clear from a field report by a Russian official from the steppe. Lieutenant Colonel I. A. Kishenskii, appointed to the viceroy's headquarters, informed the government that numerous settlements had taken over almost all lands along the Volga from Samara to Tsaritsyn. Residents of these communities did not allow Kalmyks to graze their herds there. In the past, Kishenskii explained, during the spring overflow Kalmyks moved up the Volga and its tributaries, and as the water receded they moved back to the rich pastures between Tsaritsyn and Astrakhan. Now, however, settlers had pushed the Kalmyks away from the rivers to the barren steppes, where water and fodder were scarce and poor Kalmyks were deprived of fishing. The situation was similar on the Don.[71]

Realizing the necessity of preventing further confrontations between the Kalmyks and colonists but unwilling to curb the process of coloniza-

[68]Ibid., 3.
[69]*SRIO* 67:197–99.
[70]Belikov, *Kalmyki v bor'be*, 100.
[71]Pal'mov, *Etiudy*, 5:4–5; *AVD* 3:125–26, no. 65.

tion, the government toyed with a program of dividing the territory between arable lands and pastures. Such a program, however, would have taken a long time to complete because it first required a detailed geographic and geological survey of the area and the compiling of precise maps. At the time, the authorities had neither sufficient resources nor human expertise to accomplish this task.[72]

In the meantime, another Russo-Ottoman war had broken out in 1768, and the Russian government made new demands on the Kalmyk cavalry. The empress ordered Ubashi to assemble a force of twenty thousand Kalmyks to be sent to Azov, where they were to join the Russian army for a summer campaign in 1769. The empress further expected that the remaining Kalmyks would march against the Kubans, and in no uncertain terms she instructed Ubashi to annihilate them.[73]

Anticipating Kalmyk tayishis' protests over assembling such a large army, Catherine II instructed local officials to dismiss their objections. Her reasoning displayed a fundamental ignorance of her nomadic subjects, an ignorance matched by her arrogant attitude toward officials of her own government. Referring to the fact that there were 41,523 Kalmyk tents (according to Kalmyks' own count of 1767), she argued that even if there was only one person per tent, the Kalmyks still had enough people to provide an army of twenty thousand horsemen with sufficient numbers left over to send against the Kubans.[74] Catherine II did not consider the Kalmyks' need for people to protect their own uluses from possible Kuban and Kazakh raids. She believed that Kazakh attacks against the Kalmyks were inconceivable because both peoples were separated by Russian fortresses. She angrily dismissed talk of such raids as rumors coming from people who could not read maps. Only later did she inquire whether the Kazakhs had ever attacked the Kalmyks.[75]

Despite Catherine II's orders, only ten thousand Kalmyks were ready to participate in the campaign. In March 1769 the Kalmyks led by Ubashi defeated a group of Kubans and Kabardinians near the Kalaus River, then joined the main Russian force under the command of Major General I. F. de Medem, crossed the Kuban, and routed the Kubans again.[76] In late September, the Kalmyks were reported to have left for their uluses. In the past, the necessity of attending to the herds in winter and the lack of fodder in the steppes had always compelled the Kalmyks to

---

[72]SRIO 67:199–202; Pal'mov, Etiudy, 5:4–5.

[73]Belikov, Kalmyki v bor'be, 90–93.

[74]SRIO 87:271–77, 313–16.

[75]Solov'ev, Istoriia Rossii, bk. 14, vol. 27:132; vol. 28:296–97.

[76]Butkov, Materialy dlia novoi istorii Kavkaza, 1:291–99; Belikov, Kalmyki v bor'be, 90–93; Kabardino-russkie otnosheniia, 2:291, no. 208.

end campaigns by late fall, and the empress promised Ubashi that they could return in winter. The Kalmyks, however, departed when they felt it was time rather than awaiting authorization. The government considered this desertion and called upon the viceroy and Colonel Kishenskii to punish deserters with the full rigor of the Russian military code—to administer corporal punishment.[77]

Not the least important reason for the Kalmyks' early departure was a personal rift between the Russian commander de Medem and Ubashi.[78] De Medem complained of the Kalmyks' hasty actions. A lack of discipline on the battlefield and Kalmyk tactics were also issues of contention. At this time, some tactical changes were introduced into the Russian army. One of these changes was use of the cavalry in a more direct confrontation in battle.[79] The Kalmyks always tried to avoid a head-on confrontation and instead preferred a hit-and-run tactic of guerrilla warfare. In addition to the arguments and differences between the Russian commander and the Kalmyk viceroy, de Medem's offensive personality made it more difficult for the two to agree.[80]

In November 1769 de Medem again wanted the Kalmyks to join his forces, but Ubashi declined. In the spring of the following year, Ubashi sent a small detachment to join the Russian army, and later in August he himself arrived at the Kalaus River. There he met with de Medem. Again the two could not come to terms, and a few days later Ubashi and his Kalmyks departed for the Volga.[81]

The Exodus

At various times the Kalmyk tayishis contemplated departing for Jungaria, but in the past other considerations outweighed the reasons for such a move. Most obviously the lack of consensus among the divided tayishis and the ominous prospect of a difficult and dangerous journey through the unfriendly Kazakh steppes precluded any action. In the late 1760s, this situation changed when the Kalmyks were driven to desperation by Russian colonization of the area.

[77]*AGS* 1:241–42.

[78]*AKAK* 1:84.

[79]Colonel A. P. Emel'ianov, "Razvitie taktiki russkoi armii vo vtoroi polovine 18 v.," in *Razvitie taktiki russkoi armii, 18-nach. 20 vv.* (Moscow: Voennoe izd-vo, 1957), 74.

[80]De Medem was notorious for his rudeness. In 1766 he was investigated and found to have abused the Briansk merchants by refusing to pay for merchandise; he beat some of them with a stick and slapped others in the face (Solov'ev, *Istoriia Rossii*, bk. 14. vol. 27:7).

[81]*AKAK* 1:84; Butkov, *Materialy dlia novoi istorii Kavkaza,* 1:303–6, 478–81.

After the completion of the Tsaritsyn defense line in 1718, the Kalmyks became dependent on the Russian government's goodwill to allow them to use their former pasture lands on the Volga's west bank north of Tsaritsyn. Half a century later, the Kalmyks found themselves surrounded by new defense lines of the expanding Russian state. In the west, construction of the Dnieper defense line, which in 1770 connected the Dnieper with the Don's tributary Donets, effectively sealed off the Crimea. In the south, the new Mozdok defense line threatened to cut off Kalmyk ties with the Kuban and Kabarda in the northern Caucasus. In 1770 the Kalmyks could not but feel vitally threatened and entrapped, losing their pastures to the encroaching Russian farmers and being hemmed in by Russia's newly expanded frontiers.

No one put the situation more succinctly than Tsebek-Dorji tayishi, who addressed the zargo as follows:

> Look how your rights are being limited in all respects. Russian officials mistreat you and the government wants to make peasants out of you. The banks of the Yayik and Volga are now covered with cossack settlements, and the nothern borders of your steppes are inhabited by Germans. In a little while, the Don, Terek, and Kuma will also be colonized and you will be pushed to the waterless steppes and the only source of your existence, your herds, will perish. Ubashi's son has already been ordered given as a hostage, and three hundred from among the noble Kalmyks are to reside in the Russian capital. You can now see your situation, and in the future you will have two options—either to carry the burden of slavery, or to leave Russia and thus to end all your misfortunes. Dalai Lama himself selected two years in which a migration to Jungaria could be undertaken. These two years have arrived. So your present decision will determine your future.[82]

Russia's growing control of Kalmyk administrative affairs, its excessive demands for Kalmyk cavalry, the loss of prime pasture lands to expanding military and agricultural colonies, and fear of coercive settlement and conversion were among the critical factors contributing to the Kalmyks' decision to depart for Jungaria.

Several groups among the Kalmyks lobbied particularly hard for the departure. The Kalmyk clergy and its chief lama, Louzang Jalchin, strongly supported the idea of leaving for Jungaria.[83] A group of Jungars, who had escaped the 1757 massacre wrought by the Qing armies in Jungaria and later found refuge among the Kalmyks, also favored the plan to return. At first, these refugees were harbored by Russian authorities in Siberia,

---

[82]Bergmann, *Nomadische*, 1:181–83.
[83]*Dnevnye zapiski*, 53–54.

despite Qing demands for their return. After unsuccessful attempts to convert them, Russian authorities decided to transfer some of them to the Volga to join the Kalmyks. The Jungars were sent there without an adequate supply of food, and many of them perished on the way to the Volga. Among the newcomers, one of the most influential was Sheareng tayishi, who later became a strong advocate of returning to his native land.[84]

By the late 1760s, the Kalmyk viceroy also favored migration. Hoping to save his people and herds, as well as to reassert his power over the Kalmyks, he took the bold action of publicly defying Russian authority. Plans for departure had apparently been carefully conceived and nurtured for some time. The first news of such an undertaking reached the authorities as early as 1767, when Zamyan tayishi reported it to Governor Beketov. The following year, Zamyan again informed the authorities of the existence of such a plan among the Kalmyks, but the government did not take it seriously, viewing it as Zamyan's attempt to slander his rival, Viceroy Ubashi. The government did not order the Orenburg and Astrakhan governors to take precautionary measures until 1770, when much more alarming news concerning Kalmyk plans began reaching the capital.[85]

The Astrakhan governor reported that much evidence presented by Zamyan tayishi, intercepted correspondence to Kalmyk hostages in Astrakhan, and the accounts of Kalmyk captives seized by the Kazakhs all indicated the existence of a Kalmyk plan to leave Russia. The governor suggested that six Kalmyk tayishis and zayisangs implicated in the plot should be arrested and sent to St. Petersburg for investigation.

The matter attracted the empress's attention, prompting her to write a long letter to the Astrakhan governor. The letter is an unambiguous statement of Catherine II's philosophy and ruling style. Indeed, it seems to have offered the empress an occasion to conduct a gratifying and self-consciously rhetorical excercise in political analysis. First, she admonished the governor to look beneath the surface of events and try to establish connections between causes and consequences. She then proceeded to analyze the evidence and rejected any suggestion that the Kalmyks were planning to leave. She faulted the governor for attributing too much to rumors. The empress was convinced that the Kalmyks could not possibly leave Russia because they had nowhere to go. Kuban

---

[84]*SA* 10:188, 540; 11:86–88, 98, 100, 112, 119; I. Ia. Zlatkin, "Russkie arkhivnye materialy ob Amursane," in *Filologiia i istoriia mongol'skikh narodov* (Moscow: Izd-vo vost. literatury, 1958), 310.

[85]*AGS* 1:242–43.

was inaccessible because of the continuing war with the Ottomans, and a march to Jungaria through the harsh Kazakh steppes would be suicidal. She dismissed as unreasonable Beketov's concerns and suggestions.[86] Later, in 1771, when Catherine II proved to be wrong and the Kalmyks' migration was well under way, the empress showed no signs of remorse. Instead, she suggested that Governor Beketov be removed from his position.[87]

Meanwhile, Ubashi was assembling his uluses and preparing for departure. In autumn 1770, Ubashi crossed to the east bank of the Volga. He explained the move to Russian authorities by saying that pastures on the west bank were exhausted and no longer suitable for grazing. In November, the viceroy, gathering his Kalmyk troops, informed Colonel Kishenskii that the move was a precautionary measure against an expected Kazakh raid. At this time, a majority of Kalmyks, most of them Torguts, were roaming on the Volga's east bank, while a smaller group, consisting of the Derbets, Khoshuts, and some Torguts, remained on the west bank. On January 4, 1771, Ubashi told the Kalmyk people that he had received another decree from the empress, who demanded that he send his son, five tayishis, and one hundred zayisangs to St. Petersburg and dispatch ten thousand Kalmyk troops to join the Russian army. To save the Kalmyk people from these destructive demands, he said, he chose to leave Russia. The following day, after a small Russian detachment at the viceroy's headquarters had been disarmed, 30,909 Kalmyk tents, or more than 150,000 people, set out on the long and tragic journey to Jungaria. Separated by the river, an estimated 11,198 Kalmyk tents remained on the west bank of the Volga.[88]

Nomadic peoples, seeking to escape oppression and domination by others and in search of rich pastures and abundant booty, had for centuries abandoned their native steppes of Inner Asia and migrated westward. Now these same factors compelled the Kalmyks to undertake a reverse migration eastward, making it the last known exodus of a nomadic people in the history of Asia.

By January 18, the Kalmyks, with their uluses protected by troops in

---

[86]*SRIO* 97:113–23.

[87]*AGS* 1:244.

[88]*Ocherki istorii Kalmytskoi,* 1:216; *Dnevnye zapiski,* 55. According to Chinese sources 33,000 Kalmyk tents numbering 169,000 people departed from Russia (Arthur W. Hummel, ed., *Eminent Chinese of the Ch'ing Period [1644–1912],* 2 vols. [Washington, D.C.: U.S. Government Printing Office, 1943–44], 2:659–61). The number of those who remained behind appears to be accurate. According to the censuses in the following years, the number of Kalmyk tents near the Volga was 13,063 in 1793, 13,155 in 1795, and 13,155 in 1802 (*Kalmytskaia step' Astrakhanskoi gubernii po issledovaniiam Kumo-Manychskoi ekspeditsii* [St. Petersburg: Tip. V. Bezobrazova, 1868], 163–66; *AKAK* 1:765, no. 1137).

front and in the rear, had reached the Yayik. They swept past a few cossack forts and safely crossed the river. At this point, the government began to realize that the Kalmyks intended to move to Jungaria. Suddenly, the dimensions of the crisis became obvious. The Orenburg and Astrakhan governors received belated orders to stop the Kalmyks. To pursue the Kalmyks the Orenburg governor dispatched a detachment of Russian dragoons and Bashkirs, who were supposed to be joined by the Yayik cossacks. The cossacks rebelled, however, and refused to follow the orders, and the detachment returned empty-handed.[89]

The Kalmyks, in the meantime, reached the banks of the Emba. There they remained until spring, when they renewed their journey as the new grass appeared on the steppes. While the Kalmyk people and their herds were resting, the Russian government assembled another expeditionary force in Orenburg with the firm intention of stopping the flight of its fugitive subjects. In April 1771, this force, consisting of Russian dragoons, cossacks, and Bashkirs, set out after the Kalmyks. Joined later by the Kazakhs, they began a vigorous but fruitless pursuit. Experiencing a severe shortage of fodder and food, the force had to turn back to Orenburg. In a final attempt to check the Kalmyks' movement, the authorities gathered troops along the Siberian defense line, but these troops never set out because news arrived that the Kalmyks were out of their reach.[90]

By June 10, 1771, the Kalmyks had reached the vicinity of Lake Balkhash. Most of the journey was behind them, and there was only one final stretch ahead before they reached Jungaria and the Chinese borders. But the long, rapid march through inhospitable steppe and desert had taken a heavy toll. The herds were severely depleted, many horses had fallen, and people had died from disease, hunger, and winter cold. In addition, Kazakh raids harassed the Kalmyks all along the way.

The Kazakhs had no reason to miss an opportunity to settle scores with their old foes. Among the Kalmyks moving to Jungaria there were no less than one thousand Kazakh captives, along with a large number of Kazakh herds captured as recently as the previous year.[91] Memories of the Jungar raids against the Kazakhs were still fresh, and the arrival of

---

[89]*Ocherki istorii Kalmytskoi*, 1:216–17; *AGS* 1:243–44.

[90]*Dnevnye zapiski*, 50–55, 67–70, 75–77. A participant in the expedition, Captain Nikolai Rychkov, left a detailed account of these events, as well as an earnest description of the Kazakh steppe and the life-style of its peoples. Another personal account was written by a cossack who was at the Kalmyk camp during the migration. He was captured and forced to join the Kalmyks on their journey to Jungaria (*Adventures of Michailow, a Russian Captive; among the Kalmucks, Kirghiz, and Kiwenses. Written by himself* [London: Printed for Sir Richard Philipps & Co. 1822]).

[91]*Kazakhsko-russkie otnosheniia*, 701, no. 275; *Ocherki istorii Kalmytskoi*, 1:217.

the Kalmyks in Jungaria, which suggested a possible revival of Jungar power, was hardly in Kazakh interests. When the Kalmyks stopped at the Mointy River near Lake Balkhash to gather their forces for the final move, they found themselves surrounded by overwhelming numbers of Kazakh troops. Only Ubashi's shrewd political tactics saved the Kalmyks from captivity. Ubashi engaged the Kazakhs in negotiations over the exchange of captives, and then suddenly attacked the Kazakhs at night. Ubashi forced his way through, and then decided to reach Jungaria by moving along the western shore of Lake Balkhash. This route was shorter, but it ran through the arid steppe. By the time of Ubashi's arrival in Jungaria, the route was covered with the corpses of the many animals and people who had fallen from lack of water, food, and fodder. Another group of Kalmyks chose a longer route, which led them along the north shore of the lake and then around it toward the Ili River.[92]

Many of the sheep herds, which the Kalmyks had to abandon while fleeing, fell into Kazakh hands and were later sold in Russian markets. In the years 1771–72, Kazakh trade with the Russian cities of Orenburg and Troitsk witnessed an impressive upsurge in volume, particularly in the sheep trade.[93] Even more striking was the loss of people. Only a few of those who set out from the Volga reached Jungaria. It is believed that almost one hundred thousand Kalmyks perished during the exodus. The tragedy of this event is compounded by the fact that, two centuries later, the world remains almost wholly ignorant of this sad chapter in human history.

On October 19, 1771, those Kalmyks remaining on the Volga lost the last vestige of their political independence when a government decree abolished the titles of Kalmyk khan and viceroy and thus ended the idea of a single Kalmyk ruler. All the tayishis were directly subordinate to the Astrakhan governor, who was instructed not to let the Kalmyks cross the Volga and to keep them on the river's west bank all year-round.[94]

Those Kalmyks who succeeded in reaching Jungaria arrived in a wretched condition. Qing officials welcomed the Kalmyks, provided rice, wheat, tea, clothing, tents, horses, and sheep for the destitute refugees, and allowed them to roam in the upper reaches of the Ili River.[95] Russian

[92]*Ocherki istorii Kalmytskoi*, 1:217–18. The best account in English of the Kalmyks' arrival to Jungaria is in C. D. Barkman, "The Return of the Torghuts from Russia to China," *Journal of Oriental Studies* 2 (1955): 89–115. The dramatic events of the Kalmyks' exodus were fictionalized by Thomas De Quincey in *Revolt of the Tartars or Flight of the Kalmuck Khan* (New York: American Book Co., 1895).

[93]N. G. Apollova, *Ekonomicheskie i politicheskie sviazi Kazakhstana s Rossiei v 18-nachale 19 v.* (Moscow: AN SSSR, 1960), 248–49, table 3; 292, table 13; 301, table 14.

[94]Belikov, *Kalmyki v bor'be*, 104; *Ocherki istorii Kalmytskoi*, 1:222.

[95]John L. Mish, "The Return of the Turgut," *Journal of Asian History* 4, no. 1 (1970): 80–82.

representations to the Qing court requested the return of the Kalmyks but were rejected. Catherine II was furious and threatened to reckon with the Qing at an appropriate later time. The empress claimed that the Kalmyks were Russia's subjects, and she expressed her indignation that "these rogues and traitors" had been given refuge in China. In the end, she could only appeal to the Qing emperor and called upon him to return the Kalmyks to Russia.[96]

The Kalmyks never returned to the Volga. Two years later, in 1774, a fugitive Kalmyk from Jungaria reported that they wished to return to the Volga to join those who remained there, but the Qing learned of these plans and moved the Kalmyks farther east. In 1790, Russian authorities received news that Ubashi's son, together with other Kalmyks, wished to request Russian protection.[97] The Qing grip on the Kalmyks was tight, however, and none of these plans were destined to materialize. Less than half a century later, the Kalmyks from the Volga were organized into military units and put in the service of the Qing emperor.[98] The Kalmyks had escaped Russian tentacles only to be ensnared in Chinese ones.

[96]*SRIO* 118:1, no. 2144; 31–35, no. 2166.

[97]*Ocherki istorii Kalmytskoi,* 1:219.

[98]*Ulozhenie Kitaiskoi palaty vneshnikh snoshenii,* trans. from Manchurian by Stepan Lipovtsov, 2 vols. (St. Petersburg: Tip. Dep-ta narodnogo prosveshcheniia, 1828), 1:81–84.

Conclusion

In this book I have tried to show that the history of the Kalmyks must be approached within the conceptual framework of a traditional Kalmyk-Mongol society. Such a vantage point allows one to see the history of the Kalmyks, their relations with Russia, and the history of Russia's southern frontier in a new light.

The movement of the Oirat tribes in the late sixteenth and early seventeenth centuries occurred under pressure from the Kazakhs in the south and the Mongols in the east. The westernmost Oirat tribe of the Torguts was in the forefront of this migration. At first, the Torguts moved in a northwestern direction, where they came upon Russian towns and fortresses. A few years later, joined by another Oirat tribe of the Derbets, they moved southwest, gradually taking over the pastures of the Nogays.

Several dates clearly mark the advance of the Kalmyks. In 1608 they were spotted near the Emba River. Five years later, they crossed the Yayik River, and in 1633 they were reported to have reached the vicinity of Astrakhan. This advance was limited to military detachments launching raids in the area, however, and it was not until the late 1640s that the Kalmyk uluses arrived on the banks of the Volga.

The arrival of the Kalmyks and their devastating raids disrupted the existing balance of power in the area and had a significant impact on the defense of the Russian southern frontier. Under the onslaught of the warlike Kalmyks, numerous Nogay tribes abandoned their pastures in the Caspian steppes and fled to the Crimea. As a result, Russia found its southern frontier exposed to the raids of the Kalmyk newcomers. Moreover, the fleeing Nogays, angered by Russia for the years of continuous abuse and the government's inability to protect them against the Kalmyks, had joined the Crimea in a war against Russia. The renewed force

236

of the Crimean-Nogay raids against the Russian towns and provinces made Moscow shift attention from the western to the southern frontier and compelled the government to embark on its most ambitious and expensive project of the seventeenth century—construction of the new defense network in the south.

Throughout the 1650s to 1660s Moscow made every effort to win over the Kalmyks and to ensure their participation in military campaigns against the Crimea and the Nogays. The resulting closer relations with the Russian state led to a sharp political cleft within Kalmyk society. As the chief tayishi and his supporters within the elite became increasingly dependent on annuities, rewards, and presents from Russia, contending members of the elite were compelled to form an anti-Russian party. But every time opposition rose it was crushed because the Russian government firmly supported the chief tayishi. These policies of the government, though not always consciously pursued, increased concentration of power in the hands of the chief tayishi and fostered the Kalmyks' dependence on Russia.

The attitude of the Russian government toward the Kalmyks underwent several changes. Following its initial contacts with the Kalmyks in 1606, Moscow had attempted to equate them with its other subjects and insisted that the Kalmyks pay yasak and offer hostages. Both ideas were soon discarded when the government recognized the Kalmyks' military potential and decided to harness it in return for annuities and presents. By the 1660s the government sought to put the Kalmyks on a par with the cossacks by allowing the Kalmyks administrative autonomy. This slow evolution in the Russian attitude toward further recognition of the Kalmyks' independence notwithstanding, Moscow presumed the Kalmyks to be its subjects throughout the period.

The principal goal of the Russian government throughout the seventeenth and eighteenth centuries was to reduce the Kalmyks to the status of loyal Russian subjects, willing to perform military service in return for government payments. The Russian government sought to legitimize such suzerain-subject ties through the traditional ritual of the oath of allegiance.

Several tactics were employed to achieve this goal. Throughout the seventeenth and the first quarter of the eighteenth centuries the government found it most expedient to support one strong leader. Russia had yet to develop a crucial margin of military superiority over the numerous and highly mobile nomadic armies. The country still needed to strengthen its frontier defenses and to increase and adequately arm Russian garrisons to secure the southern Russian provinces from the constant threat of devastating enemy raids.

The policy of promoting one strong leader, who could be induced to exercise sufficient authority over the Kalmyks to curb his people's raids, was, however, flawed and brought a contradictory outcome. With Russian help, the Kalmyk khan was able to augment his power, which was otherwise limited in the decentralized Kalmyk society by its independent nobility, the tayishis and zayisangs. As a result, the Russian government was able to exercise little political leverage over the strengthened Kalmyk khan and at times of confrontation had to face united Kalmyk forces.

As the situation in the area changed in the 1720s to 1730s, Russian policies toward the Kalmyks also began to change. The construction of the Tsaritsyn defense line, the capture of Azov, and an improved Russian military, better trained and armed with artillery, rendered the Russian southern frontier less vulnerable to nomadic incursions. A more confident Russian government was now less concerned with raids but rather sought increased control over the Kalmyks. To achieve this control, it resorted to true colonial policies of divide and rule. These policies, particularly as carried out by the zealous Governor Artemii Volynskii, proved to be a mixed blessing. Russia's support of various warring factions led to protracted Kalmyk civil wars, which resulted in a severe loss of Kalmyk people and herds. The government achieved its purpose of weakening the power of the khan but also undermined the economic health of Kalmyk society and Kalmyk military might, which in turn diminished the Kalmyks' ability to protect the frontier and perform military service for Russia.

Throughout the 1740s to 1750s, the government sought to balance the two policies. The balance, however, was not easily achieved, and Russian support of a viceroy or khan invariably led to his acquisition of excess power, while support of the opposition often threatened to destroy Kalmyk society. In the mid-1760s, the government decided to shift the burden of containing the khan's power to the Kalmyks themselves. The government expected to limit the power of the khan by transforming the traditional Kalmyk institution of the zargo from one that enforced the khan's will to a representative body of all the Kalmyk uluses with wide legislative authority. In her official correspondence, Catherine II referred to the zargo as a "Kalmyk government." By institutionalizing the modified zargo, the empress intended to teach the "savages" a lesson in the basics of the parliamentary system.

In contrast to Russian political expectations of a suzerain-subject relationship, the Kalmyks, from the time of their arrival on the Caspian steppes, perceived their relationship with Russia as a military and political alliance of two equal powers. In accordance with Russian requests, such an alliance was forged by affixing the signatures of the khan and the tayishis to a document written in the unfamiliar Russian language. The two parties involved in such an alliance had to render each other military assistance, and when Russia failed to protect the Kalmyks from cossack, Bashkir, or Nogay raids, the Kalmyks considered the agreement to be abrogated. Similar considerations prevailed when Russia failed to provide its annual payments, which the Kalmyks variously regarded as tribute, a display of respect, and a sign of friendship.

It was not until Ayuki Khan's death in 1724 that the Kalmyks accepted Russian suzerainty. Even then, they perceived the Russian suzerain through the prism of their own political system. The Russian emperor was only a military leader and a protector and had no right to interfere either in Kalmyk administrative and economic affairs or in their relations with foreign powers. The Kalmyks expected to be allowed to govern themselves independently, though they counted on Russian payments and protection in return for Kalmyk military service.

Russia intended to use the position of suzerain to exercise its growing control over the Kalmyks. The Russian government sought little accommodation with the Kalmyks, and their complaints elicited few responses. Not fully understanding the different needs of the Kalmyk nomadic society, the government often considered Kalmyk complaints capricious and unjustified. Even when Kalmyk demands were recognized as reasonable, the government showed little desire to meet them. Dramatically different attitudes toward the Don and Yayik cossacks show that the government was far more interested in its Christian subjects. The government's disparaging and careless attitude toward the Kalmyks was heavily influenced by the Kalmyk Buddhists being outside the realm of Russian Orthodoxy. The government proved to be accommodating only at the times when it desperately needed Kalmyk cavalry or when it felt threatened by the Kalmyks' possible departure or their alliance with Russia's adversaries.

Important social changes took place in Kalmyk society during the seventeenth and eighteenth centuries. These changes threatened to destroy traditional Kalmyk society and were a direct result of almost two centuries of relations with the Russian state. By the end of the eighteenth century, the Kalmyks found themselves increasingly incorporated into the Russian economy. At first, the Kalmyk nobility grew accustomed to Russian payments and gifts. In time, various goods, cash, and grain payments became an indispensable part of the tayishis' revenue, and competition for better payments contributed to increased hostilities among the tayishis.

The desire to obtain more Russian products and particularly luxury goods compelled the tayishis to raise taxes on their Kalmyk subjects. The continuing enrichment of the tayishis and the resulting impoverishment of the common Kalmyks polarized Kalmyk society. In the eighteenth century many poor Kalmyks frequently resorted to the only means available to them—fleeing to the Russian towns and converting to Christianity or seeking employment in the Russian fisheries. Conversion, escape, and taking up a fixed residence were responses not limited to poor Kalmyks. Certain tayishis also found it attractive to settle down under Russian protection.

Thus contacts with Russia had a profound impact on Kalmyk society. The result of Russian political and administrative interference in Kalmyk affairs was a protracted civil war and ultimately the weakening of Kalmyk military and economic power. Russian economic attractiveness to both the poor Kalmyks and the disgruntled tayishis resulted in the departure of these two polar groups, eroding traditional Kalmyk society and causing its growing sedentarization.

Its extensive experience in dealing with the Kalmyks led the government to realize by the mid-eighteenth century that co-optation and fostering sedentarization were the best ways to pacify the nomads. It successfully adopted these new policies in dealing with the Kazakhs. The government found wide-scale Kalmyk sedentarization premature, however, because the Kalmyks were needed to protect the Russian southern frontier. It was not until the conquest of the Caucasus, Kuban, and Central Asia in the mid-nineteenth century that the services of the nomadic Kalmyks were no longer necessary.

Dependent on their environment and economically vulnerable, nomads are usually the first to react to any outside pressure. Traditionally, if unable to respond to pressures by the use of force, the nomads, not bound by territorial borders, choose to move away. The Kalmyks, too, in unfavorable circumstances, often considered leaving Russia. They actually resolved to undertake such an action in 1771, driven to desperation by the colonization policies of Catherine II. Largely deprived of political and administrative autonomy and lacking sufficient pastures for their herds, the Kalmyks resorted to the last option available to them. They tried to escape the fate that was to befall the Crimea a few years later.

The departure of the Kalmyks was only the prelude to a series of events that had a fundamental impact on Russian society. The Kalmyks' unimpeded flight exposed the inefficiency of the frontier garrisons in steppe warfare and their inadequate manpower. In response to the expansionist policies pursued by Catherine II, various peoples in the south of the country became restless. Emboldened by the Kalmyks' departure, the Kubans and the Kabardinians increased their raids against small Russian garrisons, which without support from the Kalmyks were reluctant to undertake campaigns in the steppes. Kazakh raids against the Russian towns increased, the Bashkirs became rebellious, and the Yayik cossacks found their traditional freedoms threatened. Unlike the Kalmyks, the Yayik cossacks, who had no place to go, resorted to different means of protest and rose up in arms against the government. Two years later, all of southern Russia was in the flames of the largest uprising the country had ever known, the Pugachev War.

Appendix

A Kalmyk-Muscovite Diplomatic Confrontation, 1650: A Translation

A conversation that took place between a Muscovite envoy and a Kalmyk tayishi reveals much about the disparate mentalities of the Muscovite government, as expressed by its faithful representative, and the Kalmyk chief. The transcript of the negotiations shows that the Russians and the Kalmyks differently interpreted the notions of law, landownership, and their political status vis-à-vis each other.

Description of the Document

The original of the document is in the Central State Archive of Ancient Records in Moscow. It was found among records collected under the rubric of Kalmyk Affairs (Kalmytskie Dela) at the Chancellery of Foreign Affairs (Posol'skii Prikaz), no. 5. The document has been published in *Russko-mongol'skie otnosheniia, 1636–1654, Sbornik dokumentov* (Moscow: Nauka, 1974), no. 113, pp. 354–58. The original consists of twenty-nine leaves. The compilers of the *Sbornik* chose to publish leaves 1 and 11–24, omitting the others on the grounds that the information contained therein referred to the Kalmyks' relations with the Bashkirs and Nogays and was not directly pertinent to the main theme of the document. This translation is based on that publication.

The document is a report from the embassy sent at the tsar's command from Ufa to the Kalmyk Daichin tayishi. The governor of Ufa appointed Ivan Ivanovich Onuchin to head the embassy, which consisted of an interpreter, a musketeer, and a darkhan (here Muscovy's trusted Muslim subject, a Nogay or a Bashkir of high social status, who enjoyed the privilege of tax exemption). The document's dates are September 21, 1649, to July 14, 1650—the time elapsed from the embassy's departure from Ufa to its return.

The embassy arrived at Daichin's ulus on November 4, 1649, and was immediately visited by a few Kalmyk dignitaries, who greeted Ivan Onuchin and informed him that Daichin would grant him an audience four days later. On November 8, Daichin received the Muscovite envoy, who then delivered a speech according to his instructions. After the audience, Daichin spent another week in his ulus, then together with his brother Louzang, his son Namansoro, and other tayishis, he left to raid the Nogays near Astrakhan. Rumors reached the Muscovite envoy that Louzang led a detachment of two thousand Kalmyks and Nogays against the Nogays of the Astrakhan province, and, returning home, Daichin brought with him twenty Nogay captives. It was at this time that Ivan Onuchin went to see Daichin again, and the conversation translated below took place.

The Document

And when Daichin tayishi returned to his ulus with his army and captives, Ivan Onuchin went to see him and told Daichin that in the past year, 1648–49, according to the sovereign's decree and your, Daichin's, request, the envoy Vladimir Golubtsov and the interpreter Vasilii Kirzhatskii were sent to you from Ufa. And in Vladimir's presence, your best people, Dural-darkhan and Zargochi (Ziurgachei), took an oath on behalf of you, Daichin, your brothers and your children and nephews, that you and your brothers, and your sons and nephews with the people of their uluses should not wage war against the sovereign's towns and provinces and should not commit raids and capture the sovereign's people. And now you, Daichin, with your brothers, and sons and nephews, having forgotten your oath, went to wage war against the sovereign's towns and raided the Nogays near Astrakhan and the Russian people near the other towns of the sovereign and on the Volga, and captured them and brought those captives to your uluses; what, then, is your word [worth]?

And you yourself know that from early on, the Kalmyk tayishis together with all the Kalmyk people in their uluses have been in submission and obedience to the forefathers of the grand sovereign, our tsar and the grand prince, Aleksei Mikhailovich, the autocrat of all Russia, his majesty the tsar, and to the grand sovereigns, the tsars and the grand Moscow princes. And they, the grand sovereigns, showed favor and protected them [the Kalmyk tayishis] and did not permit the sovereign's military to fight [against the Kalmyk tayishis]. Likewise, in the past, Batur tayishi and Kharakhula (Karakola) tayishi and your father Urlük tayishi together with his brothers and with you, with his sons and his nephews, and all the Kalmyk tayishis together with their people were in submission and obedience under the protection of the [present] sovereign's father, blessed by his memory, grand sovereign, the tsar and the grand prince Mikhail Fedorovich, the autocrat of all Russia; and they often sent their envoys to him,—to the grand sovereign—and they served him,—the grand sovereign—faithfully. And he,—the grand sovereign,—bestowed favors upon Urlük tayishi and his brothers and upon you, sons and nephews, and he bestowed favors upon all the Kalmyk tayishis and kept them under his majesty the tsar's protection in his merciful tsar's favor and care.

And now you, the Kalmyk tayishis, having forgotten past and present sovereigns favors to your father and to you, you, the tayishis, and the people of your uluses together with traitors to the sovereign, the Nogay mirzas and the Tatars, who left Astrakhan, the sovereign's patrimony, to join you, began to roam along the Yayik, and Or, and Sakmara, and Kiyil, and other rivers, which before were in possession of the sovereign's yasak-paying subjects of the Ufa province; and you took over the lands in possession of the yasak-paying subjects and other lands along those rivers, and you [continue] to raid and pillage the sovereign's yasak-paying subjects in their hunting and trapping grounds, and to capture them and to commit all kinds of violence against them.

And Daichin tayishi, having heard this speech, said: "I was not near Astrakhan, but stayed with my military men on the Volga, and it was my brother Louzang, who with his military men raided Astrakhan's vicinity, and you know yourself that my brother roams independently from me and does not follow my orders at all."

And he, Daichin, also said: "My [Kalmyks], the Kalmyks of Daichin, went to raid Astrakhan's vicinity with my brother Louzang without his[1] [Daichin's] knowledge, and those who roamed together with Louzang and those, my [people], the people of Daichin, those who went with my brother Louzang to raid the patrimony of the sovereign, the vicinity of Astrakhan, without my knowledge, I will order deprived of their possessions according to our law, but we have no punishment other than this."

And he, Daichin, also told Ivan Onuchin: "You say, that we know that from early on our Kalmyk tayishis, together with all their Kalmyk people,

---

[1]While narrating the story, the Russian envoy often switches from the first- to the third-person pronoun.

were in submission to the forefathers of your grand sovereign, to the grand sovereign tsars and the grand Moscow princes, and that they, the sovereigns, granted them favors. Likewise, in the past Batur tayishi and Kharakhula tayishi and our father together with his brothers and with us, his sons, and with his nephews, and with all the Kalmyk tayishis were under the sovereign's protection and in submission and obedience to your grand sovereign's father. But you lied about this: our fathers, and grandfathers, and greatgrandfathers were never in submission to anyone. And our books do not say that we had ever lived in submission to anyone, and we live independently, masters to ourselves and our people. And now too we are not afraid of anyone, except God, and we dispatch envoys in the past and present for [the purpose of] peace and understanding."

And Ivan Onuchin said: "How can you, Daichin, not having stood up, make such speeches. You want to turn truth into a lie, and you say such despicable words: that your forefathers and you have never been in submission to our grand sovereigns and were not under the sovereign protection. As soon as these words of yours are known to our grand sovereign, his majesty the tsar, I expect you will not escape a punishment."

And Ivan Onuchin told Daichin: "I saw Russian and Nogay captives in your ulus, about twenty men, who were recently captured near Astrakhan. Where did you get these captives?"

And Daichin tayishi said: "Louzang's people gave these Russian and Tatar captives to his [Daichin's] ulus, to his [Daichin's] nephew."

And Ivan Onuchin told him, Daichin: "Why did you, Daichin tayishi, and your brothers, and children, and nephews not abide by your oath, and go to raid the sovereign patrimony near Astrakhan and other towns, and take Russian and Nogay people captive?"

And Daichin tayishi said: "Before this, Louzang's envoys went to Astrakhan, and a boyar put those envoys of Louzang in jail in Astrakhan. And because of this Louzang launched raids against Astrakhan and pillaged many of the Russian people of the sovereign and the Nogay Tatars."

And Ivan Onuchin said: "Why did the boyar put Louzang's envoys in jail in Astrakhan?"

And Daichin told him: "I do not know why they were jailed."

And Ivan Onuchin said: "Your envoys are sent from you to the sovereign, to Ufa and they have never known any offense, but only respect, and they were never put in jail. Perhaps, they [Louzang's Kalmyks] did some wrong."

And Daichin said: "Louzang and his people did no wrong; his envoys were detained in Astrakhan for no reason."

And Ivan Onuchin said: "I hear from the people of your ulus that your brother Louzang's people ambushed and captured the sovereign's people, a deputation of Russians and Tatars dispatched from Moscow to Astrakhan, and that is why the boyar put them in jail—for such a wrongdoing."

And Daichin tayishi said: "It was Sulbatay of the Derbet tribe and his people who ambushed that party, not Louzang's people; Sulbatay, however, roams with Louzang and obeys his commands."

And Ivan Onuchin told Daichin: "The Derbet Sulbatay roams with Louzang and obeys his commands. If not for his [Louzang's] command would he have dared to raid the sovereign's people?"

And Daichin tayishi said: "Before this we were not aware of Sulbatay's wrongdoing, and now we learned that he, Sulbatay, committed an offense, raided the people of the sovereign. The Ishteks of the sovereign commit wrongdoings without the sovereign order, and the sovereign is not aware of their offenses, likewise Sulbatay committed offense without our knowledge."

And Ivan said: "If Sulbatay committed an offense, and caused such a harm as assaulting the sovereign's people, then, in accordance with your oath, order him executed so that others, having seen this, would not entertain committing offenses."

And Daichin said: "We have no habit of capital punishment, and there is no other punishment besides depriving someone of his possessions."

And Ivan said: "And what [worth] is your word, when in violation of your oath you order your people to commit offenses, but you say that they do it without your knowledge, and you do not punish them in any way."

And Daichin tayishi did not say anything to this. And after this, the last time before the spring, the Nogays of Daichin's ulus came many times to him, Ivan Onuchin, and told us [Ivan Onuchin]: Daichin tayishi ordered war wages against the sovereign's towns and provinces.

And Ivan Onuchin, having heard that news from the Nogay people, went to see Daichin tayishi and said: "Your best people took an oath on behalf of you, Daichin tayishi, and your brothers, and sons, and nephews, and all the people of your uluses, that you with your brothers, and sons, and nephews and people of your uluses would not wage war against the sovereign's towns and provinces, and would not assault the sovereign's people or take them captive; and now traitors to the sovereign, the Nogay Yedisan mirzas and their commoners, tell us that you,

Daichin, are sending them to wage war against the sovereign's towns and provinces, and what, then, is your oath [worth]?"

And Daichin said: "I am sending to wage war not against the Ufa province, but against the Chuvashs and Maris (Cheremis) of the Kazan province, because the Chuvashs and Maris of the Kazan province are not at peace with me, but the Russian people and the Ufa Bashkirs of the sovereign are at peace with me."

And Ivan Onuchin said: "Your people took an oath on your behalf that you would not set out or send your people against any towns and provinces of the sovereign. And now you are sending traitors to the sovereign, the Nogay mirzas and the Tatars, to wage war against the towns and provinces of the sovereign, and you say that you are at peace only with the Russian people and the Bashkirs of the Ufa town, and you are not at peace with the Chuvashs and Maris of the Kazan province. But both Kazan and Ufa are his majesty the tsar's towns, and people in those towns and provinces [belong] to the sovereign alone and they are not independent; they live under protection of the sovereign."

And Daichin tayishi told Ivan Onuchin: "That is why I send to raid the vicinity of the towns of Kazan and Astrakhan and other towns and provinces of the sovereign, because I do not fear anyone of those towns, but I am on guard against the town of Ufa alone, against the Russian people and the Bashkirs, because the Russian people and the Bashkirs of that Ufa town do much harm to me; they raid my uluses, kill my people and take them captive, and the Bashkirs continually steal my horses and I can hardly protect myself. And when we undertook campaigns against them, then we all suffered losses, and in future, we shall start a campaign against the Ufa province in fall, when the leaves fall from the trees and the rivers freeze, so that it would be possible to return to our uluses before big snowfalls. Otherwise, it is impossible to restrain the Bashkirs: in summer one cannot do anything to them, but only harm himself. And I expect that the Bashkirs will come to me with peace, and if those Bashkirs begin roaming with me, then, except God, who can do anything to us?"

And Ivan said: "What can one expect to hear from you and what kind of faithfulness can one expect from you in future? Whatever you swore, all of that you violated. And what you say about the Bashkirs that they soon be yours [is not true], for the Bashkirs are subjects of his majesty the tsar from the old times, and have never committed treason and never will."

And before his departure Ivan Onuchin came to Daichin tayishi and told him: "You, Daichin tayishi, ordered your best people, Dural-darkhan and Zargochi, to take an oath according to your faith on behalf of

yourself, and your brothers and sons, and nephews, and all the people of
your uluses in the presence of his majesty the tsar's envoy Vladimir
Golubtsov; and your envoys Batur and Bastiak took an oath on behalf of
yourself, brothers, and nephews, and all the people of your uluses in Ufa
in the presence of stol'nik and voevoda, Prince Dmitrii Dolgorukii that
you, Daichin tayishi, should leave the Bashkir lands for your distant
former pastures in the Black Sands[2] and on the Irgiz River, where you
had roamed before. And you, Daichin tayishi, should remember that
word and oath of yours, and observe it firmly and faithfully, and in future
[you and your people] should not come for hunting or other matters to
the patrimonial lands of the yasak-paying subjects of the sovereign or
roam on those patrimonial lands; you should not pillage, kill, or capture
the yasak-paying subjects, or arrive in Ufa and other provinces to wage
war, or to loot villages and hamlets, or commit any wrongdoing against
the province's residents and hunters; and you should continue to roam
in your distant former pastures, but you should not roam on the sovereign land of the yasak-paying subjects between the Yayik and Volga,
where before there were no Kalmyk pastures.

"And the sovereign, tsar and the grand prince Aleksei Mikhailovich, an
autocrat of all Russia, his majesty the tsar will show you favors like his
sovereign father, blessed be the memory of the grand sovereign, his
majesty the tsar, who used to show you favors: he will not order his army
against you, the Kalmyk tayishis and your people, and commit any
wrongdoing against you, and the sovereign will order that the Bashkirs of
the Ufa province be commanded firmly, that they, the Bashkirs, should
not raid your Kalmyk uluses in order to capture horses or commit any
other wrongdoing, and should not perpetuate or initiate any hostility.
And when you, the Kalmyk tayishis, leave from those lands for your
distant pastures, then the sovereign's people will have no quarrels with
you, the Kalmyk tayishis, and with your people, and there will be no
reason for a quarrel."

And Daichin tayishi, having heard this speech, said: "Land and water
belong to God, and in the past the land, where we and the Nogays are
presently roaming, was Nogay, and not the sovereign's, and there were
no lands in the Bashkirs' possession there. And we, having arrived at
these lands, had ousted the Nogays from this place. And the Nogays after
this roamed near Astrakhan, and we, the Kalmyks, after the Nogays [had
left], are roaming on this land until now. And after we defeated the
Nogay, Yedisan, and Yamboyluk mirzas and the Tatars of their uluses
near Astrakhan, we roam together with those Nogays along those rivers

---

[2]Name of the valley in the upper reaches of the Emba River.

and valleys, because they, the Nogays, became our subjects. And before this they were roaming those lands and rivers, and why should not we roam these lands now? For we have no other land to roam, besides this one. And there are no towns of the sovereign on those lands and rivers."

And Ivan Onuchin told Daichin: "Even though there are no towns of the sovereign on that land, that land with its natural boundaries belongs to the sovereign's yasak-paying subjects: the sovereign's yasak-paying subjects gather the sovereign's yasak on those lands and rivers, and that is why the sovereign's yasak-paying subjects have bitter disputes with your people. And if you, Daichin, follow your oath and with the people of your uluses leave those lands and rivers for your distant former pastures, then there will be no dispute between the sovereign's people and you since there will be no reason for a dispute."

And Daichin tayishi said: "At the present time I am at peace with the sovereign, the tsar and the grand prince Aleksei Mikhailovich of all Russia—not only the Bashkirs may engage in hunting and trapping on those lands and rivers, they even may hunt in the rear of my uluses, and having arrived in my uluses, they may purchase supplies, if only they, the sovereign people, the Bashkirs, commit no detriment against me; and I have no other place to roam besides this one."[3]

[3]The editors omitted the rest of the document, which referred to the Bashkir captives.

Bibliography

Archival Materials and Manuscripts

BA   Başbakanlik Arshlvl, Istanbul, Turkey.
Nâme-i Hümayun, nos. 2, 5, 6, 7.
Ibn ül-Emin Tasnifi, Kharijiye.
SK   Süleymaniye Kütüpkhanesi, Istanbul, Turkey.
Mehmed Pasha, Defterdar. *Defterdar Mehmed Pasha Tarikhi*. Halet Efendi
ilâvesi 189.
Riza Efendi, Sayyid. *Al-Sab'al-Sayyâr fî akhbâr Mulûk al-Tâtar*. Hamidiye 950. A
printed copy of the manuscript is in Esad Efendi 2298 (Riza, Sayyid Muham-
med. *Asseb o-Sseyar ili sem' planet soderzhashchii istoriiu krymskikh khanov*,
with a foreword by Mirza Kazim Beg. Kazan': Universitetskaia tipografiia, 1832).

Primary Sources

'Abd al-Ghaffâr Kirimi, al-Hâj. *'Umdat al-Tawârikh*. Edited by Necib Asim. *TOEM*.
Supplement 11. Istanbul: Matbaa-i Amire, 1924.
Abul-Ghazi Bahadur Khan. *Rodoslovnaiia turkmen*. Edited and translated by
A. N. Kononov. Moscow and Leningrad: AN SSSR, 1958.
———. *Rodoslovnoe drevo tiurkov*. Translated and edited by G. S. Sablukov. Kazan':
Tip. Imp. Universiteta, 1914.
*Adventures of Michailow, a Russian Captive; among the Kalmucks, Kirghiz, and
Kiwenses*. Written by himself. London: Printed for Sir Richard Philipps & Co.,
1822.
"Artemii Petrovich Volynskii. Materialy dlia biografii." *Russkaia starina* 5 (June
1872): 934–51.
Baddeley, John F. *Russia, Mongolia, China*. 2 vols. London: Macmillan, 1919.
Bakunin, Vasilii. "Opisanie istorii kalmytskogo naroda." *Krasnyi arkhiv. Istoriche-
skii zhurnal* 3 (1939): 189–254; 5 (1939): 196–220.

Bantysh-Kamenskii, Nikolai. *Diplomaticheskoe sobranie del mezhdu Rossiiskim i Kitaiskim gosudarstvami s 1619 po 1792-i god.* Kazan': Tip. Imp. Universiteta, 1882.

Batur-Ubashi Tümen. "Skazanie o derben-oiratakh." Translated by Iu. S. Lytkin. In *Kalmytskie istoriko-literaturnye pamiatniki v russkom perevode,* pp. 13–48. Elista: N.p., 1969.

Bergmann, Benjamin. *Nomadische Streifereien unter den Kalmüken in den Jahren 1802 und 1803.* 4 vols. Riga: Hartmann, 1804–5.

"Biographiia Zaya-Pandity." In *Kalmytskie istoriko-literaturnye pamiatniki v russkom perevode,* pp.159–200. Elista: N.p., 1969.

Butkov, P. G. *Materialy dlia novoi istorii Kavkaza, s 1702 po 1803 god.* 3 vols. St. Petersburg: Tip. Imp. Akademii nauk, 1869.

Dnevnye zapiski puteshestviia kapitana Nikolaia Rychkova v kirgis-kaisatskoi stepi, 1771 godu. St. Petersburg: Imp. Akademiia nauk, 1772.

Evliya Chelebi. *Seyâhatnâme.* 10 vols. Istanbul: N.p., 1896/97–1928.

Findiklili, Silahdar Mehmed Aga. *Nusretnâme.* Compiled by Ismet Parmaksizoglu. 2 vols. Istanbul: Milli Egitim Basimevi, 1962–66.

———. *Silahdar Tarikhi.* 2 vols. Istanbul: Orhaniye Matbaasi, 1928.

"Firdaus al-Ikbal." In *Materialy po istorii kazakhskikh khanstv 15–18 vekov,* pp. 431–75. Alma-Ata: "Nauka" Kazakhskoi SSR, 1969.

Gabang Sharab. "Skazanie ob oiratakh." Translated by Iu. S. Lytkin. In *Kalmytskie istoriko-literaturnye pamaitniki v russkom perevode,* pp. 131–58. Elista: N.p., 1969.

Ikh Tsaaz ("Velikoe ulozhenie"). Pamiatnik mongol'skogo feodal'nogo prava 17 v. Translated by S. D. Dalykov. Moscow: Nauka, 1981.

Imanishi, Shunju. *Tulishen's I-yü-lu.* Nara, Japan: Tenri Daigaku, 1964.

"Istoriia kalmytskikh khanov." Translated by Iu. S. Lytkin. In *Kalmytskie istoriko-literaturnye pamaitniki v russkom perevode,* pp. 49–79. Elista: N.p. 1969.

Kabardino-russkie otnosheniia v 16–18 vv. Dokumenty i materialy. 2 vols. Moscow: Izd-vo AN SSSR, 1957.

Kazakhsko-russkie otnosheniia v 16–18 vv. Sbornik materialov i dokumentov. Alma-Ata: AN Kazakhskoi SSR, 1961.

Le Khanat de Crimée dans les Archives du Musée du Palais de Topkapi. Paris: Mouton, 1978.

"K istorii Saratovskogo kraia iz Donskikh del." *Trudy Saratovskoi uchenoi arkhivnoi komissii* 4, pt. 1 (1893): 40–59.

Knigi razriadnye. 2 vols. St. Petersburg: Tip. II Otd. Imp. Kants., 1853–55.

Korb, Johann George. *Dnevnik puteshestviia v Moskoviiu 1698–1699 gg.* Translated by A. I. Malein. St. Petersburg: Tip. A. S. Suvorina, 1906.

Kotoshikhin, Grigorii. *O Rossii v tsarstvovanie Alekseia Mikhailovicha.* 4th ed. St. Petersburg: Tip. glavnogo upravleniia udelov, 1906.

Kraft I. I. *Turgaiskii oblastnoi arkhiv. Opisanie arkhivnych dokumentov s 1731 po 1782 g. otnosiashchikhsia k upravleniu kirgizami.* St. Petersburg: Tip. A. P. Lopukhina, 1901.

Krest'ianskaia voina pod predvoditel'stvom Stepana Razina. Sbornik dokumentov. Compiled by E. A. Shvetsova. 4 vols. Moscow: AN SSSR, 1954–76.

Le Gaubil, Paul. "Relation chinoise contenant un itinéraire de Peking à Tobol, et de Tobol au pays des Tourgouts." In *Observations mathématiques, astronomiques, géographiques, chronologiques et physiques,* vol. 1. Paris: N.p., 1729.

Lytkin, Iu. S. "Ayuki-Khan kalmytskii." In *Kalmytskie istoriko-literaturnye pamiat-niki v russkom perevode*, pp. 131–39. Elista: N.p., 1969.

Materialy po istorii Bashkirskoi ASSR, vol. 1: *Bashkirskie vosstaniia v 17 i pervoi polovine 18 vekov*. Moscow and Leningrad: Izd-vo AN SSSR, 1936.

Materialy po istorii karakalpakov. Sbornik. Trudy Instituta vostokovedeniia, vol. 7. Moscow and Leningrad: Izd-vo Akademii nauk, 1935.

Materialy po istorii Rossii. Sbornik ukazov i drugikh dokumentov, kasaiushchi-khsia upravleniia i ustroistva Orenburgskogo kraia. Compiled by A. I. Dobro-myslov. 2 vols. Orenburg: Tipo-Litografiia F. B. Skachkova, 1900.

Materialy po istorii russko-gruzinskikh otnoshenii: (80-90-e gody 17 veka). Compiled by G. G. Paichadze, vol. 3. Tbilisi: Metsniereba, 1974.

Materialy po istorii Uzbekskoi, Tadzhikskoi i Turkmenskoi SSR, vol. 1: *Torgovlia s Moskovskim gosudarstvom i mezhdunarodnoe polozhenie Srednei Azii v 16–17 vv*. Leningrad: AN SSSR, 1932.

Men-gu-iu-mu-tszi. Zapiski o mongol'skikh kochev'iakh. Translated by P. S. Popov. *ZIRGOOE*, vol. 24. St. Petersburg: N.p., 1895.

Mezhdunarodnye otnosheniia v Tsentral'noi Azii. 17–18 vv. Dokumenty i mate-rialy. 2 vols. Moscow: Nauka, 1989.

Miller, G. F. *Istoriia Sibiri*. 2 vols. Moscow and Leningrad: AN SSSR, 1937–41.

Muahedat Mejmuasi. 5 vols. Istanbul: Jeride-i Askeriye Matbaasi, [1878–82].

Naima, Mustafa. *Tarikh i Naima*. 6 vols. Istanbul: N.p. [18—].

Nepliuev, I. I. *Zapiski Ivana Ivanovicha Nepliueva (1693–1773)*. St. Petersburg: Izd-vo A. S. Suvorina, 1893.

Pallas, Peter Simon. *Reise durch verschiedene Provinzen des Russischen Reichs*. 3 vols. St. Petersburg: Kaiserl. Akademie der Wissenschaften, 1771–76. Reprint. Graz, Austria: Akedemische Druck und Verlagsanstalt, 1967.

——. *Travels through the Southern Provinces of the Russian Empire in the Years 1793 and 1794*. 2d ed. 2 vols. London: Printed for John Stockdale, 1812.

Pamiatniki diplomaticheskikh i torgovykh snoshenii Moskovskoi Rusi s Persiei. Edited by N. I. Veselovskii. 3 vols. St. Petersburg: Pechatnia P. O. Iablonskogo, 1890–98.

Perepiska fel'dmarshalov F. A. Golovina i B. P. Sheremet'eva v 1705–6 gg. Moscow: Tip. V. Got'e, 1851.

Popov, A. N. *Materialy dlia istorii vozmushcheniia Sten'ki Razina*. Moscow: Tip. L. Stepanova, 1857.

Posol'stvo k ziungarskomu khun-taichzhi Tsevan-Rabtanu kapitana ot artillerii Ivana Unkovskogo i putevoi zhurnal ego za 1722–1724 gody. ZIRGOOE vol. 10, pt. 2. St. Petersburg: Tip. V. F. Kirshbauma, 1887.

Pozdneev, A. M. "K istorii ziungarskikh kalmykov. Pis'mo." In *Posol'stvo k ziun-garskomu khun-taichzhi Tsevan-Rabtanu kapitana ot artilerii Ivana Unkov-skogo i putevoi zhurnal ego za 1722–1724 gody*. ZIRGOOE 10, pt. 2: 239–64. St. Petersburg: Tip. V. F. Kirshbauma, 1887.

Rashid, Mehmed. *Tarikh-i Rashid*. 6 vols. Istanbul: Matbaa-i Amire [1865].

Reestr delam Krymskogo dvora s 1474 po 1779 goda. Compiled by N. N. Bantysh-Kamenskii in 1808. Simferopol': Tip. Tavricheskogo gub. pravl., 1893.

Russko-indiiskie otnosheniia v 17 v. Sbornik dokumentov. Moscow: Izd-vo vo-stochnoi literatury, 1958.

Russko-kitaiskie otnosheniia v 18 veke. Materialy i dokumenty, vol. 1: *1700–1725*. Moscow: Nauka, 1978.

Russko-mongol'skie otnosheniia, 1607–1636. Sbornik dokumentov. Moscow: Izd-vo vostochnoi literatury, 1959.

Russko-mongol'skie otnosheniia, 1636–1654. Sbornik dokumentov. Moscow: Nauka, 1974.

Russko-turkmenskie otnosheniia v 18–19 vv. do prisoedineniia Turkmenii k Rossii. Sbornik arkhivnykh dokumentov. Ashkhabad: Izd-vo AN Turkmenskoi SSR, 1963.

Sbornik vypisok iz arkhivnykh bumag o Petre Velikom. Compiled by G. V. Esipov. 2 vols. Moscow: Univ. tip., 1872.

Schnitscher, J. H. "Nachricht von den Ajuckischen Kalmücken." *Sammlung Russischer Geschichte* 4 (1760): 275–364.

Sibirskie letopisi. St. Petersburg: Tip. I. N. Skorokhodova, 1907.

"Spisok saratovskikh i tsaritsynskikh voevod 17 veka." Compiled by A. A. Geraklitov. *Trudy Saratovskoi uchenoi komissii* 30 (1913): 61–82.

"Spisok so stateinogo spiska Vasiliia Aitemireva, poslannogo v Krym s predlozheniem mirnykh dogovorov, 1692–95." *ZIOOID* 18 (1895): 1–80; 19 (1896): 1–58.

"Spisok so stateinogo spiska Velikogo Gosudaria poslannikov: stol'nika V. M. Tiapkina, d'iaka Nikity Zotova k krymskomu khanu Murad-Gireiu v 1681 godu." *ZIOOID* 2 (1850): 568–658.

Stary, Giovanni. *Chinas erste Gesandte in Russland.* Wiesbaden: Otto Harrassowitz, 1976.

"Stateinyi spisok pokhoda v Azov boiarina i voevody A. S. Sheina v 1697 godu." *ZIOOID* 7 (1868): 135–65.

Staunton, Sir George Thomas. *Narrative of the Chinese Embassy to the Khan of the Tourgouth Tatars, in the Years 1712, 13, 14, and 15 by the Chinese Embassador.* London: J. Murray, 1821.

Taitsin gurun i ukheri koli, to est' vse zakony i ustanovleniia kitaiskogo (a nyne man'chzhurskogo) pravitel'stva. Translated by A. Leont'ev. 3 vols. St. Petersburg: Imp. Akademiia nauk, 1781–83.

Topografiia Orenburgskoi gubernii. Compiled by P. I. Rychkov in 1762. Orenburg: Tip. B. Breslina, 1887.

Ulozhenie Kitaiskoi palaty vneshnikh snoshenii. Translated from Manchurian by Stepan Lipovtsov. 2 vols. St. Petersburg: Tip. Dep-ta narodnogo prosveshcheniia, 1828.

Ustanovleniia o soli i chae. Translated by N. P. Svistunova. Moscow: Nauka, 1975.

Vel'iaminov-Zernov, V. V. *Materialy dlia istorii Krymskogo khanstva.* St. Petersburg: Tip. Imp. Akademii Nauk, 1864.

Velychko, Samiilo. *Letopis' sobytii v iugozapadnoi Rossii v 17 veke.* 4 vols. Kiev: Lito-Tip. Iosifa Val'nera, 1848–64.

"Zapiska ob Artemii Volynskom." *ChOIDR* 2 (April–June 1858): 135–70.

"Zapiski Tulishenia o ego poezdke v sostave tsinskogo posol'stva k kalmytskomu khanu Aiuke v 1712–1715 gg." In *Russko-kitaiskie otnosheniia v 18 veke. Materialy i dokumenty,* vol. 1: *1700–1725,* pp. 437–83. Moscow: Nauka, 1978.

"Zapisnaia kniga Moskovskogo stola, 1678–79 gg." *RIB* 11 (1889): 329–525.

Zwick, H. A., and J. G. Schill. *Reise von Sarepta in verschiedene Kalmücken-Horden des Astrachanischen Gouvernements im Jahr 1823 von 26ten Mai bis 21ten August Stils in Angelegenheiten der Russischen Bibel-Gesellschaft unternommen.* Leipzig: Paul Gottheif Rummer, 1827.

Secondary Sources

Aberle, David F. *The Kinship System of the Kalmuk Mongols*. Albuquerque: University of New Mexico Press, 1953.
Akhmanov, I. G. *Bashkirskie vosstaniia 17-pervoi treti 18 vekov*. Ufa: BGU, 1978.
Allworth, Edward A. *The Modern Uzbeks, from the Fourteenth Century to the Present: A Cultural History*. Stanford, Calif.: Hoover Institution Press, 1990.
Apollova, N. G. *Ekonomicheskie i politicheskie sviazi Kazakhstana s Rossiei v 18-nachale 19 v.* Moscow: AN SSSR, 1960.
Bagalei, D. I. *Ocherki iz istorii kolonizatsii stepnoi okrainy Moskovskogo gosudarstva.* Moscow: Imp. ob-vo ist. i drevnostei pri Moskovskom univ., 1887.
Banzarov, Dorzhi. "Chernaia vera ili shamanstvo u mongolov." In *Sobranie sochinenii*, pp. 48–100. Moscow: Izd-vo vostochnoi literatury, 1955.
Barfield, Thomas J. *The Perilous Frontier: Nomadic Empires and China.* Cambridge, Mass.: Basil Blackwell, 1989.
Barkman, C. D. "The Return of the Torghuts from Russia to China." *Journal of Oriental Studies* 2 (1955): 89–115.
Barth, Fredrik. *Nomads of South Persia: The Basseri Tribe of the Khamseh Confederacy*. Oslo: Universitetsforlaget, 1964.
Batmaev, M. M. "Novye khoziaistvennye iavleniia v Kalmytskom khanstve v 40–60 godakh 18 veka." In *Obshchestvennyi stroi i sotsial'no-politicheskoe razvitie dorevoliutsionnoi Kalmykii*, pp. 23–43. Elista: N.p., 1983.
Belikov, T. I. *Kalmyki v bor'be za nezavisimost' nashei rodiny (17-nachalo 19 vv).* Elista: Kalmgosizdat, 1965.
Bembeev, G. "O rodo-plemennykh izmeneniiakh u kalmykov." In *Problemy etnogeneza kalmykov*, pp. 64–78. Elista: N.p., 1984.
Black [Black-Michaud], Jacob. "Tyranny as a Strategy for Survival in an 'Egalitarian Society': Luri Facts versus an Anthropological Mystique." *Man* 7 (1972): 614–34.
Bogoiavlenskii, S. K. "Materialy po istorii kalmykov v pervoi polovine 17 veka." *Istoricheskie zapiski* 5 (1939): 48–101.
———. "Vooruzhenie russkikh voisk v 16–17 vekakh." *Istoricheskie zapiski* 4 (1938): 258–83.
Borisenko, I. V. "O rasselenii sheretov, tomutov, chuguevskikh i beliaevskikh kalmykov." In *Obshchestvennyi stroi i sotsial'no-politicheskoe razvitie dorevoliutsionnoi Kalmykii*, pp. 44–59. Elista: N.p., 1983.
Brandenburg, N. E. "Kubanskii pokhod 1711 goda." *Voennyi sbornik* 54 (1867): 29–42.
Bretschneider, E. V. *Medieval Researches from Eastern Asiatic Sources*. 2 vols. London: Kegan Paul, Trench, Trübner, 1910.
"Bum-Erdeni." In *Mongolo-oiratskii geroicheskii epos*, translated by B. Ia. Vladimirtsov, pp. 55–102. Petersburg and Moscow: Gos. izd-vo, 1923. Reprint. Westmead, Eng.: Gregg International Publishers, 1971.
Bushev, P. P. *Posol'stvo Artemiia Volynskogo v Iran v 1715–18 gg. (po russkim arkhivam).* Moscow: Nauka, 1978.
Chuloshnikov, A. "Torgovlia Moskovskogo gosudarstva so Srednei Aziei v 16–17 vv." In *Materialy po istorii Uzbekskoi, Tadzhikskoi i Turkmenskoi SSR*, vol. 1:

Torgovlia s Moskovskim gosudarstvom i mezhdunarodnoe polozhenie Srednei Azii v 16–17 vv, pp. 61–88. Leningrad: AN SSSR, 1932.

Clauson, Sir Gerard. *An Etymological Dictionary of Pre-Thirteenth Century Turkish*. Oxford: Clarendon Press, 1972.

Darienko, V. N. "Osnovanie goroda Gur'eva." *Voprosy istorii*. Alma-Ata 5 (1973): 189–97.

De Quincey, Thomas. *Revolt of the Tartars or Flight of the Kalmuck Khan*. New York: American Book Co., 1895.

Don i stepnoe Predkavkaz'e. 18—pervaia polovina 19 veka: Zaselenie i khoziaistvo. Rostov-na-Donu: Izd-vo Rostovskogo universiteta, 1977.

Dörfer, Gerhard. *Türkische und mongolische Elemente im Neupersischen*, vol. 1: *Mongolische Elemente im Neupersischen*. Wiesbaden: F. Steiner, 1963.

Dzhangar. Kalmytskii geroicheskii epos. Translated by Semen Lipkin. Elista: Kalmytskoe knizhnoe izd-vo, 1978.

Emel'ianov, A. P. "Razvitie taktiki russkoi armii vo vtoroi polovine 18 v.," in *Razvitie taktiki russkoi armii, 18-nach. 20 vv.*, pp. 68–92. Moscow: Voennoe izdvo, 1957.

Erdniev, U. E. *Kalmyki (konets 19-nachalo 20 vv.): Istoriko-etnograficheskie ocherki*. Elista: Kalm. knizhnoe izd-vo, 1970.

Filaret, Archbishop of Chernigov. *Istoriko-statisticheskoe opisanie Khar'kovskoi eparkhii*, otdeleniia 4 and 5. Khar'kov: Univ. tip., 1858.

Fisher, Alan. *The Crimean Tatars*. Stanford, Calif.: Hoover Institution Press, 1978.

Fletcher, Joseph. "Turco-Mongol Monarchic Tradition in the Ottoman Empire." *Harvard Ukrainian Studies* 3–4 (1979–80): 236–51.

Fromm, Erich. *On Disobedience*. New York: Seabury Press, 1981.

Geraklitov, A. A. *Istoriia Saratovskogo kraia v 16–18 vv*. Saratov: Drukar', 1923.

German, Ernst. "Zhizn' Volynskogo, ego zagovor i smert'." *Russkii arkhiv* 4 (1866): 1351–74.

Golikova, N. B. *Astrakhanskoe vosstanie 1705–06 g*. Moscow: Izd-vo Moskovskogo univ-ta, 1975.

Gol'man, M. I. "Russkie perevody i spiski mongolo-oiratskikh zakonov 1640 goda." In *Mongol'skii sbornik. Ekonomika, istoriia, arkheologiia*, pp. 139–62. Moscow: Izd-vo vostochnoi literatury, 1959.

Golstunskii, K. F. *Mongolo-oiratskie zakony 1640 goda, dopolnitel'nye ukazy Galdan-Khun-Taidzhiia i zakony, sostavlennye dlia volzhskikh kalmykov pri kalmytskom khane Donduk-Dashi*. St. Petersburg: Tip. Imp. Akademii nauk, 1880.

Goody, Jack, ed. *Succession to High Office*. Cambridge: Cambridge University Press, 1966.

Gurevich, A. Ia. *Kategorii srednevekovoi kul'tury*. Moscow: Iskusstvo, 1972.

Gurevich, B. P. *Mezhdunarodnye otnosheniia v Tsentral'noi Azii v 17-pervoi polovine 19 v*. Moscow: Nauka, 1979.

Hellie, Richard. *Enserfment and Military Change in Muscovy*. Chicago: University of Chicago Press, 1971.

——. *Slavery in Russia, 1450–1725*. Chicago: University of Chicago Press, 1982.

Hucker, Charles O. *A Dictionary of Official Titles in Imperial China*. Stanford, Calif.: Stanford University Press, 1985.

Hummel, Arthur W., ed. *Eminent Chinese of the Ch'ing Period (1644–1912)*. 2 vols. Washington, D.C.: U.S. Government Printing Office, 1943–44.

Iakovlev, A. I. *Zasechnaia cherta Moskovskogo gosudarstva v 17 veke.* Moscow: Tip. I. Lissnera and D. Sobko, 1916.

Illeretskii, V. "Ekspeditsiia kniazia Cherkasskogo v Khivu." *Istoricheskii zhurnal* 7 (1940): 40–52.

Inalcik, Halil. "Giray." In *Islam Ansiklopedisi,* 4:783–89. Istanbul: Milli Egitim Basimevi, 1945.

——. "The Khan and the Tribal Aristocracy: The Crimean Khanate under Sahib Giray I." *Harvard Ukrainian Studies* 3–4 (1979–80): 445–66.

Iomudskii, N. N. "Prisiaga u zakaspiiskikh turkmen." In "Sbornik v chest' semidesiatiletiia G. N. Potanina." *ZIRGOOE* 34 (1909): 219–36.

Iorish, I. I. *Materialy o mongolakh, kalmykakh i buriatakh v arkhivakh Leningrada. Istoriia, pravo, ekonomika.* Moscow: Nauka, 1966.

Irons, William. "Nomadism as a Political Adaptation: The Case of the Yomut Turkmen." *American Ethnologist* 1 (1974): 635–58.

Istoricheskaia khronologiia Khar'kovskoi gubernii. Compiled by K. P. Shchelkov. Khar'kov: Univ. tipografiia, 1882.

Istoriia kalmytskoi literatury v dvukh tomakh, vol. 1: *Dooktiabr'skii period.* Elista: Kalmytskoe knizhnoe izdatel'stvo, 1981.

Istoriia Turkmenskoi SSR. 2 vols. Ashkhabad: AN Turkmenskoi SSR, 1957.

Kalmytskaia step' Astrakhanskoi gubernii po issledovaniiam Kumo-Manychskoi ekspeditsii. St. Petersburg: Tip. V. Bezobrazova, 1868.

Kalmytsko-russkii slovar'. Edited by B. D. Muniev. Moscow: Izd-vo "Russkii iazyk," 1977.

Kamentseva E. I., and N. V. Ustiugov. *Russkaia sfragistika i geral'dika.* Moscow: Vysshaia shkola, 1963.

Kappeler, Andreas. *Russlands Erste Nationalitäten. Das Zarenreich und die Völker der Mittleren Wolga vom 16. bis 19. Jahrhundert.* Cologne and Vienna: Böhlau Verlag, 1982

Kara, György. *Knigi mongol'skikh kochevnikov.* Moscow: Vost. liter-ra., 1972.

Kaspiiskaia ekspeditsiia K. M. Bera 1853–1857 gg. Compiled by T. A. Lukina. Nauchnoe nasledstvo, vol. 9. Leningrad: Nauka, 1984.

Keenan, Edward L. "Kazan'—'The Bend.'" *Harvard Ukrainian Studies* 3–4 (1979–80): 484–96.

Khazanov, A. M. *Nomads and the Outside World.* Translated by Julia Crookenden. Cambridge: Cambridge University Press, 1984.

Khodarkovsky, Michael. "Uneasy Alliance: Peter the Great and Ayuki Khan." *Central Asian Survey* 7, no. 4 (1988): 1–45.

Kichikov, A. Sh. "K voprosu o proiskhozhdenii slova 'kalmyk.'" *Uchenye zapiski KNIIaLI* 5 (1968): 133–34.

Kichikov (Ochirov), M. L. *Istoricheskie korni druzhby russkogo i kalmytskogo narodov.* Elista: Kalmytskoe knizhnoe izd-vo, 1966.

——. "K istorii obrazovaniia Kalmytskogo khanstva v sostave Rossii." *Zapiski KNIIaLI* 2 [1962]: 31–60.

——. "K voprosu obrazovaniia Kalmytskogo khanstva v sostave Rossii." *KNIIaLI, Vestnik instituta, istoriko-filologicheskaia seriia* 1 (1963): 3–28.

Koblandy-batyr. Kazakhskii geroicheskii epos. Translated by N. B. Kidaish-Pokrovskaia and O. A. Nurmagambetova. Moscow: Nauka, 1985.

Kochekaev, B.–A. B. *Nogaisko-russkie otnosheniia v 15–18 vv.* Alma-Ata: Nauka Kazakhskoi SSR, 1988.

Korsunkiev, Ts. K. "K voprosu o gibeli otriada Bekovicha-Cherkasskogo v Khive v 1717 godu." *KNIIaLI, Uchenye zapiski, seriia istorii* 8 (1969): 77–91.

Kotwicz, W. L. *Kalmytskiie zagadki i poslovitsy.* St. Petersburg: Tip. Imp. Akademii nauk, 1905.

——. "Russkie arkhivnye dokumenty po snosheniiam s oiratami v 17–18 vekakh." *Izvestiia Rossiiskoi akademii nauk* nos. 12–15 (1919): 791–822.

Kozlov, P. K. *Mongoliia i Kam: Trekhletnee puteshestvie po Mongolii i Tibetu (1899–1901gg.).* 2d ed. Moscow: OGIZ, 1947.

Krueger, John R. *Materials for an Oirat-Mongolian to English Citation Dictionary.* 2 vols. Bloomington, Ind.: Mongolia Society, 1978.

Kurat, Akdes Nimet. *IV–XVIII Yüzyillarda Karadeniz Kuzeyindeki Türk Kavimleri ve Devletleri.* Ankara: Türk Tarikh Kurumu Basimevi, 1972.

——. *Prut Seferi ve Barishi 1123 (1711).* 2 vols. Ankara: Türk Tarikh Kurumu Basimevi, 1951–53.

Kurts, B. G. "Sostoianie Rossii v 1650–55 gg. po doneseniiam Rodesa." *ChOIDR* 253, bk. 2 (1915): 136–37.

Kusheva, E. N. "Khoziaistvo saratovskikh dvorian Shakhmatovykh v 18 veke." *Izvestiia AN SSSR,* ser. 7, no. 7 (1929): 575–604.

Kychanov, E. I. *Povestvovanie ob oiratskom Galdane Boshoktu-Khane.* Novosibirsk: Nauka, 1980.

Kychanov, E. I., and L. S. Savitskii. *Liudi i bogi strany snegov. Ocherk istorii Tibeta i ego kul'tury.* Moscow: Nauka, 1975.

Lattimore, Owen. *Inner Asian Frontiers of China.* New York: Capitol Publishing Co., 1951.

Lebedev, V. I. "Bashkirskoe vosstanie 1705–11 gg." *Istoricheskie zapiski* 1 (1937): 81–102.

Le Goff, Jacques. *Time, Work, and Culture in the Middle Ages.* Chicago: University of Chicago Press, 1980.

Lemercier-Quelquejay, Chantal. "Les Kalmuks de la Volga entre l'empire Russe et l'empire Ottoman sous le règne de Pierre le Grand." *Cahiers du Monde Russe et Soviétique* 7 (1966): 63–76.

Leontovich, F. I. *K istorii prava russkikh inorodtsev: Drevnii mongolo-kalmytskii ili oiratskii ustav vzyskanii (Tsaadzhin-Bichig).* Odessa: N.p., 1879.

Lopez, Robert S. *The Birth of Europe.* New York: M. Evans, 1967.

Lystsov, V. P. *Persidskii pokhod Petra I, 1722–23.* Moscow: Izd-vo Moskovskogo universiteta, 1951.

Maidar, D., and D. Piurveev. *Ot kochevoi do mobil'noi arkhitektury.* Moscow: Stroiizdat, 1980.

Makhatka, O. "Diplomaticheskaia deiatel'nost' 'Sviashchennoi ligi' sredi kazachestva i kalmykov v 1683–86 gg." *Vestnik LGU, seriia istorii, iazyka i literatury* 14 (1958): 35–45.

Maksheev, A. I. "Karta Dzhungarii, sostavlennaia shvedom Renatom, vo vremia ego plena u kalmykov s 1716 po 1733 god." *ZIRGOOG* 11 (1888): 107–45.

Mancall, Mark. "The Ch'ing Tribute System: An Interpretive Essay." In *The Chinese World Order: Traditional China's Foreign Relations,* ed. John Fairbank, pp. 63–89. Cambridge, Mass.: Harvard University Press, 1968.

——. *Russia and China: Their Diplomatic Relations to 1728.* Cambridge, Mass.: Harvard University Press, 1971.

Manstein, K. H. *Zapiski Manshteina o Rossii, 1727–44.* St. Petersburg: Tip. R. S. Balasheva, 1875.

Markov, G. E. *Kochevniki Azii.* Moscow: Izd-vo Mosk. Univ., 1976.

Mauss, Marcel. *The Gift: Forms and Functions of Exchange in Archaic Societies.* Translated by Ian Cunnison. Glencoe, Ill.: Free Press, 1954.

Minkh, A. N. "K istorii pereseleniia malorossiian v Saratovskii krai." *Trudy Saratovskoi uchenoi arkhivnoi komissii* 4, pt. 1 (1893): 17–18.

Mish, John L. "The Return of the Turgut." *Journal of Asian History* 4, no. 1 (1970): 80–82.

Miyawaki, Junko. "On the Oyirad Khanship." In *Aspects of Altaic Civilization,* ed. Denis Sinor, 3:142–53. Bloomington: Indiana University Press, 1990.

Nebol'sin, Pavel. *Ocherki byta kalmykov khoshoutovskogo ulusa.* St. Petersburg: Tip. Karla Kraia, 1852.

Nogaisko-russkii slovar'. Edited by N. A. Baskakov. Moscow: Gos. izd. inostrannykh i natsional'nykh slovarei, 1963.

Novosel'skii, A. A. *Bor'ba Moskovskogo gosudarstva s tatarami v pervoi polovine 17 veka.* Moscow and Leningrad: AN SSSR, 1948.

Ocherki istorii Kalmytskoi ASSR, vol. 1: *Dooktiabr'skii period.* Moscow: Nauka, 1967.

Okada, Hidehiro. "Origins of the Dörben Oyirad." In *Ural-Altaische Jahrbücher* 7 (1987): 181–211.

Olcott, Martha Brill. *The Kazakhs.* Stanford, Calif.: Hoover Institution Press, 1987.

Pakalin, Mehmet Zeki. *Osmanli Deyimleri ve Terimleri Sözlügü.* 3 vols. Istanbul: Milli Egitim Basimevi, 1971.

Pal'mov, N. N. *Etiudy po istorii privolzhskikh kalmykov 17 i 18 veka.* 5 vols. Astrakhan': Tip. Kalmoblitizdata, 1926–32.

———. "K astrakhanskomu periodu zhizni V. N. Tatishcheva." *Izvestiia AN SSSR,* ser. 7 (1928): 317–42.

Pelliot, Paul. *Notes critiques d'histoire kalmouke.* Paris: Librairie d'Amerique et d'Orient, 1960.

Petech, Luciano. *China and Tibet in the Early 18th Century.* 2d ed. Leiden: E. J. Brill, 1972.

Popov, A. N. "Snosheniia Rossii s Khivoi i Bukharoi pri Petre Velikom." *ZIRGO* 9 (1853): 237–425.

Popov, Nil. Review of the book by F. I. Leontovich, *K istorii prava russkikh inorodtsev: Drevnii mongolo-kalmytskii ili oiratskii ustav vzyskanii (Tsaadzhin-bichig).* Odessa, 1879, in *ZhMNP* 205 (October 1879): 302–17.

———. *V. N. Tatishchev i ego vremia.* Moscow: Tip. V. Gracheva, 1861.

Poppe, N. N. "Rol' Zaya-pandity v kul'turnoi istorii mongol'skikh narodov." In *Kalmyk Monograph Series,* no. 2, *Kalmyk-Oirat Symposium,* pp. 57–70. Philadelphia: Society for Promotion of Kalmyk Culture, 1966.

Potanin, G. N. *Puteshestviia po Mongolii.* Moscow: Gos. izd-vo geogr. literatury, 1948.

Pozdneev, A. M. "Astrakhanskie kalmyki i ikh otnosheniia k Rossii do nachala nyneshnego stoletiia" *ZhMNP* 244 (March 1886): 140–70.

———. *Ocherki byta buddiiskikh monastyrei i buddiiskogo dukhovenstva v Mongolii v sviazi s otnosheniiami sego poslednego k narodu.* ZIRGOOE, vol. 16. St. Petersburg: Tip. V. F. Kirshbauma, 1887.

Preobrazhenskaia, P. S. "Iz istorii russko-kalmytskikh otnoshenii v 50-60-kh godakh 17 veka." *Zapiski KNIIaLI* 1 (1960): 49–84.

Preobrazhenskii, F. M. "Volga v Saratovskoi gubernii." In *Saratovskii sbornik. Materialy dlia izucheniia Saratovskoi gubernii,* vol. 1, pt. 1, pp. 285–344. Saratov: Tip. gubernskogo upravleniia, 1881.

Putevoditel' po arkhivu Leningradskogo otdeleniia Instituta istorii. Compiled by I. V. Valkin. Leningrad: AN SSSR, 1958.

Raeff, Marc. "Patterns of Russian Imperial Policy towards the Nationalities." In *Soviet Nationality Problems,* ed. Edward Allworth, pp. 22–42. New York: Columbia University Press, 1971.

Ramstedt, G. J. *Kalmückisches Wörterbuch.* Helsinki: Suomalais-Ugrilainen Seura, 1935.

Rerikh, Iu. N., and N. P. Shastina. "Gramota tsaria Petra I k Lubsan taidzhi i ee sostavitel'." *Problemy vostokovedeniia* 4 (1960): 140–50.

Riess, Charles A. "The History of the Kalmyk Khanate to 1724." Ph.D. diss., Indiana University, 1983.

Rubel, Paula G. *The Kalmyk Mongols: A Study in Continuity and Change.* Uralic and Altaic Series, vol. 64. Bloomington: Indiana University Press, 1967.

Sahlins, Marshall D. "The Segmentary Lineage: An Organization of Predatory Expansion." *American Anthropologist* 63, no. 2 (1961): 322–45.

——. *Tribesmen.* Englewood Cliffs, N.J.: Prentice-Hall, 1968.

Samagalski, Alan, and Michael Buckley. *China: A Travel Survival Kit.* Victoria, Australia: Lonely Planet Publications, 1984.

Sanchirov, V. P. "Etnicheskii sostav oiratov 15–18 vv. po dannym 'Iletkhel shastir.'" In *Iz istorii dokapitalisticheskikh otnoshenii v Kalmykii,* pp. 3–33. Elista: N.p., 1977.

Sazykin, Aleksei G. "An Historical Document in Oirat Script." In *Between the Danube and the Caucasus,* ed. György Kara, pp. 229–33. Budapest: Akadémiai Kiadó, 1987.

Serruys, Henry. "The Office of Tayishi in Mongolia in the Fifteenth Century." *HJAS* 37, no. 2 (1977): 353–81.

Service, Elman R. *Primitive Social Organization: An Evolutionary Perspective.* New York: Random House, 1966.

Shakabpa, Tsepon W. D. *Tibet: A Political History.* New Haven: Yale University Press, 1967.

Shara-Bodon. In *Mongolo-oiratskii geroicheskii epos,* translated by B. Ia. Vladimirtsov, pp. 232–52. Peterburg and Moscow: Gos. izd-vo, 1923. Reprint. Westmead, Eng.: Gregg International Publishers, 1971.

Shastina, N. P. "Perevod I. Rossokhinym istochnika po istorii mongolov 17 veka." *Uchenye zapiski Instituta vostokovedeniia* 6 (1953): 200–211.

——. "Pis'ma Lubsan taidzhi v Moskvu." In *Filologiia i istoriia mongol'skikh narodov,* pp. 275–88. Moscow: Izd-vo vostochnoi literatury, 1958.

——. *Russko-mongol'skie posol'skie otnosheniia v 17 veke.* Moscow: Izd-vo vostochnoi literatury, 1958.

Sheremet'ev, Pavel. *Vladimir Petrovich Sheremet'ev, 1668–1737.* 2 vols. Moscow: Sinodal'naia tip., 1913–14.

Shishkin, I. I. "Artemii Volynskii." *Otechestvennye zapiski* 128–30 (1860).

Shovunov, K. P. "Kalmytskie kazach'i poseleniia i ikh voennaia organizatsiia v 18 veke." In *Issledovaniia po istoricheskoi geografii Kalmytskoi ASSR,* pp. 13–30. Elista: N.p., 1981.

Smirnov, V. D. *Krymskoe khanstvo pod verkhovenstvom Otomanskoi Porty do nachala 18 veka.* St. Petersburg: Tip. A. S. Suvorina, 1887.

Smith, John Masson, Jr. "Mongol and Nomadic Taxation." *HJAS* 30 (1970): 46–85.

Solov'ev, S. M. *Istoriia Rossii s drevneishikh vremen.* 29 vols. Moscow: Izd-vo sots.-econ. literatury, 1959–66.

Sümer, Faruk. *Oguzlar (Türkmenlar).* 3d ed. Istanbul: Ana Yayinlari, 1980.

Todaeva, B. Kh. *Iazyk mongolov Vnutrennei Mongolii. Materialy i slovar'.* Moscow: Nauka, 1981.

——. *Opyt lingvisticheskogo issledovaniia eposa "Dzhangar."'* Elista: Kalmytskoe knizhnoe izd-vo, 1976.

Togan, Zeki Velidi. "Bashkirt." *Islam Ansiklopedisi,* 2:328–32. Istanbul: Maarif Matbaasi, 1944.

——. *Umumî Türk Tarikhi'ne Girish,* vol. 1, *En Eski Devirlerden 16. Asra kadar.* 3d ed. Istanbul: Aksiseda Matbaasi, 1981.

Tsarykov, N. "Un Voyage dans l'Ouzbekistan en 1671." *Sbornik Moskovskogo glavnogo arkhiva Ministerstva Inostrannykh Del* 5 (1893): 49–62.

Tsybikov, G. Ts. *Izbrannye trudy v dvukh tomakh,* vol. 1: *Buddist-palomnik u sviatyn' Tibeta.* Novosibirsk: Nauka, 1981.

Ubushaev, N. N. "Torgutskii dialekt i ego otnoshenie k kalmytskomu literaturnomu iazyku." *Uchenye zapiski KNIIaLI, seriia filologicheskaia* 7 (1969): 186–98.

Ustiugov, N. V. "Bashkirskoe vosstanie 1662–1664 gg." *Istoricheske zapiski* 24 (1947): 30–110.

Ustrialov, N. G. *Istoriia tsarstvovaniia Petra Velikogo.* 5 vols. St. Petersburg: Tip II-go otdeleniia Ego Imp. Vel. kantseliarii, 1858–63.

Valikhanov, Ch. Ch. "Zapiski o kirgizakh." In *Sobranie sochinenii v piati tomakh,* 2:7–81. Alma-Ata: GRKSE, 1985.

——. "Zapiski o sudebnoi reforme." In *Sobranie sochinenii v piati tomakh,* 4:77–104. Alma-Ata: GRKSE, 1985.

Veselovskii, N. I. "Peredovye kalmyki na puti k Volge." *ZVOIRAO* 3 (1888): 365–70.

Veselovskii, S. B. *D'iaki i pod'iachie 15–17 vv.* Moscow: Nauka, 1975.

Vitevskii, V. N. *I. I. Nepliuev i Orenburgskii krai v prezhnem ego sostave do 1758 goda.* 3 vols. Kazan': Tipo-Litografiia V. M. Kliuchnikova, 1897.

Vladimirtsov, B. Ia. "Mongol'skaia literatura," vol. 2: "Literatura Vostoka," pp. 90–115. *Vsemirnaia literatura,* Petersburg: N.p., 1920.

——. *Obshchestvennyi stroi mongolov. Mongol'skii kochevoi feodalism.* Leningrad: AN SSSR, 1934.

Vneshniaia politika gosudarstva Tsin v 17 veke. Moscow: Nauka, 1977.

Vreeland, H. H. *Mongol Community and Kinship Structure.* New Haven, Conn.: Human Relations Area File, 1954.

"Vvedenie buddiiskogo ucheniia sekty zheltoshapochnikov mezhdu mongolami i oiratami." In *Kalmytskie istoriko-literaturnye pamiatniki v russkom perevode,* pp. 121–30. Elista: N.p., 1969.

Waddel, Austin L. *Tibetan Buddhism: With Its Mystic Cults and Mythology, and in Its Relation to Indian Buddhism.* 3d ed. New York: Dover, 1972.

The World of Buddhism: Buddhist Monks in Society and Culture. New York: Facts on File, 1984.

Wu, Ch'i Yü. "Who Were the Oirats?" *Yenching Journal of Social Studies* 3, no. 2 (1941): 174–219.

Zhitetskii, I. A. *Ocherki byta astrakhanskikh kalmykov: etnograficheskiie nabliudeniia 1884–1886 gg.* Moscow: Tip. M. G. Volchaninova, 1893.

Zhukovskaia, N. L. *Lamaism i rannie formy religii.* Moscow: Nauka, 1977.

Zlatkin, I. Ia. *Istoriia Dzhungarskogo khanstva, 1635–1758.* 2d ed. Moscow: Nauka, 1983.

———. "Russkie arkhivnye materialy ob Amursane." In *Filologiia i istoriia mongol'skikh narodov,* pp. 289–313. Moscow: Izd-vo vostochnoi literatury, 1958.

Glossary

akche—an Ottoman silver coin. By the end of the seventeenth century three hundred *akche* equaled one gold piece.

akha—an elder or a headman of the *khoton*.

albatu—a commoner bound to the respective *khoton* and *ayimag* and personally bound to his *noyon*.

altyn—equals three kopecks.

and (*ant*)—an oath among Mongol and Turkic peoples sworn by two warriors to become blood brothers.

änge—a socioadministrative unit united by patrilinial descent.

arza—an alcoholic beverage distilled from fermented mare's milk.

ayil—a type of nomad camp involving a small number of tents, whose inhabitants ordinarily roamed together.

ayimag—a socioadministrative unit united by a patrilineal descent and sharing a common pasture ground.

ayip—a fine for an unsanctioned raid or theft of a herd among the Kazakhs.

bagatur—(literally a "hero") an honorable nickname of the Mongol-Kalmyk nobles.

bagshi—a teacher of Buddhist precepts; a head of the large *khurul* among the Torguts.

barimta (*baranta*)—a customary law, whereby an offended party was allowed forcefully to seize herds or goods to recover an unpaid debt or to revenge an insult.

bey—title of a notable among the Turkic peoples and in the Ottoman empire.

bichig—a prayer book of the Mongols and Kalmyks.

bogol—a slave.

burkhan—one of the images of Buddha.

chetvert' (*chet'*)—a measure of grain. It varied depending on the type of grain, but by the end of the seventeenth century it equaled about eight *poods*.

darkhan (*tarkhan*)—a person freed from any taxes or other duties to the *noyon*.

daruga—a steward appointed by the *noyon* to supervise various work and collect taxes.

degeley-khuyag—an armor with short sleeves.

demchi—an assistant to the *daruga* in charge of collecting taxes from forty tents.

d'iak—a secretary of a chancellery in Muscovy.

elchi—an envoy; an important position close to the *noyon*.

emchi—a medicine man.

gelüng—"virtuous beggar," or a fully ordained monk over twenty years of age, who kept the 253 rules.

ger—a tent used by the Mongols and Kalmyks as an abode.

getsul—a novitiate monk, who kept the thirty-six rules.

kalgay—a deputy and an heir apparent; the second most important member of the ruling dynasty in the Crimea.

khong tayiji—see *tayiji*.

khoshun—a military unit equated with *ayimag*.

khoton—the lowest-level socioadministrative unit politically structured around a headman.

khuduk—a well dug in the desert or steppes.

khurul—the Kalmyk nomadic monastery.

khurultay—the assembly of the Oirat and Mongol nobles.

khurza—an alcoholic beverage distilled from fermented mare's milk.

khuyag—an armor.

köteji (*kütelji*)—an equerry; an important position close to the *noyon*.

kumis (*kimiz*)—an alcoholic beverage distilled from fermented mare's milk.

küriyen—a large encampment of nomads enabling defense by means of encircling wagons.

lama—the head of the Kalmyk clergy and a regent of the Dalai Lama.

lübchi-khuyag—an armor consisting of thick wool caftan with heavy metal plates sewn on top of it.

manji—a clerical apprentice who kept the ten precepts.

matsak—a marshy area of reeds and rushes along the Caspian shores.

mirza—the title of nobility among many Turkic peoples.

"*nine*"—a common exchange unit among the Kalmyks. It usually included four head of cattle and five sheep.

nökör—a close associate of the *noyon*, who pledged to serve the *noyon* and was free to leave him.

noyon (*noyan*)—a member of the Mongol-Kalmyk aristocracy, a noble.

nureddin—following the khan and the *kalgay*, this was the third most important office in the Crimea.

nutug—a Mongol term designating a territory, pastures occupied by an *ulus* or *khoton*.

obo—a primitive temple along the Kalmyk nomadic routes.

otog—a military unit of one thousand men at the time of Chinggis Khan.

polovinka—a measure of cloth in Muscovy, equaling about forty-six feet.

pood—a measure of weight equal to forty pounds.

ruble—a Russian silver coin equaling one hundred kopecks.

saigak—a large horned antelope indigenous to the Caspian steppes.

sekban—irregular Ottoman troops armed with muskets.

shabinar—*albatu* donated to the monastery by his *noyon*.

shikhaga—an oath among the Mongols and Kalmyks taken during the trials.

shülenge—a headman in charge of twenty tents.

stol'nik—title of the fifth highest-ranking official in seventeenth-century Muscovy.

surgalin-kebün—a preparatory level for clerical students from ten to twelve years of age.

tabun—a herd of from one hundred to two hundred horses.

tayiji and *khong tayiji*—the titles of Mongol-Oirat nobles reserved only for the descendants of Chinggis Khan. In post-Yüan times it was widely used as an honorific title.

tayishi—title of a Kalmyk noble, who was a chief of the *ulus*.

tsakhan-avga—an image of the pan-Mongol deity placed on top of the *obo*.

tsorji—a clerical rank second only to the lama.

tümen—a military unit of ten thousand men at the time of Chinggis Khan.

ulus—the largest socioadministrative unit united by political allegiance to the *tayishi*; an appanage of the *tayishi*.

uzden'—title of a Kabardinian noble.

vedro—a measure of liquid, which varied significantly in the seventeenth-century Muscovy.

verst—a measure of distance, equaling 1.067 kilometers or 0.6629 mile.

voevoda—a military governor in Muscovy.

yasak—a tax paid in kind by non-Christians.

yasun—(literally a bone) a social category dividing the Kalmyks into *tsakhan yasun*—"white bone"—and *khara yasun*—"black bone," that is, nobility and commoners.

yurt—a Turkic term designating a territory, pastures occupied by an *ulus* or *khoton*.

zargachi—a counselor, judge.

zargo—a council and legislative body at the khan's headquaters.

zaseka—a defense network constructed by the Russian government along the southern frontier to prevent incursions by various nomadic peoples.

zayisang (jaiisang)—a lesser Mongol-Kalmyk noble, a head of the *ayimag*.

zud (jud)—conditions in the steppes when pastures could not provide sufficient fodder, thus causing herds to perish.

zurachi—an artist.

zurhachi—an astrologer.

Index

Library of Congress Cataloging-in-Publication Data

Khodarkovsky, Michael, 1955–
    Where two worlds met : the Russian state and the Kalmyk nomads,
1600–1771 / Michael Khodarkovsky.
        p.   cm.
    Includes bibliographical references and index.
    ISBN 0-8014-2555-7
    1. Kalmyks—History—17th century. 2. Kalmyks—History—18th century.
3. Nomads—Soviet Union—History. 4. Nomads—Asia, Central—History. I. Title.
II. Title: Where 2 worlds met.
DK34.K14K48   1992
947'.004942—dc20
                                                                    92-5282

Lightning Source UK Ltd.
Milton Keynes UK
UKHW010715290321
381018UK00013B/268